W9-BBQ-514

WITHDRAWN

No longer the property of the Boston Public Library.
Sale of this material benefits the Library

PRAISE FOR *THE ARTIST'S GUIDE TO SUCCESS IN THE MUSIC BUSINESS*

"Once again Loren has brought together invaluable information for an upcoming or even an experienced musician . . . This book is a must! . . . You will learn all that is needed to help build any musical career or take it to the next level."

—**Johnny Conga,** independent artist with Gloria Estefan, The Jackson 5, Gloria Gaynor, Paquito D'Rivera, and many others

"Loren is completely on point, capturing the landscape of the music industry of today as well as alluding to the future direction of where music could or should go. Everyone believes they are going to do something so different that they miss the point that this industry is built on a series of steps that depend on the successful execution of the previous step. Loren's writing gives that step-by-step instruction. It doesn't mean that the artist shouldn't or wouldn't benefit from hiring an experienced consultant, but this book will keep them out of trouble and give them a great direction to start with."

—**Kimo Kaulani,** Grammy-nominated producer, composer, and arranger for Maroon 5, Wu Tang, Lenny Kravitz, Geri King, Sony, UMG, and many others.

"Loren Weisman's book *The Artist's Guide to Success in the Music Business* was a really fun read for me. In addition to being informative to aspiring writers, artists, and producers, the personal anecdotes very much took me back to those times when I was that struggling kid with dreams of getting to actually make a living from what I loved best—writing music! Always interesting for me to get another's perspective on just how challenging and rewarding this business can be!"

—**Steve Dorff**, three-time Grammy nominee with nine #1 film songs and fifteen Top 10 hits, including the Kenny Rogers' classic "Through The Years"

"Loren Weisman's offering is a must-have. Time and again I see youngsters with wide eyes and desire ready to conquer the music world with something new and special. That's exactly the intent I had when I was their age and in their position. The difference between what it takes for one talented kid to make it over the fence to become a serious member of the world of entertainment and one who just can't step over, has always been fascinating to me. This book explains in detail, with heart and soul, professionalism, and passion, what that fine line is and suggests what it might take to make that difference. I applaud somebody who has taken the time and effort to make this distinction in writing and make it available to those who need it most. Finally, a book has been written addressing this very important discussion. Wishing all those who want to make music and entertainment a livelihood all the best."

—**Terry Silverlight**, drummer, composer, and arranger; drumming credits include Natalie Merchant, George Benson, and Roberta Flack; film scores include *You've Got Mail*, *Titus*, and *Frida*; television song credits include *The Sopranos*, *Burn Notice*, and *Smallville*.

"Trying to market a band, label, album, or tour is more complicated and frustrating today than any point in the past several decades. Too many choices, too many scams, and too little truth can because a "fluster cluck" of massive proportion when trying to properly plan or implement any kind of marketing or promotion effort. Luckily author, producer, and grand elder wizard Loren Weisman has survived many a skirmish in this arena and stays on the front lines of making headway towards success. His books provide plausible, realistic approaches to making sense from the chaos of 'me too' marketing, blind alleys, dumb bunnies, and evil doers, to glean clarity for those who might be led astray or fleeced in the worst ways. There are no easy answers, but those seeking wisdom will find many tutorials, proper directions to skirt the quicksand—and with the least B.S. per page than anything I've come across—in Weisman's latest guidebook. There is simply no downside to reading Loren's book more than once, to provide a proper, solid foundation for any music industry venture. Highly recommended."

—**Christopher Laird Simmons,** CEO of Neotrope® Entertainment and member of ASCAP, PRSA

"Anyone who is even considering a career in music should read this book. When finished, they should start over and read it again. Without empty promises of being fake to people or sneaking your way past the hard work, this book explains exactly the way it is. I'm not saying the way it works is fair or pretty, but it is what it is.

If you read this book and truly ponder how to make it a part of exposing your artistic statement to the world, I would almost bet my career that you will be at the point in your career that you wish. Loren is one of the less than ten people in the entire industry that I feel comfortable recommending to my clients for advice. So, buy this book. Sit down, wipe the stars from your eyes, and start reading."

—**Jason Rubal,** music producer

"If you are a musician, you need this book! Being in the music business for over fifteen years brought me to the realization that there are always the little things that you can overlook. This book will empower you with an ability to step back and look at your career in a new light. From branding your band to funding, managing to touring, pre-production to merchandising, you will gather information between the covers of this book that can lift your career to a new level!"

—**Jay Cooper,** songwriter with Treble Hooks Publishing and cofounder of Indie Islands

"Finally, a book written by a pro who has experience in basically every aspect of this industry. If you want to make music your full-time profession or a lucrative part-time gig, you owe it to yourself to check out this book. Too bad it wasn't around when I started out . . . it would have shaved off years from my 'trial and error' period."

—**Stefan Held,** owner and head producer, StevenHeroProductions.com

"Straight talk from Loren Weisman . . . loads of common sense . . . [and] insights that will save you a lot of pain, as well as a lot of time, energy, and money!"

—**Tom Jackson,** live-music producer, OnstageSuccess.com

"I have seen Loren work tirelessly in pursuit of educating the artist into becoming a businessman. His passion for the entertainment business is extraordinary."

—**Adam Gaynor**, CEO, Creationville, and former member of Matchbox20

"Loren's book is a must read for understanding and navigating the music industry of today! It's a guide, a handbook, and a daily reference!"

—**Scotty Moore**, guitarist and recording engineer extraordinaire for Elvis Presley, Ann Margaret, Jerry Lee Lewis and many more artists

"In a music industry that seems to change faster than a radioactive, mutating sci-fi movie space alien, Loren Weisman gives creative artists the most valuable thing that they could possibly need for success: the tools to make good decisions as they are hit with those changes along their road. In an industry where there is no shortage of 'pro advice' that usually is based on situations that have long passed or guesses that may never be, Weisman's guide gives a common sense approach to showing where the potholes will probably be along the various routes a career could take, and how to prepare for them when—not if— they happen."

—**Doug Perkins,** partner at jazzguitarsociety.com; Outstanding Guitarist of the Year; and former staff instructor at Musician's Institute

"Loren Weisman has written the second edition to his *Artist's Guide To Success In the Music Business* and, as with the first edition, it is a must-read for those who want to find success in this new, revamped music industry. Eleven chapters lead you through the ins and out of the industry with each chapter detailing an important aspect on the road to success.

As Loren cautions in his introduction, this is not a step-by-step guide, nor is it the end-all, be-all career guide. The lessons and advice in each chapter begin with an opening thought and close with a review of the subjects discussed, allowing the reader to close the loop on subjects from Your Band and working with Other Musicians to Music Marketing and Promotions.

What you will get from this guide depends upon your ability to see beyond where you are today to where you want to be tomorrow.

This is not a read for musicians who think they know it all and can't learn. It will benefit any musician with an open mind and the realization that you can't know everything and are open to suggestions from someone who has spent over twenty-five years making his way successfully through the obstacle course that is the music industry. Even a non-musician, like myself, came away with a better understanding of the work and sweat it takes today more than ever to make it out of your comfort zone into a new world of fans and gigs."

—**Vinny Bond Marini**, Music On The Couch

"As always, Loren doesn't hold back and tells artists the truth—it's tough out there to be a musician, but there is light at the end of the tunnel for great musicians who make an effort and market properly! Every musician should read this book, whether they are just starting out or are already having success, because it goes through all the ups and downs an artist can go through in their career. And Loren has experienced the same ups and downs, so there is no lip service here."

—**Lou Plaia**, cofounder and executive vice president of music industry and artist relations for Reverbnation

The

ARTIST'S
GUIDE TO

SUCCESS

— *in the* —

MUSIC
BUSINESS

THE "WHO, WHAT, WHEN, WHERE, WHY & HOW" OF THE STEPS
THAT MUSICIANS & BANDS HAVE TO TAKE TO SUCCEED IN MUSIC

LOREN WEISMAN

GREENLEAF
BOOK GROUP PRESS

The Artist's Guide to Success in the Music Business, 2nd Edition, is also available in
e-book versions as a full book and by chapters for download and are available as download
cards. The book is also available in audio versions by download, CD and download cards.
Visit http://tag2nd.com/ or http://lorenweisman.com/ for more information.

Published by Greenleaf Book Group Press
Austin, Texas
www.greenleafbookgroup.com

Copyright ©2014 Loren Weisman

All rights reserved.

No part of this book may be reproduced, stored in a retrieval system, or transmitted by
any means, electronic, mechanical, photocopying, recording, or otherwise, without written
permission from the publisher.

Distributed by Greenleaf Book Group LLC

For ordering information or special discounts for bulk purchases, please contact
Greenleaf Book Group LLC at PO Box 91869, Austin, TX 78709, 512.891.6100.

Design and composition by Greenleaf Book Group LLC
Cover design by Greenleaf Book Group LLC

Publisher's Cataloging-In-Publication Data
(Prepared by The Donohue Group, Inc.)
Weisman, Loren.
    The artist's guide to success in the music business : the "who, what, when, where, why & how" of the steps that musicians &
bands have to take to succeed in music / Loren Weisman.—2nd ed., 1st Greenleaf Books ed.
    p. ; cm.
    Issued also as an ebook.
    ISBN: 978-1-60832-578-8
    1. Music trade—Vocational guidance. 2. Sound recording industry — Vocational guidance. 3. Musicians. I. Title. II. Title:
TAG
ML3795 .W45 2013
780/.23   2013936454

Part of the Tree Neutral® program, which offsets the number of trees consumed in the production and printing of
this book by taking proactive steps, such as planting trees in direct proportion to the number of trees used:
www.treeneutral.com

Printed in the United States of America on acid-free paper

13 14 15 16   10 9 8 7 6 5 4 3 2 1

First Greenleaf Books Edition

*The most devastating thing artists can do to their career is get in
their own way, and way too many people do.
It's not the labels, the industry, the fans, the cities, the economy, the social
media, the marketing, the promoting, the "right time," the music, or
whatever other excuse you can come up with that determines whether you
succeed or you fail. It is you—no one else.*

—Loren Weisman

CONTENTS

FOREWORD

"Ch-ch-ch-ch-changes"

—

*"Get your motor runnin'
head out on the highway
looking for adventure . . ."*

—

Buckle up, reader, you're about to take a most fascinating trip. Actually, I'm sure you've already embarked, and with the help of *The Artists Guide to Success in the Music Business*, you'll have some important tools with which to better navigate the wacky world of today's music business.

On one hand "the biz" changes ever-so rapidly . . . jet speed nowadays. Yet at the same time, the wisdoms of personal experience, and insightful overview espoused by Loren Weisman will give you a stronger foot-hold in your quest for . . . well, whatever you wish to achieve within this industry.

I really like "straight talkers"—even if I don't like what I'm hearing, or disagree. Honesty will always be the best policy, and I can tell you that Mr. Weisman speaks from the heart—and his head. A man of integrity, and very strong views. He is a straight talker. Even better, I happen to share his views on the state of the industry, and about how to carve, engrave, etch, and gently squeeze your way into that special place that you'd like to find yourself. That could be on stage, in the recording studio, or in the many supporting roles that make up that big (and sometimes mysterious) mechanism we call show business . . . or artistry . . . or commercial success—that's your call, dear reader.

This hunk of hot info you now hold in your hand takes you through so many scenarios, many of which you will be experiencing and needing to come to terms with. It must be said at this point, that I wish I'd had an informational tool like this when I was a young "up-'n-coming". I'd have probably made a lot of the same mistakes—youth is like that, but the food for thought that the author offers here can certainly save you a lot of grief. If you're in the bookstore (or online) now, deciding whether you need this book, just thumb through some the pages—and you'll see what I'm talking about!

The first chapter is called "The Music Industry and You" and begins with five rudimentary questions. Let me tell you that as I grew into the professional music scene, my primary thinking consisted of only the essence of the first question; the others slowly surfaced as time went on. How I wish I'd been offered such a comprehensive overview at the outset.

Each chapter of this "guide-book" deals with matters of extreme importance in the growth and evolution of the artiste/band. I could spend all day discussing so many of the nuances, but hey—let the author do it. He says it with a bit more humor than I could muster up, I think. Finally, let me say that chapters 8, 9 and 10 raise issues that are unique to today's music business. These cover very fundamental "must take care of" items if your venture is to succeed. The arts/entertainment world lives and thrives through items covered here including . . . financing your venture, understanding the need—and ways to "brand" your personal "product" (making yourself a unique entity), and of course, understanding the very real "dos and don'ts" in this new age of self promotion via social networking. It's not just having the tools—it's understanding how to best use them.

I do hope that you are able to grasp just how vital all of these points are . . . if you want to succeed, that is.

Elliott Randall
Session Guitarist, Producer, Arranger, Writer—
Steely Dan, Doobie Brothers, *Saturday Night Live*, Blues Brothers, Carly Simon,
John Lennon and more.

ACKNOWLEDGMENTS

Peggy Hazlett, Ed Verner, Maryglenn McCombs, Triad Strategies LLC, Brandon Powers, Roy Wells, Thom Lemmons, Neil Gonzalez, Alan Grimes, Matthew Patin, Kris Pauls, Shannon Zuniga, Justin Branch, Angela Alwin, Madeline Meehan, Peter Fernandez, Christopher Laird Simmons, Francine Fragolini, Scott Ross, Vanessa Sommer, Mike Sinkula, Michael Manzo, Dana D. Nale, Kurt Hilborn, Elliott Randall, Scott Payne, Brian Ulery, Billy Amendola, Jim and Andrea Vidmar, Jana Pelinga, David Stoup, Phil Gent, Alicia McBarron, Andrew Larson, Peter Levy, Howard Edson, Jason Rubal, Michael McFarland, Margaret Hoelzer, Stefan Held, Swiss Chris, Hilton Hotels, Corrine Bonneau, Meghan Bonsall, Kyera Lamoureux, Elle Heinen, Steve Ceragno, Joe Kowalczyk, Cathy Corbin, Vikki Hein, Jaisen Buccellato, John Harris, Ken Robinson, Peter Kelleher, Paul Smiley, Daniel Stokes, Brandi Waite, Pam and Peter Hoagland, Rosie Caine, Kathy, Ed and Brody Powers, and everyone at Greenleaf Book Group.

AUTHOR'S NOTE

T his guide is based on my experiences over the past twenty-five-plus years, since I started drumming at the age of thirteen, through my time as a session and touring drummer, music producer, consultant, and now, speaker. Names have been changed and events have been compressed in order to honor nondisclosure and confidentiality agreements. Some of the individuals, managers, record labels, agents, and organizations portrayed or mentioned in this book are composites of more than one person or music company, and many identifying characteristics have been altered, edited, or removed.

The devil is in the details; I say that a lot in this book. If you have not read the first edition, I will introduce you to my voice, my concepts, and my angle on the music industry. I do not apologize for my approach, my views, or my ideas. From my own experiences—both good and bad—I offer you this guide so that you can apply these concepts to your own career and, in turn, make them work for you.

The changes between the first and second editions of this book are both big and small. There are some pieces of the last book that were left alone. There were some pieces that were deleted altogether. Other pieces have been updated to show changes that have happened in the industry since the first book. And there is a great deal of new material added to this second edition.

In the past few years, traveling all over North America for speaking engagements and giving private consults in support of the first book, I listened as much as I spoke and learned as much as I taught. Hearing the success stories and the failures from aspiring and professional artists, labels, and other music business professionals gave me an even broader sense of the music industry. Throughout my travels I witnessed the different music scenes all around the country and got a firsthand account of what has happened, what is happening, and where things are going. This is why I am so proud of the new edition of this book: It not only delivers the concepts, but it shares the proof of the "who, what, when, where, why, and how" of the steps artists have to take today in order to thrive.

Think of it this way: These approaches, ideas, and instructions are brought together for use as a *personalized blueprint* to create your own *customized model*: a way for *you to take the pieces of the book that you need* to achieve realistic, sustainable, long-term success in the music business.

INTRODUCTION

The Artist's Guide to Success in the Music Business, second Edition, is a detailed analysis of the subjects that all musicians should understand and apply in order to pursue a successful and sustainable career in music today. Full of practical advice, this music industry guide provides comprehensive details on how to achieve self-empowerment and optimize your success in today's music business. From production and performance tips to marketing and career-building advice, this music business book instructs and empowers artists on how to take the hard-earned lessons of a fellow musician and put them to work in their own careers.

This is not a step-by-step, instructional, how-to book, nor is it the end-all, be-all career guide. Believe it or not, as long as this book may seem, it just scratches the surface of today's music industry. Some parts you may already have under control, organized, and in working order. Other sections may be eye-openers and might make you bring certain aspects of your career back to the drawing table. Other parts might give you ideas for tweaks and refinements that could help you push down a wall that is blocking your progress. Some of this stuff you might know, other bits you might not.

My purpose is not to address every miniscule detail, but to focus on the broad spectrum of ideas, applications, and methods and lay out a solid blueprint that each artist or industry professional can adapt and recombine in his or her own personal way. My goal for this book is to give you the information that you need, information that you can personalize and apply to your career and/or the careers of the artists you work with.

In the end, it's up to you, but which *you* is it going to be? The successful or the unsuccessful? The hard worker or the complacent, lazy person? The only secrets—if you can call them that—to making it in the music industry are your reputation, your hard work, your effort, and your commitment to doing the right thing. In the end, these elements reveal the true character and heart of a successful and honorable person.

The list of what you are up against in realizing your dream of making music your career can be a long one; some people may face longer lists than others. Each individual has personal advantages as well as personal hindrances. Still, the one issue, the biggest obstacle to keeping an artist or industry professional from success, is shared by everyone and is the same:

It's you.

Most of the people who fail in this industry do so because of ignorance, ego, wrong assumptions, and bad choices. The good news is that you can choose to take the initiative toward your own success. But you *have* to take the initiative, or you'll fail for sure.

You are the one who chooses to take the shortcut that turns out to be the wrong path. You are the one who thinks there is only one version of success. You are the one who decides to not double-check someone. You are the one who pushes common sense and detail-checking away for lightning-fast, vague answers and empty promises, getting your ego stroked by someone who is using you.

You are the one who is afraid of failure, just as you are the one who is afraid of success. You are the one who lets a problem repeat itself over and over. You are the one who is not putting in the time, the one who wants everything outside of the music to be handled by others. You are the one who thought, "As soon as they hear this, I'll be big," or, "It's good enough." You are the one bitching, complaining, and whining about how you got screwed over, even though more often than not, you were the one who signed on the dotted line to allow the bad things to happen. You are the one that chose not to read the fine print—and then read it again. And then have somebody else read it.

Now on to the positive side . . .

No one wants your success more than you do. No one else will give *your* career as much attention with the same energy as you.

You *can* take responsibility for your actions; you *can* study, practice, and empower and educate yourself.

You *can* apply patience, drive, consistency, and a work ethic, putting the same 100 percent effort into the business aspects—the branding, the promoting, and the marketing—as you do the writing, performing, and recording.

You can build a solid foundation by making yourself as productive as possible with the time you have.

It boils down to this: The single worst thing you have going against you is you. But, at the very same time, the single best thing you have going for you is you.

Ask. Utilize. Empower. Learn. Practice. Problem-solve. Communicate. And *work* in the *most productive ways* to make the *most educated decisions* with the *most effective plan.*

Do this so that you can execute, take the steps, do the work, and have the patience to allow yourself to be the catalyst, the ammunition, and the fuel for your goals and dreams—instead of being the one who keeps them from becoming reality.

So, are you ready to succeed in the music business? Yes? Okay, great. Let's get started . . .

· · · · ● 1 ● · · · ·

THE MUSIC INDUSTRY AND YOU

OPENING THOUGHT

Ready to jump feet first into the music business? First, ask yourself these questions:

What is your dream?

How do you define success?

Whom do you want to be involved with?

How do you know whom to trust?

Where do you see yourself in five years?

Imagine a junior high school kid in the back of science class, drawing his dream drum set on the back of a school folder. First of all, double bass drums: They had to be twenty-four inches each. Four toms because, back in the late eighties, how could you possibly have less than four toms across the front? He draws the toms: 10, 12, 13, and 14 inches. Then two floor toms: a 16 and an 18. For those of you who are not drummers, maybe it would help to imagine a guitar or a keyboard instead. For those drummers that came up in that time, you may remember the Pearl drums advertisement for the CZX drums. I can still see in my mind's eye the shot of that tan or wood-finished kit of even, "box" sizes: 10×10, 12×12, 13×13, 14×14, 16×16, and 18×18.

Next, the kid draws the cymbals: at least four crashes—why not? Auxiliary hi-hats, two Chinese cymbals to flank both sides, and—might as well go for the gold—a big old gong, suspended behind the kit!

As you may have already guessed, I was that kid drawing those pictures, sitting at the back of Mr. Cepeck's eighth-grade science class. At the time, it was the biggest kit I could imagine, because it was supporting the biggest dream I could dream—a life in music, playing drums with a killer band in front of screaming fans in a sold-out stadium.

Of course, I now know that my dream—as sweet as it was to an eighth-grade boy who just wanted to play the drums—was full of holes. Now, I'm certainly not saying it's bad to have a dream, but if people had asked me back then to actually define success, I would have told them that they just didn't understand what I was going to be and do. "You don't get it," I would have told them.

In reality, I was the one who didn't get it.

I chased after that dream, though, and I caught it, but I also lost it a number of times. Why? Because I didn't really have a well-defined goal or a solid foundation for my dream.

Here's the moral: Dream big—to the extreme, even. But also make sure you can define your goals, and then build a plan for taking the right steps to make that dream come true— even if that takes the shape of smaller goals along the way.

HOW DO YOU SPELL "SUCCESS"?

Take a second and go back to the list of questions at the beginning of this chapter. You might be surprised—or maybe not—to know that very few artists have truly asked and answered these questions. Sadly, failing to deal with these simple, yet vital issues can destroy a career, a band, or a chance at the dream—even before an artist or a band is out of the gate.

The fact is that success in the music industry can have many different definitions. Of course, everybody thinks about the super-duper, A-list stars who achieve fame and wealth beyond imagination—at least, that's the delusion. The numbers reported in some entertainment magazines do not give the whole story of the real income and what that artist actually gets to keep after labels, investors, producers, engineers, graphic designers, distribution, booking agents, stage hands, and tons of other people are getting paid. Such numbers are far from clear, and yet everyone assumes that this defines "success" in the music business.

A perfect example of such skewed assumptions is a posting I saw on Facebook of a house with a water slide coming out of the second floor into a pool—a four-million-dollar listing, at minimum. The artist posted it and made reference to this being his new home once he sold a few thousand albums, and I thought to myself, this guy would not be able to rent this place for the summer if he only sold a few thousand albums, much less buy it.

The average artist has a naïve, unrealistic, and disconnected view of what the music industry is, how it works, what is involved in "making it," and what actually is happening behind the scenes. Too many artists take at face value what they see on some TV documentary or read in a fan magazine. Whether you are working with others in a band, looking to connect with a manager, an agent, a label, or an investor, or you just want to work in the industry, it is more crucial than ever to know what you are working for and toward.

Just to be clear: This book is not geared to helping you become a superstar. If that is all you are looking for, you might want to stop reading now. Now, it's certainly possible that by organizing, implementing, and executing a customized plan you might make it to that level, but it's a long shot: a very, very long shot.

Think of the road to success as climbing a tall mountain. But instead of just looking at the summit of the mountain—your dream of stardom—you need to pack for the ascent and plan some places on the trail to stop and rest: You work for the big goal while achieving the small ones along the way. You need to have the right boots, the right ropes, the right team to climb with, and the provisions to sustain you during the journey to continue to move onward and upward.

Maybe you don't reach the peak, but while working toward that goal, could you achieve other goals? Could you find happiness and a different definition of success that feels right for you? Maybe you're not selling out Barclays Center in Brooklyn, NY. and having records go platinum, but you are touring six to nine months out of the year and you have licensed songs in numerous TV shows, video games, and films. You have a solid fan base that comes to your shows. Maybe you are not playing to 20,000 people every night, but you are always able to pull in 200 to 2,000. Maybe you put together the right plan and hire the right agent, the right distributor, and the right promotional team. Let's say that for twenty solid years, everyone in your group is able to pull in $60,000 a year—after taxes—as well as having medical, dental, and life insurance.

How is that not successful? Maybe you didn't reach the million-dollar "peak," but while heading up that mountain path you are doing what you love and making a much better living than the majority of Americans today. Can you call that a failure?

Your definition of success is subject to change by your will and your choice, but only if you have the plan, the gear, the patience, and the drive to work toward the biggest goals while still achieving the small ones along the way.

Think about your definition of success. What kind of salary do you need to make to be "making it" in music? When you say, "I want to be a musician," what does that entail creatively, financially, and time-wise?

When you ask yourself these questions, are you also asking the question, "How can I get signed?" Are you asking yourself, "How can I succeed as an independent musician?" If you are in a band, are the expectations and definitions clear with each of the members?

Setting standards and working backward to getting there is a great way to plan. What salary would you and the other band members like to be making while getting to play, taking care of your responsibilities, and being able to afford a good life, but without the excess dreams of millions and millions? When you are able to put together the numbers that define your success, it will be easier for a music consultant, a real label, a real manager, or a real agent to come up with a plan that takes into account your goals and the beginning steps to get there.

Remember, once you have tallied up the totals and taken out the taxes, you still have to add all the considerations and costs for touring, recording, and other budgetary aspects. If you are assuming that a label or manager is doing some of the work for you, don't forget to subtract their percentage. As a very simple overview, if you want to net $250K in a year for a band—especially if labels and other people are involved—you are going to have to bring in a million to cover all the costs, pay out the investors, and take care of business. The more control you have and the fewer other parties that are involved, the more that overhead percentage will drop and the more of the gross you will get to keep.

Planning responsibly and having a nice overview of reality to go with your picture of success can help you make the best choices while still retaining as much control as possible over your own destiny.

I believe that the artists who only look at the summit are the real failures; they are often the ones who have the hardest time getting there. Those who try to shortcut the process—renting a helicopter to avoid the long, hard climb—also pay dearly. They get to the top too fast, and with too little effort, and it costs them their rights and the bulk of their profits. They give it all away just to get to the top, and often as not, they end up in an avalanche of poverty, desperation, and failure.

On the other hand, those who dream of the million-dollar mansions while patiently investing in the more modest purchases available to them, those that think about wads of cash

> Waiting to be discovered, hoping to be seen, wishing someone else would do the work, wanting to make it big, and dreaming of being rich and famous just like your heroes is submissive, passive, foolish, weak, and ineffective.
>
> Take your desire for dreams, your goals, and your ambition, then make it fuel for the fire to light your ass up; get to work on the path to make it happen. The energy, the effort, the execution, and the actions make dreams come true—not waiting, hoping, wishing, wanting, and dreaming.

but still discipline themselves to save the pennies—these are the artists I'd put my money on to make it over the long haul. Those who play with the same passion for an audience of ten as they would for a crowd of ten thousand are the ones who will find the best chance of success today. And though their images of success may change at various stages of the climb, they have already defined success by laying the best foundation. They will be the ones who can make the good decisions and see the bigger picture as they learn more about the industry and mature with the experience and information they take in.

To really work for you, your customized plan for success should lay out the "peak" aspects of your dream as well as the requirements to make that journey. You will need to alter your path and adapt to changes along the way, but the more you plan and navigate in the right direction, the more you will achieve. Planning helps you in the short term as you move toward your long-term goals, helping you remember not to waste time here or blow money there, because your aim is directed at the place you want to go.

Honestly, I wish I had learned this lesson a long time ago. I had a lot of fun, but I could have had a little less fun and could have planned a little more for the long term, arriving at the place I defined as success.

My Personal Definition of Success

To me, success in the music business means you are living your own dream, supporting yourself as you responsibly increase your ability to have the things in life that you desire. I don't put a number on it, because just like the paths to success, everyone's number is different.

My personal definition of success involves having enough money for the lifestyle I want, debt- and commitment-free, with saving and investment included. For me, success involves living securely off dividends and royalties so that I can work more on the projects I want, even with artists who might not be able to afford me—but whom I believe in. I'd like to be able to donate a few speaking engagements each month and a few consultations to those who have the drive but not the ready cash.

I have timeline goals, too: goals that include reaching certain financial benchmarks and certain benchmarks for my consulting and speaking activities. I have a time frame within which I'd like to be able to afford to reduce the hours I put in each day.

For me, in other words, "success" is defined by the different benchmarks I achieve and the different steps I take in my own personal journey. Hitting these targets along the way is evidence of success to me, just as much as reaching the end goal.

What about Music as a Hobby?

While we're talking about success, it's probably worthwhile to ask yourself this question: Do you really want to be a musician full-time? Or is making music as a hobby more like what you want to do? It's a fair question, and a lot of people are perfectly happy with being music hobbyists rather than full-time musicians.

Are you fine with the short-term wins and don't care about long-term success? Maybe you're in one of those bands that can fill a local venue over and over but just doesn't seem to break through to any bigger level—and you're okay with that. Maybe you know that person who claims to be a manager, a booking agent, or a promoter: the one who can get all his or her close friends and maybe a few strangers out to a venue, a party, or an event now and then, but never can seem to make any real money for themselves or the band.

Maybe for these folks, music is actually a hobby: a fun thing, a side project that is not intended to make anybody a living. That's fine. There is nothing wrong with being a hobbyist. It can be a lot of fun to put together fun little events, gigs, parties, or whatnot, but at least be honest and make sure everyone knows exactly what your goals are. Don't make the mistake of confusing a hobbyist—no matter how much he or she professes to know about "the business"—for a music industry professional.

Let me say it again, though: The hobbyist can still be successful. Being a hobbyist does not equate to "failure"; it is simply a different success definition for a different person—the artist who doesn't want to take his or her music or career to a full-time level and prefers it to be part-time. This may not indicate a lack of drive or ambition; these people just have different goals, different dreams, and different desires. Maybe they just do it for the art and the love of music. Maybe they want to do the work, but don't want the time away from family. Maybe their day job is too good to trade for a music career. For whatever reason, the part-time concept just works for them.

And how can you fault that? If an artist out there loves to play once a month within a very small radius of home or to make a record that might not even sell beyond friends and family, and if that makes the artist happy, isn't that success? Sure it is. Just don't confuse the hobbyist with the person who is making the long climb toward "peak" success.

YOU, THE MUSIC BUSINESS, AND THE BUSINESS OF MUSIC

The misconceptions about the music industry and how to make it in music are loud and constant. The industry itself assists in perpetuating stories of that one artist who breaks through from out of the blue and has an amazing career. Reality shows, interviews, and the Internet combine to lead many to believe that the road to success is a fairy tale. Unfortunately, only a very, very small percentage of artists get to experience that fairy tale path, and those who do very often come to realize the illusion that fairy tale truly represents.

You may even be able to think of a band you know that was playing small rooms, with each member holding a basic day job and living check to check. They practiced, recorded, struggled, and played everywhere they could. Suddenly they come out with an amazing album. Then you immediately start to see them in nicer cars and spending more money.

That should raise a couple of red flags, right there. When a larger record company, investor, management group, or agent spends a fortune on the recording of an album and gives artists things like cars, clothes, and money, this not only gives the artists an incentive but also locks them in to the people giving the stuff. What the bands don't recognize is that the record company, investor, or whoever wants all that money back—and with interest. Record labels are businesses, and they use artists' dreams as leverage to lock musicians into deals with crazy percentages. All the band sees is the light at the end of the tunnel: the ability to quit their jobs, play all the time, and live the superstar lifestyle. They don't realize that the light is an oncoming train—a terrible contract that will own and control their choices for years to come.

Whom Do You Trust?

It happens all the time: Artists sign the dotted line but do not read the contract. They hear the hype and it blinds them to the reality and length of the contract. Words and phrases buried in these contracts can restrict the artist from making choices that anyone would assume would be theirs to make. Examples include what you can and cannot say on camera; what you can and cannot do with the songs you have written; and where you can and cannot go to play or promote your music. Some of these contracts put artists into what amounts to indentured servitude. Those cool new logos, the bios, and the merchandise are created by other people, and sometimes basic merchandise profits are not given to the artists.

Artists on all levels can be badly hurt by the deals they sign. The reason it doesn't seem that way with the larger artists is because when the revenues from sales, touring, and merchandise are in the millions, the small percentages that those artists get still amount to a lot of money. But as time goes by, sales and attendance decline and even these formerly multimillion-dollar acts are now crying foul. In other words, 10 percent of hundreds of millions is not a bad deal, but 10 percent of a million is a lot less than what some of these former megastars are used to. But the contract still requires them to record a certain number of albums, do a certain number of performances, and otherwise be under binding agreements for years and years.

This can also apply to smaller labels. Sometimes bands are signed into deals with smaller companies that will make them less attractive to larger labels and managers. Many small labels will incorporate percentages into contracts that aren't justified by the work the label does. This can include long-term publishing deals, royalties, and other percentages taken from the artists' revenues. The goal for these labels is to continue to get a piece of the artists if they go big, but many of these artists will not get better or larger deals precisely because larger labels and managers don't want to deal with the hassle created by the deals done by the smaller players.

The More You Know . . .

All these cautionary tales are why I push so hard for artists to look at the business side of things as they go into the entertainment world. Learn the industry. Work to understand the loopholes, and never forget that if it seems too good to be true—especially in the music industry—you can pretty much bet that it is.

I'm not saying you should turn down every deal, but you should read the contracts and take the time to learn what you don't know. If something is unclear, don't ask the guy trying to get you to sign to explain it to you. Get a lawyer to review it. Talk to a disinterested third party, someone who is not tied to the contract in any way. And don't ask for a lawyer from the label or manager that's handing you the contract. As you review the agreement in front of you, think about these possibilities and how they would be affected by the document you're thinking of signing:

- **Look** to a realistic career and not just number-one hits and playing for thousands of people. Think about the spectrum of sales that are possible.

- **Look** to creating as much as you can by yourself so you can bring more to the table.

- **Look** to avoid having labels, managers, and agents take away from what is yours and take you in a direction you don't want to go.

- **Look** to the possibilities of licensing your songs to movies, television, commercials, video games, corporate videos, and various websites that use music.

- **Look** to how you can license your songs to other performers, or even hire performers in other countries to sing your songs in other languages.

- **Look** at the industry with a set of eyes and a mindset that still wants to go to the top in the way you always dreamed, but with the goal of achieving self-sustaining, long-term success, giving away as little in percentages as you can.

Scammers and Liars and Hype, Oh My!

In every field—from politics to entertainment and everywhere in between—there are scammers, liars, and fakes. A close look at the music business reveals a host of those who are being deceptive: who are going to try to use you, take advantage of you, and make what they can from you. Of course, there are also those that are actually in it to help you and want to see you succeed. Yes, it sucks and it shouldn't be that way—but it is. Your two best defensive weapons are doubt and honor.

First, when you initially hear it, doubt it. Make sure anyone you are getting involved with—any company, manager, agency, or contract—is clear, clean, and reviewed correctly. It is very easy to sell dreams to people who already want desperately to believe them. Artists hear that they are on the horizon of what they have wanted for years, and they bypass common-sense knowledge and red flags that would go up anywhere else. If someone is pushing you to sign on the dotted line, then and there, hoist the red flag—fast.

Doubt first; do your double-checks and your research; make sure things line up; and ask a lot of questions. Those are tips for success that can save you from getting locked into a working relationship with someone who is a liar, a user, or is otherwise going to drag you down.

Second, have honor. Be true and honest in a business that is commonly not that way. Get the reputation for being the one people can trust. This will help you along in a way you can't even imagine. An independent musician with honor and a reputation for telling the truth is going to shine brightly.

Trust and Doubt in Today's Music Industry

I used the word "doubt" above very deliberately; it can be your best friend. The fact is, trust is a scary thing in the music business. Hell, trust is a scary thing in any business or any relationship. It should be developed over time; most people need proof and good reason to trust someone—their word and their work. Trust means giving up or sharing control with someone else involving things that are very important to you and your career. When the music business is exposed to open view, you can see how trust can be a real problem.

Yet, so many people ask for trust so fast. In this ADHD, fifth-gear, Facebook-updating, Twitter-posting world we live in, people are asking others to trust them right out of the gate. They are looking for full compliance, and they even get upset when someone doesn't believe them or trust them right after meeting them. If that does not raise a red flag for you, you are in a lot of trouble. Shortcutting in this area will also cut short any chances for your success in music.

When it comes to clients that I produce or consult with, I tell them in the initial consultation: Don't trust me until I have earned your trust. Ask questions, have doubts, but work to move forward. Do your research on me and on what I am saying you should do. I believe this helps build the foundation of trust, and it forces the artists to do some homework, to form the habit of checking out other people and companies before they hire, follow advice, or sign on the dotted line.

For sure, it's still possible that things can go wrong, even with those whom you have checked out, researched, and decided to trust, but you greatly decrease the chances of a bad situation if you do your homework.

One important key is getting straight answers to your questions—answers that you can understand. If you ask a question that can't be answered right then, the other party should get back to you promptly, after getting the information you need. If the question doesn't have a simple answer, that's fine, as long as the other person tells you that up front and explains why this is the case.

Perfect example: As a music consultant, I am asked all the time, "How much does it cost to make an album with you as the producer?" Honest answer: I have no idea. But then I discuss all the variables that go into setting a budget for an album: What kind of album? How many songs? How many instruments are being tracked? How much time are you allotting for the sessions? How is the endurance of your vocalist? Are we adding in post-production, duplication, graphics, and the initial launch? Is there a preset budget? Are you going to raise the money? And about thirty other questions.

Then I follow up by offering a one- to two-hour blast consultation, where we lay out a basic budget and get a sense of different possibilities and avenues of revenue and how much it will cost. At that point, an artist can talk to me about production or they can go to another producer, but at least they walk away with the blueprint of a budget and a plan. That is much different than some producer who says "sign on the dotted line," pulls a number out of thin air, and otherwise stays very vague.

Shameless plug: The above scenario is also my most popular service.

> You are not stupid, so don't act like you are.

Bottom line: Ask questions. Ask for the details. If something is confusing, then tell the person you are talking to it is confusing. If you are about to spend money, you should know exactly what you are receiving, how you will receive it, and what your responsibilities are. Trying to act all cool and nodding your head when you don't know what is being said or you are unclear with the details makes you look like a clueless bobblehead doll—a sheep just waiting to be sheared.

If the other person gets frustrated by your questions or gives broad, vague, or confusing answers, hoist another red flag. Ask for a client list, then go out and contact them. See if they are really happy. The fact is that people can only bullshit you as much as you want to be bullshitted. They may claim to hold the silver platter of your dreams, but you have to lift the cover to see if there is really anything there.

So, as I mentioned earlier: Watch out for the people who say "trust me" right out of the gate. Words are nothing. They are easy to say, easy to write, and easy to sell. But actions are what trust should be based on. Patience and growing in understanding, seeing promises fulfilled—this is how trust is earned. Honor yourself, your music, and your art by giving trust only as it is deserved and earned.

I always tell artists I produce that I make no promises or guarantees. I was never with a single label or company as either a drummer or producer. I was a hired gun, and I jumped around quite a bit. This broad experience forms the basis for the information that I share—both the things I did right and the failures.

Chances are, there's not a single entity that can provide you with success—not even me (as much as I hate to admit it). More often you will find numerous people and various resources to help you. Just be picky. Find out who is saying it or writing it, where the person comes from, and what his or her beliefs and approaches are. This will help you build a much stronger resource list.

Anyone can tell you anything, and it's great to reflect on what you hear and always be respectful to someone offering advice. However, it takes a mature and patient mind to navigate through all the information and find the best road possible.

Opinions on Opinions

And speaking of advice . . .

In the music business there are a lot of avenues for advice, consulting, coaching, counseling, ideas, expertise, and everything in between. It's always good to research where you are getting the "help" from, but it's also important to define what you're looking for and if you're receiving information that's relevant. "Help" is a scary word, even scarier when many of those who claim to know how to help you do not have the experience, the tools, or the know-how to do it. In fact, many of those who say they are ready to help are actually hurting you.

For example, just because someone had a record deal doesn't mean that he or she fully understands the industry, though that person will likely be able to give you a wealth of knowledge about that particular record company or that particular arrangement. But that information may not be applicable to you.

Think about how you get your news. Fox has a slant and MSNBC has another slant. By finding a series of reliable, reputable sources and learning their views, including how they differ, you can come to more informed conclusions.

A very common issue with a lot of music business courses and some music consulting firms is that the information you're getting may be dated. Sure, these people were pros in the field at some point, but just as a lawyer must keep up with laws that constantly change, so must a music industry professional stay current. The past couple of years alone have brought major changes in the industry. Does your source know all the latest trends?

When you talk to people, especially if you're going to pay them, ask lots of questions. What's their current and past experience? How varied is it? As I mentioned before, who have they worked with and how satisfied were those artists? What were some of the successes and failures of this person you are talking to? Remember, someone who has had nothing but success may have some really good deals and an impressive résumé, but may not have the understanding or problem-solving skills to help you through rough patches. On the other hand, those who have failed as much as they have succeeded will often have a much wider view, which can be incredibly helpful. Watch out for promises; be wary when you're given guarantees or you're told how big you'll be and how far you'll go.

IF IT WERE EASY, EVERYONE WOULD BE DOING IT

By now, you may be thinking something like, "Wow! Is the whole music industry one big house of horrors? Is everybody out to screw me over and take advantage of me?"

Short answer: no. People can and do make it in this business—but it's not easy. Sure, you've spent years practicing, writing songs, and finding places to play. But that's the fun stuff. That's all you want to do—what it's all about, right?

Wrong.

Still in front of you is the marketing, promoting, attention to detail, problem solving, failures, losses, pain, and strife . . . Damn, I sound like some emo song. But you get the point: It's challenging—even more so if you are closed-minded or stubborn. I wish it were all about the music. I wish there didn't have to be any business in the middle of it. I would love it if you didn't have to deal with the politics and outside issues that take time away from your art, but dealing with those matters is an indispensable part of the equation of your success.

It's hard as hell. If it were easy, everyone would do it.

The point is to stop looking for the easy way out. It's going to be challenging. It will take a longer time to do it if you're doing it the right way, and—you'll love this—even when you *are* doing it the right way, it's still going to be a real bitch.

So, what's the secret? There isn't one. The bands you've heard about that just magically made it, or were seen by the right person and signed, all have their horror stories as well—they're just not publicized.

> One of my inspirations once told me, when I wanted to quit,
> 'Buck up, Binky; it's worth it, and it's a hell of a ride.'
> And you know what? He was right.

If you want the dream, it's obtainable, but you have to work your ass off to get it. It means taking stock of the time you spend each day and how effectively you're spending it.

Small Steps Can Add up to Big Progress

Ask yourself some questions: Can you cut back thirty minutes on your video games to do thirty more minutes of marketing? Can you miss a TV show and spend those thirty minutes practicing? Can you find five minutes here and there to pop up a blog, market your band online, or work on finding a new venue or another band to work with?

Sometimes doing a little each day will get a lot more done over a longer period of time. Consistency with small, daily segments, especially in advertising, marketing, or promotion, can actually be more effective than pulling a one-time all-nighter. Keep doing a little each day—every day—and then when you have days when you have hours to put into a given project, you'll be even more productive and see continuity and growth.

If you haven't seen progress, analyze what you're doing and what you aren't doing, and alter the game plan. I talk to so many musicians who say they're doing everything they are supposed to be doing, but then when I bring up a laundry list of approaches, they haven't touched one of them.

Today's musician has to learn the business side. It's crucial to have an understanding of marketing, because these days it's necessary to put in as much time promoting your songs and your band as you do practicing your music. Anything short of this is not going to work. It's a common misunderstanding that if you get picked up you will have marketing people and promotion people and agents to do all that "busy work" for you.

Don't take my word for it: Go ask any of your favorite artists who have made it in the past forty-plus years about the work and time that it takes beyond playing the music. The truth is that artists have to spend the bulk of their day on the business side of things: from radio and TV interviews to website and magazine interviews and more. Lots of bands have it written in their contracts that they must blog, update photos and videos, and tweet. I'm not trying to say put the music second—no way. In fact, we're going to spend a lot of time, later in the book, detailing the how, when, and why of making yourself the best musician you can be.

But marketing and promoting bring your audience to the music you're making. You could have the greatest chops since Stevie Ray and write the most amazing lyrics since Dylan, but if nobody hears you, what have you got?

BUILD A GOOD REPUTATION—BY KEEPING YOUR MOUTH SHUT

Artists know the importance of a good reputation with friends, fans, and followers. You want to make sure that from marketing to social media promotion and everywhere in between, your word is good—that you are not just a BS, wannabe hype machine.

So, let's say you're close to getting booked for this album or that tour, or that you just found out you have a chance to work with a high-profile artist. No doubt you are dying to share the news, and you want to tell the world. Three simple things to do first:

1. Put on the brakes.
2. Wait until it's a lock.
3. Shut up!

Too many people talk too much trash. There are so many wannabes, so many fakes, so many bullshit artists, and so many flat-out liars in the entertainment industry. No matter how excited you are about something big that is in the early stages, too many things can happen to change the outcome—or cancel it altogether. When you talk too soon and those cancellations happen—even if they aren't your doing—you are the one who looks bad, like the shit talker, the liar. Inevitably, you will be put into a category with people you do not want to be compared to.

I remember one point in my career as a drummer where I was so excited about some things that were coming down the pike: gigs, tours, albums, and what have you. Even though we didn't have social media back then, I wanted to tell everyone everything right after I got off the phone with the agent. Of course, life happens—which includes cancellations and changes. As things changed (and they always do), guess who looked bad for saying things were going to happen that didn't end up happening? Yep, it was me. If a tour was postponed or an album had to be sidelined, it didn't matter whose fault it really was; I was the one who said it, and it didn't happen.

Finally, I wised up and put on the brakes; I shut up and waited until things were secure. As much as I wanted to scream from the mountaintops about certain things, I waited. As a result, I got even better reactions from people and friends when things I talked about really happened.

> It's okay to say no. Would you rather be known as the liar or the honest one? Don't promise you are going to a show that you aren't going to. Don't tell someone you are going to do something you have no intention of doing.
>
> Don't tell someone you will call or be in touch if you have no desire to.
>
> Just be honest. I have been told I am harsh and brash for telling someone I will not listen to his or her demo or that I am not going to stay for his or her set. I am giving them the respect of the truth, which in my book is much better than lying and pretending to be nice, by making a promise that will never happen.
>
> Be real. Be honest. It will put you a step up in this industry.

With today's social media, it is even more of a challenge. People get an email or get off the phone, and they immediately post it to Facebook. When announcements are made prematurely, it sets you up for failure.

So learn to keep things under your hat. Keep quiet about the A-list artists you are working with until contracts are signed and events are announced—by someone other than you. Your reputation is crucial, especially with so many liars and fakes out there. So stop, keep your mouth shut, and wait until things are locked in.

"I Have Serious Label Interest" and Other Stupid Hype Statements

Believe me, you don't want to advertise that you're negotiating with a label, even if it's true. Label interest is nothing to write home about or brag about on Facebook or Twitter, especially to people you are trying to impress—like potential producers or investors.

Most of the time, when I hear or read the above line, I move on. I've heard artists tell me about how they're signing with Warner Brothers when their contract has nothing to do with Warner or any of its affiliates.

In this world of way too many labels that aren't working with the right people, it's better to say nothing until you actually have a deal. It is much more professional to talk only when the deal is signed and finalized. Bite your tongue, hold back, and show the results instead of telling what's coming. You will stand out over all of those that talk way too much. Instead, impress with your actions.

And for all the people claiming that what they are doing is "going to break through," "go all the way," or, my favorite, "revolutionize" this or that: Step the hell up; don't half-ass. Don't oversell what or where you are, especially in today's industry. It is easier now than ever to be found out as a big-talking beginner or a liar. On the other hand, honesty is strength; use it.

Especially these days, with more and more people calling themselves CEOs, presidents, "professional" this or "pro" that, so much of it is just BS. Be honest; tell people you do this part-time, that you are building your business. Be honest about what kind of time commitment you can give to a project; be honest about your connections. Such honesty may actually help you get new connections. People that you are working with may be able to connect you with other people who can help you. But they definitely won't do that if they catch the scent of bullshit when they're around you.

Think about it: If you are as hip, hot, together, pro, and on top of everything as you say you are, then why would you need help? The truth is that in this economy, everyone needs help, and it's not a sign of weakness to ask for it!

ALWAYS ASK: "HOW?"

"How?" It's one of the best questions you can ask as you're trying to make your way in the music business. When they are told they are getting this or being promised that by different people in the music industry, musicians and bands that ask "how" are going to find success in music a lot faster in the new music business of today.

Suppose someone is telling you how he or she can do this or that for you if you sign with his agency, her label, this management company, or that producer. The very first question you should ask is "How?" And then you must make them show you the answer.

As I've already said, there are a lot of people who will screw you over. There are also those who don't mean to hurt your career, but with their lack of experience, knowledge, or problem-solving skills, they sign artists to flawed contracts and end up hurting their chances. However, whether the mishap is brought about by dishonesty or ignorance, it could have been prevented if the artist had asked *how* these people would make this work for them. Sure, they have a cool website; maybe they've got the money to rent some really nice office space. But how, specifically, are they going to get you to the next level that they're promising you?

Here are ten of my favorite promises. Are these companies or people . . .

1. Taking over the music industry?

2. Saving the music business?

3. Changing the entertainment world?

4. Saying, "We've got the expertise and knowledge"?

5. Helping artists achieve their dreams?

6. Making bands rich and famous?

7. The next big thing?

8. The most important playas out there?

9. Going to take you to the top?

10. Guaranteeing you "thousands" of hits, friends, likes, or listens?

Every time they toss out one of these gems, you have to ask, "How? How? How?" After all, they took the time to produce the hype. Maybe they won't divulge their super-secret insider knowledge, but they should at least show you a blueprint! Make sure the answers you get are not extensions of the hype from above. Call the references; do the background checks. Ask what is going to be required of you and what is going to be required of them.

Also watch out if one of these "hype" companies tosses a contract in front of you. Many wannabes copy major companies' contracts word for word, but they don't have the ability to do for you what a major can do. Thus, the contract they point to so proudly, rather than being a guarantee of services to be rendered, becomes an albatross around your neck. This manager who has given you nothing but talk may own rights to your music for years to come. A major company has the capacity to invest large sums of money into an artist, but you are still bound to this small manager who may not have dumped in a penny. Before you even think about signing a contract, you've got to ask how.

A perfect example, though outside the music industry, is Stefanie Gordon, who took the picture of the space shuttle launch with her iPhone as her commercial flight passed over the area. She has been complaining that the photo went viral and was sold for profit by Twitter. But she posted it on Twitter, whose terms and conditions state that they have the right to use and sell any image uploaded onto Twitter. So while she did take the photo and it doesn't seem fair, there's not much she can do. She failed to ask the right questions at the right time.

Don't be sold on the hype. Ask the questions and demand the details. I have enjoyed a great career, but the biggest mistakes I ever made, the biggest losses I ever took, and the hardest times I ever had involved the times when I didn't ask how. I wanted to believe it so much and wanted it so bad, so I took "how" out of the equation—and suffered the consequences.

> ## SOME WARNING SIGNS
>
> When you question the basics, if someone . . .
>
> - gets hot under the collar;
>
> - starts to stutter;
>
> - suddenly gets much quieter;
>
> - changes the topic;
>
> - cranks out more hype; or
>
> - simply doesn't give you an answer; you should . . .
>
> - continue to go after the answers; or
>
> - get as far away as you can from this person or company.

DRIVE AND DEDICATION: ESSENTIALS FOR SUCCESS

Along with everything else we've talked about so far—along with your attention to marketing, promotion, and networking, and as you continue to ask the questions, do the research, and fact-check all the details—you must have drive. It must be constant; you cannot give up. You have to maintain it through the periods of your greatest doubt. When things are going slowly, you need to persevere. When things are looking up, you still need to keep that same level of drive. It's not an option; it's a requirement if you want to make it in this or any other business.

I'm very proud of the format that I've set up for a music business plan. With the help of colleagues and through my own life experiences, I've outlined a game plan for artists that includes every step, from preproduction and funding to release, marketing, and solicitation. The plan covers it all, except for one part: the drive.

You alone can provide the desire, the determination, the persistence, and the constant attention to detail required to succeed. These are the true core elements to your success. Period.

Drive and determination apply to all the stages of your career—especially when you start to build momentum. In fact, the most common mistakes happen when artists lighten up. They've worked really hard to get their dream recording and all the materials in place, and then the "sit back and wait" mentality begins to creep in. What the artists really need to do at that point is to apply the same work ethic to all the other elements.

You *can* succeed. You don't need some self-help, inspirational book or DVD. You just need what's inside you, remembering how badly you want it. When you were little and you learned to walk, you didn't suddenly jump out of the crib and walk. You stumbled, made mistakes, grew stronger, and learned what worked. Each day you got a little farther. You were able to do things you weren't able to do the day before, and you were proud of your achievements.

In the same way, persistence and ongoing effort can define and enable your success. Take the drive that's inside you and apply it. Get out of your comfort zone. Push yourself.

If you do this, you will succeed.

Believe in Yourself

Believing in yourself is what fuels your drive. I mean, face it: Not everyone is going to love you or your music. There is nothing you can do about that, so don't waste any effort on attempting to change this fact. Instead, apply your energy in positive efforts toward success.

Many musicians and bands tend to have sensitive personalities. This quality can help the art, but oversensitivity to others' opinions or judgments—even when they are unfair—can hurt more than help. I have been criticized throughout my career, and while I like to think I am good at taking criticism and growing from it, I have also found myself offended at times. While I am usually the first to speak my mind about a harsh attack on my playing as a drummer, my albums as a music producer, my writing as an author, or my approaches as a music consultant, I usually choose not to defend. If I need to defend against an attack, I probably do not want to work with that person anyway.

To me, this is not a passive approach. If someone has questions or has a point of view that is different and they want to talk about it, I am more than open to do so. However, when someone rips into a blog, tells me I played terrible drums on a track, or says my writing is stupid, I just let it be. The person has made a decision; who am I to change his or her mind? Why put effort into trying to change the mind of someone who has already set boundaries?

I have seen artists get into screaming matches in person and online, often igniting a flame war. My opinion is that if you are exerting that much negative energy—putting up a Facebook page about how much a particular band sucks, for example—then you really need to examine your messed-up, delusional time-management choices and shift to something a little better for your life.

Not everyone is going to love you—and that is okay. Grow your skin a little thicker. Remember, any press can be good press. When someone rips you a new one, keep that review on your home page. Hell, have two sections: one with smiley-face reviews and another with sad-face reviews. It shows character and a sense of humor. You're proving that your ego is healthy enough to take criticism or compliments and learn from both.

You have to learn to take it. You have to learn to brush off negative reactions to your music but also see when it might actually be constructive criticism or have a seed of actual honesty. When we hear bad things about ourselves, the natural reaction is to go on the defensive. But take a step back and take a breath. Before you go on a counteroffensive, take a look at what has been said or written and see if it is something you should consider.

On the other hand, there are people who are just going to be brutal. They are going to tear into you, and really, do the reasons matter? Why justify it as jealousy or a personal grudge? Who cares why they do it? Let go of it.

I relaunched my blog in January of 2013 (http://lorenweisman.com/blog) with written and video blogs. Without a doubt, my opinions are different from others, but I don't think I've ever been completely off-base in any of the articles I've produced. Nevertheless, I've received scathing comments both publicly and privately. I've been called a hack, a scam artist, and worse. Hell, one guy says my writing pisses him off more and more each week. (Note to this guy: *Stop reading*.) But for all the rude comments, I get many more that are kind and wonderfully supportive, so I keep on trucking. It can hurt sometimes, but it's better just to let the bad go.

Don't get into the habit of responding to negative, attacking people. Responding to genuine questions is one thing, but if someone says you suck, your song sucks, your picture sucks, or whatever, *let it be*.

Every time I have responded to someone being negative, the person has only become more of a jerk. I knew a guy who said it this way: "You can't win a puking contest with a buzzard." Instead, have the courage to be positive and the desire to be a part of something bigger than yourself.

And though I hate to say it, the unreasoning attacks may only get worse as you gain popularity. The more reads I get on my blog, the more kind comments have come my way, but at the same time, the number of rude and harsh ones has jumped as well. The more you play out, the more you are heard, the more you get your music, your writings, your image, and yourself out there, the more people there will be to tear you a new one.

My advice is to take it with a grain of salt—and maybe a shot of tequila. Move forward in confidence and assertiveness and create what you want to create. Don't waste time trying to turn a hater into a supporter. Spend your time going after as many people as you can to build a strong fan base that supports you. Stay sensitive to your art, but become less sensitive to criticism, or it will eat you alive. If you can't handle the scrutiny, you are going to have a rough go in any art- or entertainment-related business.

Aaron Sorkin said it best when he wrote this: "Living where there's free speech means sometimes you're going to get offended." Putting time, energy, and effort into counterattacking your critics, giving rebuttals to bad reviews, or arguing with people who don't like you or your music are all a big waste of time.

This doesn't mean you shouldn't stand by your art. In my experience, though, people who truly believe in themselves are able to take negative reviews in stride. I think it's because they know who they are and where they are going; they don't allow the trash-talking to alter their focus. They also don't have to resort to spouting hype or BS.

So, when you talk to someone—whether a manager, a venue owner, a band member, a potential label, or whomever—believe in yourself and talk straight. Sure, you can be assertive. You don't have to be an asshole, but you can be confident and stand by your opinion. Be open to hearing someone else's thoughts, but step up and stand up when you need to. If you need to say no, say no. If you need to say stop, say stop. If you need to address an issue, then bring it up.

> If your opinions, beliefs, and thoughts stand strong—regardless of whom you are in front of or who is asking for them—they not only showcase your honor, your consistency, and your views, but they also make it easier to not worry about changing your story for this person or that person.
>
> As a whole, this attitude creates a trust and sense of truth that many lack in the music business or, for that matter, any business. If you feel that you have to alter your opinions and beliefs depending on which audience you are in front of, maybe you should keep them to yourself.

By the same token, if something isn't working, don't keep doing it over and over and over again. Remember, the definition of insanity is doing the same thing over and over while expecting a different result. People who believe in themselves aren't afraid to reexamine an approach when necessary. Have enough self-confidence to take stock of where you are. Have you been playing the same room to the same size crowd for over a year? That's not forward motion. Take the problem-solving approach to continue to progress in all aspects of your career. Where can you look for new fans, and how can you find new markets in which to sell?

It takes an assertive set of ideals to be truly successful, and it takes humility to realize when things have to change. To be humble and assertive at the same time requires that you believe in yourself. Artists who believe in themselves—those who persevere, without the need for hype or for somebody to be constantly telling them how great they are—find the path to success.

ARE YOU A GOOD INVESTMENT?

I still run across a lot of artists with the mindset—or maybe it should be called a pipe dream—that as soon as the right person hears them, they'll win the big record deal and move onward and upward to million-dollar success, fame, and fortune. More often than not, these same artists have invested very little time, energy, or money in the demos they're sending out in order to get heard by "the right person." They seem to persist in believing that their inexpensive (and usually inexpertly produced) demos will showcase their amazing ability and make labels and investors want to lay down tons of cash.

I try to point out to these folks that the realities of today's music business are working against them. At a time when labels are going bankrupt or pursuing marriages of convenience, there are fewer investments more risky than backing an unknown musical act. So you need to ask yourself: Why are you worth a label's cash?

Tens of thousands of bands, all filled with delusions of grandeur, are out there soliciting labels with substandard demos, no marketing, no promotion plan, and piss-poor organization. These artists seem to hold the expectation that their raw talent ("raw" being the operative word) justifies the label's investment. Ironically, those very few who actually get the label's money and services are often the same ones who later get pissy about having to pay back all the money *with* the percentage and can't seem to understand why it's taking so long for them to see any profit.

The fact is that it's no longer about finding a label that will support and stand by you with a large investment; it's about convincing a label, an agent, or an investor that you are worth the money.

First off, don't try to shop half-assed demos or poorly recorded songs. You may be showcasing your song and your talent, but you're also showcasing that it's going to take a greater investment to record the music the right way. Studio time is a major expense: the engineer, the producer, the food, rental gear, travel, lodging, and so on. A studio recording is fraught with risk for a label; it requires money for a project that may never be released, giving it a zero percent chance of recouping the investment. So why should they take a chance?

On the other hand, if you come to a record label with an industry-standard recording, you reduce the need for funding—which, in turn, reduces the label's hesitancy. Do your homework: Find the right studio with the right engineer and the right producer. Record the album with the goal of submitting not a demo, but a finished product that's ready for the industry. Don't shortcut; if it takes a little longer to get together the money to record it the right way, then take the time. Apply that same care to the mix and the mastering. Do everything you can to make it the best product possible.

When you take this type of package to a label, you're going to leapfrog many other artists and their half-assed demos, because you have something that's going to save the label money on the front end and allow them to start making money sooner on the back end.

Similarly, if you have in place your logo, your branding, your image, and all the secondary elements of your marketing and promotion, it makes you all the more appealing to labels, managers, and agents. If you have worked to create a complete, professional press package in which everything is uniform in appearance and content, with a sharp, professional presentation, you have again saved the label money and brought them closer to making profit from you and with you.

In other words, always ask yourself: How am I helping the label?

I see so many bands that don't have the right product or high-quality recordings. They don't have a font, a logo, or the tools to brand themselves. They lack tight bios, stage plots, and other artist contract materials. They don't have a strong fan base or much, if any, web presence. These are all things that are absolutely necessary for the successful launch of a group that's looking to make money. If you don't have these elements in place, you're going to need money, time, and a development period to get them to where they need to be. These days, if you're expecting a label to invest money and time in you, you are probably mistaken.

Why not make it as easy as possible for a label to distribute you, to put you on the road, and to move your product and merchandise? In this way, you are less of a risk in a business that's taking fewer and fewer risks every day. If you want representation or to be signed, get your product and packaging up to par and beyond. Then you can go to the managers, the labels, and the agents with the type of professional package that will make it fast and easy for them to get you out to the world.

"THE BIG, BAD WORLD DOESN'T OWE YOU A THING"

This is one of the truest lines Don Henley ever sang, but people seem to have a hard time believing it. To prove this to yourself, go to any musician's hangout—a practice building, a bar, a venue, or a music store—and you'll eventually hear a rant about the music industry. People will inevitably start to talk about why they aren't where they want to be. The venues, labels, the booking agents, or somebody else in the industry has messed up their career.

I hope, if you've read this far, that you realize the truth: You can fault the RIAA (Recording Industry Association of America), you can fault managers for shady deals, you can curse agents for screwing you over, you can whine about publishing companies for not getting you your royalties, or you can even trash-talk the big names for taking away your deserved popularity—all of it is completely useless.

Complaining is a negative thing that gets you nowhere. On the other hand, actions beget actions. The ones who bitch the most are the ones who will often stay in this pathetic holding pattern and go nowhere. These are the people who feel they deserve something from the music industry and are waiting for it to come up and knock on their door.

Just like the big, bad world, the music industry doesn't owe you anything; it was here long before you were. You want success? You want opportunity? You want to make money? Then make it happen through actions, not bitching.

I've been a part of numerous tours, recordings, bands, sessions, substitutions, and productions. I've cried, I've practically killed myself from exhaustion and overworking, and I've had the time of my life. I love music; I love what I do and do what I love.

At the same time, I accept that there is a terrible and very broken aspect to things. I've wanted to quit, but I couldn't. I know what it's like to live the five-star tours just as I know what it's like to be shoved into a very small van with five very large people for a very long time—and I wouldn't trade any of it for the world. I've made a great deal of money and lost a fortune as well. I've played for thousands upon thousands and played for a single pissed-off bartender who just wanted us to go home. It's been a spectrum of love and hate, anger and joy, frustration and pure fun. I will say it again: I love what I do and do what I love—regardless of the pain I've felt at times. I accept the pain to get a chance at the joy I have received.

It's true that some labels do sign artists to awful deals. Some managers do rip off artists. Some publishers do take far too much from artists. Some producers do wrong by their clients, and some booking agents do take advantage of bands. But there are also labels, managers, agents, and bookers that are doing it right and taking care of artists. These are the people who take action and move things forward instead of putting out a stagnant, go-nowhere attitude.

Make a difference; educate yourself. Read the contracts that you get and have a professional read them as well. Advocate change by effecting change. No single one of us can change the industry, but each of us can take small steps that can amount to big ones. It's okay to be pissed off with how elements of the music industry treat musicians, but if you harness that energy into positive actions, you will create positive reactions.

CLOSING THOUGHT

Well, I never got that double-bass Pearl kit I drew in Mr. Cepeck's science class. Actually, later on in my career, I got to sit down on one of them. I thought it sounded terrible. It was a loud, heavy, gigantic kit made for arenas. I never got to play that kit in arenas, but I got to play some arenas. I got to play some small rooms, theaters, festivals, and venues of all shapes and sizes. In other words, I got to see my dream become reality—but it was a different, more realistic dream than the one I had in the eighth grade.

I never became Jon Farriss of INXS, but I was a successful session, sub, touring, and ghost drummer. I never delivered master classes like Steve Gadd, but I taught and conducted my share of drum clinics. Though my success did not reach the financial levels of guys like Gadd, Farriss, and many others, I did match one level with them both: Like them, I was successful.

Of course, my definition of success changed as my career developed in the music industry. I got a better understanding of what I wanted, what mountains I wanted to climb, and how to prepare for each ascent so that, regardless of whether I reached the summit or just got to a few of the stops along the trail, I was still able to achieve, succeed, and flourish.

When it comes to the music industry and you, planning for the realistic goals while still moving toward the "peak" levels is the best path anyone can follow. When you prepare yourself in this way, you have that many more chances of *winning*.

YOUR BAND: WORKING WITH OTHER MUSICIANS

OPENING THOUGHT

Your band (or your backing band, if you are an independent artist) is your most important professional affiliation. None of the other people in the industry—label reps, producers, engineers, managers, assistants, accountants, booking agents, publicists, publishers, stage hands, talent buyers, and whoever else—is more important to your career. The internal key to success with a band is not just the ability to make good music together; it requires being able to harmonize and resonate in interpersonal relationships just as you must with the music.

The relationship between and among band members is critical, and managing (sometimes, surviving) that relationship is a full-time job.

Bands are riskier than ever to investors and labels. These days, there are more and more successful *individual* artists out there versus the number of successful bands. Whether it's the risk of too many chefs ruining the soup, or the risk of dealing with a larger number of egos, being in a band can make things much more challenging than going at it alone.

I am not saying not to form or join a band, but I am saying that, in the music industry of today, if your choice is to go the band route, you'd better have a good idea of what you are getting into. You need to know what you will have to do, what you are up against professionally, emotionally, financially, and creatively, and some of the best ways to make sure that in the good times and bad you and the other members are protected from all the things that can go wrong.

A band's long-term, sustainable success will depend on you and the other members getting to and staying on the same page. You will often need a meeting of the minds to ensure that whenever you experience the best results, the worst, or anywhere in between, the outcomes will not benefit one while completely destroying another. It's important how you work together writing and performing—and also how you market, promote, and handle the business side of things.

The more you can understand each other's strengths and weaknesses and the more you know about what everyone is expecting, what they want, and what they are willing to do and not do, the more productive you'll be. How you communicate, problem solve, organize, and approach the music business off the stage can set the foundation for a group that can have a solid career.

PLAYING WELL WITH OTHERS

Because the quality of relationships means life or death to a band's long-term success, I begin this chapter with a fairly extensive discussion of relationship dynamics as they apply to the working band. Many solo artists and bands don't think much beyond the music, and of course, the music alone can easily take up all their time. They think about the styles, the technical approach, songwriting, and the influences of everyone involved. Unfortunately, because these are often the primary points that are looked at, bands get into fights and arguments over just about everything else. My goal in this chapter is to get you to look at the interpersonal stuff that can either tear a band apart or make it stronger.

Finding the musicians who are a strong musical fit is the first step—heck, that's what you're there for. But what about the variance in personalities, communication, problem-solving styles, and sharing? These are elements that have to work just as well to keep a group running smoothly.

Let's start by looking at your personality. Would you prefer a band that is more of a dictatorship—a group with a leader or two who run the show? A dictatorship is not always a bad thing. Some people feel more comfortable in bands where the major decisions are made by one person.

Or, maybe you prefer a democracy, where all members of the band have equal standing across the board. This requires good understanding between people and a lot of communication, which is why it is the harder route to go. Disagreements will come up more often when you have numerous people whose opinions have equal weight. In such groups, having band meetings are crucial. Planning and making decisions in advance about future strategies, such as how you may go after a certain manager or label, record an album, or take any other action, can make things much easier as you are faced with those opportunities.

You also need to think about the size of the band and the involvement of each member. Sometimes, for example, horn sections are hired guns, while other bands decide to have everyone as an equal member. There is no template that is right or wrong; this really comes down to personality and what works best for the artist or group as a whole. Now, what if you don't want to be in a democratic band and instead want the control? Maybe you would be better suited as a solo artist. There is nothing wrong with being in a band *or* with being a solo artist. But if you really want the songs to be a certain way and if you really have a vision that you don't want to alter, solo may be the best way to go for you.

There are many other options available. If you want to be a hired gun who doesn't take part in the major decisions, being a sideman might be for you. I worked as a hired gun and session player for many years and loved it. I didn't have to deal with band politics, artists' emotions, and annoying situations; I was a drummer for hire. Some think of this option as whoring yourself out or having commitment issues, but if it works for you, why not do it? I did not want to be involved as directly with artists, and by taking the hired-gun approach, it allowed me to be happiest in what I wanted to do and how I wanted to do it.

If you decide you want to be in a band, though, you must take the steps to clarify and communicate. Make sure that everyone is on the same page. As things change or ideas alter, make sure everyone is clear on what is going on. The better the communication and understanding, the less chance you will have of blow-ups on stage, group-ending disputes, and people not talking to each other while stuck in the same bus on a long tour. Trust me; I have watched all of the above happen, and every time, it came down to lack of clarification, misunderstandings, different expectations, and different desires.

Being in a band is like being in a relationship with more than one person—a scary thought! Hell, being in a decent relationship with one person at a time is hard enough; then add in your art and your passion mixed with others' opinions, egos, and stubbornness and you can have a regular World War Three on your hands. Take the steps to find out the commonalities—as well as the differences—between people to be assured that your band can survive and thrive beyond the music. In the end, you will spend more time working on things such as marketing, traveling, eating, and going over business than you will working on the music, so you really need to know you can work and deal with these people outside of the music.

CHALLENGES OF EFFECTIVE COMMUNICATION

If you're in a band with someone you cannot communicate with, it's a recipe for disaster in the long run—or maybe the short run. Often, early on when you're playing music, everything is great—not unlike the infatuation of a new romance. But you have to think about the rough times. Being in the back of the van for five hours with someone getting on your nerves or simmering issues finally being brought into the open can set the scene for an explosion.

We all have baggage—we all respond to certain situations in ways that we don't mean to. So, get to know your band mates. Knowing about their past can help you learn the best ways to approach them without triggering things that have nothing to do with the subject at hand. Read the stories about Sting and Stewart Copeland from the Police, or even more recently, the Dave Matthews Band. A few years back everyone was on a separate tour bus and not talking except when on stage.

Sometimes bringing in a therapist or a third-party mediator can help vent smaller problems before they become destructive. Other times, taking a break and creating some personal space can help mend things. Most of all, be proactive and productive instead of defensive and small-minded. It takes an open mind and a big heart not only to say what you feel but also to listen to what people say without feeling attacked.

Let's face it: Relationships of all types are a challenge. Your miscommunication and arguments will not go away overnight or, for that matter, in a week. Nevertheless, small steps count. If you really care and really want to make it work, then don't half-ass it. It takes 100 percent effort to meet a person halfway and work together to find resolution.

Relationship Expectations: Communicate, Clarify, and Try to Listen

It can be challenging to balance friendships, relationships, and your schedule when it comes to your career. Make sure you are clear in your relationships, your friendships, and with those that live outside of your world. Be certain that when it comes to anyone's relationship expectations of you, they have been told the truth about you, where you stand, and what you are about. I know this to be an issue firsthand, both for myself and for many other artists. Be clear with those you are dating and those you are involved with socially and professionally about your commitments, your dreams, and your schedule. When it comes to effective communication in life, love, music, and everything else, *be honest*.

What I ask of my friends—and I know many other musicians and bands ask this of their friends—is to understand that although we all get engulfed in work, music is a passion and a love. There is burnout, but it is a higher threshold than in many other jobs. My personal goal is to be honest about my work, my schedule, and what I can bring to the table. The more that artists can share with those around them, the better friendships and relationships can be. It will also help you avoid arguments, misunderstandings, and false expectations.

> Are you joining a conversation or taking it over? Stay aware of how you join a conversation and of your effect on a conversation. Are you complementing an existing conversation or are you being obtrusive?
>
> It is a careful balance when you join any situation, conversation, or group. The more respectful, considerate, and aware of those that are already engaged, the more you will be engaged.

Some Relationship "Do's" . . .

1. **Listen.** Listen to what the other person is saying. Don't start planning your response as the other person is speaking. That's being defensive, and it will pull your attention away from what the person is saying. Put the ego away and listen to the other side instead of preparing your response—wait until after they're finished talking.

2. **Stay calm.** Do your best to breathe, to stay calm, and to hold back on your volume and annoyed behavior. Avoid waving your arms around or making frantic movements that will only add more stress to the situation.

3. **Maintain eye contact.** It can be hard when you're upset, but try to stay connected by eye contact. Demonstrate that you are really listening, that you truly want resolution. Recognize, however, that eye contact can be interpreted as aggressive, depending on the person. This is why it's good to know the person you're trying to communicate with.

4. **Work to understand the other point of view.** Just because you see things a certain way doesn't mean another vantage point isn't equally valid. Just because you have resolution and feel content doesn't mean the issue is resolved. Look for a solution for everyone involved. You don't have to agree with the other opinion, but if you can work to understand it, you're meeting halfway and together you

can get to a resolution faster. It's not about agreeing with the other party's point of view; it's about understanding it so you can all move forward together.

If you feel slighted, give the other person the benefit of the doubt or ask the person why he or she did whatever it was that upset you. If the other says he or she didn't intend to upset you, explain how it hurt you as you work to understand that the intentions you imagined were not the true intentions of the actions. This is called trust, and you have to apply it.

5. **Keep the goals of solution, resolution, and problem solving in mind.** Remember that you're trying to fix an issue while learning to communicate better at the forefront. Don't forget that arguments will occur again, so make the next one a little better. Keep your attention on finding methods together to solve and resolve.

6. **Trust what he or she is saying.** Trust that the other person wants to solve the problem and is not trying to pick a fight or be difficult. You may be angry and you may see it another way, but if the other is coming at you honestly and you refuse to accept them at face value, your problems are going to run a lot deeper.

. . . And Some "Don'ts" . . .

1. **Do not assume.** If you don't know for sure, then don't claim to. Tell someone what the situation feels like for you; explain what you're seeing; but avoid telling others what they're doing or thinking. They might not be doing that particular thing at all, and your assumptions will only add fuel to an already tense situation. If you're unsure about something, then ask. Of course, others have the right to their feelings, their views, and their opinions, but if you ask them or tell them how it feels to you, you're taking a better step to a solution. Still, you have to be prepared at that point to hear why they see it in a different way.

2. **Do not interrupt.** Allow the other person to speak. Give the person the respect that you want when you are speaking.

3. **Do not go on the offensive.** When others are addressing an issue they are concerned about, listen and try to respond to that issue without bringing up any concerns or accusations that you might have. You may decide to bring them up later, but take one thing at a time. Respond to the issue at hand instead of

changing the topic or trying to point fingers. This, again, will only add stress to an already stressful situation. Tackle the issue at hand with the goal of better communication. When you start attacking or trying to hurt the other party, people tend to shut down and not want to listen. They begin to concentrate on their rebuttal, and you don't feel like you are being heard. You have used a form of communication that is viewed as an attack, and now the defenses are up and the ears are shut.

4. **Do not exaggerate or make rude comments.** Saying sarcastic things that you know aren't true is not going to help get you to resolution. When you're asked a question and you say, "It seems like we fight all the time," how does that help? It may be a fact; it is probably known by all parties and really doesn't need to be stated. It makes more sense to be productive than to reiterate all the issues that everyone knows are present, which will only cause frustration. Work to use only problem-solving questions and statements.

   When it comes down to discussing issues, cite examples and patterns. Don't go for the exaggerations. Sentences that start with "you always . . ." or "you never . . ." are usually false. Instead, give specific examples or patterns that explain why you believe something is a certain way. Instead of yelling, "You always use too much distortion at the end of every damn song," try to cite the exact songs in which you feel you might be hearing too much distortion and offer an alternative. Keep the creative process going by staying positive and constructive.

5. **Watch for selfish traits.** Take an honest look at yourself and watch for where you may be a little stubborn; work to find ways to meet the other party halfway. Above all, avoid the blame game. It doesn't matter whose fault it is; it's about the resolution. If others refuse to acknowledge that fact, then get out of that relationship, business, or group.

> Playing the blame game is stupid and childish. Even if it is someone else's fault, the blame game is wasted time, effort, and energy that takes you somewhere that is not going to get you anywhere. It's right up there with being passive-aggressive.
>
> Both are pointless, immature, and a waste of time.
>
> If it's broke, put the effort into the fix and the preventative maintenance to ensure it doesn't happen again.

CHECKUPS: IS EVERYONE STILL ON THE SAME PAGE?

Outside of all the performing, traveling, touring, recording, writing, marketing, branding, soliciting, and promoting that musicians and bands have to do on a regular basis, it is a good idea to set into the schedule some basic band checkups. Many bands already have the occasional meeting (usually rushed) to discuss things coming up or to review things that have just happened, but the basic checkups do not happen.

Take the time every few months to sit down and do a checkup. Make sure everyone is still on the same page, that the expectations are still clear. Are there problems with money, relationships, jobs, goals, or expectations? These are the questions to ask, and this is the time to let people speak and listen.

When I'm consulting with a band, I ask about some very personal issues. I tell them that they don't need to give me these answers, but if they want to work effectively, productively, and for the long term with each other, they need to give each other the answers in order to stay on the same page. Like mildew in a shower, small things can grow into issues that cannot be fixed. So, make sure you are on the same page not only in chapter one of your book, but check in every few chapters to make sure you are still reading together.

Communication, like any instrument, is something you will never truly master but should practice every day. I am still having my issues with it. Any artist I have done a full album or long-term project with has gone around the ring with me in a couple of verbal bouts. The difference is that the artist and I both realize the argument is about the long-term resolution and the success of whatever is being worked on; this usually turns the argument into a productive conversation.

The best relationships, the greatest loves, and the most wonderful creative connections take effort. Compromise and work hard on the small steps to better communication. At the same time, recognize the efforts of the other person. Move forward together, learn together, grow together, and then experience the benefits of all that work—*together*.

THE BAND HOUSE: PARTY CENTRAL OR CENTER OF STRESS?

The wonderful world of living together—or not—as a band is an age-old dilemma and not one that has an easy answer. For some groups, the band house can be an amazing experience, but it can be a very negative situation for others. This really comes down to the collective of the group and how it can best mesh together.

Just because you practice four times a week, play on two or three other occasions, and spend lots of time together in cars, vans, and buses doesn't mean a total living situation is the best option. There are a lot of questions that need to be considered. People are definitely different at home than they are on the road, and some of these "jump the gun" living situations have actually broken up bands that should have stayed together. Not all groups that work well professionally can also successfully live together.

Knowing the traits of each member's lifestyle, beyond his or her role in the band and on stage, is necessary. Also, if you can get out on the road and get a solid tour under your belt—something at least three weeks long—that can show you how you live as a group and how you handle yourselves in a tighter, more private environment.

Begin by asking yourself these questions about the group:

- What traits do you like about each of the members?

- What traits do you dislike?

- Do you like each person's friends outside of the band?

- Do you have hangups about sharing, or do certain members have a more communal sensibility than others?

- What rules would you want in place in your living situation, and what rules would other members want you to abide by?

- When you have to compromise on different subjects or details—and you will have to compromise—do you feel it is an even compromise, or will it cause animosity amongst you?

- What are the band members' needs for personal space, and will the house allow for that?

- What about other people living in the house with the band? If there are extra rooms and it is a larger house, do you want to rent the other room or rooms to people outside the band, and if so, to whom?

Remember: You are now taking life with the group to a 24/7 level, bringing a number of creative people into a place where you are all practicing together, playing together, and living together. It really comes down to looking at both sides of the coin before committing to something of this scale. The pros may outweigh the cons, but even a few simple cons can cause a member to be pissed off, which can have an effect on the music as well as the future of the band.

Sometimes a couple of members already live together, and too often it is assumed that it will therefore be an easy transition for all to join in. But think about it: Two is easier than four, five, or six. The two who already live together could have an established friendship outside the band. This will not necessarily make it an easier transition for the rest. Some bands have even experienced anger or jealousy when a couple of members click in a living situation and spend more time together than with the others. It may sound sappy and stupid, but it happens a great deal.

It would be smart to put together a checklist in advance to review whether it will work or not. Also, decide ahead of time on the costs and who's paying what.

That said, what about the positive side of bands living together?

- All the gear goes back to the same place.
- You save on rent, food, electric, gas, and other bills.
- You have a center of operations for the band. You will potentially have an office and a rehearsal space in the same location.
- If your band is a business, you can take advantage of tax deductions.

Sharing a house also gives you a place to hold band meetings, to have everyone around for practice, and to problem-solve issues that are a lot easier to resolve when everyone is under the same roof. This can make it a fun experience. It all comes down to weighing out the options, the people, and the mix that is created by everyone being under the same roof.

Ask questions of each other. Spend time talking about the best and worst roommate experiences that you have had in the past. Each of these questions will help give you a better sense of your bandmates, which will not only help you to see if living together is a good idea, but also bring you closer together by giving you a better understanding of the people you perform with.

ROMANCES TO BROMANCES—AND EVERYTHING IN BETWEEN

The last couple of relationships I have been in were nothing short of train wrecks. I don't imagine myself as the easiest person to see in a romantic fashion, and I know that I put music first in most cases. I tried very hard in my last situation to put someone else first, but it did not end up how I wanted. But who really wants to hear about my love life?

What I know from the bands I have toured with and the relationships I have witnessed that were most effective is that they were, as I mentioned before, based on clear and concise communication and expectations. If music is number one to you, then tell that to the person you are seeing. The more that is clarified from the start, the better things can be. Talk with your date or partner about what it means to be with a musician. Talk about your dreams, your goals, and what you have to do. Explain that the hours are awkward and different; that rehearsals are part of your job; and that the weekends will often be packed with shows. The more that's understood up front, the fewer fights down the line.

As far as intra-band dating, I've always found it to be a no-no. The line we used to say was, "Don't Fleetwood Mac each other." You are living and breathing music with your group; it can only make things harder if there is a romantic relationship occurring in the middle of that dynamic as well.

A number of years ago, I was on tour with a band in which two romantically involved bandmates did not speak in the van from Chicago to Houston; their only interaction was on stage. Those ten days in the van sucked—for all of us. You could cut the tension with a knife, and the worst part was that the rest of us had to deal with that tension as well. We practically killed each other by Oklahoma City. The guitarist who was involved with the keyboardist had packed his bags before the show in New Orleans and planned to quit after that show; by the end of the night, they worked out their differences.

Not that it made it all better: The rest of us then had to deal with lovey-dovey crap until we reached San Diego, when the guitarist and keyboardist started hating each other again, by which point we found the animosity a relief.

Leave the significant others out of the practice space and the studio, most of the time. Let them visit now and then, but think about it: Would you go to someone's office or workplace to just hang out and watch all day? Don't let that happen with your band. Also, significant others' opinions should be kept quiet unless requested. You don't need someone's squeeze sitting in the middle of your practice and asserting how the music should go and why.

It's hard enough to date, much less be in a steady relationship. When you add an artist or a musician to the mix, it can become downright challenging. I'm not trying to be discouraging; I know that there is hope for those who see musicians. From what I have witnessed, it's all based on communication and trust. But if you're not up-front and honest, it can become that much more of an issue after the initial infatuation is over—not to mention what it can do to the rest of the group.

THE LAST STRAW: HOW TO AVOID DRAWING IT

I was sitting in a coffee shop about a year back and watched a guy walk in and sit down at a table with a woman. He did not look very happy as he walked in and yet she looked fine, though inquisitive as to his expression. Though I didn't know it in that moment, I had front-row seats for the last straw.

They spoke quietly for a few moments; I did not catch any of it, and was trying to avoid listening in. However, a few moments later, she was loud enough for the whole shop to hear. She said it was the last straw and they were through. Then she went on a tirade—in a public place, mind you—about all the things she hated about this man.

This all happened not five minutes after a kiss and "I love you, and I missed you today," which quickly transitioned into "You are worthless, a loser, and I have wasted too much time on you." The fight then moved outside and the scene was over.

It made me think about musicians and bands, though. I thought about many of the dysfunctional relationships I have either been a part of or have watched as a music producer or even as a music consultant, trying to play mediator.

How Solid Is Your Relationship with Your Band?

Unfortunately, one of the things I spent the most time on in many of my productions was refereeing between band members who were so far away from being on the same page that it wasn't even funny: business arguments, fights over songs, screaming matches about money, alcohol, girlfriends (the Yoko types), and you name it.

Still, watching the last-straw coffee shop event made me wonder: If a relationship is really down to the last straw, what does that mean for the band? Maybe it is time to work on communication, to discuss and try to problem-solve issues before everything explodes.

If little issues are starting to arise, address them before they compound into larger issues. If you are seeing a pattern start, get it on the table before it becomes stressful and while it can be talked about in a cool way—while you still have a box full of straws.

MEMBERS WHO QUIT OR GET FIRED: HANDLING THE AFTERMATH

Do you remember the first band you were in? The one you were convinced was going to change the world? Do you remember those rock star fantasies you had when you played in a basement or bedroom? You knew that you were the bunch that was going to go the distance. Mine was a group called Orenda. I still remember all their names: Kurt Hilborn on bass, Jon Zahourek on guitar, Bill Murphy on vocals, and me on drums.

It's interesting what we remember and what we forget. I have played with tons of people and tons of bands over the years. I have forgotten a number of those band names and especially the members, but I don't think I will ever forget Orenda or those guys.

We were not good. And when I say that, I mean we were really bad. We had no original songs, only covers, yet we were going to rock those covers harder than anyone else in the world—or at least that's what we thought at the time.

> How long do you think you can pick up the slack for the band members that are slacking on everything from the music side to the business side? Do you have such limited vision that being signed, being managed, or making all this money will make it go away?
>
> Carrying someone else's weight is only going to weigh down on you and add stress, frustration, and pain. Choose who you work with and play with wisely.
>
> Making it these days means a lot more than just playing the music, and unless you have the financial means, you are going to need to share, delegate, and be responsible and accountable for all the work that has to be done. If someone in your band is not there, you might want to look for someone else that is.

We seemed to have more band issues than good music. We replaced the bass player and fought about the direction of the music (keep in mind that we played covers, not original music). Then we got rid of the vocalist, and the band imploded—we "orended." Yet for some reason, I still often think about Orenda.

I also remember standing on the porch one day with a musician who had been, in a way, a mentor to me for some time. He was in a Boston band that blew up and then evaporated almost as fast. He told me that I should plan on being a part of many bands in my lifetime. He reminded me that I was only fourteen and if I were going to make music my career, I should plan on breaking up with just as many bands as I formed or joined. I have not spoken with him in years, but watching and learning from him helped me out a great deal, and his advice to me that day was no exception.

The point of this little rant is to prepare you for those scenarios in which a band member quits or you have to fire a member. As much as you think it will never happen, it inevitably will. It's an extreme rarity for bands of musicians who have never been in other bands to actually stay together for the long haul. The only way you are going to survive the inevitable splits and departures is with the best communication, clarity, respect, and honesty. Mix that with trust and you will have a solid time together and a less challenging separation, when that time comes.

DEFINING YOUR DREAM AND PUTTING THE BAND TOGETHER

Now let's turn from understanding relationships to thinking about the different possibilities for your band and the territory you want to stake out in the music world. It's really important to make sure everybody is thinking of the same territory!

I have met a lot of artists and bands who have worked together for months, even years, and when I ask certain questions like, "Do you want to tour?" or, "Would you prefer to stay local?" you would be surprised at how many different answers are given. You'd be even more surprised at the shock within the band when members look at each other in disbelief of each other's answers.

Just because you have a dream of what you want and how you want it to go, you can't assume that the rest of the group shares it. It is a smart and very helpful idea to have a band meeting or a talk about what everyone wants and what everyone is expecting. These meetings also should happen over and over again as time passes, because where one member might have had a similar vision to yours six months ago, it doesn't mean he or she does now. A girlfriend, a new job, a kid on the way, buying a house, or just burning out can change the place where he or she was. So right off the bat, check in with everyone, see where people's heads are at, and make sure you are all on the same page.

Sometimes when a band has been together for a long time, a deal falls through, or even when nothing seems to be on the horizon, attitudes and ideas can change. Staying on top of attitudes as they evolve will make life in the group, and life in general, much easier and help to avoid surprises and personnel changes.

So, whether you are a solo artist, a member of a band, or the leader of a band: What is your dream and what do you want?

There are so many avenues and opportunities in music today, and the market is still growing. The chance to make a solid and sustainable living is better than ever. Remember: When I say sustainable, I'm not talking about being a rock star, making millions, or for that matter, even playing in front of millions. I'm talking about all the different avenues out there that will allow you to do what you want on a realistic and financially secure level.

Do you want to tour? For how long? Would you rather teach? Do you hate traveling and prefer to play only locally? Would you rather do sessions? Would you rather run a studio? Do you really love songwriting, and if so, would you prefer to write songs, jingles, or maybe soundtracks? If you think you will do it only for a while before calling it quits, how much time do you want to put in?

All these questions can help you find the answers that will help get you where you dream to be. It doesn't start with understanding the music business; it starts with understanding yourself. The clearer you are on your dreams, your goals, and your aspirations—from best-case scenarios to just getting by—the better you'll understand what you have to learn and what direction you have to take.

Each step you take toward your own clarity will define the opportunities and approaches that you will need to take. These steps may also help you know what to look for in other musicians—beyond their playing.

Hiring or Adding Musicians to Your Band

Whether you are forming a band yourself, replacing someone, or adding a member, the first step in finding the right musician for your group, after satisfying yourself of their musicianship, of course, is to make sure you all have a clear understanding of what you are looking for and what your expectations are. As you are looking for the right players, you have to make sure you are getting the right personalities as well. Are you a good fit together? Do you have things in common outside of the music? Remember, even successful bands usually spend more time together at marketing events, traveling, or doing music business and promotion than they do actually playing. You will be stuck in hotels, backstage, and just hanging around very often. Being in that situation with someone whom you aren't comfortable with is a total pain in the shorts.

It's all about the music in the end, but if you can only play together and otherwise can't stand each other, then either it will be a short-lived relationship or you will be hating life pretty quickly. Naturally you are going to want to gel musically and in the creative, improvisational, and technical aspects, but you also are really going to want to like the guys or girls you are playing with; they are not only coworkers but, ideally, friends as well. Make sure the dynamic is there.

Let's say you need to place an ad in order to fill a spot in your band. Here are some questions your ad should answer for the people who respond, as they size up what you're looking for:

- Who are you (as a band or as a hiring artist)?

- Who are your artistic influences?

- What are looking for in a player? What musical skills should the applicant bring to the table?

- What are you looking for in a person? How will you expect the applicant to fit into the group personality dynamic?

- What is the musical vision of the group?

- What is the background of the group? What skills and experiences are already present?

- When are you looking to get together and get moving?

- When are you looking to practice and how often?

- When are you thinking about recording?

- Where is the band based?

- Where do you want to play or tour?

- Are you planning to keep the band going part-time, or are you trying to go pro?

- Why are you looking for a musician?

- Why did the last person leave (if applicable)?

- What is your approach to marketing, recording, and band ownership?

- How open are you to change and switching up the vision?

Yes, it's a truckload of details, but a strong ad that includes all these elements is going to get you better responses from the types of players that you're looking for. The same goes for any other services you might be looking for: from distributors to producers to studio players to selling or buying equipment. The details should be there, and they should appear professional.

Write your ad and edit it carefully. Don't come off cocky; that can turn away the kind of players you'll want to talk to. Hell, let's face it: You're writing an ad to find a missing piece, so don't come off over the top. Include links to websites, samples, or social networks so that someone can see and hear you. Leaving holes leaves questions.

You want to have the strongest players possible supporting you and complementing your music to bring it to the best level it can reach. Across the board, you should go for people who are welltrained and wellversed in a variety of styles. The more styles they know, the better they can supplement your sound and give you verstility. Whether it is a bassist, a pianist, a guitarist, a horn player, or a singer, make sure the person has good timing and can play to a click. Players who can read music and have the ability to play to a click make for quality takes in the studio, getting you what you are looking for much faster. You may pay a little more, but it will save you money in the end.

Make sure the professionalism is there apart from the instrument that they play. Players who are on time, sober when they play, call if they're going to be late, and are well organized make the difference and stand out above the rest. You should set these expectations early and often with anyone you bring on board your band.

If you are looking for a solid keyboardist, make sure the person knows piano, too. Preferably he or she has both classical and jazz training. The classical background comes through in technique and theory, while those trained in jazz have a solid sense of improvisation and a better sense of how to voice chords.

This can ring true for bass players, guitarists, and singers as well. Depending on your style, it is not essential that everyone you hire be able to read note for note on a chart, but having the foundation and the background as well as the experience in different genres, styles, and ensemble or band types will make a big difference and add a lot of versatility to what you can accomplish musically.

Having the right gear is also important. Your musicians should take care of the instruments that they play and come with their gear in the best shape, maintained to a professional standard. You can have the greatest keyboard player in the world, but if he is playing on an old, broken-down Casio, it's not going to sound as good. The keyboardist should have a quality keyboard with the ability to give you a wide number of sound options. Make sure the drummer has an array of cymbals and snares. The bass player should have a fretted electric, a fretless, and a nice upright. Musicians should also have backup gear and the skills and tools to repair things. I used to say as a session drummer and hired gun that I was not paid to record; I was paid to be able to solve any problem that could arise.

And Speaking of Drummers . . .

I want to go into a little extra detail about drummers, and not just because I am one. A good drummer can really make the band, regardless of the style, and a bad drummer can really hurt the band. A drummer should have solid time—should not rush or drag—and feel comfortable with a click track. When you have a drummer who can keep the band in time and stay solid, it helps the foundation of the music. It will also make things go worlds faster in the studio. Often when I am producing a record on a serious time budget, the first problem we run into is a drummer who is not able to be solid with the click, and that person is the first to be replaced in the studio.

When you put up an ad or you talk to a drummer, explain what you are looking for. While you might not be able to afford a session drummer, if you display yourself, your music, and your career as something that could be going somewhere, you might find a drummer who will dedicate time without charging you for rehearsals or too much for shows.

This may seem obvious, but drummers should have drums that sound good. They do not need to have some brand-new, top-of-the-line kit, but their gear should be well maintained and sounding great. The drums should be in tune, and the drummer should know how to tune them. It sounds obvious, but believe it or not, a lot of drummers do not know how to tune their drums.

Dynamics are another big key. You are going to want to find someone who can support you not only with energy and excitement, but also with the ability to be quiet sometimes. When I have helped artists audition a drummer for a tour or for a band, I've asked them to play a really deep, in-the-pocket, hard-rock feel at a higher tempo, and then I like to see if they can play with the same feeling, emotion, and energy at half the volume. This is a great way to see how the drummer can handle dynamics. If he or she can't maintain the groove without playing loud, look for someone else.

Something you are also going to want to look for is consistency, patience, and taste. Can the drummer lie back, sit on the groove, and not embellish at all? Can he or she just play the groove and fill only when needed—not when he or she feels like it? A lot of drummers who have the chops and the technique will display both at the wrong times. Pull out a stopwatch and ask a drummer to play a simple beat. Use a beat that has a repeating bass drum pattern, a simple two and four on the snare, and a basic eighth note pattern on the hi-hat. Now here's the trick: Have them play this for three minutes. Can the drummer play a solid groove with no extra dynamics, no fills, and no changes? This is a great test of the basic abilities of a good drummer. It sounds simple, but I have seen many drummers who have not been able to do it.

Lastly, even though there are a million other elements to look at with drummers, it is good to look at their understanding of different styles. When you have a drummer who has a solid foundation in many styles, it can help you find the pattern or beats that you are looking for in a given situation. It's crucial not to settle for lower quality. The drummer is often one of the most expensive personnel in the band. But considering time issues, recording issues, dynamics and volume issues, and loads of other issues, if you want to save money, stress, and time while improving your sound, you need to have a drummer who can support, supplement, complement, and carry the rhythm. You may not always be able to find the perfect drummer or be able to afford to pay the drummer you want, but try to make sure you have the drummer you need on the big shows and on the recordings.

New Blood in the Band: Who Are You Bringing into the Fold?

Way too many bands make the mistake of bringing someone in as a full member too quickly. It's not about distrusting the new guy or girl; it's about developing, over time, the kind of trust that is needed. You wouldn't move in with someone after just a week of dating, right? So why do so many bands audition and bring in a new member that quickly?

When you list an ad for auditioning a new artist . . .

- Be detailed.

- List your influences and your approach.

- Explain the plan or concept of the band.

- Be clear about expectations for rehearsing, investing, writing, recording, and time commitment.

- Find out about the person's social life. Does he or she see this as a hobby? Does the musician have a controlling partner or spouse who could make things difficult?

- Does the performer have a job that will not allow the time to tour? Does he or she have a criminal record that may make it difficult to get a visa to play out of the country?

- What is the credit situation of the potential member? If you bring the person into the band and into the business side of things, will it affect the band in a negative way?

- Is this person committed to any other projects that might get in the way? Is he or she just out of a band and might try to get back with it? Are you sure you would keep this person if your former member wanted back in?

Look at it like a personal ad instead of a music ad. It will inevitably come down to how your personalities mix anyway, and by taking the proper steps to get to know your new member and also letting the person get to know you, you will have a better chance of building a long-term partnership that can be successful.

Trial Period

If you're starting your group at ground zero, letting someone in as a full member is one thing, but if you already have merchandise, recordings, bookings, and other tangible assets and structures, I strongly recommend a trial period. This is the time when you observe the following: Does the new member come to practice on time? Perform well on stage? Come prepared? Do his or her part? What are some of the core issues for you as a group? Is the band vegan? Political? Is there some other social or moral viewpoint that is very important to the group? How does the new member work in with these issues?

Allow yourself the time to review and observe before committing to a new member. The same goes for a producer, a booking agent, management, or any partner you are going to be involved with. See how things go; see how you feel working with that person. Watch for warning signs and red flags and address them immediately.

Lastly, decide where you are able to compromise and where you will stand firm. If there are elements that you can bend on, define them, just as you should define the elements that you will not bend on.

Taking the time and building trust will make adding a new person to an already established group an easier transition and, in turn, will not overburden you with the normal stresses of the new-blood syndrome.

Keeping the Band Together in the Best and the Worst of Times

As I said at the beginning of the chapter, communication is an essential part of being in a romantic relationship, in a friendship, and especially in a band. Many problems that occur in a band are caused by misunderstandings, miscommunication, and assumptions. Such issues can cause anger and frustration and become a huge debacle if you don't feel as if you are being heard. Just make sure you are listening as well.

Connect Outside of Music to Better Connect Inside the Music

Sometimes people communicate in rhythms, notes, and phrases instead of words. Many musicians and bands have the keen ability to know each other musically but still have no idea how to understand where a band member is at personally. The ability to communicate in a mature and professional fashion has to grow stronger as a group finds more and more success in music, since they have to spend more and more time together.

Lots of artists have written songs about the fact that on tour, it can seem like the least amount of time is actually spent on the stage; the bulk of it is on the bus, in interviews, traveling, eating, in the hotels, and in meetings. Being able to make sure that the band is a team and that team cohesion is well in place will help to prevent a number of problems down the line.

One of the things I like to recommend to bands who may have those external conflicts is to get the band to do team-building activities outside of music. It may sound crazy, but I have seen bands that I sent to try those types of events actually grow and understand each other that much more as a unit, both on stage and off.

I'm not necessarily talking about group therapy, though that can help. It is more about experiencing things together outside of music that teach everyone about each other. Sports, challenge courses, board games, or anything done together completely outside of music can bring a group closer and develop a better understanding of each other musically, personally, and professionally.

Communication . . . Again

Passive-aggressive communication is not the best way to achieve problem solving. It is also a real douche-bag approach to arguing your point. Music is a hard career in which to make it and stay successful. That's a simple fact. You have to have a hard shell; you have to be prepared to run into uncomfortable situations and not run from them. You need to be prepared to develop problem-solving approaches, to get past internal issues as well as problems you may have with producers, managers, labels, booking agents, venues, and most everyone else you come in contact with.

Passive-aggressive approaches can be a leading part of why problems continue to resurface. Many people use a passive approach to keep things stable and nonconfrontational, but this can make things more and more problematic and overwhelming, as issues will continue to occur every time something similar to the initial problem comes up.

Taking a more assertive, open, proactive approach to issues or disagreements can help solve the issue at hand more quickly and can also build the foundation for better communication, along with bringing a greater understanding of expectations and how to address a particular person in the most effective manner.

Listening Even When You Hear Things You Don't Want to Hear

Take a few steps back from the normal day-to-day things you do—writing and practicing songs, marketing online, postering for upcoming shows—and think about how you listen, how you learn, and how you communicate.

Listen with ears that want to understand, no matter how hard and confusing things may sound. Any interaction that consists of two or more people with strong views, opinions, and personalities is going to involve disagreements. It's human nature, and sometimes that just *sucks*. You're going to have confrontations. You're going to have disagreements. You're going to get frustrated and upset. So why not work to learn the best ways to communicate, and the best ways to argue, so these problems can be easier to deal with and a little less stressful?

One of the most important abilities in communication is the ability to listen, even when what you're hearing is not pleasant or what you want. You don't have to agree, but you have to hear it out.

Don't Waste Time in One-Sided Arguments

This line from a Max Cohen song still rings true: "It doesn't matter how much you scream, when they've chosen not to hear you." If you are dealing with someone who will not listen, will not accept that things may not be the way they think, why try to convince them? If someone is not going to listen, then all you are doing is wasting time, creating frustration, and making things worse.

A little while back, I had to back off on some consulting recommendations. While I am not always right, nor claim to be, I have a pretty solid background and some solid ideas and approaches. But while I was trying to help certain artists, they were fighting me on things they claimed to be true, but could not prove. I had had some very personal experience with the items being discussed and had made these exact mistakes in the past. I didn't want to see them fail or make the mistakes they were about to. But they were right, they knew everything—and in the end, they got nailed by something that could have been prevented, had they taken my advice.

I don't waste my time anymore. I am here to help independent musicians. I want to share tips for success. I deliver reason, experiences, or explanations for my recommendations. But I don't argue anymore with those who believe they are always right. This is not to say I don't hear their side or views, but if they are not willing to hear mine and we are not having a two-way conversation, then it's game over.

If you are coming to the table with an open mind, would it be worth the time to sit down with someone that is locked down, already convinced they are always right? Look at patterns that emerge when you argue. What are things that set you off? What are things that set the other person or people off? It's very common to find that many arguments reoccur not based on the item or issue but based on how people are communicating and approaching that issue. If you are constantly saying or hearing, "We always have this fight," or, "It always goes here," then maybe it's time to look at the patterns of communication and make a two-way effort to work out the issue being brought up.

It comes down to trust and respect. Can you and your business partners, your band members, or your spouse trust that no one is trying to belittle anyone else? Agree that neither party will attack, that you are aiming for a solution, not just a fight. Add to that the promise that everyone will do his or her best not to become defensive, jump the gun, overreact, or assume. This will help communication during tense moments as well as day-to-day conversation.

Watch yourself for patterns, just as you're watching others. Avoid telling people what they're doing and why they're doing it. After all, you don't know everything, and that approach can come off as condescending and assumptive, which will almost inevitably anger the other person. Identify things together, but listen to each other. You may have a conclusion as to why so and so always does this or that. You may have identified some patterns, but what if there is more to it? Don't claim to know everything. It will only force the tension to a higher level. But if you'll keep these principles of communication and trust in mind, you'll build a foundation that will make everything work better together—especially the music.

TAKING CARE OF BUSINESS—LEGAL AND OTHERWISE

Now let's spend some time thinking about the various legal and business aspects of putting your group together. A little time invested here in learning a few of the ropes can save major hassles later in your career.

Picking a Name

One of the first decisions that bands typically make is deciding what they're going to be called—the name under which they'll work and with which they'll begin to create their space in the music marketplace. But picking band names is a pain in the ass. There. Done.

I mean, it really is a pain, and there is no simple way to get to a name. There are stories of bands that have actually gotten into fights—fisticuffs—over a name. Come on! I mean, what's in a name?

I always wanted to be in a fusion project called Chocolate Orange Thunder Monkeys from Mars on Boats. What a surprise—no one has ever gone for it!

Truthfully, these days there is a lot in a name, and when you are coming up with one, of course, you want to see if it has already been taken. Sometimes just searching online to see if there is another band is not always the answer. Certain bands do not have great optimization, so you might want to look through some of the band name registries, copyrights, and trademarks. Make sure to review the legal rights. If a name is trademarked, don't use it. The hope is to get popular, isn't it? While people might not catch you at first, if you have to change a name later after you have been building a career and marketing with it, it can be a tremendous setback. On that same note, don't settle for a name until you decide on one you like. As soon as you start a website, your social networking sites, and then performing, that should be the beginning of your branding and marketing. So work to find the name that you want. With all the importance of branding, marketing, and promotion, you want to make sure you have that name locked in early on to create the best foundation for long-term recognition.

As you're coming up with the name, think from a marketing and branding standpoint. Is it easy to spell? Will people be able to remember it? Is it too long to make an effective logo? Is it available as a domain name? Is it available as a name for Facebook, Twitter, YouTube, ReverbNation, and Pinterest? Branding the name and the uniformity across social media sites will make you that much easier to discover.

Does the name work in the font you have already been thinking about? Or have you even thought about the font or the lettering for the name of your band? Think about all those fonts, lettering, and graphic spellings used by groups like Metallica, Megadeth, the Who, the Rolling Stones, and many others. Think about the fonts of brands like Dunkin' Donuts and Coca-Cola. Taking into account all the different elements can make it easier to figure which name will suit you best.

Often I tell members of a band that is in its early stages to separate and individually come up with keywords or even just words that they like. Find books from their favorite authors, chapter names, characters, whatever they enjoy or like. Is there a theme, a story, something they want to tie into the name? Think about these things separately and then come back together as a group. Bring lists and go over everyone's words. This is not necessarily where they will find the name, but they will find commonalities that may lead them to it.

If you have some initial names or off-the-cuff ideas, put them on one list. Your keywords go on another. Finally, create a list with your themes, ideas, or other bits of information that you might want to use. When you know your theme and have begun to find words that seem to work, take those words and ideas and step away again. See what you come up with separately for the next time you meet up.

Keep a pen and pad at hand. I always have a pad by my bed so I can write down ideas that come to me while I'm sleeping. I always keep a couple of extra blank cards in my wallet for ideas, lyrics, or things I want to jot down. If you're the technical type, use your iPhone, BlackBerry, or some other smart phone. I prefer to write things on paper.

Don't be rushed; spread out the words over time and see what is working for you. As you meet again with the group with your edited list, begin to find the band name. As you collectively weed out what you don't like and hold on to what you do like, you can usually find a name that will work for everybody. Take your time finding your name. Work on ideas, together and separately, and think about every issue associated with the name, from the name itself to branding and marketing and even the way it will look with a logo. When you take these steps, as you try to figure out a name, it can make things a lot easier and a lot less stressful.

Nicknames, Stage Names, and Name Changes

Nicknames, stage names, and dubbed titles have been a part of the music business for years. When it comes to branding great nicknames, it can be a dicey thing; it's not good music marketing to make or imply large claims before you actually get large. Still, musicians and bands can have fun with nicknames and they can help your social media promotion in different ways.

Sometimes I tell people they may want to consider a different name that is easier to spell, pronounce, or find online. My advice is to stay away from self-dubbing; let a nickname come to you from another source or from a series of other sources that are not directly related to you.

Regarding stage names, sometimes you can find a name that is better for online optimization or choose a name that differentiates you from someone who already has a presence. For example, David Bowie was really Davy Jones, but when he was coming out in the business, a little band called the Monkees was making it tough for him to keep his given name.

You can also search out names or phrases that have low competition for searches, which you could take over fairly easily as well. And in a closing thought on names, here are ten of the great dubbed nicknames for some artists that you will recognize. Use these as inspiration and food for thought:

Aretha Franklin: "Queen of Soul"
Iggy Pop: "Godfather of Punk"
Donna Summer: "Queen of Disco"
James Brown: "Godfather of Soul" as well as the "King of Soul"
Neil Young: "Godfather of Grunge"
Eminem: "King of Hip-Hop"
Ozzy Osbourne: "Godfather of Heavy Metal" and the "Prince of Darkness"
Michael Jackson: "King of Pop"
B. B. King: "King of the Blues"
Benny Goodman: "King of Swing"

On the other side of the nickname is the stage name. Here are my favorite top artists and their real names. Browse this list and see if any of these inspire you:

Jon Bon Jovi: John Francis Bongiovi
Bono: Paul David Hewson
David Bowie: David Jones
Cher: Cherilyn Sarkisian LaPiere
Alice Cooper: Vincent Furnier
Elvis Costello: Declan MacManus
John Denver: Henry John Deutschendorf
Flavor Flav: William Drayton
Flea: Michael Peter Balzary
Faith Hill: Audrey Faith Perry
Joan Jett: Joan Larkin

Geddy Lee: Gary Lee Weinrib
Huey Lewis: Hugh Cregg
Barry Manilow: Barry Pincus
Marilyn Manson: Brian Warner
George Michael: Georgiòs Panayiotou
Joni Mitchell: Roberta Anderson
Gene Simmons: Chaim Weitz
Slash: Saul Hudson

Work-for-Hire Contracts: Getting It in Writing

The main function of a work-for-hire contract is to stipulate that the person being hired is performing the outlined duties or tasks for pay only, not for any percentage of ownership, royalty, or anything else. As a session and touring drummer, these were the contracts I signed 90 percent of the time. They were clear, clean, simple, and easy. Even as a music consultant and music coach, my music consulting agreements side with the artists: I put in clear and simple wording that states I am an independent contractor and that everything I do for an artist, management group, or label is exclusively owned by the person or company who hires me.

A basic work-for-hire agreement shouldn't be expensive. There are numerous templates available to cover the freelance or work-for-hire contract. The easiest version is the clear-cut, pay-for-work-performed: no percentages, no points, no royalties, and none of the trimmings. These contracts can easily be less than a page in length—hell, they can be less than half a page. You simply want to state that a session or tour player is being paid for the service and that he or she has no standing percentages, points, options, royalties, or anything else coming beyond the agreed fee.

As simple as such an agreement is, not having it in place—in writing—can set up a world of hurt down the line. They become a serious cluster-fuck when someone starts making money—especially if it's a *lot* of money. The lack of clarity, understanding, and agreement then comes back to bite you in the ass. "This person owes me this"; "I was never paid that"; "I was promised this if such-and-such happened"; and especially, "Well, I normally charge X, but since you are doing well . . ." The preventative maintenance is to put it all in writing.

It doesn't matter if it is one song or an album; make sure everything and anything having to do with your career is clearly laid out in either work-for-hire contracts or some kind of binding agreement that will help keep things from coming undone just as it all finally comes together.

And here's a word to artists who sign work-for-hire contracts to provide the service: Go into the job with the attitude of performing and playing as if you were in an ownership or equity position—don't act like a hired hand. After all, if the band or artist who hired you does well, chances are they'll need your services again—or they'll be in a position to refer other people to you. Approach every job as if it were your chance to break into the big time—it may be! Don't forget that Chet Atkins made his name as a sideman and session player long before he became one of the most influential people in the music business.

Feeding the Legal Beagle: Internal Contracts, Copyrights, and Publishing

Lots of great books cover the legal details of internal contracts, copyrighting music, and publishing, as well as setting up your own publishing company. *The Business of Music*, Tenth Edition, by Krasilovsky, Shemel, Gross, and Feinstein (New York: Billboard Books, 2007); *Legal Aspects of the Music Industry*, Revised Edition, by Richard Schulenberg (New York: Billboard Books, 2005); and *Making Music Make Money: An Insider's Guide to Becoming Your Own Music Publisher* by Eric Beall (Boston: Berklee Press, 2003) are some great books. I especially recommend that you dig into them for details of publishing and contracts. You can also go online and search for specific, up-to-date legal agreements. Use the template forms found at the Legal Zoom website (www.legalzoom.com), but also get someone to review the exact details to make sure they cover the contract you are looking to create.

The point is that you must act on the legal details. You need to take your copyright activity beyond the standard, do-it-yourself method of mailing a song to yourself. Just as you pay attention to the musical, communication, and organizational details, you absolutely, hands-down need to take care of the legalities in the professional and correct manner.

It's true that aspects of copyright law fall into the realm of "common law." It's also true that it can be very tricky—a downright pain in the ass, in fact—and you may have to go over things with a lawyer or a consultant to make sure you have everything you need and want correctly written and organized. But it will make your life much easier, especially when you start to do well and people other than yourself begin to care about who really owns your creative output. I guarantee that you do not want to go into the ring with some publishing company's $200-an-hour lawyer with nothing in your corner except "I mailed it to myself, so it's copyrighted."

The books listed above, as well as information on the websites of ASCAP (www.ascap.com), SESAC (www.sesac.com), and BMI (www.bmi.com), will walk you through the steps (if you are a US citizen, these are the three organizations you will be affiliated with). I personally believe you should not only copyright but also set up one or more publishing companies (Neil Young is one major artist who agrees with this), but others may advise you to publish your music through someone else. That comes down to personal choice, but make sure you understand all the details of the contract if you choose to publish with another company.

Pay attention to the details, read these books thoroughly, and if you do not understand something, find someone with the right knowledge to clarify it. You need to be proactive and detailed. Consider where you stand when you are happy and content with the members of your group (if you are in a band) but write these contracts and organize as if you are breaking up and never speaking to each other again (more on this later).

Make sure your copyrights register who wrote what; do not just share in the creation of the songs. Avoiding this detail can cause major problems down the line if you break up and begin to argue about who the song belongs to. How you copyright it is how it stands. The same goes with publishing, so you'd better make damned sure that you list each party exactly as you want. Your friends or partners of the moment may become bitter enemies down the line—I've seen it happen time and time again. And by the way, in case you think sharing credit is a minor detail; take a look at all the songs on which Elvis Presley is listed not only as performer, but also as co-composer. Colonel Tom was no fool, and he always made sure his boy shared in the royalties of everything he recorded.

Everyone says it will never happen: No problems will ever arise, and if you fight, everything will be made up. Friends forever, Care Bear Power, and all that cheesy stuff.

Wrong answer. Plan as if things are going to go to hell to ensure that you will be taken care of under all circumstances. I'll cover this in a bit more detail later in the chapter, but you should take the time to discuss—and document in a contract—what will happen if someone chooses to leave, dies, quits, or whatever. Discuss the rights to continue to use or not use the music. Figure out how people will continue to be compensated or not. The more you can put on paper—from copyrights to publishing, performing to breaking up, people leaving, starting other formations of the band, and so on—the better. Does someone have rights to the band name? The logo? Do you have an agreement stating that the dirty laundry can't be aired publicly? Does someone have rights to license the music, and does that person get a separate cut for getting the deal before royalties and payments are split?

Have a brainstorm session and think of every issue that could possibly come up. Then do some research on problems that either broke bands up or gave artists serious problems or hassles. Lay out everything clearly, professionally, and legally. Make sure you are protected and that the group as a whole has a crystal-clear understanding of how things stand legally. You will be much happier in the end, regardless of best- and worst-case scenarios.

Who Gets Paid Back What? Questions to Answer before Money Complicates Everything

Many band arguments—while they are together, when they are breaking up, or amid personnel changes—arise over who gets paid back for what. Some examples . . .

The band replaces a cymbal that the drummer broke or buys a microphone for the singer or an amp for the bass player. In the moment, it was a must-have, but who is owed what and who owns what? Is this sharing the wealth, or is someone keeping tabs? Then after the purchases happen, who gets what? What are the financial expectations for band costs and eventual returns?

As a music consultant, I advise bands to clearly lay out how every purchase is made and who will get what in the end. Is the band paying for something for an individual expecting the person to pay it back? If you are not 100 percent sure, you might want to sit down and discuss it—prior to the purchase.

The bands who have clear agreements—on paper—about purchases of instruments, PAs, or whatnot experience less stress, less tension, and less fighting amid breakups or changes in personnel. Be clear on who has what, who is paying for what, and who is expecting what. This will save much bitching when something goes bad.

Left Behind: If the Act Starts to Take Off, Do You Get to Go Along?

Are you and all the other members in it for the long run? If someone offered some kind of deal to the singer or the guitarist but not the rest of the band, what would happen? You never know what will happen when somebody gets an offer until it actually happens. Therefore, you need to have these discussions early on.

I had a meeting a while back with a band who hired me for a mediation; a group of guys had put the last three years of their cash, their work, and their efforts into a group with a singer. Unfortunately, the singer got a solo spec-development deal, and the others got left behind. Sadly, there was not much they could do—nothing was in writing. Now it was just an ugly situation that I couldn't really help with.

So what do you do? Are you only in it for the lean times?

You have to ask yourself: Are you in the band, and are you sure? When I was coming up as a drummer, I spent a lot of time as a session player and a sub. I was the backup guy, and I was fine with that. I did get the left-behind treatment a couple of times, but I was prepared for it. So how do you handle it? What do you do to avoid being left behind? It is actually simple.

Since you never know what is going to happen or how someone might react to a deal, to money, or to an offer, it is best to have something in writing early on. These kinds of deals are less and less frequent now than they were in my day and the days before, but that still doesn't mean you shouldn't be prepared for the worst. If you are going to invest your time and sweat, whether you are fronting the band or you're the drummer, put your expectations in writing for the scenarios that could leave one or more people behind while the others move on.

Write out the expectations: Who would get what? What kinds of working arrangements would be in place? Do you require advance notice? Would some kind of separation fee be required? What about rights to any cowritten music? If you don't have this stuff written down, you've got nothing to stand on legally. These guys I spoke with lost a friend, a lot of money, and any chance of profiting by the eventual success of the singer who took off. The more you prepare for both the best- and worst-case scenarios, the more you will reduce the chances of getting screwed and being left behind.

Really, what a lot of the above comes down to is this:

BEFORE THE HONEYMOON IS OVER, PLAN FOR THE DIVORCE —OR FOR WORSE

It may sound defeatist, but the ending is something you should be prepared for at the beginning. Whether you are firing a member or a member quits, it's crucial to have a game plan for how the situation will be handled. It's not absolutely necessary to have a legal contract or template; you can set it up yourselves—a prenuptial agreement, of sorts. However, it's even smarter to have a lawyer or someone with a legal background review the agreement. Setting up scenarios for each member leaving the group by choice or by force will make life a great deal easier if and when this does occur.

And as awful as it may be to think about, it's also a good idea to make provisions for the true worst-case scenario: death. What happens if a member dies? Handling it like a will that is to be probated will ensure that you address issues such as royalties, ownership, and who has rights to what, even in this very sad situation.

It sounds a little morbid, but make sure you have a clear plan for what is supposed to happen if a band member or someone on your tour passes away. Does everyone know whom to contact, including someone who can verify the contingency plan? Does that plan include canceling remaining tour dates?

It may sound harsh, but as someone who was on the road with a group where someone passed away, I can tell you that it can be a very confusing, frustrating, and even frightening process. Have a simple plan in place where everyone knows what is supposed to happen if someone passes away or if they are hurt in an accident where they are unconscious and cannot make decisions for themselves.

The fact is that attention to detail and planning for those worst-case scenarios will allow you to recover quicker if things go wrong. Think of it as disaster insurance; if the worst happens, you'll have a backup plan.

Here is a checklist of items to address with individual members. The band should decide the details; the specifics will differ for each group:

- Songs, copyrights, and publishing: Who has the rights to which songs, and what happens if someone leaves?

- Are you paying group fees for management or solicitations, such as press packs, that you have already purchased? Will you give a percentage back to the exiting player? Or are all monies nonrefundable?

- What issues surround the label, if you are on one? What happens on the business side if someone leaves?

- Band gear: The band bought it, so how do you want to handle it if someone leaves? Buyouts? Do you want to give the gear in question back to the exiting member, or pay them a depreciated rate for their share of the purchase?

- Merchandise and sales: What percentage should the exiting member get and for how long? Should there be a flat buyout of monies invested in the product?

- What kind of notice needs to be given if someone is leaving, and how long should the departing artist have to play before a replacement is found?

These are some of the key elements to think about. It gets a lot more detailed as you sit down to make the decisions that will create the contracts, but having a plan will facilitate a much easier transition if a member leaves for some reason. Such agreements can also help if a band dissolves. If you incorporate as a business, you can lay these out as bylaws. Just make sure everyone is on the same page, and put these agreements in place—and in writing.

TIPS FOR TIGHTENING YOUR SOUND AND SONGS: PRACTICE MAKES . . .

Let's focus now on the reason you got interested in this whole business: the music! Throughout your career, it's vital for you to continue to grow, progress, and develop *as a musician*—that's what keeps you alive and focused.

Whether you are preparing for a show, getting ready to go into the studio, or just looking to tighten up a new song in rehearsals, it's important to take a professional approach to practice. Don't neglect the details that can get in the way of making the most of precious musical rehearsal time. You may be surprised to hear me say this, but it's really not about how much time you practice. To tell you the truth, I am never all that impressed when people tell me they practice for five hours a day. You can waste lots of time in practice or rehearsal if you are not using your time as effectively as possible. I am more impressed when the bands I produce put together game plans for rehearsing and preparing materials.

Sitting in a room and just going over songs is pretty pointless; you're only reviewing the song. But if you work on different elements inside the song and switch things up, you can really develop the strength of the tune, the performance, the approach, and the creativity you bring to the song. Also, preparing the songs for performance will give your live show an extra edge, that little something that people will not be able to define but will register as special and different.

Bands need to be aware of each other and how each player brings his or her piece to the song. Even the untrained ear knows when a band is sounding really good together—and when it's not. Practicing builds the strength of the songs, but also helps develop the communication needed to play songs the right way. This same communication skill set will also help you cover mistakes, problem-solve any issues that can arise on stage, and make on-the-spot changes without an audience even noticing.

Here is the top-ten list that I give to musicians for effective practice in preparing for the studio and live shows and for working on new and old materials in rehearsals.

1. **Tempo alteration.** Practice with a click. Make sure the tune is where you want it to be. Especially when it comes to the studio, you are going to want to have that song dead to click but also comfortable, so you don't give it a robotic feel with a robotic sound.

   Try the tune faster and slower in order to create the "pocket" of the song. Take the tune up ten beats per minute and work through it faster on one day; then the next day practice it ten beats slower. This can help you feel exactly where the tune's tempo should lie and give you a new sense of what it feels like when the song is beginning to rush or drag.

   Now and then, make a dramatic tempo change. Set the click radically slower than what you are used to. This method will really help each person feel his or her part and define the parts that are being played. This helps a lot with the development of solo sections, time keeping, and an awareness of the little intricacies that are lost when it's at the faster, normal tempo. It forces you to focus on the details of the tune—and that's a good thing.

2. **Song section loops.** Anyone can practice song after song, counting in the tune from the beginning and taking it to the end. Not surprisingly, many songs, especially new ones, really sound great in the beginning but then become weaker as the song progresses. By starting the song in different places, you can work the sections to a point where they all become a lot stronger.

3. **Start the song from a different place.** For instance, play the last verse out and then loop it back to the beginning and up to the starting point. Play a verse, chorus, or section over and over again. As you come to the end of it, just loop it and repeat it. This forces you to hear the song differently and to pay attention to things that might otherwise be glossed over.

   Try transitions that don't exist. Play the bridge into the intro and loop that a couple of times. You may never actually play the song this way, but you are familiarizing yourself with the different sections and increasing your understanding of each transition.

   Play it backward: each section from the end to the beginning. This will also help you feel transitions in a stronger way.

   After playing through these variations, play the song straight through as originally written. You will feel a greater control of the form of the song.

4. **Practicing song transitions.** Test the waters between songs. Have a rehearsal that is just about song transitions. This can help you decide on the best set-order sequence for live shows or the order of songs on an eventual CD. Take the last twenty-five seconds of a song and the first twenty-five of the next song and play through a set of just beginnings and endings of songs.

   Or, take five seconds from the end of the tune that you have started and then launch into the beginning. Be aware of the tempos, the keys, the feels, and the relative levels of energy of the songs you are coming from and then heading into. Spending the time on this will really help to mold different sets to have different effects, making your show that much tighter and stronger.

5. **Practicing in other keys and modulations.** You're comfortable in a certain key for certain tunes, and that's fine. But why not try them in other keys? This can help your chord voicing, phrasing, and understanding of the song. You may even discover that there is a better key for the song than the original, due to guitar voicing or your singer's range. By modulating and using different keys,

you can also open up ideas for different types of solos and additional creative approaches for the song.

6. **Practicing staging, locations, and setup.** Bring in the video camera or a normal camera for this. Find out: How do you look on stage? What kind of setup works best to help the band members communicate with each other? What bad habits or silly faces occur and on what songs?

By watching yourself in rehearsal, you can help format the stage show to look the way you want it to. Does the guitar player always look down? Does the drummer play with his mouth open on certain songs? Looking at your rehearsals from the audience's perspective can help you go for a more natural approach or change things up as needed to better suit your music. Having an idea of what you look like and how you are delivering your music visually can take your show to another level.

It just makes sense. After all, actors and dancers practice in front of a mirror so they can see how they really look, not just how they imagine they look. You're putting on a performance that has visual as well as musical elements; why not give yourself every advantage possible?

You can also address how you get on and off the stage and even how quickly you set up and break down. Attention to these elements demonstrates a higher level of professionalism and raises the bar for your performances.

7. **Practicing set alterations.** Whether you are preparing for a rehearsal or a live show, write it all down! Write down every set—for rehearsals as well as shows. Afterward, cover what felt good about it and what felt bad. In reference to the song transitions above, think about overall set transitions. What seems to work the best and what doesn't?

8. **Use a spotter.** Add that fifth Beatle to a rehearsal or a show to watch the band. By not playing an instrument and only concentrating on the band, the spotter may be able to point out small things that need to be altered. Having someone watch the crowd reactions—when the crowd seems most excited and connected in contrast to when they seem distant and uninterested—can help you make the band that much more aware and that much stronger on stage.

Compile the data and figure out what works best. It will make a difference.

There are also books and videos from guys like Tom Jackson that are worth checking out to help your onstage presence and delivery.

9. **Practicing worst-case scenario arrangements.** Rehearse for problems that might occur live. Preparation will help the show to recover quicker when those unexpected scenarios happen. Whether the drummer breaks a stick, a guitarist breaks a string, the monitors go out, the vocal microphone shorts, a pedal breaks, an amp shorts out—you get the idea. By working through such situations in rehearsal, you can have a backup plan.

   Practice some plans to keep your songs going or to do something to get out of the tune without showing the audience that everything just went wrong. Have a joke ready, along with secondary arrangements or solos, to enable a quick recovery. Have a cue for each person so anyone can alert other band members that he or she is having a problem and that a backup plan needs to take place. Things go wrong—they always will—but when you handle an unexpected problem without showing that there even was a problem, you will raise the level of your performance significantly, and even when things do screw up, nobody will care. Instead, your audience will be impressed with your professionalism and skill.

10. **Time signature alterations.** This is a great practice tool that will make you think about your songs in a different light. It will also really help define songs in their original time signature. Switch the time of a song for a rehearsal: Play a song that is in four in three instead; try adding a beat or a two, then subtracting a beat or a two. This will help you sense the form and the chords that you use when it is in the normal time signature. It will play with your head a bit, but it's a great exercise.

11. **Style alterations.** Try altering the style and the feel of a song. Take a tune that is jazzy and play it with a hard-rock feel. Then take a quieter tune with soft dynamics and play it in a style that is really loud and brash. This can help you feel the dynamic and approach differences to the tune and make you more aware of the foundation of the song.

12. **Minus-one rehearsing.** Sometimes as musicians, we habitually cue into certain instruments or certain ways of playing a tune and find ourselves not listening or not as aware of others. Do some rehearsing without any vocals at all; make

sure the group knows the changes without the vocal cues. Rehearse without the bass, without the drums, without the guitar, and so on. This will help each player feel the songs in a fresh way and become aware of aspects of structure and instrumentation that he or she might not have been paying attention to before. It also may help bring to light wrong notes or chords that one instrument is playing that were hidden when everybody else was playing.

13. **Of course—last but not least—practice and run the sets straight through as you would perform them!** While freshening things up by altering certain aspects is valuable and will improve your mastery and understanding of your music, you also need to have comfort and familiarity with the way your sets are going to run. So, do the one without neglecting the other. Your shows will be tighter, your audiences will be more enthusiastic, and you'll continue to grow as a musician.

Try applying some or all of these techniques to different rehearsals. They can really help to tighten up your songs and, at the same time, make rehearsing more effective and more fun. Some of these techniques may even find their way into performances. Maybe certain nights you can take a song and switch the time signature, the tempo, or the stylistic feel to change things up, just for an evening.

Summing up: Practice and preparation are not just about the amount of time you put in but also about the way you spend that time and how effectively you use it.

Individual Musicianship—Outside the Group

It's important to practice as a band. Of course you want to be tight; you want to have the songs as strong as possible, both while performing live and recording in the studio. The ensemble needs to click together, to know the beginnings, endings, changes, and transitional sections of a song.

Still, musicians often forget to work on their personal musicianship, ability, and technique. It's stereotypical for a guitar player to set up his gear and go into a chop frenzy during sound check, showing off riffs he or she already knows—but could never really use in a song. The same can go for the drummers; I know I've been guilty of setting up and then starting to see how fast I could move around the kit.

Some say this is warming up, stretching out, or even practicing; it really isn't. Just as you need to exercise to stay in shape physically, it's key to keep your technique, ability, musicianship, improvisation, and creative knowledge in shape as well.

> Making music is more than just going into the studio with a producer and making beats. It is more than just having your voice washed over with every effect from Auto-Tune, to compression, reverb, and equalizers. It is more than shit-talking hype.
>
> You want to be a singer? Then learn your craft and learn an instrument. Understand basic theory; comprehend chords, keys, and harmonies. Learn the basics of recording.
>
> Too many "artists" rely on others to make the art. That's like saying you want to be a chef and all you do is bring out the food.
>
> Put in some effort. Learn the basics so you can advance and don't need to rely on everyone else all the time.

I used to maintain a very steady practice routine, always keeping up on the basics while mixing in new styles and different techniques. Practicing with the band is not enough. It will help the band and help you some, but you need to continue to grow on your own. If you are not growing, you are shrinking in skill sets, abilities, and knowledge, and sooner or later this will harm the band and your career.

Keep working on the technical exercises that give you the rudimental skills needed *for* the band and *beyond* the band. Practice styles that you find challenging, or create your own challenge; working out of your comfort zone will make you grow. Work with metronomes and take lessons. Just because you're in a band doesn't mean you shouldn't take lessons, and just because you're on the road doesn't mean you can't connect with a local teacher and work on different methods and approaches.

Listen to a new song in a style that you aren't used to, one that might not be your favorite. With iTunes, Google Play, YouTube, ReverbNation, Spotify, Pandora, SoundCloud, Bandcamp, and all the other sites, you can find more music of more different styles easier than ever. Expose yourself to new sounds and styles, even if it's only for ten minutes a day. This can really broaden your ears and your musicianship. Hearing how another player in another genre might approach something can really impact you and inspire new ideas. After all, the truly great artists—Sting, Paul Simon, Zappa, Bob Wills, Led Zeppelin, Jack White, and the list goes on and on—have absorbed influences from a wide variety of genres, then fused them together to create something unique and important.

Now, don't go over the top: If you hear some kind of riff that's way out there, you don't have to learn it and add it into a song that really doesn't call for it. Still, it can become a source of reference for new and different ideas and approaches.

Work on your reading. If you don't know how to read music, learn! Use the time you have and the musicians around you to gain knowledge in areas in which you are not as proficient.

Buy different books on music; rent documentaries or educational DVDs. Read interviews of your favorite musicians, articles about your principal influences. Bring more to the table as a complete artist who is working on his or her own craft to enhance the band as a whole. Also, encourage the other band members to take the initiative to better themselves individually; this, in turn, benefits the group.

> Grow, learn, develop, study, and aim to be better than you already are.

There are players, and there are bands that have players. Also, there are musicians and groups that have musicians. My favorite artists and bands are composed of musicians who continue to work on their craft and develop their voices individually while being a supplementing voice and player for the other artists they perform with.

TAKING CARE OF YOURSELF AND THE MUSICIANS AROUND YOU

The musician's life can be rigorous: on and off tour buses (if you're lucky—most bands travel jammed into somebody's car or van); in and out of hotels; weird hours; the stress created when a booking agent or event promoter doesn't do what is promised; financial pressures; the constant need for improvement; creative slumps . . . The list of obstacles and challenges faced by professional musicians is long and tedious. The daily wear and tear of life on the road or in the studio can really start to do a number on you and the people around you.

That's why it is crucial for you to nurture yourself and the people who are important to you—not only the others in your group, but your family and friends, as well—by recognizing the unique challenges you all face. In this section, we'll look at a few of these—thought not all, by any means—and suggest some ideas and things to watch out for as you maintain the investment in your most important piece of equipment: you!

Leggo My Ego: The Waffling of the Musician's Confidence

You might have heard this one. Q: How many guitar players does it take to screw in a light bulb? A: One hundred—one to screw in the bulb and ninety-nine to say how they could have done it so much better.

There are a dozen jokes like that representing the egos and competitive natures of musicians. Words like egomaniac, arrogant, egotistical, and pompous have been used to describe some musicians. Some are based on stereotypes, but too many are accurate. In fact, many of those who present themselves in this way are actually very insecure people; the only way they can feel good about themselves is by making everyone around them feel inferior.

Musicians with confidence and healthy egos go much further than those with egos that are out of control. The music sounds better, communication is usually better, and the individual musician's reputation is almost always enhanced.

But too many rock, rap, and R&B artists add an excess of ego into the lyrics of their songs and their marketing as a whole. These days, in a larger scale market, the ego has to take a back seat; otherwise, you are just another artist with attitude, and there is little original about that. Instead, present yourself as confident but respectful, and your attitude will open a lot more doors in the industry.

When you are working up your bio, your tagline, and your basic marketing, think humbly. Don't use words or phrases like "innovative," "new," "never been done before," "best," "greatest," "can't be compared to anything else," or anything similar. Instead, think about how you would describe your sound, your album, or your band if you were standing in front of one of your biggest inspirations, one of the people you have looked up to.

You want to put across an image that is . . .

- Confident without being cocky

- Strong without being arrogant

- Descriptive without going over the top

- Humble, with respect for those around you and those who came before you

It's not about playing yourself down or being underwhelming. It is simply about taking a few steps back and designating your music, your image, and your materials as something that is a little different, a little more respectful, and a little more aware.

Don't overembellish; avoid exaggerating who you are and what you have done. Most people in the industry are more impressed by artists who talk less and show more—through their performance. Highlight the facts and showcase the talent and the concept. The public doesn't need to know many downloads you get or how many friends you have on this or that network site; this data should instead go on a stat sheet.

Don't make up a label if you don't have one. Don't talk about showcases for labels and how you are right on the verge of breaking through; just define the simple truths.

If you're not incorporated or you're not a business, don't claim to be one. People check that stuff out, and when they do, you have then made a bad first impression. If you don't have a copyright, go file for one and then post your music. Don't lie about the details—your lies will come back and bite you in the rear.

It's one thing to look professional, but it's quite another to merely pretend to be. You'll look the fool when people check you out. Humility is the foundation for a greater gain than any wordplay or arrogant statement. Stay humble; it will take you higher and further than attitude and ego.

Being Stubborn: Knowing When to Stand Your Ground and When to Move

I run across a lot of stubborn artists. It's a big part of the reason for the initial client question form that I require from all potential clients. It's a long, three-page form with repetitive types of questions that help us get an initial view of the artist. Anyone that fills it out gets a free consultation, but even the length weeds out a great number of people, and if the attention to detail is not there, I don't take them on.

A couple of the questions hint at the ideas of how hard a client wants to work and how open a potential client is to learning new methods or updating old ways that aren't working. If a client is coming to me for consulting or wanting to work with me as a producer, it's usually because what he or she has done so far has not worked effectively or the artist wants to learn and develop more. I don't have time for people who aren't interested in learning and motivated to make changes, if necessary.

You need to understand that sometimes, standing your ground in stubborn arrogance will prevent you from moving forward. Admittedly, artists in general tend to have strong egos, strong opinions, strong feelings, aggressiveness, and an all-around obstinate persona. I know this not just from those I have seen; I carry those traits as well.

But a stubborn artist who has a set of beliefs or views that cannot be adapted or altered is an artist who is going to fail. Adapting, changing, learning, researching, and reviewing different ideas and ways to execute are fundamental to success.

If you're not prepared to bring those attributes into play, then keep the day job. Period. And don't think that just because you saw an idea on TV or read it in a book, magazine, or interview that you've got it all figured out. Many of these elements may be good, yet oftentimes they can transition to bad execution plans when the artist does not look at the entire scope.

Every element, every approach, is different and has to be individualized for the specific artist. From there, it must be fine-tuned for the style, sound, and plan. This is where the shortcuts occur and the failure ensues.

Whether it's recording, production, advertising, touring, marketing, branding, fundraising, practicing, or anything else, you need a plan. But the plan must be carefully specialized for the specific situation. Just because you sit through a ninety-minute lecture or clinic from an artist who made it big doesn't mean that you shouldn't further research and analyze the points that he or she gives you.

A good example is "Band A" (name changed to protect the innocent), a successful platinum-selling group with videos, tours, groupies, the whole bit. One of the members of "Band A" was on a music panel with me a while back. We were talking to independent artists about the best approaches and plans to succeed in the industry.

As I sat next to this guy, I listened to his story, which was really pretty interesting. I learned about how the band actually formed and about its road to success. I knew a fair amount about the band because of its popularity, and the assisting producer is a friend of mine from San Francisco, but it was cool to hear the information right from one of the members.

But as the question section of the panel began, I had to continually drink my coffee and cover my mouth to keep from screaming out, "Really? You actually are telling musicians to do that?"

"Band A" is one of the .007 percent groups. They were seen at a show and quickly signed to a manager. What their member didn't say to the audience at our panel was that the manager owned a major percentage of this band and still does. When he brought the members to the label they are on right now, he penned the deal with the label, since he had exclusive bargaining rights—a little thing the band signed away to him in the small print of the management contract. He cut the deal, giving himself, the label, and the new touring agent—who also became a part of the deal—the upper percentage and long-term rights to the band as a whole.

Now, some people don't mind this concept and would take it in an instant for the fame, immediate money, and success, but this band is going to end up in debt to the label for at least three more years. Although they are making money and they have fame, they are owned by this same label for five more albums and seven years—with no "out" in their contract.

The advice that the member from "Band A" was giving these independent musicians could not have been more wrong. What he was telling the audience was what *he* had seen and what *he* was doing. He wasn't even aware of the promotions, marketing teams, and infrastructure being built around him and the rest of his group. He was not aware that their initial promotional rollout was a $45,000 campaign involving interns galore.

I took a few questions and explained some elements along these lines. I carefully explained how another band actually did it the way just described, being careful not to say to my panel colleague, "Dude, that was how it worked with your band, and you had no freaking idea?"

But he immediately chirped up and said, "No, that's not how the music industry works."

This is where his approach switched from unaware to stubborn. A guy who was in five local bands and who was picked up and controlled by management, a label, a touring agent, and a public relations firm—a guy with one album under his belt—was telling me, a person who has worlds more industry experience in a much wider variety of circumstances, "This is not how it works." I don't claim to know everything, but it seems to me that experience in a spectrum of groups, positions, labels, and albums—ranging from platinum to never released—should outweigh that of a person with a single album and the single experience of playing with one major group.

After the panel was over, he signed lots of autographs, but to his surprise, people kept coming over to talk to me and three others on the panel who were a lot more versed in the various ins and outs of the industry.

As I talked with him in the car on the way back to the airport, he continued to explain to me how the industry works and how his band made it. As we were now in private, I asked him about his producer and the teams that worked with him, from the label to the PR people. He waved that off, saying that it was the shows that brought them to where they were. This was a conversation that I knew was going nowhere, so I took my own advice (as presented earlier in this chapter) about not continuing an argument with someone whose mind is already made up. I changed the topic to sports. I am a Red Sox fan and he is a Yankees fan. We had a much more enjoyable argument from that point forward.

The point of this story is that stubbornness can hurt you. To avoid this, look at all the facts. Even if something looks like a good thing, don't be impulsive.

Go through a checklist first:

- How will it help me in the short term and the long term?
- Who has it helped so far?
- When is the best time to execute this plan or opportunity?
- Do I need to have other elements in place to make this work?
- What will it cost in the short term and long term?
- Have I checked and connected with the references of this person or company?

It doesn't matter if you have a studio that offers you all the time in the world. How good is the engineer, and what are the costs? You might get into an amazing, famous studio, but instead of a seasoned engineer, you might get assigned to an intern. Just because you're in an industry-standard studio does not guarantee that you will get an industry-standard recording.

What if you get a web designer who gives you an amazing price but doesn't set up the site to allot you the most options and opportunities on the web? Even if you have a service or a person who is more than up to snuff with what he or she can do and has done, does the person understand the details of the project you are creating? Is this a service or person you should back-pocket until he or she can be of maximum use, or is this person someone to use right out of the gate?

These examples illustrate why you shouldn't be stubborn about the elements and facts; don't claim to know what you don't. Mixing stubbornness with arrogance is a recipe for disaster and also sets you up to incur unnecessary effort and expense.

Instead, look to those with a wider array of experience. Remember that many of the high-profile overnight successes don't have a clue about the details of what got them there; they can't tell you about the tens of thousands of dollars of behind-the-scenes investment that you won't be getting.

In the end, patience and awareness are your best assets. Educate yourself and learn from others while continuing to do your research. Your artistic enterprise needs to be maintained as a well-oiled, well-rehearsed, strongly communicating, problem-solving, marketing, uniformly packaged, content-creating, always-promoting, fan-interacting, regularly performing, selling machine. You can't build that kind of organization if you're too stubborn to learn from anyone else.

Drinking and Drugs Within the Group and in the Music Business

It's not a newsflash to anyone that drinking and drugs are an issue in the music industry. There are extremes in both directions: both those who overconsume and those who freak out if you are having a sip or doing drugs around them.

I'm not going to tell you to do or not do alcohol or drugs. It is not my place.

Personally, I've stayed away from drugs. I'm not claiming to be any kind of angel; I've done my share of pot and even the harder stuff a few times, but I mostly keep it to alcohol, and I stay in control when I do drink.

I was very young when I saw drugs kill two people close to me and two other musicians I admired. For me, this was a deterrent, showing me a path I didn't want to end up on.

On the other hand, I think people can take it too far in the other direction. Every person and situation is different. If a shot of whiskey loosens you up and gives you a better performance, then take the shot. If you need to have a *bottle* of whiskey on stage and then you act belligerent and drunk, forgetting words and parts to songs, maybe that's not such a good idea.

It comes down to responsibility. Can you have a whiskey, a glass of wine, a beer, or a shot and not be adversely affected? If so, I don't really see the problem. If you can't function *without* these things, then it's time to take a responsible look at what you are doing.

I did a test with myself when I was on the road and drinking every night: I decided to stop cold turkey. I stopped the morning after a show in Chicago and told myself I would not have a drink again until we reached Orlando. For me, it was easy. I actually felt I had a little more energy and stamina during the day, and I found that I was able to warm up before shows a little faster. So I cut back the drinking some, but I did continue to drink.

That's my unique experience; it's different for everyone. If you did that test and found yourself needing to drink, then it might be time to address the issue and whatever issues might lie beneath. Rather than telling people not to drink or do drugs, I'd rather tell them to take note of the habits that they and their band members have developed around drinking and drugs.

Prior to touring or as you're forming your group, if you have strong opinions on drugs, state them up front. I've been on tours where we actually signed a contract stating we would not drink before a show and would not have a drink until we had completed the gig. I had no problem with this. This was how the bandleader wanted it, and I wanted that tour, so I did it.

There are other people who are recovering alcoholics and can't handle alcohol around them. If you like and want to drink but are in a situation where someone is going to be on your case if they see you drinking or smell alcohol on your breath, that really isn't something you can change about that person. It might not be the right fit for you. Otherwise, you will likely get very upset with each other and want to go for blood. I saw this on one tour and it wasn't pretty.

My personal belief is that alcohol and drugs should be avoided in the studio, where I think people need to be at their sharpest and most aware. I like people to have stamina and to be able to maintain a coherent energy level that is productive, effective, and positive. I do not try to draw the lines or figure what is the right amount for a person; that is not my job as a producer. I just usually like to say "none of that" in the studio and leave it at that.

There are exceptions, though. I have gotten whiskey for some singers toward the end of a session. I know some vocal coaches that are going to send emails about that statement, but that was what we needed to do to get the job done. One of the editors of this book happened to be a consulting and production client of mine. He remembered a session in 2010 when I had him go for a walk to get some fresh air and a bottle of whiskey to loosen him up before a drum track.

In the end it's a very personal thing. Whether you are looking at drinking and drugs and the effect they might have on you or the rest of your band or you are looking at another member and wanting to bring up your concerns, it can be a hard thing to do. It requires a specified and individualized approach. Sometimes having a mediator work with the group can make discussions easier.

If you're wondering how much is too much, think about how drug or alcohol use affects you in practices, on stage, and on the road in hotels. Work on figuring out why you drink—whether it is for fun or out of necessity. I have told a couple of musicians to videotape some of their performances and then play it back to see just how they looked and sounded on stage. Two guitar players I suggested this to went from feeling that they were on top of their game on stage to realizing they were not playing as sharply or looking half as cool as they thought they did.

Figure out what you want, what works for you, and how alcohol or drugs affect you in the pursuit of that. If you need to be in a group that doesn't drink or do drugs at all, then state that right from the get-go. At the same time, don't go to the opposite extreme and try to sell your drinking to others. Every person handles alcohol or drugs differently. You are not the shrink; you are a member of the band. Discuss your thoughts on the matter as your opinion, not as an ultimate authority.

One time I heard a comedian say, "I don't have a problem with Jesus, and I don't have a problem with Elvis . . . It's just some of their fans that piss me the hell off." There are super freaks on both sides of the spectrum: people who say that drugs and alcohol make you more expressive and free, and those who say you can't touch a drop or take a hit. There's a middle ground that doesn't need to be sold to anyone or overly explained; that's where you are personally. So keep it personal; be honest and be true to yourself and the others you perform with. Be open to talking about issues as they come up, and stay away from the soapbox. Everyone is different. Accept that.

Supplemental Income: The Best Jobs to Take as an Aspiring Musician

So you can't quite support yourself on the music alone yet? Although it would be much more gratifying to give 100 percent of your time to your craft and your dream, there is that whole thing about paying for the roof over your head, keeping the heat on and the water running, buying food, making car payments, and doing all those other adult things that demand fiscal responsibility. This means that you have to either continue what you're doing for a day job or find the right job to counterbalance your craft and your sanity.

It's not just about having a job and making the money you need until you can cross over to the full-time status of musician. It's about finding the right type of job that will enable you to perform in what you have to do for the job at hand *and* allow you the energy and the stamina to spend another day's worth of work on your craft.

First you have to make the decision about the job at hand. Is your goal to leave your job and become a full-time musician? It may seem like a stupid question, but the answer for many musicians is no. There are a number of people out there who are too scared of the concept and will continue to maintain their day gig.

Here are some questions to help you decide what the best job is for you. Are you a morning person? Can you get going on little sleep? Does an early afternoon nap give you enough stamina for the rest of the day? If so, early morning jobs like a barista, a packer, or other early-morning manual gigs can be a good idea. These are often shifts that get done early in the day and give you the rest of the day and evening to practice, play, and work on your music. These types of jobs can also allow for certain days off for performing or out-of-town shows.

Whatever the job, be up front during the hiring interview. Explain what you are doing and how you are looking to work until you're able fully to support yourself musically. While some people want to hide this from bosses and potential employers, it can sometimes actually work in your favor, showing that you have drive and desire, which can be very attractive to a potential employer. Ask the employer about time off. Mention that you may be doing some short or long tours, and find out if the job will allow you to leave early on a Thursday and come back late on a Monday. The jobs are out there; you just need to do a little more research to find them.

From there, work to figure out the finances and decide whether you have to go full-time or part-time. Do you have the option of a part-time job, and will it make you enough to get by? If it is part-time and hourly, can you work somewhere where you can put in a surge of hours on one day and work less on another?

Watch out for later-day or evening jobs. Those tend to be the most problematic with bands. Though jobs such as being a bartender can bring in fast cash, you can run into scheduling issues on nights that you might need off to play.

If you're in a band, try to create the same basic working schedule. If everyone is working mornings, then it will be a lot easier to practice, play, and work. However, as helpful as it may be to have the same schedule, you might not want to have the same jobs as other band members. As much hassle as a job can be, it can also serve as a little downtime away from the band. Not only that, but it can be more difficult to get time off if several people need time off at the same time from the same employer, as opposed to only one person.

I generally advise against artists working together or working the same job. I know it's okay for some people, but I really find that having time apart from the group can be helpful.

Stresses at work can enter the band dynamic, which is something you don't need. Even worse is when a band member is working for another band member. This can create serious internal frictions and affect the whole band.

Remember: It's not just a job to pay the bills. It's a transitional job that you can do to make the money you need while being productive and effective with your music. This focus will help move things faster toward getting you out of that day job and achieving the goal of making music your full-time job.

A Life Outside of Music Can Help Your Sanity—and the Music

When I was first starting out, I practiced an obscene amount of hours. I would practice every day for anywhere between five and eight hours. I traveled two hours, once a week, to study with my drum teacher, Gary Chaffee, and I was also playing with four groups at the time.

I was living and breathing drums—my dream. I wanted to keep getting better, to learn all I could. My car was filled with albums that were very drummer-oriented, and I was renting or buying every drum video that I could. I did grow during this time as a drummer, but at the same time, I was stagnant in other ways. I was living the life I dreamed of, but I had no life outside of it.

Then I began to notice that certain things I was working on weren't getting any better past a certain point. I found myself becoming more mechanical than I wanted to be. I felt my approach was becoming stifled, though my technique and awareness still grew. I was obsessed with being as good and prepared as I could be for my lessons, but I was not thinking of the outside elements that supplement music. Even my drum teacher told me to pull back some on the practicing.

Then I got to do a session with an amazing saxophone player whom I had looked up to for many years, and we had dinner after the session. I was in awe of his performance and thrilled to be hanging out with him. The first question he asked me was, "What are your hobbies?" As I was going to answer him, I realized everything I was about to answer with were either things I wanted to do or things I had done in the past. Right then, I didn't *have* any hobbies. In fact, I didn't have any life; I didn't do anything outside of music. It was eye-opening.

Then he asked me what I would like to do that would relax me, outside of music. As this guy explained his hobbies and talked about how they affected his playing and his music, I began to think about ways to make some time for things I enjoyed, other than music. I got back to exercising, which was fun for me. I got back into the Red Sox, my favorite team, and I got back to comedy (I'm not funny, but I love comedians and comedy venues).

The most interesting thing was that when I started practicing less, the practice time actually became more effective. I was growing again, both in my technique and conceptually. I was also finding a life outside of music, which brought more to my music *and* my playing.

Here's the point: It's crucial to experience life, to experience relationships and feelings outside of music, and then to bring them to the music in the best way possible. Don't use outside interests as an excuse not to practice or work on your craft, but use them as a supplement to expand your craft. This especially applies in songwriting. If you are only writing music about music, you may not be capturing the fullness of life in your work—and probably having less impact than you would hope for.

I prefer to see artists, musicians, and producers who not only work to hone their professional skills but also have a life outside of their work. I've gone back and forth at times, but I have found that when I can get away for a while, even for a few hours, I'm much more effective in the studio. Oftentimes at the end of a full session, I'll pop out to a bar to get away from all things music or just to get together with people who have nothing to do with the industry—to recharge.

I also love catching Red Sox games, walking, and people-watching. I've gotten back into swimming, hiking, meeting people, and making new friends outside of music. I am reading again, even books not related to music.

The point is, even in the flurry of living the lifestyle I love, I'm taking the time to live outside of it. Hobbies help me relax, clear my head, and make me better at my work. Make sure you take the time to balance your life. You won't regret it.

Depression and Maintaining Good Mental Health as a Musician

Music, like any other field in the arts, can bring the most pleasure and, at the same time, the most pain. The despair that artists and musicians have faced over the years has been revealed both privately and publicly—now more than ever, with the paparazzi capturing every move. In the past six months you couldn't turn on a TV or read a newspaper without seeing something about an entertainer who had either taken or tried to take his or her own life, gone too deep into drugs and alcohol, or been viewed as "losing it" or otherwise going nuts. In fact, as I am writing this, the entertainment industry is mourning movie director Tony Scott, lost to an apparent suicide.

Mental and emotional problems have resulted in tours and shows being cancelled, with millions of dollars lost. Yes, the alcohol, the drugs, and the party lifestyle contribute to the problem, but the root, more often than not, is depression, anxiety, and despair. Very often, these emotions turn musicians to drugs, to alcohol, to gambling, to violence, or to unhealthy seclusion.

Depression occurs at all levels, whether because of the stress and strain of popularity and fame for those who are higher up in the industry or the hopelessness of musicians who have been trying for so long and can never seem to catch a break. It can be brought on by the stress of recording, being fired from a group, having to fire someone, losing a deal, abrupt highs and lows in sales and attendance, feeling like the dream is never going to happen, internal arguments, the strain of outside relationships, and more.

Sure, the life of a working musician is amazing, but at the same time it's loaded with challenges. I don't want to be too blunt or harsh, but if you think you're a little weak of heart, weak of mind, or weak of soul, the music industry is not for you, nor is any other entertainment field. If you cannot accept or prepare for terrible depressions, ongoing doubts, fears, and disappointments, you're in the wrong field.

Even planning and awareness will not prevent the emotional rollercoaster of the music business. Regardless of how much you prepare, you will go through it; it's part of the deal, period. But if you can take the right steps, you can make it easier and a little less painful.

Let's take a single element: performing on stage. Earlier in the day, you probably felt the anticipation, but you had to do other things, whether you are on tour and waiting to pull into the city or you're working your day job until you can get home to load out and get to the gig. After you get to the venue, you set up and get to play for a few minutes during sound check; then there's the waiting game, which can last for hours. Finally, you get to your performance, and it can be amazing, but it only lasts so long. After the emotional spike of the music and the crowd energy, you're loading out your gear to go either home and work the next day or to a strange room in a strange bed in a city you might not know all that well.

That kind of shifting and swinging of energies can really do a once-over on your general mood. The wild high followed abruptly by the lowest low is a hard change to take. I remember after playing one of my best shows as a drummer—you know the situation: The stage was amazing, the crowd was packed in and screaming, the lights, the sound, and everything else were just perfect—I got such a high off it, and then it was over. I was alone in the hotel room in a strange city that night, and I remember feeling like I just wanted to die. I was so sad, and I couldn't figure out why; I was in the middle of an amazing tour, I was having a blast, and yet the lows were so excruciating that they tore me apart.

As a result, I did my share of drinking and I did my share of partying. For that matter, I did a couple other people's shares as well. I found that by drinking, partying, and sleeping, I could close the gaps and stay on a constant high.

This was not the healthiest approach. The answer eventually came from a balance, from understanding myself and the way the moods and feelings would swing based on what was around me.

When I controlled the high of the stage, it in turn controlled the countering low later at night. I was not enjoying the stage experience any less or taking away any of the energy; I just didn't let myself get lost in the high, thus balancing out the low. I also paid more attention to my diet. I made sure to eat the right foods that would energize, always making dinner a lighter meal, to avoid a crash after a show.

The better the balance during the performance, the better the balance was on the front and back sides of the show. Just because you control how high you allow yourself to go during a performance doesn't mean you won't be able to have as much fun. Think of it like controlling the amplitude of an effect or the volume of your instrument: It's not any less powerful; it's just the way you're approaching that part of life.

DIVIDE THE WORKLOAD FOR THE BEST RESULTS IN THE SHORTEST TIME

Whether you are a single artist or a band, the work that has to be done to keep things moving onward and upward can be intimidating and overwhelming. A big problem that I often see is that an artist or members in a group look at everything they have to do as a massive, single item that just seems impossible to get done, so they shove the day-to-day, administrative work under the rug, accomplishing only the scraps—the small things that seem doable. Meanwhile, core elements are being ignored, becoming more and more problematic and harder to solve.

Of course, if you are a band, you can divide up the workload among members. The question comes down to who does what and when. But for right now, I am going to discuss dividing the workload over time and days as a single artist.

You are not going to sit down for three hours on one day and be able to knock out all the things you want to; most people cannot commit that kind of time. With day jobs, rehearsals, girlfriends and boyfriends, and life in general, a lot of artists can't pull that out of a day. But sitting down for half an hour is something that can be scheduled into a day and can actually happen.

The key point is to work smarter and more effectively over a series of days instead of trying to knock out everything in a single day. Let's look at the basic administrative list that artists should be covering in a given week:

- Marketing
- Promoting
- Booking
- Rehearsing

- Maintaining equipment and gear

- Networking

- Advertising

- Administrative

And the list goes on. But this is the basic core, and now we can begin breaking those elements down into bite-size chunks. First of all, let's flesh out each item on the above list:

- Marketing online via website, Facebook, Twitter, Pinterest, and other sites to draw new friends and fans to you

- Promoting for shows; promoting your recording or latest merchandise; promoting sales; keeping content fresh with blogs, picture updates, and schedules; printing up the posters and ordering and keeping stock of your music and merchandise for sale

- Booking shows; preparing tours; organizing press packs; soliciting and submitting to festivals, concert promoters, managers, venues, and talent buyers

- Rehearsing your old material; writing new material; working out arrangements; and getting songs ready for recording or the stage

- Taking care of the gear that takes care of you: allotting the time to maintain, clean, repair, or just check your gear to make sure you don't run into problems on stage or in the studio

- Networking; reaching out to the manufacturers of the gear that you use to begin to build relationships for endorsements; meeting other bands and connecting with groups you could share a bill with: finding ways to market and connect with people and media in places where you are playing to find different avenues of exposure; talking with management groups and record labels or agents that you may want to be involved with, so that someday you don't have to do all this stuff and someone else will!

- Advertising your group; getting the group up on different sites; getting reviewers to do stories about you; postering, organizing, and stickering around the country and world; buying ads in different markets and different media channels

- Administrative details include tracking your receipts, your spending, and your profits; making sure your taxes, bank accounts, and other finances and contracts are in order; double-checking about shows; making sure the hotels are booked for the overnight shows; dealing with everybody's schedules and personal or calendar issues; keeping the paperwork organized and up to date

By now you may be thinking: I really just wanted to play music! Well, unless or until you are part of a label, management group, or agency, you are going to be responsible for all these elements.

Sure, everybody hopes that they get so big and so busy that either they get picked up by a label—whose personnel will perform the above tasks—or they can afford to hire someone to take care of all these administrative worries. However, I think everyone needs to spend some time early on handling these elements. By doing so, you will not only get a full sense of the inner workings, but you will also gain an understanding of what needs to be done and what to ask of a rep, manager, agent, or label. You will also have an idea of how hard people are working for you or, for that matter, how hard a manager or label should be working for you. Knowing these ins and outs will make you a more complete professional, so that when that great day arrives and you are negotiating with a label, an agent, or a management group, you will go into the process with knowledge and confidence, instead of being a "gee-whiz" novice with stars in your eyes.

Now, back to the dividing up of this massive amount of work. As in any situation, the first step is to know what you have to do and then clearly set in the game plan to get it done. The more organized a plan you have for how you divide or delegate the responsibilities of promotion, solicitation, booking, content posting, rehearsing, and everything else, the easier it will be. Get your music business plan or music marketing plan in place so that everyone knows what needs to be done, when it needs to be done, who is doing what, and how it is being done.

The next step is to designate each section to a day or the allotted time needs. For example, when I was drumming, I would spend fifteen minutes a week just going over my kit: oiling the pedals if they needed it, making sure all the lugs were in place, wiping it down with a rag and looking for any problems. Once a month, I would take a half hour to really clean the kit and go over everything with a fine-tooth comb. Then, every six months, I would plan for a couple hours where I would strip the kit, take off all the heads, check the edges of the drums, and really give the kit a "day at the spa."

You can approach any of the items on the above list in the same way. What can you do for five minutes a day? It may feel like a beast of a job, but step back and allot five minutes per item, six days a week. It totals out to three hours of solid work each week across the spectrum of things that need to be done. Five minutes may not feel like it is enough, but it amounts to a half hour of work if you do it for six days. After a month, it equals two hours of work on whatever you have designated that time to.

So now the list, but in five-minute intervals for the single artist in a single day amounting to only a half hour:

1. **Marketing—five minutes.** Go add a new friend or connection on one of your social networking sites. Post info about a show in a new forum or message board or a site related to the topic. Link a new band or a new company to your site and then send an artist, a fan, or a venue a quick email just to check in.

   That's five minutes down!

2. **Promoting—five minutes.** Find three social networking sites where you can advertise a scheduled show—maybe a few sites that are local to the area you are playing—and just add in the date, time, and place of the show and your basic info.

   Another five down and still effective in a short amount of time.

3. **Booking—five minutes.** Research a new venue or booking group. Copy down the info and save it for networking, or email a press kit to a new agent, venue, or festival.

   Fifteen minutes in, and you are grooving!

4. **Networking—five minutes.** Research and make a new contact every day: What are they about, what can they do for you, what can you do for them? Pop out a basic email. One contact attempt a day—that's all.

   Twenty minutes.

5. **Advertising—five minutes.** If you have the money, buy an ad once a month in some kind of media outlet, newspaper, website, or radio station. Add your banner to a new website, join a new web group, or contact a new postering group for a city you play that is too far away for you to poster yourself.

   Twenty-five minutes—and almost done for the day!

6. **Administrative—five minutes.** Update your files with some of the info you collected that day. Make sure it is organized and saved in the right databases. Set the calendar for the next day's plans and the things coming up.

   Thirty minutes—done!

It might seem oversimplified, but it really isn't. Being effective for short spurts of time on a regular basis brings results. As you do small amounts of work each day, it adds up. Your databases for venues, contacts, and all sorts of information will grow, and it is all done in a reasonable amount of time. On certain days, if you have more time to commit, then do so, but don't neglect any element.

KEEP YOUR MESSAGE, YOUR MARKETING, AND YOUR PROMO ASSERTIVE

I have been reading quite a few band bios lately, as well as observing updates to websites and social networking. I see a lot of inflated résumés with information that is particularly beneficial. We've already discussed toning down the ego for the sake of professionalism; use that same approach in your résumé and your online and other promotional materials. Don't highlight singular events that might make you look unprofessional or inexperienced to the people who really matter.

Be relatable; be the artist garnering interest, the artist or band that will draw continued interest in a humble yet assertive way. Backward comments like, "Wow! I have this many followers on Twitter," or my recent favorite, "This celebrity is following me," come off stupid and weak.

The celebrity more than likely has a team working his or her Twitter account focused on following more and more people in order to grow the celebrity's base. Furthermore, you disrespect those who actually follow and read you by highlighting someone and leaving out the others.

Take a minute and think about what you say and how it could be misread, misunderstood, or seen as confusing. Ask people outside of the group for their views. An overly embellished résumé or bio can look really good to friends but carry a bad tone for booking agents, managers, labels, and other industry professionals. I told one artist to tell the girl he wants to impress about the big show he played, but make the bio and the website impress the industry people who will do the booking and promoting.

Sometimes, artists get concerned that they don't have enough to fill up a bio or the promo materials, and they add things like playing a venue or winning a battle of the bands. These are not strong marketing points. Try to look at things from an industry stance; think about what would make someone want to do a story on you.

Some aspects of the "fake it 'til you make it" philosophy apply, but the industry has become loaded with so many phonies, and social media has cranked up the volume. This means that trying to make a cool first impression can actually make you look like a poser, getting you completely bypassed by a potential fan.

You can and should use the Internet to your benefit, however; solicit for reviews around the country and not just your backyard. Look for music blogs that might not have the largest number of readers or visitors, but will write reviews and add information about you. You can always replace a smaller review with a larger one down the road.

The other big no-no is talking about the likes, followers, plays, or friends you have on Twitter, Facebook, or any of the networking sites. Putting out posts or bragging about numbers of Facebook friends, views, hits, "likes," "retweets," or plays has been outdated since Myspace. With the ability to buy friends, likes, views, followers, and anything else, these are no longer really something you want to advertise. If anything, it makes you look cheap.

Even if your résumé is small, work to build it from the foundations of what you are doing. Talk about the songs, the group, the shows, and the steps you are taking toward your dreams. As more things come into play, you can add them; just make sure you're adding elements that are going to highlight you in a strong way to the industry instead of impressing some girl or guy.

It's better to push what you have done and the things that matter than to inflate things that the industry as a whole will not care about. Consistent content in the form of blogs, videos, photos, samples, and quotes, along with your uniform branding, will grow your brand, your reach, your awareness, and your fan base.

One final warning: While it is crucial to keep your promo assertive, make sure it is not too aggressive or disrespectful, and above all, avoid attempts to tag onto topics that aren't really related to your group or your music—a shady tactic sometimes referred to as "newsjacking."

For example, in the days surrounding the horrific killings during 2012 in Aurora, Colorado, Happy Valley, Oregon, and then Newtown, Connecticut, some very tasteless, dishonorable, and flat-out disrespectful artists used hash tags to market ideas, plugs for shows, downloads, and materials that had nothing to do with the events themselves. It's bad enough when somebody posts a promo link on a Facebook group or a discussion list that has nothing to do with their music, but these idiots chose to newsjack in connection with these heartbreaking calamities, just to gain some exposure. Not eight hours after the Boston Marathon bombings, I saw three artists use that to promote Boston songs . . . in memory. What B.S.! Such events are obviously not the right place or the right time. Stay away from newsjacking on social media or in your marketing, especially in the wake of terrible tragedies.

CLOSING THOUGHTS

The volume of material presented in this chapter may seem overwhelming to you. Keep in mind that the idea is not to discourage but to encourage an artist or a band to sort out the details that it takes to be successful. Whether it's looking for the right members, to healthy communication, to having an exit strategy for a single member that wants to quit (or that everyone else wants to fire) and even for an individual who has passed away, you need to have a plan. These are the types of things that too many see as unnecessary—until something happens.

Here are a few more questions to ponder. What would you do if:

- Someone is stealing?

- Someone is put in jail?

- A label wants someone replaced?

There could be a million more questions floating around in your head. Reel them in, put them on paper, and address them as a group.

By coming together and laying out the basics on the "what ifs," you will have the best chance of parting ways—when, not if, that happens—with the least hassle, the fewest lawyers, and the smallest loss of money and time.

So, plan for the divorce before the wedding. Take care of yourself and your collaborators. Continue to develop as a musician and as a person. And above all, get everyone in your band on the same page for all the aspects of what could possibly fail. In the end, this will make it that much easier to succeed.

3

DEFINING AND REFINING YOUR SOUND

OPENING THOUGHT

How do you create your sound? How do you define and refine your sound as you seek opportunities to perform, record, tour, and receive backing? How do you write hit songs that will work on stage and in recordings? How do you formulate a sound that becomes the "brand" that people will know you for?

The answers are different for everyone: There is no magic pill or cookie cutter. It just makes sense; the sound you are creating is going to be built from a mix of your musical influences, your technical ability, your writing ability, and your interpretation. But it doesn't stop there. Your sound comes from how you communicate with others, how you listen, and how you hear the different parts, the transitions, the dynamics, and the melodies.

Sometimes I hear music coaches and teachers claim that there is only one answer or one way to learn, listen, play, or grow. Usually, the stated or implied message is that this "one way" equates to their way.

I believe this is completely wrong! Everyone comes from different places, different backgrounds, different influences, and different views and opinions on what they want to create. Trying to jam every artist into a single mold is, I believe, a colossal mistake.

Don't get me wrong—I am completely in favor of listening to what others have done to develop their sound—how, why, when, and where they did it. Tuning in carefully to another artist in this way can serve as a learning tool and inspiration for your sound. A little later in this chapter, in fact, I'm going to talk about the absolute importance of listening to other artists if you really want to grow.

But you have to personalize and customize how those elements will work for you, for the way you write and play. Copying someone else's exact way of creating their sound or how *they* approach writing, practicing, performing, and recording is probably not going to work, even if you are going for that exact same sound. After all, you're not the same person. How could you expect identical results?

The most important factors are what you focus most on and what you listen least to. Your sound also comes from how you are affected emotionally, physically, and mentally as much as how you react creatively, dynamically, and technically.

Your sound is your art. From the similarities with others to the differences, you create your sound, either by yourself or with others who will draw from your inspirations. Your efforts will be enhanced by your experiences and your style of learning, communication, improvisation, and execution. What results will be your own, unique sound. It may be categorized and labeled with genres, taglines, or summaries—which it needs—but it will also be yours, and fans will be able to connect with you on a much deeper level.

SONGWRITING: WHO ARE YOU MUSICALLY?

"What makes a hit song?" This is a question I've heard many people answer. I've read some articles that address the question—many of which give downright embarrassing answers. I think what makes a hit song can be measured more by opinion than an actual formula, and even if you complete a formula, what kind of hit song are you creating?

Some say success lies in the melody; some point to lyrics; others point to hooks and turnarounds. In my opinion, they are all correct. The hit song can be based on any one area of a song or it can be based on a meshing of different sections. I think it's a bad idea to sit down and decide that you're going to write a hit song. Many times the contrived mindset of this approach can send a song down the tubes. For every person who has a formula for a hit song, there are ten people whose hit songs break all the rules.

Read up on your favorite songwriters and their approaches; learn their structures and ideas, and don't set any particular artist's formulas or methods in stone. Many who do so end up sounding just like the artist they studied—except worse, because they aren't perceived as original. Using established artists' formulas or favorite practices as writing exercises can be a good tool for understanding a particular approach. Don't forget, however, to mix the inspiration with the improvisation and creativity that you have in order to find the songs that mean something and belong uniquely to you.

A hit song may be commercially successful, but at its root it is still a mixture of ideas and formulas. There are basic rules in the theory of music, but when it comes to creating that hit song, the guidelines are few and far between—that's why songwriting is an art, not a science.

When I produce a client's song, I try to pay attention to the song as a whole, making sure that each section is clearly defined and developed. Along with the definition of a hook, the clarity of motion in each section is also important. Most imperative of all is the way the pieces fit together. Just as in cooking, you want to make sure you have all the right ingredients separately—fresh, and not stale or spoiled. Sometimes songs have verses that might be better if they were the root of another song.

So, as you work on your songs, make sure you add the right ingredients at the right time in the right amount and in the right way. You want to create a song that not only works in each section by itself but also clearly transitions from one section to another. Sometimes small nuances that repeat throughout the song can tie sections together. Sometimes certain rhythmic or melodic fills can tie elements together, giving the whole an identity that pulls the parts together in unity.

But consider a different angle: What do you mean by "hit song"? Are you looking for a chart-topping, million-dollar masterpiece that will garner airplay ad nauseam? Or maybe you mean a key track that helps you sell your album, but also gets decent airplay. You could be talking about a tune that gets licensed to a soundtrack or used in a commercial. It's interesting how artists pore over what song will be their hit track and then spend all their time trying to push it to the charts, usually with no results.

It's good to remember all the alternatives. A single song could be sold as a download or as part of a full album. It could be licensed to a movie, a TV show, a commercial, a video game, or perhaps to someone overseas who will sing it in another language. In such a scenario, even if the song doesn't go to number one or, for that matter, even hit the charts, you'll be seeing some solid royalties as you get exposure and make fans you would never have made if you didn't have the song playing in these channels. Using many channels is the most productive way not only to get your music out there but also to make money from royalties and placements instead of depending solely on album sales and downloads.

Push every song to its utmost potential in order to receive exposure and accrue payments. Maybe it will cross over to a hit song. I believe, though, that if you create a song, you can either go after the large-scale fame of a hit, or you can make it a hit by taking all the smaller steps and pitching the song in every avenue it might fit. If the song is bringing in royalties, percentages, or even a one-time payout, that makes the song a hit. It's a success; it has generated revenue and carved one more notch in your résumé.

THE BEST TRANSITION AND MOTION APPLICATIONS FOR A SONG

Even the smallest part of a song can be a big part of its flow, structure, and foundation. Various songwriters may emphasize the intro, the outro, the verses, the choruses, or even the bridges. Often forgotten are the mini-bridges, or the transitions between each of these larger sections.

Just like a bridge, but a lot shorter, these transitions can last a couple of beats, less than a bar, or even a single accent. The transitions don't have to be a separate part; they can be the very end of the section before. When I listen to an album, I listen for the song and the sections, but I pay a lot of attention to the flow, the way the song moves as a whole from beginning to end, and how each section moves from one to the next.

Here are a few points I always address as a producer when talking to songwriters:

- Is the ear being carried through the changes, or are sections of the song transitioning a little too abruptly? Sometimes you might want some abrupt and dramatic changes in your transitions, but make sure that all motions, fast or slow, have the flow and the strength to keep the ear of the listener connected.

- Keep the foundation of the song present and well established. Reminding the listener about the foundation of the piece dates back to early classical music, where the theme was always prevalent in more ways than just the chords. Listen to for Bach's *Goldberg Variations*. He creates very interesting motion and movements in all the voices while still reinforcing the core theme. You can be in a totally different key and a totally different section but still hint at the foundation of the tune. For example, Bach would use a motion or a melodic movement in the alto and then copy it a number of bars later in the bass voicing.

- Solidify and clearly identify each section. Is the motion of the song— from chords to instrumentation to lyrics—defined in each section? Does it move forward? Again, it's not about being boring or obvious; it's about defining the tune.

- Establish the transitional leads as their own hooks to the previous and following sections. If you have a clear transition from the bridge to the chorus, use it again, or maybe have that rhythm or note set played on another instrument when that section comes around again. Think in terms of themes and variations.

- Identify the active, dominant voice of the transition. Which voice is it coming from and which voice it is leading to? For example, if the transition is a drum fill and it opens up into a chorus where a female is singing a high note, make sure the final hit of the fill does not conflict with the first note of the voice. High notes from females and males can get washed out in cymbal crashes. It's not about changing things too much; it's about being aware of the qualities.

Don't get too wrapped up in the mathematics of it, either. Sometimes writing from a completely technical level can serve as a good exercise, but when you are getting too technical in your writing, it can take away from the flow and motion of a song. When I was at Berklee, I wrote a four-part piece for a traditional harmony class. I was tired and did it in my room instead of in front of a piano. The melodic, harmonic, and rhythmic elements were all dead-on and followed the rules of music theory, but when the piece was played in class, it sounded like cats being tortured.

> It's not about the amount of time you put in, it is the way you spend the time on the work you need to get done. Saying that you worked ten hours on something that went nowhere is not really anything to brag about.
>
> Focus on what needs to be done over the time you are putting in. That way you can work to optimize and make the most out of the time you spend on any given project. This goes for practicing, promotion, marketing, and anything else.
>
> Focus on the result and the actions getting there over the time it took. It will make the whole experience greater as a whole.

You want to keep yourself in a creative zone. The old rule that I was taught by Gary Chaffee was to learn the technique, then forget the technical aspects to be able to apply it in a musical way on the drums for the song. What I recommend to artists is to look at a song in a couple of different ways as they play it. Listen one time for the form, listen another time for the transitions, and listen a third time for another element. Study the art you have created from a number of different perspectives, and you will create a well-rounded piece of work.

DEVELOPING YOUR SONGS FOR RECORDING STUDIO SESSIONS

Below are ten of my favorite approaches that I suggest to artists who want to develop their songs a little further in preproduction. I also apply these in the studio with bands.

1. **Chord inversions where the fifth becomes the root of the transitional chord—or just working on different chord inversion options.** Sometimes inverting a chord so that the fifth is on the bottom and using that as the root for the transition can make for a smooth movement. This is a simpler, more open technique, but it can give a nice, easy exchange without complex changes. For the drummers, it's like that extra note to the hi-hat, kick, or snare that keeps the beat driving but adds a solid and simple embellishment to mark a change.

2. **Single-note voice transition.** If you are transitioning through a single line or note, doing a transition from one instrument to another can be very cool. On Sting's album *Nothing Like the Sun*, he does a cover of Jimi Hendrix's "Little Wing." At the end of the guitar solo, a note is held and taken over by the soprano sax. It is a smooth and slick transition into the turnaround of the solo before the repeat. Alternatively, you can use a number of instruments and mix them into one another. You can use voices as well.

3. **Rhythmic pattern or rhythmic theme in another instrument or voice.** If a certain rhythm is used as an ostinato, or repeated phrase, by one instrument or even with the whole band hitting the accents, you can bring a sense of that section back without the accents by having a single instrument repeat the rhythmic phrase in a different section of the song or as an intro to the accents that will be hit by everyone.

4. **Panning and fades.** Panning across different instruments or fading certain voices and instruments up and down can bring a very ethereal change that is not as noticeable or up front, but is definitely felt.

5. **Fills on drum, bass, percussion, guitar, etc.** Basic fills from any given instrument or mix of instruments is a common transition. A fill, perhaps played by the guitar into the first chorus, could be played by the bass into the next, keeping the same notes and form while bringing a different sound into play. The drums can do the same pattern as well. Repeating the rhythm, even using different instruments, creates a sense of identity and familiarity for the element that gives the song a feeling of unity.

6. **Silence or obscure removals of instruments and voices.** Dropping out the bass and the drums, killing the percussion, or bringing out a guitar in a transition can create an abrupt yet smooth change. Changing up the tones and the microphones (with the recording mix) of the instruments in a different section can help with this as well.

   Even something as simple as killing the bass drum and the bass or going to only room microphones on the drum set can create a motion for the ear that will draw the listener in even more.

7. **Added pads or long notes and chords of other instruments—brass, strings, backing vocals, etc.** Fading in and out basic pads in the transitions can add a supplemental element to a song, even if it's just for the transition. It can add another layer and hint at something coming or going in the tune.

8. **Dynamics.** The most obvious and simple yet effective and often-used way to transition a song is to pump up the volume of the band or bring the band way down. You can also bring up or down the dynamics of a couple of instruments. Another way to play with dynamics is to have one instrument get softer or louder.

9. **Doubling with secondary voices and other instruments.** Almost like padding, you can double an existing voice or instrument with itself or with another instrument to bring a richer texture. If a guitar line is descending into the chorus, maybe add a horn or an acoustic guitar, even a vibraphone, to join and complement the run down into the chorus.

10. **Reverse effect on existing voices or instruments, or additional samples or instruments.** Flip it around. Try reversing any sound, from a snare drum to a cymbal to a guitar hit—to anything. In certain places, a reverse lead-in can bring a cool, dynamic tension into a new section. Sometimes piggybacking or putting a couple of reverse effects or samples on top of each other in the mix can deliver a fuller, rounder sound and can really emphasize an element. By turning a cymbal around and then leading it into the original crash you can really open up a section and offer a different type of transition.

Play around and have fun. You don't have to use every trick in the book. Think of these as embellishments to play with, not requirements. Don't go too over the top in the same song with these, or you will blunder into the world of overproduction, making a song that will be impossible to re-create live. There are also a lot more ideas than just the above ten. Play with concepts yourself and read up on how others approach production and songwriting.

These are just a few ideas I think of when I listen to songs I am working on that might need something more. Sometimes the writers exert so much concentration on the chorus, the verse, the bridge, or the hook that they don't think about the leading and transitions in each of the sections. As a writer, review the changes of your tunes. Listen to other writers—not just the sections but also the transitions. Study and learn about other producers and their ideas. Listen to other styles of music and how the sections transition. It can really help you in your own writing.

ODD TIME IDEAS AND APPROACHES: NOT JUST FOR ODD PEOPLE ANYMORE

Odd time signatures can be fun and can give a unique feel to a song. When people hear it, they can't quite put their finger on what's different, but they know something is. Because of our mostly Western European musical heritage, most Americans feel a comfort in three or four, but not many other time signatures. In different countries around the world, feeling time signatures like 5/4, 11/8, and 15/8 is commonplace, yet the average American feels the main pulse on the downbeat and needs to hear some kind of upbeat that's evenly divisible by two or three. So, careful use of an asymmetric meter—one that's not evenly divisible by two or three—can give a song a memorable touch.

Many progressive-rock and fusion artists take a very purposeful approach to writing in odd meters and putting sections of songs through a number of different time signature changes. Yet in the mainstream, the mass buying population is all about hearing things in four or three time. Peter Gabriel, with his song "Solsbury Hill," is one of only a handful of artists to chart a tune in 7/4 in the *Billboard* top twenty.

Now of course, if you ask most drummers, they will reference Neil Peart and Rush, as well as many other groups that are a little more progressive and often a little more open with time signatures. They talk about great feels in odd times, but often when I hear groups trying to work in odd meters, it ends up feeling very contrived. I believe the best approach to working in odd meters is to be comfortable; treat the odd meter as if it's a normal meter. Record yourself—especially the drummers! Do you notice that you are overaccenting the one? Would you do that in a normal, even meter? If not, work to find that comfort zone.

There's no special secret to odd time and meters. It's all about being able to execute comfortably and being able to play phrases with a full awareness of where the beat is in the bar. In a normal bar of four, most people easily feel the "one" as they land on the beat—when it's about to come around and when they're leaving from it to the two. This comfort zone allows the drums—or for that matter, *any* instrument—not to need to accentuate the "one" on every bar or turnaround. Younger artists (or artists who are not as comfortable with odd times) will punch the "one" on every bar, sometimes every other bar, but it's much more prevalent and in your face than those same parts being played in a normal four or three bar measure. Much of the time, these grooves in an odd time signature lock up and become stale or dry. Sometimes, with the lack of prowess or comfort in an odd meter, the drummer, especially, will become robotic.

The best approach to succeed at these odd times is to subdivide. When I was drumming in five, I actually never counted to five. I would count in my head 1–2–3, 1–2. So I would combine a three-beat and two-beat pattern in my head. This helped me feel a pocket a little more. It also allowed me to work on developing phrases that were not based on landing solely on the "one." I also would phrase it as 1–2, 1–2, 1 to create a more bouncy feel in the middle of the phrase. To get a more full, staccato phrase I would count out 1–2–3–4, 1. Different techniques work for different people. I really recommend reading articles about your favorite musicians to see how they approach odd times. It may help you have a greater understanding of their approach. You might also listen to music by people like Don Ellis, a jazz trumpeter and band leader who often featured works by people like Hank Levy and Milcho Leviev (a Bulgarian musician who grew up counting in 15/8).

Also, try taking songs that are in even time, stretch them out to odd times, and see what could be added. Or take a song in four, drop it to three, and see what could be taken away. The more you play with moving phrases, melodies, and time, the more comfortable you will find yourself in odd meters.

Listen closely when you are playing in the times you are most comfortable with. Listen to how you phrase, how you accent, and how you move across the bar. This is a great exercise in both technical practice and in gaining a greater understanding of your personal approaches to writing or performing. The goal, then, is to work in the odd meters to achieve those same results. When you can feel the pulse of eleven, fifteen, nine, or seven in the same way you can feel four, you will be able to execute a much more solid feel and groove in those odd times. This will also give you additional strength in the even times.

Odd times are tricky, but add them to your regimen of practice and writing. Work to phrase in the meter you are attempting, and try to avoid the biggest pitfall: phrasing an even meter idea with beats either subtracted or added. I started working on the odd meters of five, seven, and nine when I was first exploring odd meters, and slowly I became more comfortable with the ideas of time that strays from the usual. Test the waters with five. And again, for the drummers, do not crash or accent too hard on the "one" every time. Remember: Odd meters still swing—it's just that one leg is a little longer than the other.

One more idea: Go back through things you have written, maybe something you have tossed or thrown away—something that just didn't seem to fit a song or section you were working on. If it had an extra few beats, or if you took away a beat or two, could it work? You could have a song or section that you have already phrased to work in an odd time, and you didn't even know it.

Play around; expand your time vocabulary, both as a performer and a writer. Perhaps the bridge of a song that's in an even time isn't working because you have it phrased in something that would work better in an odd time signature. You don't have to start right out of the gate writing full songs in odd time. Maybe sections, like bridges or codas, could be in an odd time. Even just dropping a bar at the end of each chorus can give the tune an interesting friction that pushes and transitions it well into the next verse. Have fun, mess around with the possibilities, and test the waters. Sometimes going odd is better than normal.

SAMPLES: SHOULD YOU USE THEM, BUY THEM, OR CREATE THEM YOURSELF?

Samples are a prevalent part of the music industry today. You can go online and buy beats, loops, grooves, effects, sounds, parts, and even sections of songs. You can find iPad apps that are beat generators and loop factories. You can also go and steal them, which is becoming too common these days.

I'm not a big fan of taking samples from other people. I don't like it when artists download samples, whether purchased or stolen; it's something I ask artists to avoid at all costs if they want to work with me. I much prefer that artists create their own loops and samples. I know: "Old school" was built off samples, but with the changes in technology, I like artists to create the samples they want to use instead of using somebody else's creation. It also ensures that every penny of profit belongs to the artist.

If you hear something fun or a sound that you like, try to re-create it. If you want that car-start sound, go out with a microphone and sampler or mobile recording rig and grab the sample yourself. I find it better for the music as a whole, both musically and from a marketing standpoint, to be able to say it is all you—your creation and your samples. I would rather see artists be able to say truthfully that they recorded the album themselves—all the tracks and all the samples—as opposed to pulling this sample from here, stealing this sample from there, and buying this sample from somewhere else.

Make the Samples and Loops Yourself!

This is for some of the older musicians: Remember the Akai S950? Remember that heavy beast that you had to load those old floppy discs into that could only hold 1.5 megabytes? You had to bring a whole bunch of discs to operate it for a live show? Nowadays, you can sample off of a phone and still get a decent sound quality, then put the sample on your laptop to develop it. Amazing how things have changed, huh?

My point is that now it's easier than ever to make your own samples. Create your own loops. It costs less. And, why bother sampling someone else's work if you are an independent artist?

Here are three reasons I believe you should create your own samples:

1. The technology to sample is lighter, cheaper, and easier than ever.

2. If you made it and created it, then *you own it!* You don't have to pay out to buy it or pay royalties on it. On the other hand, if you stole it, you constantly have to watch your back in case the song gains momentum and someone catches you. And trust me: The better your song is doing and the more airplay you're getting, the more your theft is going to cost you.

3. You can add a cool marketing angle of saying that all loops, all samples, and all music is organically and totally yours from start to finish.

I do understand the convenience of the other side—I get it. But these days, to really stand out, to *really* make the mark and spend as little as possible while retaining as much as possible, when you make your music, you should make it *all* your own.

Then the Fit Hits the Shan: Busted for Sample Stealing

Lawsuits over samples are common and extremely expensive. These suits can grab percentages of what you have already sold, in addition to fees and costs associated with stealing property. Don't do it! I push artists to own all their music and avoid covers for recordings, and I think of samples in the same way. Adding a sample to a song, whether legally or illegally, is like adding a cover song written by someone else to your album without handling the legalities and permissions. Even if it's now a part of your song, it's something you didn't create. In fact, I think it's ironic how musicians who use such heavy sampling brag so much about what they've created.

By the same token, I'm much more drawn to sample-heavy R&B and hip-hop albums that state on the back cover that all samples are the creation and property of that artist. This tells me the album is that much more creative. As I said, it's just one more marketing element to make you stand out and show what you're made of—and what you have made.

Spend some time outside the studio to think about why you want a sample and specifically what it will add to your recording, and then find the sample you like from something that already exists. Next, figure out how you can record it yourself to get that same sound or effect or loop. Take the steps to make it yours.

As a drummer, I did a number of sampling sessions for different hip-hop artists. I would set up, we would get the microphones up on the drum kit, and I would play a number of four- and eight-bar phrases with some different feels and ideas. Then those artists and their producers would add the effects and the mix tones to my drums to create the drum loops or samples they wanted to use. I was not there for more than an hour, and they had tons to work with—which they owned, free and clear.

Open your mind and awareness. As you're going for a walk, what sounds do you hear? How would you capture them? How would you make a normal musical instrument sound a little different or give it a touch that would sample well and create something that's yours? Work to find those sounds and inspirations from the world around you that you might be hearing every day but not focusing on.

This is how a lot of artists thought when sampling was new, and it's a great mindset to keep. We have had harmonica players play into toilet bowls to get a different sound. Even Paul Simon sampled a snare drum in an elevator shaft to add that powerful explosion sound in the choruses of "The Boxer"—and that was in 1968! Try flanging the sounds of footsteps, playing on trashcans, or doing anything you can think up. Anyone can go online and grab samples and loops that enhance a song. Take the road that's a little harder: Create your own. Make them yours.

I know there are producers out there who will disagree with me on this. I respect the use of samples and have many albums with lots of samples on them. I just believe that when you are creating your own music, you should also create your own samples. I believe it's much more rewarding musically and a great marketing bullet point to add in postproduction that you are the author of the music, the samples, and the album as a whole. It will help make you stand out in a world in which artists steal, grab, buy up, and—in all honesty—cut corners to create tracks that could be so much better if they'd just taken a couple more days to brainstorm and figure out how to enhance a song by making the samples themselves.

Yes, you may use session players and others—musicians, a producer, an engineer, other members of your group—to assist you, but these are all people directly involved in your songs and your work; you've recruited them to help you get to where you want them to be. Take that extra time to create your own specialized embellishments and supplemental sounds. They are your songs, so keep them that way: each instrument, each voice, and each sample.

WHAT ARE YOU LISTENING TO? IS IT MORE THAN JUST YOUR FAVORITE MUSIC?

What music did you listen to today? Was it one of your favorite songs, albums, or compilations? Was it something you listen to often? Beyond practicing your instrument, writing your music, and managing the business side of things, how are you nurturing your ears and your inspirations? Just as you needed books in school to provide you with a vocabulary that would allow you to write, you need music to expand your artistic reach. Connect with what you like, but understand where it comes from. The more you are listening to, the larger the inspirational, technical, and musical palette you have for your songs, your writing, and your performing.

Listening to a variety of musical styles is like taking artistic vitamins—musical supplements. While you might prefer big-band jazz, you can educate your ears by including pop, country, and Latin, to name a few. Even crooners like Frank Sinatra listened to and even covered artists like the Beatles. It's about understanding what inspires you but also about being a student of music, which means listening to as much as you can, even the stuff you don't like (yet).

While you might not enjoy this style or that genre, you can benefit by listening to it, just like eating your vegetables when you were a kid. They didn't taste that good, but they were brain food, and they helped you grow big and strong . . . you know the old hype. In the same way, listening to something you don't particularly enjoy could become brain food. Songs or styles that you normally wouldn't choose can give you a better understanding of its successful elements and clarity in why you don't like it. Personal knowledge along these lines will make you a stronger musician, writer, and communicator when you're asking someone to play something a certain way or even describing it yourself.

With YouTube, Spotify, Google Play, iTunes, satellite radio, subscription services, and countless artists' websites, it's easier than ever before to listen to and find music. From song samples to full albums, there's a pretty good chance it's on the Internet or possible to get. Researching music is much easier as well. Since it's literally at your fingertips, why not commit at least ten to fifteen minutes a day to finding, learning about, and listening to both new and old music?

I get it: Everyone has favorites, and I know there are times when I can put on an old album and just listen to it a few times in a row. That's one of the joys of music and that, too, can also be educational. Still—add the learning, the exploring, and the searching to your day. Find out about the past. Figure out the influences of your favorite bands and check them out. Hell, find out the influences of their influences and dig back even further. You might be surprised at what you learn and also what you like. As they say, try it before you say you hate it. Some of you probably didn't mind the cauliflower after all—once you finally ate it.

Scott Ross, one of my favorite engineers and the owner of Elliott Bay Recording Company in Seattle, sums it up perfectly: "If you are going to be in the music industry, you have to know some damn music history. You don't have to like Elvis, but you better know who he is. If you are a drummer, you better know who Gene Krupa is. If you are a bass player, you better know who Abe Laboriel Sr. is, and no, he's not Paul McCartney's drummer—that's Abe Laboriel Jr., Abe Sr.'s son, and a guy worth checking out as well! If you are a trumpet player, you better know who Maynard Ferguson is. If you don't know who these people are, how can you connect yourself with the history of your instrument to know where it came from yesterday and where you are bringing your sound, approach, or ideas to today?"

Scott is dead right; it's crucial to know the past. There are many different opinions on what drummer was the most talented and who was the best bass player and so on and so forth. It really doesn't matter. It's not about learning who was the best, the most famous, the most this or that, or spending too much time absorbing an entire catalog of music, though you might find an artist or musician who inspires such a pursuit. The point is to become familiar with these artists and to have a basic understanding that allows you a broader view as a whole and will make you a better musician, listener, and student of music.

I often hear people claim they're doing something that has never been done before. They talk about how they can't be compared to anyone at all and they are totally original. I have talked to way too many artists who claim they sound like no one else, and once I turn them on to a track or an album from some band they never knew about, even they can hear the similarities. This can go for bands, artists, and even individual musicians. It's the same old story: The more you know, the more you know how much more you don't know.

I remember many years back, when drummers were first going nuts over Carter Beauford. Now don't get me wrong: The guy burns. But there was all this hype from drummers claiming he was reinventing the drums and doing things that had never been done before. I'm not taking anything away from Carter; he's a badass drummer. But if you study drums, you can hear the influence of Tony Williams, Buddy Rich, and Papa Jo Jones ring very clearly in his playing. When I checked out Carter for the first time, I was not surprised to find him state that those were three of his biggest influences.

By learning about the past and musicians you've never heard of, you'll be able to compare, contrast, and explain where you're coming from, what you sound like, and what you're looking for when connecting with other musicians. Why do you think Sting includes melodies from people like Prokofiev in his music ("Russians," 1985), or why Frank Zappa was a student of people like Varèse and Stravinsky?

An understanding of your musical roots can also help you develop your promotional materials. I know everyone wants to be original, but we all take from other places. If you can pinpoint influences or specify that you sound a little like this or that artist, it can potentially draw a new fan to you. If you have an array of artists, the mix might inspire someone to check you out who might otherwise not have.

To put it more bluntly, if you truly think you are re-creating the freaking wheel, you don't know history. It was probably done thirty-some years ago. Maybe not with the same effects, but no, you didn't invent it. Same goes for your supposed incomparability with anyone else. If you can't be compared to anyone, you either don't know your music history or you listen to a very limited amount of music.

It's not that there aren't innovators or people who create new things, but a completely new thing really hasn't been done in a very long time. Since there are only so many beats in a bar, so many notes in a scale, and so many alterations of a chord, there is a pretty decent chance that, while it may not be exact, you are in the ballpark of someone who came before you. And that is okay. Just be humble enough to acknowledge the fact.

So, find out all you can about as much music as you can. Use the Internet; use your friends' collections. Try listening to something old or new every day. Give it your attention and see what you love or hate about it. It doesn't mean you have to own the entire catalog, and you don't have to spend hours upon hours studying others, but get familiar with as much as you can. It will broaden your horizons and help you in more ways than you know. There's no right way or wrong way to do it; just expand your horizon, your vocabulary, and your ears. You might even enjoy it and be inspired by all sorts of things you never knew were out there. The wider you expand your spectrum of listening, the wider you grow your vocabulary of sounds, ideas, colors, and textures you can add to your music, your writing, and your creative arsenal.

PLAY NAKED: STRIPPING DOWN FOR CREATIVITY

There is nothing like connecting with your instrument when you are naked. Okay, maybe I should explain: I'm talking about switching up your routine by stripping it down to a much more raw and elemental form of your actual instrument, to reconnect with the way you work with it. Practice naked by removing certain items you are always setting up or using. Try taking away some of the gear for a day or a week.

For instance, if you are a drummer, take off the toms. If you are a guitarist, remove a string. If you are a piano player, tape up some keys and do not use them. The idea is to take away something that may be a crutch and see how you create and perform without it. Success in music and growth on your instrument is all about switching it up. As a music consultant, when I attend rehearsals, I will pull off strings, take away cymbals, and try different tricks that will be annoying at first for the musicians and bands. But after a while, these omissions will spark a lot of creativity.

This technique can open up a new world of ideas, a new way to form chords and approach your instrument. Also try moving things into different places, such as restringing your guitar with strings in different places, and see what new ideas and embellishments you come up with. Take a little recess or playtime in your practice to get weird and creative in a different way.

Take away some notes: Play a seventh chord in one of your songs in a different inversion, or remove a couple notes so it ends up being just a simple interval. What stands out? What seems cool and what feels really weak? What ideas come to you for supplementing in new ways? Drummers, try playing a song straight through with just the groove—no fills or embellishments. Then try it again with just the groove, and when it is time for a fill, just stop and leave it empty. This can be a great method to see if that fill you normally use is the best one for the song—or if it is needed at all. Then maybe you might find another spot that could use an accent or some kind of push or pull from the drums.

Get naked when practicing alone or with others. Find out what it sounds like when things are missing or reduced. It can be very eye-opening and make you aware of new ideas. It can also highlight older problems in a fresh way. Too many musicians just practice their songs, their technique, and their instrument in a very static, routine way. Be an artist, be creative, and open yourself to trying things that are a little different. Get naked to reveal things that can creatively move you forward and to identify elements that have been holding you back.

Missing a String—or Not Missing It at All

This also goes for tuning, setting up, and practicing. Guitarists, have you ever worked on your songs with one string missing? How would you rephrase the chord or substitute for that chord if you were missing a string? Would it make you approach your solos in a different way? Do you find yourself creating or finding new licks from having that string missing?

Why not try it over a period of six weeks; each week, remove a different string. Run through your tunes, your practicing, and your improvisation to see what happens. You may find you're more prepared and able to continue playing during performances, even if you break a string. In fact, Paganini, the nineteenth-century violin virtuoso—he was one of the first rock stars, actually—used to fray one of his strings just before a concert so that it would break while he was on stage. He did it to showcase his ability to play just as well on three strings as he could on four. Hey, it sold lots of tickets and got him into even more cool parties. It might work for you, too.

PLAY WITH YOUR FOOD

Many artists strive to get the best gear, the top equipment, and the most stuff that they can possibly cram onto stage or into the studio. Whether it's that drum or this effect pedal or that additional instrument, many musicians today have too much stuff, and most of them don't even know how to use half of what they have. So play with your toys. Mess around with buttons, sounds, tunings, setups, etc. You may know the basic sounds, but what else can you do to find out even more about your gear?

When you purchase a certain effect or instrument, it's as if you have purchased a whole kitchen's worth of supplies and food. When you only use a certain configuration or a certain setup, it's the same as using only one kind of food from the kitchen. I have a favorite food, but I also like variety, and I like to know what all my options are before I prepare or order what I want to eat. Why not apply the same ideas to your gear? Change the settings; do something different. You never know what you may discover. Take a little time each day to experiment with your gear and/or instrument to find out what might inspire something new and different.

Write It Down

Don't spend time worrying about losing your settings and the ones you like the most: Write them down. List where you have knobs turned to or settings placed at. You can take pictures if that helps—use your smart phone! Then write down the different settings you discover while playing with your toys. Keep a diary of different settings and their effects, what you like, and what you don't like. It will help you learn how to find and remember the sounds you like and help you learn what you don't like and how to avoid it.

And don't just settle for the sounds you know. Take chances, take time, and add some effort to learn the full array of the gear you have. Understand how you can change sounds and how those sounds can change your playing. Turning knobs, taking away a string, removing a drum, and anything else you can think of—all these are ways you can research, listen, and think of different ways you can express yourself. You already invested the money in the gear; now invest the time to know it inside and out.

CLOSING THOUGHT

A single word summarizes your sound and the best ways to develop it: communication.

The better you know yourself, your sound, and the best ways to write, record, and perform, the more you'll be able to look at the song as a whole, the different parts of the song, and the different instruments as you see the pieces coming together. From supplementing to complementing; listening to learning; analyzing to just letting go and drawing in the connections of your life, your music, your technique, your story, and the stories of others; you will connect that much more with every aspect of an album, a song, or even that overdubbed instrument in the far back.

Those who work to learn as much about themselves musically and creatively as they do technically and theoretically will hear where the changes belong, will hear those dynamics, and have those moments in performing with others where you all just knew where the other person was going. Were you born a psychic? No. You were paying complete attention to all the details while letting them all occur simultaneously. You allowed the song to happen. You learned and had a complete awareness of everything, and yet you were free to create a song or put colors on a sound canvas with yourself and others in a way that gave you the freedom to explore while remaining within the blueprint.

Your sound, in the end, is you: who you are, how you play, how you hear, how you communicate, how you react, how you write, how you feel, and everything else that inspires and transpires from the musical, personal, improvisational, theoretical, and technical sides of you. Whether it is the sound you bring to a section of a song, a whole song, a whole album, a live performance, or a recording, your sound develops from how you voice everything that you have built up in your vocabulary of experiences, education, communication, and contemplation. Those who dig in deep to learn themselves and music as a whole will be able to hear everything with a better set of ears. They will also have a whole lot more to say.

4

MANAGING, PERFORMING, AND BOOKING GIGS

OPENING THOUGHT

Whether it is a performance in front of a small bar crowd, opening for a national act, or headlining a festival, gigging can be a great way to get a band ready for a tour or to build your fan base.

But gigging needs to be thought about with the best business and marketing sense before, during, and after the show. Remember, you are marketing with your performance.

So, it's important to prepare for a gig from a technical and business standpoint. You need to know the best etiquette when you arrive at a venue: That's how you show respect and consideration to the house, the manager, sound people, and any other bands.

Premarketing, set lists, double-checking contracts, tipping the sound guy, mentioning your band's name during the performance . . . These are all ways to put you and your band in high demand with fans *and* with the venue—to set yourself above and beyond the other acts out there.

Whether it is a single show, a weekend's worth of shows, or a tour, gigging is a core part of the dream. To be out there in front of an audience, performing your songs and playing for the crowds, is fuel for the rush that keeps most musicians going.

But sometimes the gig is all musicians are about, and they don't want to deal with any other aspect of the business. Artists have to understand that a lot goes into a successful show—even more so for a series of shows—beyond just showing up, setting up, and playing.

Organization, planning, and attention to detail are required to make a gig successful. Marketing, contracts with venues or booking agents, set lists, loading in, stage etiquette . . . You must execute well in each of these areas in order to be as professional and efficient as you need to be.

GREAT GIGS DON'T JUST HAPPEN—THEY'RE BUILT

The better your performances get, the more you will be asked to play. The more crowds you draw, the longer you can stay out on the road and the larger the number of people who will get to hear you or hear about your band. The days are long gone when you could get by with pulling into town ten minutes before you go on stage, have a couple of shots and a beer, and slowly let the night get sloppier and sloppier. Today, to find a sustainable level of success that will allow you to gig more and more as well as tour and sell your music and merchandise, you must take a new approach to the gig itself.

Successful gigs begin well before the first note is played, even before the mic check. To make sure each performance is successful and propels you further in your career, you've got to start preparing well in advance of the gig.

Of course it's still all about fun, creativity, improvisation, and doing what you love. While there are aspects of the business in marketing and web work that are always going to suck, playing live on stage for a good house is what makes it all worthwhile. For this reason, you should give ample time and planning beforehand to make it the best show possible from an organizational and business standpoint.

A gig should not be viewed as a one-time event or "just a show." Every performance should be seen as the part of your career that you love the most; you should project that love of playing whether you are in front of ten thousand people or ten. Whatever the size of the venue, you need to fill the seats or the standing room and move product so that you can continue to play. You need to consider all the logistical elements that ensure a successful show—artistically and financially.

Even while you're on stage performing, you need to make sure you're marketing and promoting your band: mentioning the name of your band, your products, and other merchandise. This is how you convert listeners into fans. When you're taking all these elements into consideration as you plan and perform, you're being the most productive and effective you can possibly be, which will allow you to play more gigs and to tour longer.

The more you can organize and plan in advance, and the more you can form habits that enhance the success of every facet of a gig, the less you'll have to worry about come show time, and the more you can enjoy performing. Gigging, touring, and performing are the best parts of being a musician. If you take into consideration all the details—the checklist of everything that should be done before, during, and after the show—then each show will help you grow larger audiences, lead to better shows, and allow you to enjoy performing that much more.

HOW TO GET GIGS: CREATE WINNING SOLICITATION LETTERS

Are you pitching yourself in the best way possible to booking agents, venues, talent buyers, or whoever is hiring you or your band? Do you have one or more effective solicitation letters? Are you approaching potential bookings in a way that demonstrates that you are on point, a standout act? Do you have a tight, professional pitch email, letter, or package?

Connecting, contacting, and networking are integral to getting your name out there, gaining representation, and booking gigs. The good news is that the logistics of making those connections have gotten a lot simpler. In the last ten years we have shifted from those big promo packets that used to have to go out, to emails and even download cards that fit in the palm of your hand, each one holding all the information needed to book or hire a band.

However, at the same time the process has gotten easier for you, it has also gotten easier for everybody else. These days, it comes down to delivering your message both professionally and as fast as you can.

A few do's and don'ts:

1. **Make sure you include an opening that is individualized.** Address the note to that venue and to a specific contact person, and personalize it. In other words, *do not* send mass emails to numerous venues or contacts at the same time. Show the respect and put in the effort to focus on the exact place where you are going after a gig.

2. **Summarize and make it brief.** Give the who, what, where, when, why, and how of your band. Include links for more information; give them the bullet points and then the options to learn more about you. This is where those one-liners and taglines you developed while brainstorming your band name will work

well for you. *Do not* write a book. *Do not* give them dozens of reviews or tons of excessive information that does not summarize you quickly and easily.

3. **Set up links in your email that will take the addressee to your music, your videos, your pictures, and your promo materials.** Make it an easy decision to book you. *Do not* send attachments! Skip the MP3, JPEG, PDF, WMV, MOV, and any other type of file. Do not fill up an email inbox that is probably already stuffed. If they request it, send it; otherwise, make it a link.

Here are some things to think about as you develop your email pitch:

- What can you do to make it original and eye-catching?

- What can you do to make them want to save and then click on the links to find out more about you?

- What can you do to make your group stand out?

- What can you do to make it a special event, a step above the average show?

The email needs to project the same excitement and fun that you bring to your live performance, so make sure the letter and the content is strong. Think about what you can do to help the venue. What can you offer? Most bands are looking for something and not offering anything beyond the music.

Here are some ideas:

- Consider asking for a lesser rate to prove yourself, and be willing to negotiate. (With everyone asking for top dollar, you will stand out, showing you want to not only prove yourself, but also develop a long-term relationship with the venue or agent.)

- Take an opening-act billing instead of a headliner spot to show what you are capable of.

- Describe how you will work to advertise and market the show to get people to the venue.

- Think about a special giveaway or some kind of marketing stunt for that specific venue.

- For the booking agents, how about offering a higher percentage for a period of time to get them booking you faster in new markets?

The point is to make it a solicitation letter that stands out, is informative (but brief), and provides a strong overview with links to all the additional details. It should deliver everything someone needs to know, all in a brief and solid way. You want to showcase yourself in a way that makes you the best and easiest option to book and hire.

BUSINESS CARD OPTIMIZATION FOR THE MUSIC BUSINESS

Bare minimum, if your card does not have your logo, your name in the font you use for everything, phone number, email, a social media network, a website, and either your title or your tagline, you are missing the boat and potentially missing opportunities when you hand out a card.

By minimizing the risk to the venue by going the extra mile, and by delivering all the answers to the basic questions, you will get the best results.

THE DANGER OF THE REGULAR GIG: PLAYING TOO CLOSE, TOO OFTEN

Another decision you have to make—before you ever take the first step on stage—is what type of engagements you're going to accept. For newbies, it may seem that any gig is a good gig; after all, the idea is to get out there and start playing for somebody—anybody—right?

Not necessarily. There are some types of engagements that can put you in a loop of repeating gigs that, while nice for their security and dependable income, can actually lock you into a segment of the business that will almost guarantee that you'll never make the type of name for yourself that you want. Let me explain.

The Paragon is a great Seattle restaurant that has live music on the weekends and a few days during the week. Often they have a series of bands who rotate over a period of weeks. For a place like the Paragon, that can be a great thing; they have a solid, consistent set of acts that people are expecting. They're not paying these groups a large fee, but at the same time, the restaurant is supplying the stage, the marketing, the consistency, and a regular crowd.

For the bands, however, this model is more of what I call a general business model, as opposed to working on wider recognition and a bigger future. Now, there's nothing wrong with general business gigs, and if you prefer more stable shows, there are many avenues: cruise ship work, casino gigs, private parties, weddings, bar mitzvahs, weekly performances, open mic hosting, and the coveted hotel house-band gig. But you need to understand: Often it's one or the other. "General business model" performances don't mix well with trying to get your music out there to a bigger public.

Think about it. If you're playing every week at a restaurant or bar, listed as a group that can be seen at any time at the same place, why should anyone come when you try to play a larger show somewhere else? Why would they buy a ticket to see you at a concert or festival when they can see you every week, often for free?

But some people still want the predictable income of the weekly gig. One effective strategy, if you want to try to have your cake and eat it, too, is to play the weekly gig under another name. Work it from a different angle than your other marketing; keep the promotion about your band separate.

Nevertheless, if you're trying to become a sustainable band that tours and draws larger crowds, I discourage the weekly gig. Some artists feel they're building a fan base by playing them, but it's usually a very small and localized following that doesn't really multiply. In my experience, constant playing in a local venue will keep you local, giving you a niche following that won't come out when you're playing at the venue where you really want them to see you—especially if there's a cover charge or ticket and they already know where to see you for free. In the end, weekly gigs are not going to take you where you want to go; they'll just keep you playing in circles for the same circle of people.

"TOURING SCHEDULE" VS. "GIGGING SCHEDULE": CALL IT WHAT IT IS!

I have spoken with a great number of musicians and bands as to whether it is better to use the words "touring schedule" or "tour" over "gig schedule," "dates," "appearances," and so on. While it can sound cool to tell people you are on a tour, it can also potentially hurt you in the eyes of some event planners, talent buyers, booking agents, and management groups.

Now, I'm not talking about the bands that are actually out on the road on a real tour and playing at least ten dates without going home—or those playing a series of dates that take them out of their zip code with at least fifty miles between dates. What follows is more about musicians who go "on the road" on the weekends. I'm not saying this is a bad thing—many have to hold a day job—but a "tour" that is only a few dates a week is not a tour; these are gigs.

My advice is to "dress for success" in music: Stress your strengths and let others see you on a higher level. If your schedule includes three dates a week for a full month, that is an impressive schedule. But if you call that same schedule a tour, though it might impress some friends and fans, industry folks will see it as weak.

Keep a good reputation in the music industry. After all, you never know who might be checking you out or considering you for opportunities. Showcase your strengths by sticking with the truth; you will find that you create a much more impressive résumé. Ditto for higher-echelon distribution deals: Just because Sony distributes you does not make you a major-label artist.

Avoid lies and capitalize on your promotions by looking strong to your fans, your friends, and the industry—at the same time. The little things that help you—and hurt you. So stay aware. Make sure that a "touring schedule" is actually a scheduled tour.

WATCH OUT FOR REDUNDANCY IN YOUR SHOWS AND APPEARANCES

Pick up one of those weekly magazines you'll find in most cities and look at all of the bands listed for performances. You sometimes see them listed as playing three nights in a row in a radius of fewer than fifteen miles. These are the same bands that wonder why they have such a bad draw on the last night and a mediocre draw most of the time.

It comes down to getting out of your backyard. You also need to think strategically about how many gigs should be booked and how best to draw a crowd. I heavily recommend that bands think from the perspective of the audience members that they want to see at their shows.

If you play every weekend in Seattle, as many Seattle bands do, you'll end up oversaturating that market and creating a lax fan base. When people begin to see you constantly listed in the local papers, you're no longer the must-see band; you become the "hey, I can catch them whenever" band.

Oversaturation of the market occurs in every city with thousands of bands. They all look from the angle of "the more gigs the better," even if it's all in a tight radius. This is a bad move.

The best way to attract an audience for any city or venue is to be the artist or band everyone wants to hear. Or, think in terms of supply and demand: Spreading out your appearances—limiting the supply—will make you more desirable for the people in the area who want to hear you—heightening the demand. Over time, your fan base will move things around in their schedules to make sure to see you because they know that if they don't catch you on a given night, they won't be able to see you for a long time.

This approach can also make booking much easier. When they know that loyal fans are watching for your appearances, venues and booking agents will bring you into better-paying shows and larger rooms. If you are able to tell them that you are appearing for the first time in, let's say, nine weeks, then the venue, manager, or agent gets the sense that the market will want to see you, since you didn't play down the street the night or weekend before.

In presenting at a venue a fifty-mile-plus radius from anywhere you've played in the previous nine weeks or more, you have a better chance to pull a larger crowd. Certain venues even have it written into their show agreements or deal memos that you're not supposed to play for a certain number of weeks or even months before and after your booking with that venue. This is how some places prevent the negative effects of oversaturating a market.

The number of weeks between shows can vary, but I've found that the bands who draw the most and have the best responses are those that play in a given fifty-mile radius no more than every nine to twelve weeks. No doubt, some readers will think I'm crazy, but a nine-week spread really is the best for constant promotion and for packing the rooms you play. Doing a press release five weeks out from a show is best. Then at the two-week point, get the posters out and start building the hype leading up to your show.

After the show, you disappear for a month. It's the best tease possible: You had a great show, tore up the room, and gave 100 percent. People are going to want more. Four weeks after, a press release comes out about the next show, coming in five weeks. You are maintaining interest, staying connected, and remaining on your fans' radars. At the same time, you are not oversaturating your audience. And, once things get better and bigger, spread that nine-week period to four or five months between shows!

It's a strong and effective formula that works with the marketing concept of people *needing* to see you when they can, as opposed to seeing you whenever they want. A month doesn't really allow enough time for the best marketing and preparation for a show. The nine-week window works well.

So, where to play on those other weeks? Venture farther out. I was based in western Massachusetts for a number of years and was surprised that bands would play every damned weekend in the smallest radius. I remember seeing a posting in the *Valley Advocate*, a great local arts and entertainment magazine for western Massachusetts, of a band that was booked on a Thursday not two blocks up the street from where they were playing on Friday. Then I overheard them complaining in a local music store in Northampton about the lack of crowds at both places. Foolish—that's all I can say. Especially when western Massachusetts is so close to so many great music towns. In western Massachusetts, you're twenty-five minutes from Springfield, two hours from Boston, an hour and fifteen minutes from Albany, three hours from Portland, two from Providence, four from the Big Apple, five hours from Montreal, four from Stowe, Vermont, and forty-five minutes from Hartford, Connecticut.

So you've got nine playing markets right there over a nine-week period:

- Albany, New York
- Boston, Massachusetts

- Hartford, Connecticut

- Montreal, Quebec

- New York City, New York

- Portland, Maine

- Providence, Rhode Island

- Springfield, Massachusetts

- Stowe, Vermont

Even if you didn't want to journey out of a five-hour driving radius, you could still play every weekend in nine different markets, without even considering the smaller markets you could play the night before or after those larger markets. This technique would allow you to increase the strength and numbers of your fan base, since you're are not returning to the same rooms night after night and week after week. You'll create new fans who will seek out chances to see you and put your dates on their calendar.

Think about it: If they were planning to see another band that plays in their area all the time, but you're showing up, that other group becomes the "I can catch them whenever" group and you become the "must-see" for that night. This is the advantage of performance marketing as opposed to oversaturating a market. Tease them, but maintain your mystique: Play, then go away for a while. When you come back, the fans will, too, and your base will grow stronger and more enthusiastic.

GIG ESSENTIALS TO MAKE YOUR GROUP ESSENTIAL TO BRING BACK

Okay, now that you've got the gig, the next step is to make sure you make yourself indispensable to the venue. Here are some good rules to live by when you are playing a show. If you are professional and present yourself well on and off the stage, you will be invited back. Many of these ideas are simple, and you have probably thought of them, but applying them will ensure your popularity with both the audience and the venue.

1. **Market the show well in advance.** Promote and market your shows well in advance. Promotion brings people out, and even if you do not have a budget to market, you can still go grassroots and be effective. Use press releases, Craigslist, social network sites, local radio, and local websites. Start with releases five weeks out. This will allow the time to get stories about the show and the band. In addition, make sure to reach out to the venue's talent buyer

or marketing staff and offer any assistance that you can give for the show. This is a great way to butter up, but it also confirms your professionalism and desire to truly have the best—and best-attended—show possible.

2. **Confirm the date with the venue two weeks in advance.** Call the venue's management office or talent buyer to confirm the show and double-check arrival times. Find out if there are any last-minute changes that you should be aware of. This highlights your professionalism and reassures the management that you and your band will be there. There are many times when a venue double-books by accident or a band just doesn't show up. Confirming the date will ease your mind as well as the venue's. Create a show-tracking form; add a column for confirmation and check it off as you call each venue.

3. **Tip the sound person.** The person handling your sound has the ears at the front of the house. Take care of this person, and he or she will remember you. When I was on the road, we often gave a ten- or twenty-dollar bill to the sound tech, and any time we came back, he or she took extra special care of us.

4. **Be early; be prepared.** Know the room and where you are playing. Learn the potential traffic problems of the area. Get there early and double-check that you have all your equipment, your merchandise, and your contract (if required). Print out the directions and contact information so you can call the venue if there are problems. Know when load-in time is and make sure you are there and ready to go. These small details will make all the difference.

5. **Do a last-minute poster run of the area.** Grab some posters during the preshow downtime and hit the vicinity of the venue. Do some quick promotion, hand out some leaflets, and see if you can book a radio interview between the load-in and the performance. Dead time between sound check and the actual show can be filled up with effective marketing.

6. **Be nice; be aware.** Show respect to the venue, the staff, and the other artists. Some gigs may not be in the nicest rooms or on the best stages; still, showing respect is paramount. Don't talk trash about the room, other bands, or anyone else! If someone is talking trash about you, take the higher road and keep your mouth shut. Venues, managers, agents, and staff will see this and, in turn, will want to work more with class acts—like you.

If you have problems with your monitors, your agreement, or anything else, address it in a respectful manner. There is no need to go "diva," and it doesn't make anyone want to help you. When you approach someone with respect, most of the time you will get respect in return.

7. **Organize yourself and your gear.** As you unload, get your cases out of the way. Find out where the green room is or where you are supposed to store things, and try to consolidate and pack your stuff tightly. If it's a shady place, bring the cases back to the cars.

THE BIKE CHAIN TRICK

If you are playing in a venue where things often seem to go "missing," you can apply the bike-chain trick to make things just a touch more secure when there is no one available to watch your stuff. Buy an extra-long bike chain or cable lock and, wherever you are storing your cases, run the chain through all the handles. Now, instead of someone being able to pick up a drum case, a guitar case, or hardware case and just walk away with it, the "borrower" would have to drag out all your cases.

Count up your merchandise; make sure to track everything you need to go over. Talk to the sound person about issues or important things that he or she might not be aware of. If you are bringing certain sound equipment, make sure it is well marked and not easily mistaken for the venue's gear; the same applies to cords and power supplies. It will make your life a lot easier.

8. **Get on and off the stage quickly.** If you're doing a load-in during the set, organize your gear to the side of the stage. Figure out an order for the gear, and find the fastest way to get it up on the stage and ready to go. If there's a band on stage before you, ask if they need help loading off. Too often people waste time standing around, which backs up the sets and ends up either cutting bands' sets or creating needless delays.

Load off quickly as well. If there's a band coming up, move pieces off the stage immediately after you are done. Don't take a cymbal off its stand on stage; take the stand with the cymbal on it off the stage. Unplug and move! Show respect to the venue and the next band. People remember things like that. Don't go have a conversation, get a drink, or hang out. Clear the stage first, and then be social.

9. **Market on stage.** Have a great show and have a good time with your audience, but don't forget to market while you're on stage. Mention the band name numerous times; get it into the audience's head. Talk up the website and the primary social network you use, and tell them the name of your album or merchandise that you have. Tell the audience where you are from. Brand your sound and your name so the crowd knows how to find you after the show is over.

10. **Have fun—or at least look as if you are enjoying yourself!** Whether there are five, fifty, or five hundred people, play the same show. Showcase what you're about by displaying that, regardless of how many people are there, you're having fun, delivering a great performance, and making the most out of whatever situation you're in. Connect with the audience, no matter how large or small, and you'll continue to build a fan base. Every show is your next step toward your goal. Perform with that in mind and you'll see results.

Make eye contact with the audience! I can't stress that enough. Look at the audience and connect with them. This is where you're going to build your reputation—where the buzz about your shows and performances gets started. If you make them walk away wanting more, they'll come back and then some the next time you play. Make the audience feel like a part of the performance and a part of the band. Engage them, connect with them, and draw them in with your music, your performance, *and your eyes*.

THE ARTIST CONTRACT: GETTING IT IN WRITING AND MAKING IT LEGAL

As you start to play better shows—higher-paying shows with greater exposure— it's important to take your professionalism and organization up a level, too. Many times, especially when you're starting out, arrangements are low key, with verbal agreements or very crudely drawn-up contracts in the bodies of emails. While these work fine for some of the shows you play, it's crucial to have an artist contract available to maintain the professionalism and organization you need as a group and also to secure information, promises, and dates in a top-notch manner. I strongly advise using an artist contract for all shows and, for larger shows, the next step: a full technical rider (which I will cover later in this chapter). The artist contract governs the show between the artist and the venue, talent buyer, or booking agent who has scheduled the show. Having a contract makes things cleaner all around; it means both parties are legally responsible to make the show work.

How many times have you been in the back of the room and heard the story change about what you are getting paid? How often have you been surprised and disappointed when you thought you had things taken care of but found out that there was a misunderstanding about the venue—or the booking agent or promoter just downright lied? If you have an artist contract, all of the terms are clear and in writing, and if something suddenly changes without your awareness, you can enforce legal consequences if need be.

> Choose those you give your trust to carefully. Be caring; be loving; be creative. But also be careful.
>
> Too many music relationships show red flags early on that are ignored or not addressed.
>
> Your honesty, candor, and questions can allow for much calmer seas in times of tension, stress, and anger.

Now, some venues and agents will not sign contracts—which should be a red flag, right from the start, that things could get dicey. Also, some booking agents and venues will sign very oversimplified contracts with loopholes you can drive a truck though, allowing for complex problems to occur with nothing clearly written to protect you.

I recommend having a basic artist contract that you can present to a venue, agency, booking agent, or promoter. Present your contact with a well-organized document that considers all parties involved. It can be up for discussion and not carved in stone; you don't have to be a diva or ask for things that are unrealistic or over the top. But it's just good business to have a basic contract that covers all the core issues. From there, you can make mutual edits and agreed changes with whomever is booking you. If you present the contract as negotiable to some extent, there is a better chance that you will not intimidate a smaller venue or booker and still secure core elements for your protection.

In the contract, the stage plot, the input list, the sound and light info, and the backline requirements, you should list all the details, embellishments, and nuances important to your group; you can then take away requests or parts as needed. It's a lot easier to trim back on the front end than to add on down the line.

Talk to a lawyer who specializes in music law and create a personalized artist contract. You can also download one from the Internet; there are some decent general contracts that you can use until you can spend the money to get a legal document that fits you to a T. Often when inexperienced bands put together a contract, they end up using wording that does not actually say what they really had intended to say. I know: freaking lawyers, right? But, you are eventually going to need one to write the contracts correctly.

Another way to save money and still have a solid legal artist contract is to use a down-loaded template or example. Fill it out to the best of your understanding with all the specific elements that pertain to you. Take it to an entertainment lawyer with the outline and the key bullet points you are looking for, allowing him or her to create the document faster and cheaper for you.

Following are the basic points that I make sure to include in an artist contract (which some booking agents may call a deal memo or contract face). While some seem obvious, it's still good to get that information, and get it in writing. This is also a good cheat sheet to have for yourself to summarize all the important details.

Make sure you can easily mark down the following:

- Date
- Venue
- Venue/booking point of contact
    - Email
    - Phone number
- Venue address
- Venue phone number
- Venue fax number
- Venue website
- Venue social networking sites
- Opening for/opening act(s)
- Info on other artists or venue
- Load-in time
- Set time(s)
- Payment/fee agreed
- Method/time of payment
- Merchandise split
    - Soft goods
    - Music: CDs, download cards, USB sticks, vinyl, etc.
- Additional percentages of profit

- Lodging/amenities
- Catering budget or meal buyouts

Setting up these basics right out of the gate, putting them in a contract, and confirming them will make life a lot easier. Also, having this list for yourself will keep everything clear, and if problems arise, it will be that much easier to deal with.

While the venue's social networking site is not something crucial, knowing it makes it easier for you to advertise to its friends and fans. This will help you with the marketing and promotions for the show. Posting a link to their Facebook or Twitter page can be a good thing, but make sure you check with whomever is handling their social media before making an announcement directly on their feeds and updates.

Next, make sure you are covering the details for cancellations. What happens if you have to cancel? What happens if the venue cancels? What does the contract stipulate if a cancellation happens last-minute as opposed to a month out? This section should cover all these elements.

Another section should cover how you would handle inclement weather as well as something called *force majeure*—also known as an act of God. Most contracts cover this, and you will want it in yours. What do you do if there's a hurricane, tornado, or blizzard? Do you have a plan or agreement in place? These are the details that would involve things you wouldn't ever expect but should absolutely be prepared for.

The terms-and-conditions portion is next, giving a basic overview of the agreement as a whole. This is followed by signatures, which complete the contract. You now know what's planned, because it's all on paper with signatures. This may seem either oversimplified or over the top to you, but you must believe me when I tell you that it is so much better to be safe than to be sorry.

While the artist contract will not guarantee an end to all disputes and problems, it will move things along faster and clearer for all parties involved. And remember, these artist contracts go both ways: for the artist and for the venue. As you're securing your rights and what you want, you have to make sure to secure the rights and desires of the venue as well. Again, just think back to every time something has gone wrong or been misunderstood: Every time you felt ripped off, screwed over, underpaid, or taken advantage of. In most of those cases, if you had in writing what you thought you were supposed to get, you would be a great deal happier and things would've probably gone a lot smoother for everyone. On the other side of it, think of the times when a venue or booking agent was upset with something you did or didn't do that was unclear or undefined. The artist contract is for both parties to clearly understand and have in writing the who, what, when, where, why, and how of a performance and the expectations and responsibilities of everyone involved.

PAYMENT STRUCTURE: BEFORE THE GIG, DECIDE WHO GETS PAID WHAT

Speaking of contracts, who gets paid what? This very common question needs to be addressed before the gig or session—not afterward. In chapter two, I talked about who gets paid what when it comes to gear, but now we're talking about performances.

If you didn't nail this down when forming the band, do it now. What type of situation are you coming into? Are you a hired gun at a hired gun rate? Are you getting an even cut? Does the person that booked the show get an extra cut? Do the flyering, advertising, and promotional costs come off the top? Does a specific gig have an allotted amount that is set to pay back a member of the band for gear, gas, food, or other expenses?

Musicians and bands who ask all the questions and put the answers down *before* the show will be fighting a great deal less and have a better understanding of what everyone is expecting. Assumptions, miscommunication, and confusion are inevitable when money comes into play prior to any discussion.

As a music consultant, I always bring up the money questions and ask each member of a band how they expect things should go. More often than not, various members of the band will have different answers. Notice that I didn't say anything about the right or wrong answer. What matters is that a band is on the same page before a check gets cut; this avoids all sorts of annoying issues.

TECH RIDER: STAGE PLOT, INPUT LISTS, AND SOUND AND LIGHT REQUIREMENTS

Okay, so now you're ready to go to the gig and rock the house, right?

Not so fast. While we're still thinking about contracts and getting things in writing in advance, I want to cover a really important aspect that will help the show go smoother for you *and* for the venue. Many larger organizations want to make booking as easy as possible, and if you have your tech rider (stage plot, input list, sound and light info), backline, and even your hospitality requests in order, you streamline the process for the venue. The easier you make it for them, the more they will want to book you.

For starters, remember that all your documents must stand alone, even if they are all presented together with the contract. The supplemental documents mentioned above may be given to different staff members, depending on the size of the venue. It doesn't take that much time to set up a simple letterhead with your logo, adding a basic header with your name, tagline, and website, along with a footer containing your contact person, address, email, phone, and fax. Then, regardless of who has received this sheet or that document, they always know who it is for. Use this same template for all documents.

A stage plot and input list should be part of any promotional and booking package. The stage plot and input list are blueprints for your technical. While not all venues expect you to have them, they are appreciated by sound people, both front-of-house and the monitor engineers. It also presents you in a more organized, professional light. Some places like input lists, others prefer stage plots, and some will ask for both. I also advise having a sound and light information sheet as well. Though they are not as commonly asked for, it is a preference for some.

When you walk into a venue with a stage plot and input list, you make the engineer's world a happier place. The sound tech can more easily set up the microphones and monitors and get you to sound check faster. Some of the better rooms will ask for these materials in advance (hopefully, they already have it because you made sure it was emailed during your production advance). You can also send them a direct link to a downloadable PDF, JPEG, or protected Word document. Send them clearly named and well-defined links rather than attachments. By clearly named, I mean something you can read and know what it is supposed to be, like this:

Stage plot PDF for Michael McFarland scheduled to perform at your venue on 7-03-13—http://michaelmcfarlandmusic.com/stage-plot

Not like this:

http://bit.ly/10hNrzg

Sending links that are intuitively named with titles and detail preceding them gets you appreciated.

When you know what you're bringing, what you need, and the basic aspects of technical, setup, and sound issues, you become an easier band to work with and one that the venue or booking agent will want to have back. Think of it from another angle: So many venues have to deal with so many bands that may be good musically but can make life incredibly difficult technically. The groups that are easier to work with are the ones that have the supplemental materials prepared, organized, and presented in the most professional fashion. The music, of course, is the staple and the foundation, but with the proper documents, just like with the proper promotional and marketing materials, you will be able to open more doors faster.

Now, let's take each element in turn.

The Stage Plot

The stage plot—a diagram of your stage layout—is the most commonly requested document. It helps define the space and the equipment locations. There are several ways you can set up a stage plot. I find the following style to be the most effective, professional, and informative.

Start with the header: "Stage Plot." Yes, that's obvious, but many people often don't take the simple steps. From there, provide a clear, concise layout with the basic descriptions of each instrument that you have for your group on the stage. This gives the reader an easy blueprint.

> Getting a stage plot to the engineer or producer in advance
> of a recording session can also make your studio time more efficient.

Draw the diagram in a simple, clean, and size-proportionate way. Take some time with it and get it right so that it will be an easy document for people to use and understand. If you are a solo artist or a small band, you can always combine the stage plot and input list; I advise adding a small box on the stage plot with the basic input list information.

> For an example of a full band stage plot, visit
> http://tag2nd.com/stage-plot

The Input List

The input list is more an informational document than a picture or diagram, usually created in Microsoft Excel or a similar spreadsheet program. You are going to want to have the basic channel number and the instrument and microphone preference. Next, add a column for microphone stand preferences, insert or effect preferences, and a blank comment section that can be used by the engineer for notes. Some artists add a basic symbol section to abbreviate certain items, but many sound people and front-of-house crew have their own symbols and abbreviations. Most front-of-house engineers prefer the input list for a reference point, and often a monitor engineer or the stage technicians will want the stage plot. To a certain extent you will get the sound the house can provide, but the more you communicate your preferences on your input list, the better your chances that a sound person who doesn't know you can get your sound right with what is available at the venue.

Include a numbering system for your microphones. For the drums, show the basic placements so the sound person or engineer can prepare the microphone setup, the monitors, and the basic layout before you arrive. Have a column that designates the location of the microphones. I suggest three-letter designations such as USL (upstage left), DSC (downstage center), and so forth. This lets the engineer reference the location of each channel to its microphone and solve problems much faster should they occur.

I also advise adding FOH # (front-of-house) and MON # (monitor) columns that can be used by the engineer to list the channel the specific instrument is in. Just because you're using eighteen channels doesn't mean that the lead vocal will always be a certain channel number on every board, especially when more than one act is playing that night. Some engineers who have larger boards will reassign channels, and others will use a different channel altogether. Either way, adding a FOH # column and a MON # column will let the engineer designate the correct channels for your gear and for your monitors.

Finally, have a notes section where you can add your requests or core preferences, such as separate monitor mixes or specific sound requests. Don't go over the top, and don't be surprised if you don't get every microphone you're looking for or every wish you put in writing, but it never hurts to ask.

As with the stage plot, I recommend putting the input list on the band's letterhead with a clearly defined header: "Input List." I also recommend having a definitions table on the bottom to make sure that your definitions for your particular acronyms are understood.

As a final touch, you can also add a column for band member names and instruments so that when the front of house is calling out to you, he or she can call you by name.

> For an example of a full band input list, visit
> http://tag2nd.com/input-list

The Sound and Light Information Sheet

This sheet is the least commonly used in the set, but many if not most higher-level touring bands have this in their performance contracts or supplements. The truth is this: Unless you are a higher-echelon touring group with a sound engineer, you're generally going to get what they give you. Yes, there are great techs that want to go the extra mile and make your night at their venue the best night for you, but they are few and far between. House sound engineers are running the front of house on their own abilities the night of your show and are putting in more effort to have the overall sound right than to tailor their efforts for your songs or your band. Independent artists may choose to give a description of what they would like to see, but they should be humble and respectful, realizing that in most cases, they won't get it. Still, by having that information ready, those who want to go the extra distance for you will have a guide.

For lighting it's the same; most of the time, you're going to get the simple, in-house lighting rig. Sharing with the lighting director (if the venue has one) that you do not want a Madonna dance party or 1970s disco tells them that you are aware of what you'd like your set to look like without coming off arrogant or expecting a Fourth of July light show.

> For an example of a full band sound and light requirement sheet, visit
> http://tag2nd.com/slr

The stage plot, the input list, and the sound and light information sheets are three simple documents that you can put together to ease your life and the lives of the venues and crews who help you. They can help you get a better sound, a faster setup, and a better matchup among you, your music, the sound person, and the room you are playing. Go for the basics that you really need, and always remain open to adjustments and alterations. If you're an artist who performs with different-sized bands, create these documents for the largest-scale group you would play with, then edit and modify based on the personnel for the specific shows.

Make your life easier, prove that your group is well organized, and show the venues, talent buyers, and booking agents that you are ready to play—from the smallest venue with no PA to a hall with a top-of-the-line sound system—and you will see the payoff. Think of it this way: If they are on the fence about your music but see these documents in place, you have a much better chance to get booked.

BACKLINE REQUIREMENTS: WHAT SHOULD BE THERE BEFORE YOU GET THERE

The backline requirements sheet is usually reserved for large-scale acts and musicians who fly to shows with limited or no gear. This sheet covers all the needs in detail, down to the bare bones of what is required. Backline requirements are supplemental attachments to riders and artist contracts. Having your backline list available for download from your website highlights your organization to others, and will help you know exactly what you need for a show.

You may also find that having your backline together with the other tech riders will get you bookings that you may not have gotten otherwise, such as certain festivals and corporate shows that have a budget and can supply backline or afford to fill a backline order.

Don't get cocky or overzealous when addressing your backline. Make sure it has what you play on and what you actually need. It's also a good idea to mention that you are willing to make adjustments and changes upon request. Finally, this document can act as a nice supplement to a potential endorsement package, showing that you use certain gear exclusively, if that's the case, and that it's a part of your rig regardless of where you play and where you travel.

As with your press kit and other promotional, marketing, or logistical materials, make sure that the document stands on its own: properly labeled with every piece of contact information, including addresses, phone numbers, emails, websites, fax number, contact person, and your logo.

I'll say it again: Every sheet, every document, everything you are sending to anyone should have *all your contact and identifying information*! Think of someone's desk, stacked with piles of stage plots, input lists, sound and light information sheets, and backline requirement documents. Then, imagine a gust of wind coming in and blowing all those papers all over the place. If a single separate sheet were picked up, would that person know it is for you or your band? If you answer that question with "no"—fix it! Whether a full package or a single page, it should clearly, easily, and uniformly identify you!

If you list all your gear in a clear and concise backline requirements document, and if you take pictures of the gear you own, it can also help with insurance issues for you and your band. It becomes an inventory document for the band.

My Old Backline Requirements Sheet

Below I have the information from my personal backline that I used when doing sessions and sub drumming gigs to which I was either flown or otherwise connected with when I was not going to be bringing my own kit. I requested, in detail, the drums I wanted: by size, the heads I wanted on them, and the miscellaneous items that would allow me to do my best for the gig.

Seventy-five percent of the time, it was filled to the T. I would show up and find the gear that I'd requested. I was able to add my cymbals, which I always traveled with, and get ready very quickly. The other 25 percent of the time, I would be contacted and asked if certain existing backline drums would be a problem, and I was glad to adapt. But I would always initially ask for the kit I was most comfortable with and the setup I used when I was carrying my own gear.

This was the complete rig and the largest I would use. I never used it for jazz; I usually formed a kit specifically for the music I was playing, often by subtracting elements. I found this layout could handle any type of style and every need I had.

To the drummers who are about to scrutinize me for the size of the kit: Go suck it! This is all the stuff I would ever need for any situation; I'm plenty happy on a four-piece, too.

But if you still want to give me crap, go look at . . . well, we are going to leave his name out of this book. But go search for a drum set where the drummer has two seats! (I'm talking about his old setup.) You can search him online. No one knows what the guy looks like because he's behind a small city of freaking drums! Don't get me wrong—I still think he burns—but, really, dude? I mean, if it takes you longer to set up and strike your kit than the time you're playing on stage, cut down on the gear. This guy's kit is so big . . . how big, you ask? Like I said before, he has two thrones. I always want to ask him, "Hey, man, do you bring that rig out if you don't have a drum tech or three?"

I'll admit it: When I didn't have a tech, my kit was kick, snare, rack, floor, three cymbals, and hi-hats. So again to the minimalists who are going to feed me crap for the list below—get over yourselves. Besides, it's fun to rant for no good reason sometimes, isn't it? And the kit wasn't that big.

Anyway, here's my old backline sheet.

LOREN WEISMAN BACKLINE SHEET FOR FLYING AND TRAVEL DATES WITHOUT PERSONAL CARTAGE

Drums and Hardware:

- 1—20" × 18" kick drum—double headed w/microphone hole in front
- 1—12" × 9" rack tom—double headed
- 1—10" × 8" rack tom—double headed
- 1—14" × 14" floor tom—double headed
- 1—14" × 5.5" snare drum wood shell (maple preferred)
- 1—double tom stand for rack toms or two tom holder clamps
- 5—cymbal boom stands with five arms for cymbals
- 1—hi-hat stand
- 1—snare drum stand
- 1—DW5000 bass drum pedal or equivalent
- 1—Throne or high-quality drum seat—low base
- 1—floor carpet to be placed under the drum kit
- 1—Meinl cowbell or equivalent and attachment to cymbal stand

Miscellaneous:

- Please make sure all cymbal stands have felts for above and below the cymbals.
- Gretsch or Taye drums preferred. Remo drum heads preferred.
- Please make sure all drum heads are new.
- Drummer travels with cymbals and sticks. No cymbals or sticks are needed.
- Please supply duct tape, a Phillips screwdriver, flat-head screwdriver, and a small can of WD-40 oil and a small bottle of Vaseline pure petroleum jelly. (Note: The Vaseline was for the drum lugs; get your mind out of the gutter!)
- Supply one towel for the stage as well as a fan.
- Hiring party or persons are responsible for the pickup and the returning of all gear.

As you can see, items are covered across the board. For a band's backline requirement, just add the list for each player and the needs of each. As I mentioned before, don't get cocky; ask for the things you really need. Most of the time, listing what you already have is a good idea. For the items you own that are custom or outrageously expensive and hard to find, ask for either equivalents or realistic alternatives. Also realize if you're playing a smaller market or a smaller city, they may not have all the gear you need. Be flexible!

Your backline requirement sheet helps you define exactly what you need. It can also get you some cool shows booked by large-scale companies. Understand that bands at these shows have their logistics in order. If you have a great sound and a great production package, you could be the one getting booked!

> For an example of a full band backline sheet, visit
> http://tag2nd.com/backline

PRODUCTION ADVANCE: A BEFORE-THE-SHOW, LOADING-IN, AND SETTING-UP LIST

Now you're at the venue and it's time to do the final prep for the show. But there are still some hurdles to overcome.

The biggest problems around sound checks, loading in, setups, and all the other steps from "A to Play" are miscommunication, misunderstandings, and assumptions. From the venue owners to the booking agents, the sound people, and the staff at any given venue, I consistently hear complaints from both sides of the fence. I remember early on, being a musician and also being young and stupid, blaming everyone else when things went wrong or ran behind, when in fact it was usually on me and the rest of the band.

Now a little older and a little wiser, I advise bands to have a production sheet. This document goes into a little more detail than just the venue address, sound check time, gear storage, and performance time. It is chock full of solid details that can help ensure a show goes off the right way: that the artist not only gets to the right place, but gets there on time. Assuming you don't have a road or tour manager, pick one person—the most responsible and organized member of the group—to be responsible for calling the venue to collect the information and create the production sheet for each day or show. This document is called a "production advance."

Before the show, hammer out the details. Know all the extras and create a template to apply to all your gigs. By creating a production advance for each show and following it, you will build a reputation for reliability that will give you a leg up with venues and agents.

Following is a production advance checklist to ensure the best results. And remember, every venue is different; each music manager, owner, and agent may have certain preferences. Knowing them in advance will help you be that much more prepared.

Production Advance Information

- Date of performance
- Venue name
- Street address
- Website
- Social media site
- Email
- Phone (land line or cell)
- Other supporting acts
- Talent buyer (who booked the date for the venue or promoter)

Schedule

- Departure time
- Estimated drive time
- Traffic considerations
- Parking considerations (does venue have a dedicated parking location?)
- Description and location of stage door or loading door

Technical and Production

- Production representative
- Phone/cell
- Sound person
- Lighting director
- Backline available (if any)
- Gear storage location
- Merchandise setup location
- Confirm merchandise split percentage

- Meal consideration, drink tickets, buyouts, menu
- Closest food locations (if not supplied)
- What you may need to bring or what the venue might lack

And the most important question: Who will be paying me?

This might seem like a lot of things to find out, but knowing each of these items can prevent problems at the gig. I've watched road managers who used these detailed production sheets and observed how things went off without a hitch, or, if there was a problem, it was resolved fast. By comparison, with the managers and bands who had less complete information and relied on guesses and assumptions, when those fires started, they turned into out-of-control blazes.

So, get the details; know the ins and outs. If you have emails for the venue's talent buyer and production rep, take the time to send them your technical sheets via links. Tell them to review it in advance of your show and contact you if they have any questions. Ask about one-way streets, alleys, names of cross streets, etc. This really helps, especially if you're pulling a trailer. Knowing the location of the load-in door and any available parking can really reduce stress at the end of a long drive. Do not put total trust in your GPS, your map app, Google Maps, or a Garmin. There are no stupid questions, only stupid mistakes and assumptions.

> Hint: Keep your production sheets on file (or in a folder in your hard drive). They'll be handy when you return to the venue for a future gig, and you can also use them to send thank-yous. Remembering people's names and things that happened at the gig will make the staff feel good about you being there again. I guarantee that staff remember those who were really nice as much as they remember those who were total divas. You want to be on the former list!

FIRST AID BOX FOR THE STAGE: PERFORMANCE PREVENTATIVE MAINTENANCE

What do you bring on stage with you? What do you keep in your cases? Most people have the gear they need and occasionally some backup stuff, but many don't keep the essentials needed for worst-case scenarios.

But unless you have a tech who's sitting side-stage with a tool belt and his handy box, you should prepare like a tech for the problems that can occur on stage. Having that first aid kit in arm's reach can help keep the flow of the show going in the face of the problems that often arise. Sure, it's one more item to load in and load out, but your emergency kit can be just as important as the gear you use; it can keep your gear happy and operational.

Go through a mental checklist of your gear. Come up with a list of items you might need to fix—anything and everything. Obviously, you can't always carry a second amp around in case your amp blows up—too big to put in your emergency box. But think of items that you'd need as a first responder, not a trauma center surgeon. This is your first aid, mend-the-scratch, and cover-the-cut kind of box.

Every musician's needs are different, and every box should be individualized to that player and his or her needs. It should contain the things that will keep the artist and his or her gear functioning. Small hint: Use a black case to carry it in, since black can fade into the background of just about any stage.

Here are the contents of my first aid for the stage box when I was on the road without a tech. This is for drums, so figure out the equivalents for your instrument or needs:

Backup Stuff:

- Backup beater (1)
- Backup drum lugs (5)
- Backup kick drum lugs (3)
- Backup kick pedal springs (2)
- Backup cymbal felts (4)
- Backup hi-hat clutch (2)
- Backup drum-tuning key (1)

Most of these were the physical backups of items I needed. If a head broke, I usually had a second snare with the kit, so that switch was easy. Yet I still wanted to problem-solve and usually had heads in the bottoms of my drum cases or in the bus. If a head broke on a tom, I just wouldn't use that tom. I never really was the head-breaking type, but you never know when something will break.

Here's another list of stuff I kept in reach at all times:

Mr. Fixit Stuff:

- WD-40 (for the pedals)
- Vaseline pure petroleum jelly (for the lugs)
- Phillips screwdriver (for loose drum nuts or bolts)

- Flat-head screwdriver (for loose drum nuts or bolts)
- Wrench (for hardware repairs)
- Pliers (for hardware repairs)
- Allen wrench set (for drum or hardware repairs)
- Duct tape (for everything!)
- Small towel (for spills on gear and sweat)
- Rope (for slippery stages or when there's no rug to keep your kick from sliding away)

Then there's the stuff that you need . . . just because. Take a lesson from the Boy Scouts; be prepared by having these in your kit:

Personal Stuff:

- Flashlight (if the stage is dark or it's hard to see, a small Maglite helps)
- Band-Aids (if you cut yourself)
- Advil (if you . . . come on, duh!)

Items for other players can include batteries (especially for effects pedals and switches), extra tuners, extra cords, strings, and a backup microphone. And nearly every musician needs assorted screwdrivers, pliers, and other tools to make last-minute repairs or adjustments.

You may think having a list and a box like this is over the top, yet I know many musicians who not only do this but also continue to build and add to their boxes. A good emergency kit can also be useful on off days as you do maintenance on your gear. Each problem you can solve quickly under pressure will showcase your skills as a musician who can keep the show going regardless of setbacks. So, learn how to be your own tech when you need to be. Plan ahead for potential problems, and as a result you will solve them more quickly and often with an audience none the wiser. The ability to problem-solve is important in many aspects of the music industry. When you have a handy box to solve certain problems faster, you will be a step ahead of most and more prepared than the rest.

YOUR BEST LIVE SHOW: EFFECTIVE STAGE COMMUNICATION AND INTERACTION

Finally! You've done the prep, nailed down the details, and now it's time to deliver the rocking performance that the audience has come to see. So many musicians and bands talk about how you have to see them live to truly get them, and it is true in many cases. I write a lot about the business side of the music industry and the best steps to take for getting that crowd to come see you live, but now that the fans are there in the room and listening to the music, are you using the most effective communications possible?

Are you telling people your band name? Are you plugging your website, mailing list, social media site, and band products—CDs, download cards, T-shirts, travel mugs? Are you interesting? Are you drawing in the crowd, interacting with them to make this the best live show they have seen in ages? Are you keeping them engaged and connected, not pushing them away from the stage or your music? Are you delivering the type of show where people do not want to go outside for a smoke or leave their spot to get a drink?

Captivate them with the music, but make sure the communication and interaction is alive and kicking as well! Talk to the audience like friends; have fun with them. Stay away from stale intros: "Well, I wrote this song years ago when I was young . . . blah, blah, blah . . . Ask people about situations they might know, relate to, or may have experienced themselves. If you mention that you wrote a song about a girl that broke your heart because of X, Y, or Z, ask if anybody in the audience has been there. Engage, relate, and connect on a higher level.

Think about having a conversation with an audience rather than talking to them. Draw them in between the songs. Try not to sound like those singer-songwriters that go on and on with ten-minute, barely intelligible stories that everyone endures until the next song starts. Try to make them need to listen to the space in between the songs. Interact, react, share, and just make it that much more fun.

> The best sound for your shows will come from the understanding of how you get your favorite sounds and the specific compromises on how to get those sounds in each room you play.
>
> Every room is different; every room has its quirks, its hot spots, soft spots, and feedback angles. Talk to the sound person and talk to the employees of the venue; ask what makes for the best sound possible.
>
> Those who take the steps to learn a room and figure the best ways to get their sound to work in that room will have the best-sounding show in that room.

Do Unto Others

Be a good fan while you are waiting for your turn to perform. Hush, and be the type of audience that you would want for your band. Take it from Elmer Fudd: Be vewy, vewy quiet.

Whether it's the band before you, the one after you, or just a group who could use the support of the type of audience that you would want for yourself.

You'd think the above paragraph would be unnecessary, but I remember an open mic I attended not long ago. I was grabbing a drink and watching some very talented artists, from beginners to semipros, performing and sharing material. The room was intimate—or, if we aren't going to be all PC and shit, we will just say it was a sparse audience. Anyway, this one guy was making all sorts of noise—actually tuning his guitar right in the middle of the room! He was yelling to people coming in and giving no respect to an amazing female vocalist and guitarist on stage. A good audience member? Not so much.

Here is where the HMS *Irony* set sail. When he got up on stage, in front of a few more people than the woman who had played a couple songs earlier, this king of double-standard douche bags stopped in the middle of a song to tell the audience to stop talking and pay attention to him. He lectured the audience about respecting the performers. Hmm . . . really?

> If you are not practicing what you preach, then you either need to change your practice habits, change your practice, or just shut up.

It made me think about how musicians and bands need to consider others who are performing. I understand that a band may need to deal with loading in and other issues that may keep them from watching a performance, but when the work is done, give the attention to the band on stage. Present yourself as respectful and you're more likely to get the same in return.

I SPY . . . MYSELF ON STAGE: VIDEO YOURSELF TO SEE WHAT THE FANS SEE

Do you ever wonder what you look like on stage? Do you wonder what kind of faces you make when you solo, when you end a song, when you react with the crowd? Why not video yourself and find out? Plus, you can use that live footage for promotional videos. So why not have someone shoot a video of you for the entire night? You can see for yourself what you look like, how you appear, how you are working your instrument, and your posture from the audience's perspective.

When was the last time you videotaped or digitally recorded yourself on stage? When was the last time you watched yourself perform, scrutinizing the playback for performance issues, pros, cons, or just an overall review of your stage presence? Most people never have. Recording video of yourself is a great way to critique yourself, to see things you might want to change or things you might want to reinforce. Will Calhoun of Living Colour used to video a large number of his shows and watch his footage to see how he was hitting the drums and to look for different issues in his playing.

Self-videoing can be an instructional tool to help you refine your stage presence, tighten your musical technique, and even straighten your slumped-over, emo posture. So, get in front of the lens and record yourself. Learn about your stage show, including all the stage habits you have—good and bad. Studying yourself on stage can help you present a better show and point out problems that may be occurring that you don't even realize until you see them for yourself. Approach the video playback the same way you approach your audio playback. Watch, analyze, and learn. It will help you in more ways than you could ever imagine.

Lights, Camera . . . Action?

Set up cameras in places where there are unobstructed views. Sometimes having a camera on a tall stand above the mixing board (or somewhere close to someone trustworthy) will help you greatly. Having others shoot you can work well, but make sure they understand that they're shooting for your benefit and not to become the director or creative genius behind a music video for the band. It's also a good idea to have a couple of cameras if you can. Or, if you only have a single camera, concentrate on different members of the band for each show so you can see all the different elements that are occurring.

Talk to the venue about adequate lighting, or shoot in rooms that already have good lighting so that you can clearly see and review the video instead of squinting at a dark mashup of the stage and some shadowy figures on it.

Remember, you are recording yourself so you can review your performance. Take into consideration all the aspects of lighting and placements, and most important, make sure you or someone is turning the cameras on and off. It sounds stupid, but bad communication and lack of preparation can mean you have some great camera angles that aren't even turned on. Oh, yeah . . . take off the lens caps, too.

A side note: Check with the venue before setting up any video equipment. Explain that it is for archival, educational, or staging purposes. Some venues will get bent out of shape if they see you setting up cameras, and other venues may ask for a fee if they think you are filming something for profit. It is better to ask than to have your hands slapped, especially when you are working on building new relationships with venues. If they say no, then just do it another night at another place.

Man, I Look Good on Video, but What Else Am I Looking For?

Okay, get over that little ego flare of watching yourself on stage—especially guitarists. Yes, guitarists, I'm picking on you. Many stereotypes are based on common occurrences, and this one's no exception (end of guitarist rant). After you get over the fun of watching yourself perform, it's time to get down to watching for the core elements that can help you develop the best show possible.

1. Technique, Posture, and Exhaustion

How are you performing with your body and your instrument? Look for signs of bad posture that might indicate early fatigue. Are you moving around like a wild person for the first half of the set and then pretty much stationary for the second half? Then maybe you should spread out how often you are moving or how active you are, to be able to have the best level of endurance for the show.

Certainly, you'll want to watch for the technical aspects of your instrument. If you're a drummer, how's your posture affecting your endurance? Are you tiring out too fast or can barely finish the set? Maybe your posture or certain flourishes are actually detrimental and needlessly tiring when you're playing live. Reviewing from this perspective can help you with your performance, your technique, and your endurance. Whether you're holding your bass too low or jerking your neck while singing, this first review can help clean up such undesirable mannerisms.

2. Appearance, Interactions, and Reactions

How do you look on stage to each other? How do you look to the audience? Do you look as if you're having fun? Are you interacting with the members of the band and the audience? Is the stage balanced? Is the main action centered? Does every part of the stage get played throughout the performance?

Sometimes having a camera pointed from behind the drum set and out to the audience can help you gauge how the audience is reacting to your performance. Watch for the point when they are most connected and try to figure out why. What songs are getting the best reaction? Which ones are getting the worst? When, as a whole, does the audience look disinterested, and when are they hanging on every note?

Watching the audience can help you design better set lists or become a little more aware of when things are moving too slowly. Remember, you want to keep the audience involved and connected. Videos will help you dial into these specifics.

3. Eye Contact, Recurring Technical Issues, Marketing, and Other Miscellany

In this last review, watch for both good and bad habits that might be occurring, from eye contact to marketing. Notice where you're looking. Are you connecting with the other members and the audience? Are you always looking down, closing your eyes, or staring in one particular direction? Watch for technical issues as well. What constant or common problems have to be addressed with your equipment or your setup on stage? What can be streamlined, adjusted, or taken care of before a show to keep those time wasters down to a minimum?

And what about marketing? Are you saying the name of the band? Are you promoting while you're on stage? Are you keeping it short and sweet and keeping the show moving? Do people know where to buy merchandise or where to sign up for a mailing list? Make sure you're not talking too much or for too long. Watch for moments that slow down or delay the pace of the show. Analyze them thoroughly. Refine your performance and keep an audience connected with you from start to finish.

Again, just as you review your audio to ensure you're delivering the right sound, review the video to make sure you're delivering the performance you intend to give. Most artists perform a great deal more than they record, so it's absolutely necessary to review all aspects of your stage presence. Lights, camera, action—and then review. Increase your awareness of what's happening onstage and use that knowledge to heighten and tighten your show to deliver the best performance possible.

HOW TO OVERCOME STAGE FRIGHT—OR AT LEAST REDUCE IT A NOTCH

Stage fright, performance anxiety, being scared shitless before a show, or whatever else you want to call it—it happens to more people than you realize. Some of the celebrities you think never could have it spent a lot of time asking questions about how to overcome stage fright. To be honest, I think it's a bit like masturbation: Everyone experiences it and never talks about it. I believe most people deal with some kind of stage fright at some point but do not talk all that much about it.

For those who have it in a really bad way, there are books that can help. I would suggest that you search a few and read of the first few pages online to see whose communication style you connect with.

For onstage performance growth and confidence, as well as putting on a better show, I am a big fan of Tom Jackson and his Onstage Success information. It is filled with great tools, tips, ideas, and approaches for the independent musician. You can find out more about Tom at:

http://tomjacksonproductions.com/

Though I do not touch on stage fright too much as a music consultant or music producer, there are three key tips I have used with people who have stage fright or recording-studio anxiety issues:

1. If you know you need to work on your nerves and the pressure, cutting back on caffeine, soda, or heavy, sugary foods is a good idea. While caffeine can somehow strangely calm some people (which, for whatever reason, works for me), it can make it worlds worse for others.

2. Try to do something calming before going on stage. Some people get pumped up so much before they take the stage that their excitement can shift to fear and anxiety. Sometimes, just lie down and meditate or stretch before going on stage. It worked for me by centering my mind, and it gave me a better show all around.

3. This is probably not in Tom Jackson's books or anyone else's for that matter, but early on when I was feeling any kind of performance anxiety or needed to overcome stage fear, I would look at the lights. I would blind myself somewhat in the spotlights by staring directly into them for a few seconds. The stage felt a little smaller and a little more comfortable.

Regardless of how you approach it or what you have to do, just remember: You are not the only one who has had to deal with stage nerves. Also remember that nervous energy can be harnessed and used for your benefit and improved performance.

OPEN MIC NIGHT: GOOD IDEAS TO FOLLOW AND BAD TRAITS TO AVOID

Open mic night is a chance to test out songs and performing ideas, to listen to and network with others, and to have a good time. Whether pro or hobbyists, all musicians and bands should be treated equally and respectfully.

Don't use open mic as a time to show someone up or take someone down. Instead, use it to meet other musicians, see newbies take to the stage for the first time, and hear seasoned pros test new material.

Here is some solid open mic etiquette to make it a better experience for you and others. Bear in mind that though some of these might seem to be written by Captain Obvious, they are missed or forgotten by beginners and pros alike.

1. Be prepared to take the stage and get started.

Tune up in advance of your performance; if you have a guitar, have your equipment with you or ready to go on the side of the stage so that you can get started as soon as possible. On any given open mic night, there are a lot of people who want to play, and you are wasting time for those coming after you by taking too long getting ready. A lot of open mic MCs will announce who is on deck or coming up next, so listen up or ask, so that by the time someone is done, you are ready to get up on stage and play.

2. Play the number of songs you are told to play (know your brief set list).

If you're allowed three songs, then play three songs. If you want to do a song that is extralong, then cut it to two songs and, most importantly, don't try to sneak in another song. Don't be selfish; you wouldn't want that from the artist that went before you, so why do that to the artist waiting in the wings?

3. Do not order drinks to the stage!

I actually saw this happen at an open mic. Not only did the band take forever and a day to get ready, but they also requested drinks to the stage before they started. Un-freaking-believable! If you need a drink on stage with you, order it in advance. But honestly, it's not a set; it's a few songs. Leave the drink at your table or wait until you finish. It is not *your* show, *your* stage, or *your* set. Play and share nicely with others. This goes with the whole vibe of what you would want from the act going on before you.

4. Settle some for the sound, and be aware of yours.

When you are on stage at an open mic, a very overworked and underpaid engineer has to run around all night. Ask for the bare-bone basics. You are not going to get the greatest sound in the world, and if you are getting a monitor mix at all, you should be thrilled. You might not get the greatest mix and sometimes you might have trouble hearing yourself, but *do not* yell at the engineer and *do not* take up a song's worth of time adjusting your sound!

Also, be aware of your volume and keep an eye on the engineer. If he is signaling you to turn down or you hear "turn down" in the monitors—do it! What it sounds like to you is not what the audience is hearing. Be aware of your volume, your dynamics, and the sound person, who has a better sense of what your volume and dynamics sound like in the room.

5. Say your name.

Let's see, did I mention this already? Seriously, say the names of your songs and tell people if you are looking for other musicians or if you have a show coming up. Tell people who you are. Whether you are up there just for fun, testing out a couple of tunes, or promoting an upcoming show, talk to the audience. Connect!

Different places have different rules, and unusual situations can occur. The above ideas mostly pertain to full houses and long sign-up lists. Things do change when you have a thinner crowd, a bigger stage, or an acoustic-only stage, but overall, these are good rules to live by.

Lastly, just because others aren't following these rules, don't drop yourself to a selfish level. Stand out with your respect, your consideration, *and* your music. Success in music comes from a mixture of the music and the way you treat other musicians and colleagues in the business. You will make better contacts if you're respectful—and you might even influence others to follow suit.

SET TIMES AND SONG PLANS: A BLUEPRINT FOR THE PERFORMANCE

Set lists are often altered by bands, depending on the time they have on any given night. If you have to fill up a couple of hours, you're looking to stretch things sometimes or add extra songs you don't usually do. On the opposite end, if you only have twenty-five minutes, you have to trim the set. It's really important to set up song plans logically, creatively, and effectively—to create set lists that showcase the songs and present them in the best order for the time you're allotted to play.

Now on the long side, if you have a full night to fill up, deliver more rather than less, especially if you're playing to new people and building a fan base. Some of the jam bands who spend twenty-five minutes on a song can really bore listeners. Fans as a whole have attention deficit disorder, especially when it comes to new things. Keep a set moving with new songs and mood changes to keep the attention of the crowd. Pay attention to the keys and tempos. Though a song that's in the same key and close in tempo may seem so different to you, it might seem like the same song to someone not paying close attention. In your set lists, spread out the songs that are in the same keys and same tempos.

Keep the show moving. If you need to add a couple of extra cover songs, then add them in and spread them out. If you're playing a really long night, say three or four sets, you can bring back some of the songs from the first set. Also, as you start a set, make sure you give the punch to let them know, "Hey, here we are! Now listen!" On the same note, as you finish a set, give a nice solid ending to the last song. Make sure it's a clear-as-day finale and tell the audience you'll be back. Mention where your merchandise is being sold.

On those long nights, keep the breaks limited to exactly what you say they are. If you're taking a fifteen-minute break, stick to it. So many bands will disappear for way too long, losing audience members and pissing off the venue owners. If you say fifteen minutes, make it fifteen minutes. Tell them what time you'll be back up on stage. I know some bands in New York that actually hang a little "Back in Fifteen" sign on the microphone, showing the returning time. I thought that was cute and pretty effective.

Playing more songs in a long set is more effective than stretching songs, as far as the attention span of the audience goes. As you build up your audience and fan base and want to explore things further, you can start to stretch a little. The more you give people, the more they can take in and feel as if they're getting something new.

Now, I'm not saying don't take solos, but unless you're doing jazz or fusion or music that's based on soloists and solo interaction, keep to a single solo or two short solos for two people per song. If you don't have the material, learn covers to spread across the set.

For newer artists and bands just laying the foundation, make sure to identify the originals as well as the covers. If you're mixing them up, certain covers everyone will know, but make sure that they know it's yours when you're playing an original. Every gig you play is about marketing your music to the audience, so make sure they know it's your song, the name of the song, and the name of the band. You can make it a little funny, too. Maybe say something like, "That was 'Peg' by Steely Dan, and right now we're going to switch gears to a tune we wrote called 'Stuck in a Moment' by the Acme Band. Oh, by the way, we are the Acme Band—just in case you hadn't heard."

Throughout the night, talk to the audience and show the CD you're selling or any merchandise you have. This should be part of your set; it is very important! Write into the set list where you hold up a disc. Then, a couple of songs later, hold up a download card, a sticker, a T-shirt, or whatever. You have their attention; they're all looking up your way—at least you hope they are. When you display the products, you're giving them visuals, so showcase your stuff; make it part of the show. If you have a sexy tank top for girls with your band name and logo, have someone wearing it, maybe a cute girl, and have her come up on to the stage at the end of a certain song and cross the stage wearing it. It sounds hokey, but it's effective.

The most common mistake is picking a couple of songs and then just tossing them into a random order. If you're given a very tight window, such as twenty-five minutes, or in some cases even less, you have to be time effective. Make the plan and time the set. Allow for getting on and off the stage and a brief couple of seconds for some applause. Give them as much as you can in the amount of time you have. Don't look at it as if you only have time to do five songs; consider how you may be able to cut a solo or shrink a section—maybe cut an intro or outro. Lose a verse. All this allows you to fit more music into the set and thereby present more about your group in a shorter amount of time.

In short sets, try to stay away from really slow songs. Since many short sets happen when you're playing with a number of other bands, make sure they know who you are. Allow the audience to clap, but get right into the next song. Try to have very little silence between the songs, and if you have a short intro that you can talk over, do it! It may not be the perfect scenario, but it is the most effective and productive. Mention your website, social network sites, where they can talk to you after you get off the stage, and where your merchandise is. It's a lot like speed dating; you have a certain amount of time to make an impression on someone, and then after the bell rings, you move on.

Of course you want time with an audience, and you want to share the music the way you wrote it to be delivered, but if you adapt to the situation at hand, you'll have a much better chance of bringing new fans to see you in a place where the performance isn't as rushed and the focus is on you and a longer set. So, whether you have ten minutes or two hours, prepare accordingly. Time your sets; write into set lists what you will discuss or promote between songs; figure out the orders that work best; and keep the audience attentive and engaged. Work on the set lists; work on your songs and how you can alter and adapt them for different gigs. Make sure to also save these set lists with comments on them about what really worked well and what didn't. The more versatile you are in arranging and organizing your shows to the time and situations you're given, the more fans you will be able to attract and keep.

STAGE SETUP: WATCH AND LEARN FROM OTHER BANDS

Many musicians spend a great deal of time researching different ideas for their stage setup. Whether setting up the drums, the guitar amps, the keyboards, or any other instrument, musicians and bands often try to find that perfect setting, microphone placement, or angle on a drum. Therefore, one of the most surprising answers I get when I ask bands what they thought of the drummer's kit from the night before or how the guitarist in the opening band had his pedals set up from a show the week prior—is that they didn't notice.

If you are out there playing live, you are playing with other bands more often than not. Whether you are the headliner, the opening act, or one of the many bands in any given night, pay attention to what the other musicians around you are doing.

I grew up watching and reading about my favorite drummers in *Modern Drummer* magazine and often wanted to emulate their setups. I was a big Simon Phillips fan and loved what I saw of his setup. I tried copying it, but I found it challenging. When I got to see Simon deliver a mind-blowing, incredibly informative, and amazing drum clinic in Boston, I realized that I stood almost a foot taller than him! I got to sit at his kit, and it didn't work! Then, when I had a chance to sit down on Gregg Bissonette's drum kit, it inspired me to move my china cymbal into a position that felt so good, and I haven't altered it since. I remember sitting down at Carter Beauford's drum set from the Dave Matthews Band and was amazed at how far away his first floor tom was away from him. It was interesting to watch his approach to playing and why it worked for him, but for me, my floor tom was always right there, practically touching my leg, so I could do faster side swipes from the snare drum to the floor tom.

My kit has changed through the years, but the basic angles fell into place, and whether I was on a small three-piece or an excessively large, thank-god-for-drum-techs kind of kit, there was a uniformity to angles and basic placements that I locked in after a number of years of playing around. But talking with other drummers, sitting at other kits, and asking questions helped a lot, too.

Regardless of the instrument, it is great to pick up or try out someone else's setup and see what works for you and what doesn't. You are around tons of different musicians from different backgrounds with different ideas. Ask questions; see if you can sit down on a kit or look over a guitar rig; find out why that person does what they do. You might find some great ideas to try for yourself while sharing your approaches with others. Hands on, sitting down at, picking up, or testing out is always better than just reading up on it. Test-drive other people's setups to see what might work for yours.

LOAD-IN AND LOAD-OUT: THE SUPER FUN PART OF EVERY GIG—NOT

Loading in and out of a show, your rehearsal spot, a house, or wherever is just about the worst part of being a musician, especially if you're the drummer. I used to joke with a band that hired me, telling them that I practice for free, perform for free, and record for free; what I get paid for is carrying all this crap in and out of all these places.

I played in a group with a keyboardist who played on a Rhodes piano. Basically, it was the two-person load instrument. The bass player had to have his double-stack amp, and at the time I was all about this drum kit that I did not have any reason to carry around. Yet there I was, lugging it in and out, up and down, and all around.

The first time I got a tech, I remember thinking it would be hard to go back to carrying my own stuff. During one particular tour, I continuously increased the number of drums, cymbals, electronics, and other miscellaneous toys I used. It was ironic how much smaller my kit became and how much less I needed when I got off that tour and was hooked up with a band in which I had to carry my stuff by myself.

There's no way to get around the loading in and out, unless you get techs to do it for you. Some of you have those faithful few who come to every show and will carry your things for a few beers, but most everyone in the low, mid, and even basic pro levels is trucking his or her own stuff.

There's got to be an easier and more effective way, especially when you go from weekend warrior to playing four to seven shows a week. And when you perform at a radio station or on a TV show during the day and then have a show that night . . . the dreaded quadruple load! And that doesn't even include what you brought into the hotel, or wherever you were staying that night, to protect the gear.

Solo artists, this is not really for you. Most of you are only lugging a solo setup that's not too bad or too much. This is geared toward the bands and the groups who are lugging guitars, keyboards, amps, drums, basses, merchandise, and whatever else. The key point to making load-in and load-out bearable is to get the damn singer actually to help! Okay, maybe it's a stereotype that singers don't help carry stuff, but I know that a truckload of you know exactly what I'm talking about. It definitely happened a lot with some of the people I played with.

Here are the key points to getting through the hell that is loading in and loading out:

- Simplify the job.

- Maximize the loads.

- Work as a team.

- Practice the plan.

I know it seems obvious, but trust me; I've watched and been a part of bands that got this down to a science, and it made life so much easier for everybody. Think of the job as loading for the band and not the individual. When you're only thinking of you and your stuff, it doesn't help the process go faster for the group. If you're in a band, you need to realize that you play together as a band, so you should load in and out as a band.

1. **Simplify.** Figure out what you're loading—not just your equipment but also the band's gear as a whole. Ask a few simple questions to simplify the job for the group.

   What takes the longest to set up? Are you working with your own PA? Who has the most gear, and is it brought in a van, a truck, or a number of different vehicles? What's the heaviest, or what requires two people to load? How do you set up it all up on stage? When you answer each of these questions, you can come up with the most efficient way to load in certain gear first. For example, bringing in the monitors or frontline items and placing them on the stage first is a bad idea if you have to load in the backline of drums and amps that go behind them.

2. **Maximize.** Once you figure out the venue setup and what needs to load in first, pack the transporting vehicles accordingly. Do you have to load in on a street corner where only one vehicle can be? Then load in one car at a time as another person finds parking; other members unload the next vehicle, and so on.

   Some places work better for security purposes if you daisy-chain the gear. In other places, you might all have to grab a load, lock the vehicle, carry it inside, and then return to it. In other venues, you might want to have a loading team structure: someone at the vehicle, a couple people carrying in, and someone to begin unpacking and placing gear for setup on stage all at the same time. Be ready to work the variables.

3. **Work as a team.** This goes back to thinking of the load-in as a band thing and not a "my gear" thing. Numbering the cases and listing points where they go can help with the organization of how stuff is loaded into vehicles and back out again. You can also add simple stage terminology on the boxes like the big boys do, such as USC (upstage center), where the drums most commonly go. This can help to tell people exactly where something should go when you are lucky enough to have an extra stagehand or two assisting. Having the boxes numbered and coded can also help you keep track of your items when you're not loading right onto a stage or when you are playing a venue with a series of other bands.

   Distinguishing markings on your cases can help as well. Luggage tags are always a good idea, as well as numbers, but adding some extra item that identifies them as yours can really do you good—a large logo of the band or even a red stripe, something that would distinguish your cases from others. Think of the luggage collection at the airport. Have you ever noticed those bags that look like everyone else's but have some distinguishing tag or band around them? Notice how they stand out?

4. **Practice.** Practice a load-in and load-out from your rehearsal space to the car and back in. Figure out what system works best and quickest for you. Once again, the more organized you are with load-ins and load-outs, the more professional you will appear.

Work on your setup and getting yourself ready as quickly as possible. Especially on the nights where there are a number of bands, the faster you are up and down, the more you'll be noticed by the venue or the promoter. Trust me; this is an area in which you'll want to impress. Venue owners, booking agents, and other bands will take notice. If you're moving fast and keeping things on schedule, you're going to be asked back faster than a band that is screwing up the schedule because of their disorganization on and off the stage. Best of all, you can get it done and over with quicker, because even with the right plan, the professional appearance, and the faster results, *it still sucks*.

Stage Setup and Strike: Best Ideas for Getting on and off the Stage

Most bands get into the groove when it comes to setting up and tearing down off stage. The more you practice your music, the better it gets, and the same is true of stage setup and breakdown. But what about those items on stage that are more, let's say, perishable?

You bring drinks on stage; you break a string or a drumstick, drop it on the stage, and get back to the songs; you have a set list taped up somewhere and leave it behind; maybe you have a bad cable, quickly replace it, and abandon it on the stage. All these things and whatever else you might leave behind can make the stage a mess.

Just as you're loading off your gear, load off your trash. It might be one more trip to and from the stage, but it's a trip that will give you a better reputation with the venue, the sound person, the stage crew, and the other bands who might be playing with you that night. Do as Mom says: Clean up after yourself. Most don't, so when you do you'll be remembered.

Of course a venue wants to pack a house, but a venue also wants to have bands that are easy to work with—respectful and not selfish or over the top with the egos. Unless you're sporting your own techs, pick up your mess. Leave the stage as you found it.

On that note, if you're playing with a number of other bands and either some of the gear is backline or you're using someone else's gear, take care to leave things as you found them.

Sometimes headlining drummers will lend a kit to the opener so they can have things in place for a faster transition. If you have to make adjustments, make small ones. Try not to mess with the kit or the setup too much. If you raise a stool or a seat, drop it back to the height it was originally when you're done. Try to put things where they were before you moved them. If you're borrowing an amp and make adjustments, try to get the settings back in the ballpark of where they were before.

These are the little things that will be remembered when a band is looking for another group to play with or a venue is looking for someone to fill a slot or a date where they want good music but also need the utmost professionalism. It's more important than ever not only to deliver the best music but also to take care of business before and after the show. Step up, clean up, and get out of the selfish mindset. Be aware of the other bands, the venue, and the employees who work there. The extra effort and respect will be returned tenfold in most cases, since so many musicians skimp on these little extras.

Acknowledge, respect, and be aware of the staff. Whether it is just the sound person and a bartender or you have a crew—someone running monitors and someone else running lights—these are the people, the professionals, and the team who are going to help you sound your best. Do not give off the higher-than-thou vibe; do not talk down to them and do not expect them to be at your beck and call for every single thing.

> Tip, tip, tip! If you received good service—tip. Seems obvious, right? And yet so many artists will tip poorly while still having the expectation that everyone should buy their CDs and merchandise and tell all their friends to do the same.
>
> Just as you could use the sales after a show, waitstaff could use the tips. What comes around goes around.
>
> Respect those who serve you; they might be the same people, a night later, that you are serving on stage.

There's a good reason for asking for the name of the sound person (and if you're lucky, a separate lighting director) in your preshow contact info: When you arrive, you know exactly whom you are looking for. By knowing and remembering the staff's names, you are already taking a step toward a great show.

Tip the sound person; thank the crew when you are done. You will almost be guaranteed the royal treatment on a return visit. With all the jackasses who treat crews like crap, you will be remembered and the staff will want to go above and beyond for you and your next show.

SAFETY: PROTECTING AND SECURING YOURSELF AND YOUR GEAR

Musicians often overlook the safety of people and gear—until something bad happens. Playing on the venue circuit, the theater circuit, and even the arena circuit involves hazards surrounding the people who come to the shows, the people in the neighborhood, and the time of day or night.

Most shows occur at night and don't finish until late, so the band inevitably is getting out even later. Loading out can be dangerous and downright frightening in some of these neighborhoods. People get attacked, things get stolen, and anything and everything can go wrong.

It doesn't matter whether you're female or male, big or small; incidents happen. Most of the time they occur when you aren't paying attention and are taking things for granted. A number of years ago in Seattle, I was walking home late one night and got jumped by two guys. Now here's the kicker for those of you that don't know me: I stand six foot four and weigh about 255 pounds. I'm broad shouldered and generally not someone who gets messed with.

Anyhow, one guy grabbed my bag. The only problem for him was that I never let go, so the other guy smacked me with some kind of stick. It happened really fast, but the next thing I knew, they were running across the street and I still had my bag, my wallet, and an adrenaline rush like no other. I think these guys were on drugs and pretty amped up. I'm not a tough guy, but no one takes my bag. It contains, on any given day, production notes from sessions, backups from sessions, my laptop with everything I write, and everything else.

The point of the story is that things happen when you least expect it. Things can go from usual to unusual in a split second.

The corners that we cut to save time and effort are the same corners that can cut us in an instant and when we least expect it. Think about the things you take for granted in the loading-in and loading-out process—when the van or truck is unlocked and you'll be right back out. Come on, everyone's done it! Or when you're loading out from the venue and everyone is taking a load of stuff out, leaving a ton of gear sitting inside. What about when you're storing cases with a bunch of other bands' cases or gear? Or when the merchandise boxes are sitting somewhere unwatched while you're doing sound check? What about leaving clothes hung in an unwatched backstage area? Or when you run down the street late at night to grab a coffee or go into a convenience store after a gig and leave the van running—or carry on you the cash from the gig? These are all common things that occur and don't faze you until something goes wrong.

There's nothing earth shattering or revolutionary here. These are just the simple, stupid rules that will keep things from getting simply stupid:

- Leave someone with the van as you are loading in and loading out, and leave another person with the gear inside. It's the safest way to go. Whether one person stays out there or you rotate, keep someone with the gear at all times.

- Make sure you double-check the locks on your doors, and chain your hitch if you have a trailer. Save up for a security system, and keep your merchandise and other expensive items locked up.

- Take pictures, get serial numbers, and inventory your gear. Make sure that if something happens to it, there's defined information or markings that show it belongs to you.

- Watch your back, and in the bad cities and neighborhoods, travel in twos. It may not stop everything, but it will reduce the chances.

- Have a clear system of knowing everything you have loaded in and everything you have loaded out from a venue. Track your stuff; otherwise someone else might.

- Find out if you have a place that's guaranteed to be secure in the venue. It's rare to stash your cases and gear where the public has access; however, if you don't have a secure area or security guarantee, be prepared to watch your own stuff.

- Keep your wallet and personal items with you. I know artists who will actually bring personal items on stage and store them in amp racks and by the drummer. It may seem over the top, but when something happens to your personal items, you might change your mind.

The overall idea is to solve problems before they occur and to avoid common shortcuts in security. These initial measures can help prevent the negative situations that too many run into.

Is Your Money Safe? Waving Cash Onstage Makes You a Target

I read an article about a band with a song about money, and the singer decided to flash a decent-sized wad of twenties during the song. Four hours later . . . Who woulda thunk it? The police report actually mentioned that the singer was "surprised" by an attacker who asked him for all his cash in the alley where they were loading out. Duh! Is your money safe in any back alley of any city at any time? I think it is safer to always assume not.

Carrying cash is dangerous enough. I tell bands to try to do as many electronic transactions as possible and avoid having cash on them, especially in the rougher neighborhoods. It is not about your size or about how tough you look or don't look. I am pretty sure the whole you-look-cool vibe while waving cash is old and outdated anyway. Leave it be or be funny with it: Wave Monopoly money!

Musicians and bands need to focus on their safety and their profits after a show. I remember being told if I was ever paid in clear sight of anyone to maintain a look of disappointment and be very careful to not let anyone see the money in my hands. Also, counting money in a place no one can see you is another good idea, and if you can settle the night and be paid somewhere private, such as a production or bar office, that is even better.

Be careful: Don't wave it, don't brag about it, and don't make yourself look like an easy target, because if you do, you deserve what will come eventually; you were asking for it.

THE POSTSHOW FOLLOW-UP: STAYING CONNECTED WITH VENUES AND AGENTS

The show rocked. You just got off stage after playing a great set. The audience loved you, and everything that was supposed to happen actually happened. You load out, get paid, and are either on your way home or to the hotel to sleep before driving to the next show. However, there's one more step that will close out the show, but it doesn't take place till a few days later. This is the "postshow follow-up" and it will not only help you stand out but also helps solidify your contacts and connections for future shows at that venue or with that booking agent.

Remember when your mom or dad had you write thank-you notes after your birthday and holidays? Maybe you are not old enough; I am talking about the time before email when you had to actually write a thank-you note, put it in an envelope, address it, add a stamp, and then physically mail it!

You wrote those notes and sent them out to people who gave you crappy socks or sweaters or things you wouldn't want in a million years. It was the good thing to do, the right thing to do—and it's something you should do after any gig, especially those venues to which you'd like to return. Up to this point, I've discussed how professionalism in your marketing, load-ins, load-outs, and stage performances will make you stand out. By adding the postproduction follow-up, you will have put the cherry on top.

Write an email and thank the venue, the booking agent or talent buyer, the sound person, and whoever else was there. Use your letterhead for the note and look back at your production sheet to make sure you have the correct names. This will bring your professionalism to a more personalized level and show consideration to the venue and staff after the fact. If you want to take it a step further, write that letter and actually mail it out!

Never Coming Back

If the venue was bad, the people were awful, and you have no intention of playing there again, just skip the note altogether. *Don't* go sending letters scolding venues, giving them a piece of your mind. As much as it may be true, you don't want it in the hands of people who might spread it around and make you look like a diva.

Not Perfect, But Would Return Again

Even if things go wrong—sometimes it's not the booking agent's or the venue's fault—don't use this letter to gripe or sound like a princess. You can still send a nice note to keep the connection with the venue or the agent for future opportunities.

Thank them for whatever was good. If there were problems, try to address them in a positive and considerate way by emphasizing how you would like to make things better for both the venue and the band.

These notes make a difference in the long run. For larger shows and bigger agents, make the effort to send out that actual, physical letter along with the email. For the smaller ones, you can stick to emails. Thank them for the night and talk about how you would like to return.

I usually recommend sending out a note to arrive on the Monday or Tuesday a week after you played, if you can time the postal service. More things are reviewed and more mail is opened on those days as opposed to the show days or busier nights late in the week or on the weekend.

The follow-up can help foster a stronger connection with that venue or that agent and get you back in there again—maybe on a better bill or with better stipulations around your show. So, as Mom said: Be nice and send a thank-you note. Keep the mindset that every gig starts at the booking and ends with the follow-up.

CANCELLATIONS AND RESCHEDULING: HAVE PLANS B, C, AND D

So the show got cancelled. Whether it was your fault, the venue's fault, the manager's fault, or the weather's fault, it really doesn't matter. It's strange to me that when something goes wrong, people seem more concerned about figuring out who did something wrong and assigning blame than with problem-solving and doing what they can to make the best out of the situation.

Mistakes happen. Gigs are going to get cancelled or rescheduled. There will be times when you're going to be double-booked. You can take the steps to organize and track things the best you can, but problems occur, and sometimes they just can't be helped. I've heard bands scream and moan about this booking agent or that manager messing up. Then I've seen the online postings where bands blast venues and then the venues blast the bands. This really doesn't solve a single thing, and it takes up time you could use to reschedule, put into place preventative techniques, and reach out to your fans and people who were going to come to that now-cancelled show.

First and most important, it's about the fans and not your bruised egos and placing blame. Get the word out once you know there's a problem that can't be solved, so you can be in communication with every fan possible—hopefully before they come out to the show that's not going to happen now.

Some bands have text mailers, others have emailing lists or use the various social network sites' invitations through Facebook. Some still use Myspace. Some use the ReverbNation mailers or sites like Evite and other invitation-style sites. Some may use Twitter as well as all of the above. Use whatever site or format you have available to inform people the moment you know a show has been cancelled. Get the information out to your street teams if you have them. The show may be cancelled, but don't see the cancellation as taking you off the hook. Make that time useful by reaching out to the fan base that's intending to come and see you. Ask the venue to post the cancellation on its website, and visit any pertinent music and entertainment sites in the area to get the word out that you're not playing there that night.

With today's social media and our connected lifestyle, you have no excuse for not getting the word out to prevent someone from making a trip they don't need to.

Be respectful and diplomatic in these efforts. Explain that the show has been cancelled and will be rescheduled to that venue or to another location. Don't bad-mouth the venue, manager, booking agent, or whoever is to blame; be the bigger person. Just explain what's happened without attacking or coming off rude. It doesn't even matter if you're completely right and the other party is completely wrong; be the more respectful person.

In fact, try to spin the cancellation in a strong marketing way. If people bought tickets, tell them to bring the tickets to the next show at the same venue. See if you can make the reschedule work in both the band's and the venue's favor. If your next time in town is at a different venue, offer a discount for merchandise to those who can show they purchased tickets for the previous cancellation. Maybe create a raffle drawing for people to bring their tickets and win some of your more expensive items. This will show you care about your audience and may draw more people to come out to see you.

Remember, cancellations do not mean you assign blame and end the night on a bad note. Reach out to every person you can through every media source. Get on the Internet, on the phone, and in the streets to get out the information. Buy a big felt-tip marker to hit some of the posters in the area of the venue, stating that the show was cancelled and more information is available on your website—it's a simple and smart idea.

Next, take steps to ensure mistakes don't happen again, but keep your focus on your audience and you will see them return the next time and the time after that. Think effectively, execute expediently, and communicate clearly to keep everyone in the know. Display that you care about the people coming out to see you. It will set you a notch above; most bands just pack up and go right home.

CLOSING THOUGHT

The more prepared you are for the show, the better the show will be. This will also make life easier for the crew, other bands, and the staff. Pushing aside ego and arrogance will make a show work better on all levels for all the bands and artists. Larger-scale artists who have been difficult to work with are often not invited back to some venues, even though they have massive draws. The reason? They are not worth the trouble for the money made. Work as a team with the venue, the stage manager, the other bands, and the booking agents to get everything as prepared as possible. This, in turn, will allow you to have the best gig possible. Take the trouble to be aware of other people's jobs and think about what you can do to help them help you.

If you look at spectrum of gigging—from the creative to the business sides—and take into consideration all the elements and all the people that it takes to put on a show, you will have the best chance for the best shows. Not only are you addressing and preparing to make it the best time and the best performance, but when you are working, respecting, and putting in the effort to help all those around you to create the best show possible, those people are going to work just that much harder for you.

5

SOLO OR BAND TOURING

OPENING THOUGHT

It's one of the biggest parts of any musician's dream or goal: to be on the road, playing to crowds all over the country or all over the world. All the hard work of recording, branding, promoting, and marketing is done to be able to get out and play in front of fans every night. But whoever realized that the dream included a team of people not only to book a tour, but to maintain and sustain that tour?

Now, the dream is still alive; don't give up on it. I can still remember walking back to the hotel room, knowing how lucky I was to have played that show and thinking how I would get to do it again tomorrow. But touring is no longer about that one-city, one-night, one-show mindset. You have to think about touring as a multifaceted beast that needs to be fed every few days, but you can still keep that animal out on the road: happy, making money, and being invited back.

By creating excitement about the show, engaging and entertaining fans before and after the show, and building a network of relationships everywhere you go, you will be able to be successful on the road and on tour.

GETTING AND STAYING OUT ON THE ROAD

Touring is a good thing. You want to be out on the road, supporting your music and your secondary products, as well as establishing your marketing and branding your name. Touring to keep your band and your business operating is a smart way to approach things. But to tour and perform while being able to pay the bills and even profit is where the business elements come into play. Remember: Touring is expensive.

Think about all the costs associated with touring. You need gas—which is a killer—you have lodging, food, and instrument upkeep. You have basic hygiene items, clothing needs, and vehicle upkeep, like oil changes and maintenance. There are tolls on certain highways, you'll need Internet access, and many times you'll have to pay for city parking, since free parking isn't always available. Don't forget about laundry; you're going to have to keep your clothes clean. Then those on-the-spot marketing costs like printing up flyers and posters at local copy shops. There are also postage fees to send things home or have things sent from home to wherever you are. Don't forget about ordering products and merchandise to be shipped ahead to a venue so you can keep selling those items. Then add in the fact that you still have your standard bills for rent, electric, water, cable, credit cards, phone, insurance, medical, and costs like student loans or other monthly debts. But wait, we aren't done! What about those little morale boosters like movie tickets, going to a bar, or visiting a tourist attraction or historical location that might cost you a little cash?

Touring suddenly seems a little more expensive than you may have initially anticipated, right? There are ways to trim back and prepare, but the point is that you need to make sure you're working on selling your band, your music, and your other products to make this a realistic and sustainable venture. Some nights you'll get a good amount of cash, but most nights you're barely going to make enough for gas money; it's the reality of the industry. So the answer is to tour *and* market the product as intelligently and as effectively as possible. Do your advance marketing and promotions. Once you get there, do some additional postering, see if you can get a couple of CDs in a popular local store, or hand out some download cards. Know about the local music rags and newspapers so you can contact them the next time you swing through that particular town. The more steps you take to make every stop as effective as possible, the more sales and audiences will grow. The tour will get longer when you can sustain yourselves on the profits that are coming in.

Carefully plan your driving hours; the more time you're on the road, the less time you have to work the next destination with marketing, flyering, and researching local TV, radio, newspapers, and other media. Some bands and booking agents will try to book only larger markets and have you driving for hours. I remember being on the bus for nine hours straight some days and thinking, "Okay, there isn't a city or market we could hit within nine hours—really?"

Now, it's easier to be on tour and traveling long distances when you're on a nice tour bus, but only a very small percentage of artists today have that luxury. For those traveling in smaller vehicles with larger numbers of people, it's a good idea to be on the road for shorter distances if possible. Find the smaller markets you can play between the bigger metropolitan areas. With all the social networking out there, this is easier than ever. If you're traveling a maximum of three to five hours a day, it can allow ample time to get into a city or town, do some marketing and research, hit sound check, and then continue to promote the show locally up until you have to go on.

That also means no sleeping in! Or at least only rarely. Many who try to live the rock star lifestyle—drink until four in the morning and leave at the latest possible checkout to arrive just in time for sound check in the next city—are wasting valuable hours that could be used to make every stop better and set up a bigger show the next time they return.

Instead, commit to working every city and every town. Enter the local media information you gathered into a spreadsheet about that city. Track the venues, new and old. Find out who the hot bands are; if they can pack a house, make nice with them by email or through a social networking site. If you find a band to open up for (if you're lucky, someone who can bring in five hundred people) that gives you a bigger crowd to play to, sell to, and potentially gain as fans. This is much more effective than playing a headliner in front of a room of twenty-five. Sure, being an opening act can be a great thing. But is your goal to be a headliner, or is your goal to play to as many people as possible and convert them to fans who buy your music, see your shows, and stay connected? If you never headline but have success as an opener or warmup spot, is that so bad?

I was in a band whose manager would hand us each a couple of CDs, a T-shirt, a hat, and a truckload of stickers after sound check, and we would go to the local restaurants and bars to talk about the show and hand out a couple of free items. This really helped. If you're playing during baseball season in a city that has a baseball game in the afternoon or evening, head down to the ballpark. You don't have to go to the game or pay to get in, but you can hand off a flyer to an excited baseball fan, and—you know what they say—if the team wins, people don't want to stop partying. Maybe they'll continue that party by coming to see you. Ask if the venue will give an entry discount for people bringing a game ticket stub. There are tons of ways to work the city you are in before you play the stage.

When you view touring as a marketing opportunity, a chance to grow your fan base, perform, and sell merchandise while learning about local media, venues, and key people, your return dates will become even more productive, effective, and lucrative.

WHERE ARE YOU BASED? LIVING LOCATION VS. DRIVING DISTANCES

Where is home base for your music career? Are you in a location that can get you to more places faster, cheaper, and easier? With the changes in the music industry, social media, and oversaturation of both bands online and bands that play live, it is more crucial than ever for musicians to get out on the road and perform as much as possible. Being constantly on tour, reaching as many people and as many cities as possible, is hands down the best-case scenario. Still, many independent artists are not financially stable or secure enough to be able to tour. This is all the more reason to base in a location where you can get to as many places as possible faster and cheaper. Success in music is no longer about taking over a city; it is about taking over the country and reaching as many cities, towns, and music markets as possible. So when you consider the question, "Where are you based?" make sure you are thinking about the bigger picture rather than a single city for a single reason. This means it might be time to calculate driving distance to key markets and think about where you should call home, at least for a while. If you are able to base yourself in a hub or somewhere close to many cities, you will save a fortune. Maybe a personal example will help illustrate my point.

As I started to do more college speaking appearances, I found that it was harder to travel from Seattle to dates on the East Coast. Many told me I needed to be in Philadelphia, but traveling in and out of Philadelphia was a major pain in the ass. I found that being in a smaller area made it easier to access airports, roadways, and trains much more quickly. When I lived in Boston and had a session in New York City, it meant a whole crazy day of getting out of one city and into the next, with all the traffic. So, I went back to being based in western Massachusetts, in Harrisburg. Getting to either city took half as long.

In fact, when I calculated the mileage between cities all over the East Coast and how fast you can get into and out of a city, I found Harrisburg to truly be the center of the East Coast. Now, admittedly, Harrisburg is in no way a music city. Still, getting anywhere on the East Coast is faster, cheaper, and more effective from Harrisburg than anywhere else on the East Coast. One website shows that Harrisburg is a twelve-hour drive from 75 percent of the population of the United States. I still call Seattle home, but I am based here for a while as I launch this book and travel for speaking dates.

The point is, where are you based is an important question in today's music industry. You must play as many markets as possible and avoid playing the same markets too frequently. When you live in a place that allows you to get to more places easier, faster, and cheaper, you are going to be able to build your audiences larger, wider, and faster.

When my first book came out, travel for speaking and appearances was breaking the bank. Flying from Seattle to locations mostly on the East Coast took a toll in time and expense.

During a nine-week promotional run, I was looking for filler dates and music conferences to limit some of the down days. I found that the Millennium Music Conference in Harrisburg, Pennsylvania was a very close jump from where I was going to be a few days before and a quick hop to the next speaking date after. I was previously unfamiliar with both Harrisburg and the conference, but I looked up the Millennium Music Conference and was impressed by the layout. John Harris, the founder of the event, scheduled me for a full, one-hour seminar as well as adding me to a few panels and giving me a table to "coach" and sell books. Long story short, his conference ended up being much better than just a filler date.

Clearly, Harrisburg is not like Miami, LA, or NYC. But for bands and musicians who need to get everywhere as often as possible for as cheaply as possible, it is hands down the best city to be in! I researched everything from the airport to the train station, the highways getting in and out of the town, and the cost of living. I found that there was no other place on the East Coast where you could

- get in and out of a city easier and faster;
- reach any city on the East Coast by air in under three hours;
- reach 75 percent of the US population within twelve hours by road; and
- be less than three hundred miles and under a five-hour drive from well-populated cities or college towns.

CITY AND DISTANCE FROM HARRISBURG AREA

- Baltimore, MD   80
- Philadelphia, PA   110
- Annapolis, MD   115
- Washington, DC   120
- Dover, DE   130
- Scranton/Wilkes-Barre, PA   130
- Atlantic City, NJ   170
- Newark, NJ   170
- Jersey City, NJ   170
- New York City, NY   175

- Binghamton, NY   180
- Pittsburgh, PA   210
- Stamford, CT   210
- Charlottesville, VA   210
- Richmond, VA   220
- Ocean City, MD   220
- Danbury, CT   235
- New Haven, CT   250
- Syracuse, NY   255
- Rochester, NY   265
- Lynchburg, VA (six colleges) 280
- Newport News, VA   285
- Hartford, CT   290
- Albany, NY   293
- Buffalo, NY   298

By contrast, the three-hundred-mile radius of major markets around Seattle, where I was previously based, included Vancouver, British Columbia, and Portland, Oregon. That's it.

Do I miss Seattle? Yes. Will I return? Most likely; but I will go back when I do not need to be traveling like this. Until then, I am basing myself in the hub of the East Coast, where I can get to the most venues, cities, schools, and people to promote my book and my speaking.

As you think about your career, wouldn't you want to be where you could best afford to get to more people more often? Wouldn't you want to be developing a fan base all over the East Coast and central United States? Wouldn't you want to reach more places where you could make it home the same night? If you were flying, wouldn't it be better to be able to leave a city to head to an airport an hour and a half before a flight rather than dealing with traffic and an airport that ends up taking over an entire day? If you are touring and performing and aren't tied to your present location, you should get to Harrisburg, Pennsylvania.

PERFORMING LIKE A DEFENSIVE DRIVER

Are you a good defensive performer on stage? Are you a good problem solver, someone with a smart eye for detail and issues, before and during the show? Switching to a sports metaphor: Effective quarterbacks study videos of the opponents' defense, looking for patterns, consistencies, or certain methods or moves that appear often.

Hello again, Captain Obvious! While the above probably makes sense to most musicians, many do not take this logic to the stage with them when they are performing or on tour. In my experience, you often see these three types of performers:

- Type 1: "If it sounds good where I am, then it sounds great everywhere."

- Type 2: "If something is wrong, it is the sound people's fault and they should fix it; I am not responsible."

- Type 3: "I don't know all that much about live performing, but I don't want to look stupid by asking questions."

These are the opposite of the "defensive driving" approach to live performing. In fact, these three attitudes are what I like to call "the stupid trifecta"—recipes for failure.

Ask questions to find out what it sounds like out in the house! Ask the sound person, ask the audience—just ask! You could be hearing something that no one else is hearing. Tell the sound person what your issue is and ask them if they are hearing it.

Be respectful when making requests! The sound people are not your slaves; they are working with you to deliver the best sound to the audience. Treating them like crap is not really going to make them want to jump up and help you out.

Besides, even if the sound tech is screwing up, in the end, the blame is going to be placed on you. The average person does not know all that much about sound, and when something sounds off, wrong, or weird, it is going to be viewed as your fault. If you just let it ride without trying to help to resolve an issue with the sound, most will assume this is just what you sound like. Don't be a jerk, but communicate as best you can to see what can be done to help the sound person get a better sound for you.

Finally, if you have questions—ask! Some of the most experienced people do. Before the show, ask if there is anything you need to know: Any hot spots on the stage where you shouldn't stand? Any tips to getting the best sound in that room, on that system, and using their microphones? You may have that setup that you love and you prefer to be just that way, but if you can make simple, advised adjustments, you may sound worlds better.

Preventative Maintenance and Advanced Problem-Solving on Stage

Like the quarterback studying the other team's defense, if you are going on as the third act in a three-band night, watch and listen to the first two acts, even if only for a couple of songs. What is happening in the room? Are you noticing any hot spots or places where there is feedback? What tips, ideas, and hints are being presented that you can use to make your set a little better? You do not need to be a sound pro to keep an open ear and listen for numerous issues that could put you in a little more control of your sound and your performance.

Certainly, you will have your share of nights with just flat-out terrible sound people; this is unavoidable. Your sound is going to suck on some nights. Worst yet, this bad-sounding night may happen in front of new audiences. Trying to problem-solve is the best answer, but if it is just not going to happen, *keep your cool!* Getting pissed off and yelling at a sound person, blaming the venue, calling people incompetent, and ripping them a new one on stage and online is not going to help you build your audience. Stay cool and try to deal with it the best way possible. Just as in driving, you can take steps to be a smart defensive driver. You won't avoid all the wrecks, but you will minimize the damage.

CASES: PROTECTING YOUR STUFF AND YOUR LIVELIHOOD

Good cases can be expensive, but they are worth the cost for the peace of mind in knowing that your gear will safely get from hundreds of point A's to point B's. Think about it: Would you rather shell out the money to protect that really nice guitar, snare drum, horn, or whatever, or would you rather pay for constant repairs?

Your instruments —your livelihood—spend more time in travel mode than on stage in playing mode, so be good to them. Protect them and invest in them by putting them in solid cases so they can be around for a long time and cost you less in repairs, especially when you are touring or on the road.

Casing the Joint

Cases are the key to protection, transportation, and storage of your gear and instruments. Still, are they being as effective, protective, and informative (yes, informative) as possible? Whether you are using soft cases, hard plastic cases from companies like Protechtor, or you have the big, heavy-duty Anvil-style road cases, there is a step that people often miss. Many know to put their name or the band name on the case, but as GI Joe would say, that is only half the battle. More often than not, when gear is misplaced, stolen, or grabbed by accident, the name of the person or band isn't enough.

Number your cases as "1 of 7" or whatever total number of cases you have. If all the cases are numbered together, it makes for a much more secure load-in, stage load, and load-out, especially when others are helping you carry the cases. On those nights when you're exhausted, if you can at least account for every case by number, you are in good shape—as long as the gear is really inside!

Next, somewhere visible on the case (many use the bottoms), using stencils and spray paint or in some other permanent way, add the contact info, but *not as a sticker that can be removed*. If the case is found, the finder should have your phone number, email address, website, Facebook site, and your physical street address. This will help if you're lucky enough to have your case found by a person with morals; it will get that case and its contents back to you all the faster.

Lastly—and especially with the bigger standard cases that might be easy to repaint to look like they do not belong to you—make sure you have a marking that only you know about. Keying or knifing a phone number into a plastic case or entering information behind some foam or padding that you might either Velcro or glue over gives you the advantage of truly being able to identify the case as yours, should a question arise. If you come across a case that shows markings or damage but is clearly yours, being able to show a picture of the case and its damages or special markings is crucial to proving your ownership. In the late nineties I had a purple spray-painted message in the bottom of my Anvil hardware case under the floor shelf: "Not Yours." I was able to prove it was my case during a festival tour where there were nine other cases that looked exactly the same.

TOUR PACKING: WHAT TO BRING AND WHAT NOT TO BRING

Every tour is a new adventure, whether it's the first or the tenth. You're stretching out your base and expanding your music to more people in more cities and towns. The playing is the same, the loading in and loading out is the same, but the rest of it can be worlds different.

Let's look at a middle-of-the-road kind of tour: a month out on the road, which is realistic for a lot of aspiring bands. Chances are, everyone cashes in vacation time from day jobs, maybe even taking a bite in pay for a few weeks, to do a full, four-week stretch. You probably have been playing for a good while and have the load-in, load-out, and packing down, but what about clothes, supplies, and backup needs?

Before packing equipment and personal items, consider the order in which you pack, to make unloading and loading easier. If you're in a bad neighborhood and unable to check in to your hotel before the show, bring your personal bags into the venue. Trust me: You don't want to learn this by having someone steal all your personal items and clothes.

If you're in a van or have a trailer attached, I always advise having two packing methods down pat. The first is for when you're going to the hotel room first. When you're loading to leave, make sure your personal bags are closest to the door of the trailer or the van so you can take them out easily and quickly. This will save you time and grief in the parking lot when you're trying to dump your personal stuff and get to the venue for sound check.

On the other hand, if you're doing a show before you get to your hotel room or if you're doing a radio promo on which you're playing early in the day, load the personal items and the clothes in the back of the van or the trailer. This whole process will avoid unnecessary unpacking and repacking.

Color-Coordinate Your Cases and Luggage

The above suggestion may sound silly, but things often get lost in the transitions of loading in and loading out. So, just as you add better cases with numbers on them to make the load-ins and load-outs easier, you can also do the same for personal items. If you have a band with four members, assign a main bag and a backpack or side bag for each person, each with a different color. This way, regardless of who's loading the van, you know that all the personal gear is packed and accounted for. If everyone knows every item that's supposed to be in the touring vehicle or vehicles, it's more likely that it will be there or at least asked about if it's not seen before you leave any city.

Suck It Up

Vacuum-seal bags are great to consolidate clothes or pack dirty laundry. You can get one of the little minisealers, so you don't need a full vacuum cleaner. You can store dirty clothes with your clean clothes without spreading the odors. Even better, after a good run of days and all the sweating onstage, the van will not stink! It also compacts your stuff in a situation where space is always at a premium.

Keep It Clean

One of our old tour managers took us to Costco the night before we left for a tour and bought us an industrial-size laundry detergent bottle. He then gave us a hundred dollars in quarters for city and highway tolls, parking, and laundry. Whenever we had to do laundry, we had the quarters and the detergent; we saved a lot of time and a small fortune. Sure, quarter machines are always at laundromats or hotels, but ask any musician how much trouble it is to find quarters while on the road. Also, ask how many musicians have gotten ticketed during sound check because they didn't have the quarters for the meters. So carry your own detergent—and keep that stash of quarters!

What to Pack?

When you play that one-shot gig or that local bar, you don't pack a suitcase—unless you're trying to be Queen. You know how to pack the van or the cars with gear for gigs and short runs, but how do you pack for a tour that is four weeks or more? Think of where you are going, and pack light.

Plan to do laundry once a week, minimum, to keep the basics clean. If you do it more, you can bring fewer clothes; you don't have to worry about being seen in clothes you wore two days ago in another town, so get over yourself. Think about what you want to perform in and then what's comfortable to travel in. You want to look the part on stage, but remember to pack for the majority of your day, which is traveling. You're going to be on the road, in the van or bus, setting up and tearing down, in hotel rooms, diners, and truck stops. Pack and dress for that; it's the bulk of your tour. Don't get me wrong; I got a thing for a good-looking woman in a spandex suit. It's hot—Catwoman when you add a mask—but do you really want to be wearing that catsuit into a Waffle House in front of a whole bunch of truckers at three in the morning a few exits away from South of the Border?

Packing a cooler can be a good use of space and a great way to save money as well. Buy an Igloo, and when you're at a supermarket, pick up the essentials for snacks and the basic road eats. It will save you from spending too much in truck stops and fast food joints. While you're picking up the detergent at Costco, grab large packs of energy bars, vitamin mixes for water, and so on. This keeps more money in your pocket! Set aside an extra bag that contains all the stuff you don't need in the hotel room or for the gig—the extra drumsticks, boxes of guitar strings, and wires, cables, and backup repair items. Even better, these things can be put in small, tight bags and shoved under seats so they can be accessed when needed but out of the way in the meantime.

Finally, use the US Postal Service, UPS, or FedEx. If there are items you don't need or you amass purchases, mail them home. Save space and loads going in and out of hotel rooms. If you head to a warmer climate and don't need your cold-weather clothes for the rest of the tour, consolidate them, pack them, and mail them off. Use a couple of those vacuum bags to scrunch them down tight, and send them packing! The longer the tour, the smaller the van, cars, or bus will become. The more room you can make, the better for everyone.

Plan for the tour, think about what you need and what you don't, and keep in mind that the tour is, unfortunately, more road time than stage time. The better you prepare for the realities of the road, the better the road time will be, which in turn will make the performing that much better as well.

HOTEL ETIQUETTE: GROUND RULES FOR SLEEPOVERS

Sorry, kids: Gone are the days of destroying hotels. The fables of debauchery—Led Zeppelin fishing for sharks out the window of a Seattle hotel and Joe Walsh creating doorways with a chain saw—are ancient history. I was a good, respectful boy in my touring days, but I can't say that for others I was with. I will not name names, but I knew many musicians who used to steal various items from each room they stayed at, almost as competition. These guys created collections of towels, ashtrays, alarm clocks, glassware, and many other items. They never really destroyed anything, although one time a bass player and guitarist of an unnamed touring group stacked everything in the hotel room on top of the bed—I mean everything. The hotel couldn't trace them, because the room was paid for in cash under a fake name. Thank God.

You shouldn't pull that kind of crap anymore. For one thing, it's a lot easier to get busted. With advances in the Internet and communication among hotels, it will catch up with you. In fact, it's now a good idea to incorporate a few elements of hotel etiquette when you're on the road. Just as a hotel will report a person, a band, or a group for doing bad things, they will also note the good stuff you do.

When you book a room, don't book each night separately. Booking rooms in advance for a number of nights through a chain or affiliate hotel groups will save you a fortune—seriously. You can also join rewards programs or find other deals with a little research. Think smarter: Think about the whole tour and not just each night.

> I highly recommend Choice Hotels International. They book for
> Comfort Inns, Comfort Suites, Quality Inn, Sleep Inn, Clarion, Cambria Suites,
> Mainstay Suites, Suburban, Econo Lodge, Rodeway Inn, and
> Ascend Hotel Collection. The website for Choice Hotels International is:
>
> http://choicehotels.com/

Keeping a good relationship with a chain or hotel group is helpful. If you're a frequent guest, you can get hookups and perks. An old road manager once gave us a very strict list of hotels to use, and as a result, some nights we were upgraded to top-notch suites for nothing extra. We received free meals, free nights, and more, all because we followed some simple rules of good hotel etiquette.

Here's my Letterman-style Top Ten List of hotel etiquette tips:

10. Be quiet.

You're obviously going to be coming in late at night. Leave the party at the bar and try to keep it quiet in the hotel room. I had a tour manager who used to request the rooms by the stairwell or the rooms that were the most separated from the rest of the hotel. Bands have stereotypes about being loud late at night and partying till all hours, waking the other guests. Many hotels will report you. At the same time, when you're quiet and respectful, that gets around, too.

9. Park your vehicles in locations with the most lighting.

Whether you have a van, cars, or a bus, try to park in a well-lit and more public area. Thieves are less likely to try to steal from vehicles that are easily visible. If you can get parking in front of a hotel or somewhere with good visibility, that's best. You like the spotlight on stage, so make sure your vehicles get the spotlight later that night.

8. Strip the bed and towels.

It sounds crazy, but when you leave, strip the sheets and put them in a pile on the floor with the towels and the trash. Hotels notice this, and the maid service will love you. We used to get a lot of our perks because we did this. It takes two seconds and it's a good thing to do.

7. Bring the sensitive gear into the room.

Don't leave the really small and expensive stuff outside. Bring it inside and inventory it, just as you inventory when you load it out. This will also enable you to rest easier.

6. Bring your own pillow.

This was one of my tricks. You sleep in a truckload of different beds, in different rooms, in different hotels, in different cities, states, and even countries. Give yourself some continuity by bringing your own pillow if you can. It really can make a difference. If you can't pack the pillow, bring the pillowcase. This can actually reduce insomnia on the road.

5. Avoid room service, pay channels, and the charge food in the refrigerator.

Make money on the tour! Avoid the pay food stash that's in the rooms. You can easily go to a supermarket and buy cookies for five nights instead of opening the cookie pack in your room and paying five dollars for it. When you avoid additional charges, it will also allow for faster checkout the next day.

4. Leave a tip.

If you are in a room for more than a night, leave a tip for the maid service. *USA Today* recommends only about two to five dollars per night in the United States. Three dollars is normal for midrange hotels, and five dollars is usually only given in high-end, luxury hotels. If you do this, you will be better taken care of.

3. Bring and share air mattresses for the floor.

A four-person group can book a single room and rotate people from the floor to the beds on different nights. If you are trying to stay out longer on a tight budget, bring a couple of air mattresses; it will save you a small fortune. You will sometimes get nailed with overoccupancy in a room, but many hotels will give you a cheap additional rate that is less than getting another room. You can also request rollaway beds.

2. On the days off, give each person alone time in the room—for sanity's sake.

On tour, you will be in a van, a single room, on stage, in restaurants, at gas stations—pretty much everywhere—together . . . constantly. If you're not on a tour that allows for individual rooms, nerves get frayed. Taking a walk alone is great, but to be able to have some quiet time alone—in the shower or just sitting in solitude—is a very helpful and healthy thing.

Schedule times for everyone else to be out of the room so each member has a little time to take a shower, take a nap, or just have a place to hibernate, meditate, vegetate, isolate, contemplate, masturbate, exfoliate, regenerate, lubricate, celebrate—for an hour or so. The tour and your collective mental health will be a lot better for it.

1. Leave a recording, merchandise, or swag products with the management.

For the cities where you do best and in places where you've established a good audience and relationship with a venue, do the same for the hotel. Drop the management a CD, download cards, a T-shirt, or some kind of merchandise. It will set a good tone and help you develop a relationship with that hotel for the return trips.

As you leave the hotel, take down the name of some of the staff just as you would with the venue staff or the local media. A lot of musicians forgo collecting information about the places they stay, but it's one of the most expensive costs on any tour, so pay it the attention it deserves. By making good contacts with some of the hotel staff and management, the reputation you build can save you the next time you come through that city or stay at that hotel.

SOCIAL MEDIA PROMOTION AND UPDATING WHILE ON TOUR

Stay active with your social media when you are on tour. This means much more than just listing the dates and locations you are playing. Use Facebook, Twitter, Google+, the check-in sites, and Pinterest with the places you visit, such as restaurants, rest stops, and other things outside of music.

Say you're at a restaurant in Ohio where you send a tweet saying, "Try the mac and cheese at this place." You've helped your overall social networking. Taking a picture of a bed and breakfast you stayed at can be effective for your promotion, too.

The easiest way to sum up social media and online promotions is to look past the show. Fans and followers will get bored with the same old posts about schedules, shows, and locations. But on the other hand, if you are the band that is sharing sites, places, stores, restaurants, and more, that's going to draw in a more interested and engaged crowd, whether they are coming to see you play on stage or just following your adventures online.

Take that extra step when marketing online and using social media. Develop contests, games: something fun and interactive. For example, take some pictures of the band in front of the "world's biggest ball of twine" in Cawker City, Kansas. (There's another one in Darwin, Minnesota; Weird Al sang about it—go figure.) Post a picture on Pinterest and start a short campaign where the first five people that come to the any of the next five shows with a ball of twine for the band get a free T-shirt and CD. Now you have a contest, more content to put up, and you can call it "The Twine Time of the Tour." Maybe you even get in touch with the people in Cawker City and ask if they would donate some tickets to the Twine-a-Thon (not even kidding; look it up.) Point is, use what is around you to draw interest to you and your band to keep new and old fans staying connected and looking out for not only where you are playing next but also what you are posting next.

KEEP A MUSIC JOURNAL

Yes, I am talking about a real journal that you can keep on your computer or actually write out by hand. The difference between this and a social media post is that you keep it to yourself! I talk to a lot of bands who claim they don't have anything interesting to post online, and yet they tend to post everything about themselves every day.

Keeping a music journal can help a lot with social media promotion. Think about some of the things you might do every day and how they can become interesting patterns over time. A blog about something that has occurred twenty times in the last twenty days or after twenty gigs could be viewed as a lot more interesting than just posting the same thing over and over.

I advise artists to write it all down and then work with it later to create and build content that is that much more interesting. You do not have to post every little thing, but when you look at all those little things and then add them up, you might find something to draw from to interest your friends and fans.

Don't think of a music journal as something to be posted every day. Remember when we used to have private thoughts that we could collect together and then share if we chose to? Sometimes too much information all at once is just that: too much. Still, collecting, cataloging, and using that information to construct good marketing posts for blogs, videos, or other promotional elements can be effective for you in the long run.

WELLNESS ON THE ROAD

Just as you oil your pedals, change your strings, or tune a piano, you also need to maintain your body. A musician's life can wear on the bones—literally. Long hours followed by sleepless nights of driving, alcohol, fast food, smoke in the air . . . the list goes on. As much fun as the road is, it can become draining and even depressing at times. You can change that and make the experience more exciting and even more invigorating by taking some simple steps to stay healthy while you're out on tour.

> Pack the cooler on the longer trips. The average four-person band can save a lot in a day by packing a cooler with snacks, a carafe or pot of coffee, and water bottles prefilled. So much money is wasted at rest stops that can be used to pay artists or be put toward your music. Use the rest stops for rest.
>
> Pack the food and the drink in advance and save the expenses for the gas and other costs that are harder to cut.

First, make the right food choices to maintain and improve your body. This involves accepting what is around you and balancing what your body actually needs. What if you could get everything your body needed anytime you needed it, at no additional cost, and it was all fresh and tasted great? Well, that's not going to happen, especially on the road, unless you're working with one of those wild technical riders where you can request a bowl of all-green M&Ms and get sushi every other night (I have done the sushi but never asked for the M&Ms). But there's an in-between. You can find the right foods in certain places and bring them with you. I used to keep a lot of my per diems (daily or weekly cash allowances) and go to a supermarket or Whole Foods store to stock up. For example: Why eat those crappy roadside fries and donuts when you could have a healthy snack of carrots, broccoli, hummus, or peanut butter? I also love those Clif Bars. I used to buy them by the box to have around for shows and the road. The wholesale stores are great places to shop, even if you don't want to go quite as healthy as I mentioned above.

Healthy eating isn't always about cutting foods out; it can also be about replacing or having better choices available. When your body is being fueled by the right foods, it will handle the stress of the road much better than if you are eating fast food every single night.

Sleep

Everyone needs a good night's rest, but on the road sleep can be erratic at best. As I've said, pack your pillow or pillowcase. I also recommend bringing along a basic toiletry bag with the items you like the most. Sometimes having your favorite soap or shampoo can make things that much better. The smallest items really can make the biggest difference. Speaking of the smallest things, earplugs are not just for the stage! They can do you very well when you are in the car trying to take a nap or when you are dealing with snoring or other noise in the hotel room.

Exercise is crucial, but finding a gym can be difficult while on the road. Fortunately, there are things you can do in your hotel room. Try to work out when you can. Stretch every morning and every night; it's good for you and for your body. I found that a mix of yoga and Pilates worked wonders for me, and when I was somewhere where there was proper gym equipment, I would jump on a treadmill or try to get in a solid workout. Otherwise, I would try to get out for a good walk, just to get the cardio going and to see the city or town I was in. If you do go for a walk, make sure you know where you are and how to get back. I've screwed up now and then and gotten lost (oops!).

The point is to take care of yourself. A great tour, a record contract, or an amazing gig is not going to mean that much if you are slowly killing yourself. Find a way to work cardio into your daily routine. Look at the labels on the food you eat and on tour; watch the sodium levels. Try to stay away from or limit the soda, hydrogenated oils, corn syrup, refined white sugar, refined white flour, and fatty fried things. Skip the fast food places when you can. They may not always be avoidable, but keep them to a bare minimum. Also, stay hydrated! Make sure you drink plenty of water on stage, on the road, and while you are just sitting around. If you're going to drink alcohol, do it with moderation and make sure to stay hydrated with water to make the next day easier on your body and your memory. Energy drinks are not the best things for you. Although B vitamins are good for you, too much of the good B vitamins and sugar can make your body "B-have badly."

Following these steps will make the road an easier place to be. You will have more energy and more stamina. When you treat your body like your instrument (assuming you care for your instrument), you will be able to maintain better health and demeanor. When I cut the crap out of my diet and added exercise, I noticed I was warming up much faster on the drum pad, I was less tired after shows, and I was sleeping better at night. The cases felt lighter as I carried them to and from the venues, and I was a happier person all around. Think about the changes you can make. They don't have to be all at once, but taking small steps can bring you a new awareness of your body and how much better you can feel every day. Don't see it as a daunting task; see it as caring for your craft, caring for yourself, and attending to what your body really needs. Put down the Snickers and reach for a Clif Bar. Drop the soda and have some water. Experience the difference in how you feel. If the changes come fast, it will become easier to adapt to a healthier lifestyle, both on and off the road.

LEARNING ANOTHER LANGUAGE . . . OR ENOUGH TO FAKE IT

I got to see a band from Italy a while back that had this grungy, pop punk thing happening. They were in the states recording an album with Jason Rubal, a music producer based in central Pennsylvania (also the guy cutting the audio version of this book). They were clearly not too solid with the English language, but they put in the effort to learn some basic phrases in English. It was cool to hear them, even though they stumbled through. I appreciated their effort to learn another language.

However, I see this more often with foreign bands in America than with American bands that go abroad. The effort to learn some of the language of the country you are going to play in shows respect and gives you a sort of music-ambassador role. You will stand out over the truckloads of bands that either don't try or don't have a translator with them.

Any band heading to another country should get someone to translate some of its content to the language of the country as well as learning a good set of phrases in that language in order to connect with the audience. Give each member a few phrases to learn, so that everyone is communicating in some way. This engages the audience and breaks down the language barrier, and you stand out that much more.

CLOSING THOUGHT

Touring is much more crucial for an artist today and requires organization, time management, and economy. The more an artist or band can be out on the road touring, connecting, engaging, and growing a fan base, the better the attendance will be, the more sales there will be, and the longer the artist or band will be able to stay out on the road.

Connect with fans; maintain relationships; develop networks; and convert new fans to sales, word-of-mouth to online followers, first-time listeners to dedicated fans. You should also base in a location that will allow you to reach the most markets at the least cost for travel.

Today, effective, profitable, and productive touring requires a multifaceted conversion effort—for every show. The linear mindset of one town, one night, one gig has to go away. It is no longer effective and that mindset is bankrupting musicians and tours, keeping them off the road, and not letting them thrive in their dream. Instead, those who take a broader approach will get to tour that much more, reach that many more people, and build that much larger of a fan base: people who are waiting for them to return again and again.

6

THE MUSIC BUSINESS PLAN

OPENING THOUGHT

You've probably heard the old saying, "He who dies with the most toys wins." The music business equivalent would probably be something like, "He or she who has the most products with interesting variety, and freshness for new and existing fans, wins." And your entire product line begins with your music business plan.

Your product line should include the optimal mix of your primary product—your music (digital downloads, CDs, and download cards)— with your supplementary merchandise— posters, videos, and stickers. Auxiliary merchandise includes coffee cups, T-shirts, water bottles, hats, beer koozies, condoms, and whatever else you can dream up. But it all is driven by your music business plan.

Make sure that your name, logo, website, and tagline show up on all those products being created. After all, you want your merchandise to keep selling and promoting after it is bought.

Utilize the principle of exclusivity. Offer specials and produce certain items only at certain times or on specific sales sites. Remember: People love limited editions. Have one song available only on the CD, and make sure that one song or even a couple songs are only available online. The more creatively you think about your products, the more interest you will draw. Sites such as CafePress that allow for one-offs or single sales of products allow you to test interest in the items before you order in bulk.

Again, do not forget the product that is at the foundation of it all: your music business plan.

A PLAN IS YOUR FIRST PRODUCT

When you think about your products, how do you define them? How do you define the various avenues of profit potential, and how do you create, control, track, and decide on the right products? When it comes down to it, your products are much more than just your songs or recordings. It's a strange but common mistake: People concentrate heavily on the primary product—music—and then skimp on all the secondary products that will actually support the primary product.

It's important to have a detailed music business plan for all the phases of a recording and its release. If you're organized with the right plan and the right producer, it will allow you to focus on the music as you are simultaneously executing and creating all the complementary aspects of profit, promotion, and potential support products. With a solid music business plan, you are laying the best foundation for sales and success.

A well-organized and optimized music product with every sample, non-vocal versions, and additional mixes will allow for even more opportunities to license music to commercials, movies, corporate videos, video games, TV shows, and other places where your songs can bring in revenue.

That's only the first step, though. Your product also includes the CD, its cover, your press and promotional package, and every item in it. Your product includes every aspect, every document, every item that will either bring you revenue or contribute to the marketing, promoting, or recognition that sells your physical or digital products. Your product is your logo, your tagline, your font, and your secondary merchandise, such as clothing, stickers, posters, novelty items, and whatever else you create to brand, market, promote, and profit from.

All this means that your products—in the broadest sense—have to be organized and created with the same attention to detail as your music. You need to budget and then track your costs and profits to know what's working and what isn't. The last step is understanding your conversions: where the sales are coming from and what makes them rise and fall. The artist who is on top of all this can make the best decisions for advertising, marketing, and promotion to keep the conversion rates and profits on the rise.

CREATING YOUR MUSIC BUSINESS PLAN

A well-written, well-budgeted, and well-organized music business plan is a key element in the success of any project. Two common problems that show up most often are plans with an unrealistic budget or none at all, and artists with inadequate focus on detail who rush through the process or take a lazy approach. Be warned: Every time you cut a corner, skip a detail, or ignore an element, you reduce your viability, sustainability, potential longevity, and success rate.

Big-label artists have detailed music business plans with everything laid out before the first step is ever taken. A full plan needs to consider everything from preproduction costs to branding and development, and it needs to be in place before the first single is cut. Advertising, launch, and initial touring will, more often than not, cost more than making the recording itself. But only when you have all these costs formulated and presented in organized fashion will you be ready to present your plan to investors or a label. The first step toward the plan is usually taken by the label or the investor supplying the startup capital, and the cost of its creation will be paid back by the artist at some point—sometimes this is a major cost. For these reasons, I encourage artists who are ready to put their money and time where their mouths are to work with a producer or consultant who has experience and knowledge to create a customized, personalized, and specialized plan for each project and artist.

Full disclosure: This is a shameless plug. Hey, it's my book; I'm allowed. Business plans for individual artists, management groups, labels, and investment groups are one of my most popular services. I build budgets and plans for artists, labels, and managers to help them clearly define the money that has to be raised and to validate the money that is going to be spent. Documenting these details reduces risk and increases the project's chances of being executed effectively—with the required capital.

But check this out: 90 percent of the time, the rate I charge a label or investor to create a music business plan for an artist gets marked up dramatically in the payback plan. In other words, if the artist had started with a plan that only needed small-scale adjustments, he or she could have saved thousands down the line.

When I create a business plan for any given project, I work with the artist over a series of weeks—before a single note is played—to discuss the exact details of not only the recording itself, but also the project as a whole. Outlining, detailing, explaining, organizing, and allocating expenses and projected revenues, and then providing the reasoning behind everything, is worlds more effective than jumping into the studio and recording a song that you hope gets picked up and signed.

And don't forget: If you do get signed, you are going to need a plan anyway. So wouldn't it make more sense to work on the front end with someone to create the best plan for you? Regardless of your funding status, are you taking all the best steps toward your goal?

Look at it from the investor's viewpoint. If you had ten thousand dollars and a friend wanted you to spend all that money to just create his CD—paying for the studio, the band, the mixing, mastering, and duplication—how do you feel about your chances of getting your money back with some interest? If you know the band members are all carrying day jobs to pay the bills, how is that product or project going to go anywhere? Are you really going to just blindly invest in them? Of course, any investment in music or entertainment is risky, but isn't it worlds riskier if there is no plan to distribute, market, promote, or advertise?

On the other hand, what if you were presented with a plan—even one with a higher price tag—that clearly listed all the expenses and projected revenues? You could see, from start to finish, how the project would be handled, along with contingencies for problems that could occur. Which option would you be more inclined to fund with your hard-earned money?

We all know that the music is the root of it all, but these days you can't just walk up to the type of investor or label who could fund you, hand them only a CD, and expect to maintain control of your career.

Bottom line: No investor is going to give you a penny without a music business plan. Like any business, if you don't have a plan, you aren't going to get funded.

Even with a plan, it's not a sure bet. But this plan is the basis, the road map, for how you will make everything happen. Whether working with investors, donors, a combination of both, or a record label or a management group, a business plan will set you worlds above the rest.

The Music Business Plan Broken Down: Building the Beast

Just as a recording includes many steps, from preproduction through the final mix, a music business plan has multiple parts. The more you research the initial information in the proper way, the easier it will be to create a plan that answers the questions and limits the risk.

Below is a list of the primary elements that have to be addressed in any effective music business plan. Additionally, each section needs to be customized, individualized, and personalized. Using a template is a good start for figuring out what questions you need to answer. However, copying someone else's music business plan can lead to disaster.

- **Executive summary**—What is the who, what, when, where, why, and how of the project as a whole?

- **Objectives**—What do you intend to achieve and what are the basic time frames from start to release?

- **Mission Statement**—What are your goals and intended results? How long will it take, and how will it be done? Is it an album or EP? Will a tour support the launch of the recording?

- **Keys To Success**—What has to happen for this project to be a success and pay back the investors with the agreed-upon interest in the projected time frame?

- **Artist Summary**—Who is the artist or band? What type of branding or marketing is already in place?

- **Artist/Organizational Ownership**—Who is getting what? Who wrote what? Where do debts and percentages currently stand? What previous debts or percentages does the band or project owe?

- **Products and Services**—What products are being created? What kind of shows can be played: full band, solo performances, acoustic, electric, opening act, headlining? What merchandise, licensing opportunities, downloads, and physical products are included?

- **Market Analysis Summary**—What is the market for the artist or band in comparison with other acts? Who is the competition for this project or group?

- **Web and Social Media Plan, Marketing Strategy, and Summary**—What is the plan for content, search engine and social media optimization, uniformity, and content creation? What is the strategy for advertising and networking online? How will the artist or band convert web and social media contacts into sales?

- **Branding, Graphic, and Development Requirements**—What is needed to implement the existing logo, including physical and online graphics—posters, merchandise, online and print ads, and other uses?

- **SWOT Analysis**—What are the project's strengths, weaknesses, opportunities, and threats? This section is often one of the most grueling for artists, but it is also one of the first a potential investor will look at. If you are realistic and detailed with what can go wrong, you are more prepared to prevent it from happening.

  o **Strengths**—Don't get too crazy here. Be honest about why this investment can work and how you can achieve success in this venture. Include both business and creative strengths.

- ○ **Weaknesses**—Go to town here. The music business plans that get the best funding take into consideration all the problems. What are the vulnerabilities that could make the project fail?

- ○ **Opportunities**—What are the unexploited openings in your market? What kind of touring, products, publicity, and promotion are you putting in place?

- ○ **Threats**—What could make things go downhill fast, whether inside the band or in the industry? To give you an idea, imagine the headline "Band Dies in Car Crash." Is there a plan to sell or license the music if everyone were killed? The artists who have these horrible yet possible scenarios planned out see financing a lot more often than those who don't.

- **Marketing Strategy**—A major section of the plan! How are you going to get it heard, distributed to the masses, and sold, especially with so much market saturation?

> Note: "As soon as they hear it, we will blow up" is not a marketing strategy—or at least, not a good one.

- **Advertising**—What is the advertising plan and budget? Where is it going to be spent and how is it going to be adjusted as things go well or don't work? What is your budget for launch advertising, and how much of your profit will be allotted for advertising as you pay back your investors?

- **Promotion**—This is different from advertising. What is your strategy for public relations, press releases, street teams, appearances, shows, interviews, and product giveaways?

- **Marketing Team**—Who is going to head up your marketing? Although the band will have to be greatly involved, who is going to track the conversions, schedule the advertising, and follow the numbers to decide what is effective and what is broken?

- **Sales Strategy**—When is the album relcased? The single? The video? Where are the CDs and downloads available? What kind of touring are you doing? Have you budgeted for the musicians you need on the road? What kind of merchandise is available, and where? When are the special sales and promotions? How much is given away? How are you tracking your promotion and advertising to create conversions to sales and profits?

- **Milestones, Timelines, and Goals**—When are you going to complete the recording? What are the timelines for the release, the first money to come in, the return on investment, and then the profit? How will you keep the investors informed about all this?

- **Management Summary**—Who is going to oversee the investment and allocation of funds and keep the budget in check while reporting back to the investors? Who does what, and who reports to whom? Remember: If it's everybody's job, it's nobody's job.

- **Expenses**—What does it all cost? This includes every single cost of every single item previously listed. Have you factored in a buffer percentage, in case your estimates are off?

- **Revenues**—What are the realistic revenues and projected profits from performances, tours, products, and promotions?

- **Startup Funding/Investing**—Considering all the above, what are you going to need initially to get started, and where do the first monies go?

- **Break-even Analysis/Investor ROI**—When do you break even? When do you pay back investors and pay percentages? Remember, you may have to consider long-term percentages after the return on investment, but artists, smaller labels, and management groups with a correctly organized business plan can avoid the excessive percentages the majors try to assess.

As you can see, there are a lot of questions to answer, and those answers need to be personalized, customized, and specialized to your exact project, band, and plan for the best chances of funding and success. When you take the time to address all the questions before someone asks, you are positioning yourself in a more professional way than most. By identifying these elements and demonstrating that you have really thought through the crucial details, including all the things that can go wrong, you ease the mind of a potential investor.

> If it is important to you and you are really committed, you will find the time to make it happen. Too many bitch and whine over not enough time in the day.
>
> There is plenty of time in the day.
>
> The day's length has not changed, just the drive of some people who don't know how to work it. Yes, things get crazy, but if you truly need to, want to, and have to do it, you will find the time.
>
> You might not be able to give 100 percent or as much time as you want; you might not be able to get everything done you want; but there is always time in the day to make forward motion. Work! Execute the effort to move toward the finish line, closer to whatever dream you are going after.

Keep in mind that just because someone in your band has a business degree and is familiar with business plans does not guarantee that they know how to create the best possible music business plan. Yes, they are well ahead of the curve, but do not get cocky with your ability to create a professional business plan. Ask for help, or at least get someone to give a full review of the plan you have built or are building.

I would advise any musician, at any level and with whatever level of business experience, to use the above list and questions as a starting point. Use bullet points and short sentences to answer each of the questions. Talk with the other members of the band, and as you address the questions you feel you can answer, note the questions you are unsure of for later review with a consultant or producer. This can give that professional the best idea of where you are and how much work needs to be done. One size does not fit all when it comes to music business plans, and just as you can't really ask how much is it going to cost to make an album, the same can be said for a business plan. If an artist has the creative and business mindset together, the process gets faster and easier. So keep an eye out for those who are boxing you into a budget and a plan that might not fit you at all.

Organize your plan of attack. Are you going to present to labels or management groups for someone else to take the reins? Or are you going to try to fund it yourself? If you are taking the do-it-yourself route, you will need to bring in a lawyer to take care of agreements, and if you are setting things up with investors, you will need to set up the final plan in accordance with Security and Exchange Commission (SEC) regulations to execute the plan legally.

It may seem overwhelming, but the truth of the matter is that if you want to make it in music, all these elements are going to need to be addressed at many points in your career. The next time you record, tour, or whatever, they will need to be addressed yet again. Learn about the various elements of what it takes to create a solid and professional music business plan. Whether you are going for full funding or just laying the groundwork, you will have a solid plan that can be edited, adjusted, and used again for another album or project.

Building a Plan on Gossip, Rumors, and Assumptions = Bad

Stupid assumptions and the music business seem to go hand in hand. More people claim to know more about the music and entertainment industries based on rumors, half-truths, gossip, or outdated information than many other business fields out there. Many people call themselves experts without any apparent experience, knowledge, or understanding. Following their recommendations can set you up to make some really bad business decisions.

In consulting sessions, people tell me with great conviction how this or that works in the music business. I have even been told "information" about things that happened in the studio on albums that I was playing on or present for. It gets even more interesting when I say, "I was there," and the individual insists I was wrong because he "read somewhere it was different." At this point, I generally walk away.

Anybody can have a blog; anybody can start a rumor, whether it's in entertainment, politics, or any other field. Those who want to make the best decisions will look at the whole story and the sources for the story. Fact checking and verification are part of any worthwhile decision process. Use common sense and dig past the exciting celebrity gossip.

It is also important to understand that things that were correct once might no longer be true. This applies to many success stories based on what worked ten, fifteen, and twenty-five years ago. Most of those models cannot be applied anymore. Your music business plan has to be current with present industry trends. You can use examples of the past, but you need to be focused in the present and aware of the developments that will determine the future.

In consulting sessions I have heard people say, "Well, so-and-so said it is this way," or "I saw this article that said this was true," or "I visited this website that showed these numbers." Seriously? Did those sources of information offer any proof? If not, do you want to base your career on half-ass truths? Just because someone posted numbers means nothing. Who came up with them? Can they be verified? It is your responsibility to ask the questions, especially if you are going to put time, money, and effort into that model! Humility, truth, and honor build trust; don't claim to know what you don't. You can give a best guess, but if you don't know, say you don't know.

You can and should verify everything I write in my blogs, talk about in my videos, and discuss in my book. I present facts, but I also write about trends I see and ideas that I believe in that are best guesses based on a lot of research, interviews, and years of hands-on experience.

Despite all that, I have no problem saying, "I don't know." I have found that I have been able to build stronger relationships with clients by backing up what I say, and if I am not 100 percent sure, I will say, flat out, "I don't know," or "I am not 100 percent sure."

I know that industry rumors can take on an aura of truth. I'm old enough to remember when everyone "knew" Paul McCartney was dead, and they proved it by the clothes the Beatles were wearing on the cover of *Abbey Road*. For a more current example, a couple years ago in December 2011, when hundreds of websites and thousands of social media users said Jon Bon Jovi was dead—that didn't make it true, did it?

When you build your plan, make sure your facts, numbers, and approach can be backed up. Deliver the best information you can find. Make sure the comparisons, the numbers, and the plan are pertinent to what you are doing.

> "Call Me Maybe" exploded across the charts in 2012 and made a lot of people a lot of money. But, if you are a singer-songwriter with morose songs, male, twenty-eight years old, and not eye candy, using the "Call Me Maybe" model is not such a good idea. If you're not familiar with the song, check it out on YouTube, and you'll understand what I mean.

Make sure you are making comparisons to relevant models or artists when you discuss comparisons or expectations. Get away from assumptions, second guesses, and statements like, "This song will break the mold." The more you ground your music business plan with the facts and stay away from fiction, the better the chances your project has to fly.

AVENUES OF PROFIT: PLACEMENTS, SALES, SHOWS, AND PRODUCT OPTIONS

There are many avenues for profit and sustainability with a recording that is well made and prepared for the most options. By executing the right music business plan that prepares for the most possibilities and products, you will have a primary product that gives you the maximum means for revenue.

Many musicians and bands do not consider the widest array of options for revenues. By doing this *before* the recording, you can create many more items that leave the studio with you. This keeps you from having to go back into the studio, pay more money, and spend more time on remixes, edits, changes, and adjustments.

Below is a list of physical and digital products and various avenues to license and sell your music in other ways than just a single or an album. Finally, there are secondary and auxiliary products and merchandise items that can be forms of revenue but also act as additional marketing items to promote your music and the music products.

1. **Digital download sales of singles, full albums, or sales sets.** You know this one.

2. **Physical CDs.** You know this one, too.

3. **Download cards.** Love these things! The lowest-cost, highest-profit physical items. You can build a series of different cards as different products, and you can also create full promo packs on these cards. Dropcards is the way to go: I love this company, these people, and their products. Get connected with Dropcards at http://dropcards.com/

4. **Vinyl.** Vinyl is on the rebound, but it is also very expensive. This can be a nice limited edition item, though.

5. **Tapes and eight-tracks.** Cassettes have become a niche item—go figure! And for the seventies revivalists, eight-tracks are a cute option. Yeah, I said "cute."

6. **Physical and digital sales on compilation recordings.** Make sure the compilation is legit!

7. **Shows and touring, including openers, headliners, festivals, and so on.** That's pretty self-explanatory, Binky!

8. **Basic supplemental marketing merchandise products and items.** T-shirts, hats, water bottles, coffee cups, beer koozies, etc.

9. **Secondary marketing merchandise.** Posters, stickers, bottle openers, mouse pads, memory sticks.

10. **Auxiliary and specialized marketing merchandise.** Band name on existing products such as coffee, beer, wine, obscure products, etc.

11. **Nonvocal versions of songs for licensing.** Not just for karaoke! You can license and sell these that much easier if you already have them in the can and ready to go.

12. **Licensing to video games.** Maybe parts or pieces of your music can show up when a Mario-like character gets the mushroom to power up. Other more modern games use full songs with and without backing vocal tracks.

13. **Licensing to television.** From segment sections to opening and closing credits, licensing to television has become a large avenue to make money and to market your music and your band. Some shows specifically showcase the music they use and mention the band in the credits.

14. **Licensing to movies.** Movie placement with your music is another broad-range revenue angle. Make sure that you are working with a reputable agency or publisher who can lock in opportunities, instead of signing with the wrong publisher who will lock up control of your songs and keep you from potential profits.

15. **Licensing to corporate or educational videos.** Remember those videos you watched in science class or the training videos for a day job? What about the music when someone walked out on stage for a seminar or speaking event? There is a large market for licensing and sales for corporate and educational videos and presentations.

16. **Licensing to sports teams, complexes, and corporate and nonprofit organizations.** What about sending or writing music for minor league teams and sports venues?

17. **Performing for academic or student activities programs.** There are opportunities and options to connect with education-based groups that can bring you into the school systems. You can also align with organizations like NACA (National Association for Campus Activities), which can help you connect with various colleges for shows and events at campuses around the country.

18. **Military, cruise ships, hotels, and overseas options.** Connecting with the USO (United Service Organizations) to play for troops and bases around the world, as well as sending packages to cruise lines and hotels for longer-term residency gigs, are great options if you're looking to play every day. There are also international management groups and venues that book you to perform in other countries; many will assist with obtaining working visas and cover the other details.

19. **Backing band work and other general business (GB) playing opportunities.** Your band could back up other artists coming through town. As mentioned, you can work a number of repetitive gigs such as a hotel gig or as a function and event band. Similar to casino residencies, it is kind of like retiring for the touring musician not ready to quit but who wants to stay home or in one place.

If you want to get into scoring and licensing for TV shows, commercials, and movies, try building a video résumé on a YouTube channel with a visual demo of your work. Take a clip of a TV show, a commercial, or a section from a movie, and put your music over it.

Having a secondary YouTube channel for potential licensing opportunities can give music supervisors and other industry professionals an idea of not only what you do for music but also what your take might be on existing scenes and existing commercials (with the normal music muted and yours added in).

This is one extra step in the process that can pay great dividends in the long run.

With all the new products coming out and becoming popular every day, there are many ways to derive profit from your music and merchandise. Do your research and keep a finger on the pulse of what items are selling and what items seem to be fading. Look around you. What are people wearing, using, buying, and liking? The artists who keep an eye out are usually the first ones to get their name, logo, and branding on it. Remember, if your auxiliary items are created and branded right, they will not only make you profit but also help to turn more people on to you, your music, and your shows, which of course are the main avenues of revenue that you want to sell and promote.

BULK ORDERING FOR BETTER PROFITS

Merchandise is expensive, and while some items like download cards are cheaper, you can still increase your margin by buying in quantity. On the other hand, products like vinyl or certain clothing items can be very costly, and buying these in bulk is just a bulky cost that may not readily convert to profit.

Before digging in too deep about buying in bulk, let's touch on the individual products. It can be a great idea to test products by using those one-off sites like CafePress (www.cafepress.com). You can upload your logo, font, website, and tagline to a series of different products to test the waters. While you have your toe in, you will also need to understand these are very shallow waters for you when it comes to profit. You are getting the opportunity to print product on demand, but there is a very high charge for that single print and limited order. Think of it as market research, not a long-term supplier relationship.

Finding the money, investor, or budget for a larger supply of products like T-shirts and other easy-to-move items will allow you to turn debt to profit, while putting money back in your pockets faster.

Wouldn't you rather borrow a certain amount, pay that person back quickly, and then maintain larger profits down the line, instead of making tiny percentages over and over? Yes, it costs more on the front, but it allows ten-fold the profit to you on the back end.

Think about the cost per CD if you order a run of a thousand discs. Then make the comparison to the cost if you order five thousand discs. Right there you can keep a more sellable price point and you are going to make more money in the end. Try to take it one step further: With the masses going digital these days, another option that might allow for higher profits is to purchase a CD duplicator and printer (with some extra printer cartridges and some blank CDs). Take it another step further—you've written this into your plan ahead of time, right?—and make the design on your CD simple, informative, and easy on ink. Then you will need fewer ink cartridges, making each CD that much more profitable.

For other merchandise items, check out companies like Jakprints (www.jakprints.com) and Branders (www.branders.com) to fulfill larger bulk orders. They can also set you up with better deals if you are ordering more items at the same time.

Think out of the box and take the approach that you might need to order that many more boxes of this product or that product, to not only sell at an affordable cost to people in a tight economy but also to be able to make as much *bulk* profit as possible.

GET YOUR INFORMATION OUT THERE—EVERYWHERE!

The information about your primary product, whether on the front and back of a CD jewel case or on the CD itself, should be informative and should draw in the potential buyer. This is even more important for digital downloads. Most sales sites provide a number of fields to add information about the recording, yet many artists just put up the track and hope for the sales. Huge mistake!

I have long been an advocate for putting the best information on CDs to make them easier to buy. Fill in every blank possible on the various streaming and sales sites and on all the social media sites. You have so much information about your music, its creation, and all the elements involved that you should be sharing. All of this will lead more people to your music and optimize the words online about your music and your product. Most people are going to read about you before they hear you. Share all that great information about the recording in a uniform way that will become optimized across search engines and social media. In turn, this will bring the audience to you that much easier.

For the images, go artsy, have fun, and do your thing. Just make sure you use the font of your band logo in a legible size on the front side along with the album name. Think about the cover art shrunk down to thumbnail size for Google Play, iTunes, and the other stores—is it still clear? Brand recognition of your name and logo and your cover art is a good thing. The *Sgt. Pepper* cover is a perfect example. What amazing album art! That, of course, translated to an even more amazing poster-size print. However, if you see that cover in a thumbnail, it is next to impossible to make out.

Also, it's a great idea to have secondary images for individual songs. Staying with your branding and theme, you can post subsidiary album or song images for each track that can pop up with the primary image for the complete EP or album.

If you are printing out CDs and inserts, the same goes for the inside of a disc. If you want to spring for a pamphlet that has fourteen pages, every single lyric, and thank yous to the guy who delivered pizza on the second day of the sessions, that is totally your choice. Just realize that it doesn't make a difference for sales; if someone is looking at the inside of your disc, that person has probably already bought it and is listening to it.

The back of the disc cover and the disc itself are crucial areas that should be marketing and selling you and your music. People often lose the covers or the inserts, and for those who still have CDs, they're putting them in travel cases with hundreds of other discs—make sure the disc identifies and markets you! As for the back of the CD case, if someone is looking at a CD in a store—yes, folks, people still buy CDs in stores—it likely has a plastic wrap or cover film around it. This doesn't allow the potential buyer to sift through your small book inside. The only information they have is what can be seen on the back. So combine the two: For that person going through a friend's disc case or the guy or gal in the store looking at a plastic-sealed disc, use the back side of the case and the disc itself to properly advertise, market, and promote your group and the recording.

If the listener likes you, wouldn't you want to provide all the information needed to be able to connect with you, join your social media sites, and make it easy to get in touch? But most artists don't think of it and provide minimal info on their discs. Bad idea! #Fail!

And don't forget that many of the booking agents and talent buyers who still accept CDs are usually loading them into their computer, separate from the cover. This is another reason why it is important that the crucial pieces for promotion are on the physical CD. For those loading discs into their computers—many of whom will rip the music to their media players and possibly never again look at the actual disk or its packaging—make sure that the information on the actual song on the CD is filled out before you go to duplication. That way, regardless what program or player they are using, your name, the song title, and your information pops up on their computer, instead of . . .

- Untitled track

- Unnamed artist

- Unknown album

Now, I'm no Sony, and I'm not with William Morris Endeavor. I have a small, very independent production and consulting company, yet we still receive close to a hundred solicitations a month, both in CD and digital form. Think about those larger groups—the labels, the management firms, and the touring agencies. They receive thousands of CDs, links, attachments, and solicitations a week.

Stand out! What if your package and cover are lost when they put your disc in? How are they going to put together your disc with your package? Take the smart approach. Make the disc *a promo package in itself.* Yes, it's a lot of information, and yes, it takes away from the art you might put on the disc, but you tell me: Would you rather have (1) an artsy disc, or (2) a disc that provides the information to draw the most interest from a potential fan, booking agent, talent buyer, or music industry professional? (Hint: I would go for option number two.)

Here's the layout I give to artists for the most effective and informative discs and downloadable digital tracks. Each element listed below displays your organization, your professionalism, and your attention to detail. This is smart, effective marketing for anyone who sees your disc, including labels, booking agents, venues, talent buyers, management agencies, licensing groups, TV and movie music supervisors, reps, and more.

Use this not only for your CD, but also for your websites, your social media sites, your streaming sites, and so on. Make it simple to cut and paste the information, especially on the digital side. Leave no field blank. The more information you compile online, the more ways you can be discovered online!

Here are the elements you are going to want to have on the disc and the back of the disc cover:

- Name of artist or band (in the correct font)

- Title of album

- Song titles and durations

- Writing credits

- Copyright credits

- Publishing credits

- Produced by
- Recorded at
- Engineered by
- Mastered by
- Album short description—single-sentence summary
- FBI/copyright warning
- Compact disc graphic
- Representation/contact name
- Representation address
- Representation phone
- Representation email
- Representation website
- Logo with tagline
- Website/social media site

On the back of the disc cover, I advise all the above, as well as:

- Barcode and Universal Product Code (UPC) number
- Short bio for the band and brief description of product

I know it's a lot of information. It takes away from the art element. It does give a very businesslike look to your disc.

But . . .

Isn't that what you need in the beginning? You can still be artistic. You can lay out the information in an organized way in a small font. But if you are a new artist trying to launch into a world with millions of bands, why not stand out better than most? Open the door for every opportunity by making your package, whether it be the physical or digital one, the easiest, most organized, and most professionally prepared possible. Take serious steps so you'll be taken seriously. The extra time spent on the details in the beginning make it much easier in the end.

Think about all the various products that can be built off of the music product. Just as you create the music business plan as the detailed blueprint for your career, you need to do the same with the recording.

Remember, your product is one of the key factors connecting you with the media and the public. It is crucial to make sure this product represents you musically, creatively, and professionally while at the same time serving as a promotional and contact device.

Adding informational elements to the physical and digital products and your promotional materials is important. More online places with uniform information about all aspects of your recording equals more optimization across the web. You can also maximize your online content by putting up blogs or posts with the lyrics every couple weeks. You can post diaries and images from the sessions. Fresh content propels interest in the recording for online searchers. More people find you, find out about you, and connect with your music, your recordings, your other products, and your shows.

But it all starts with the business plan and aligning the details for your recording and all the products associated with it. Uniformity of content and marketing makes it easier to reach more people and create additional products that will bring in the profits for you across the board.

CLOSING THOUGHT

Creating the detailed music business plan—covering all the elements from recording the primary product to branding all the supplementary products—is crucial. By branding all these products with consistency and uniformity of information and promotion, every product you release and sell to one person has the chance to become a marketing and promotional tool for many other potential fans.

Your products, devised in the most creative, organized, and branded ways and sold at the best prices, will allow the best chances of continued sales and interest that will keep your existing fans connected while inviting new ones.

Your music business plan—your first product—correctly laid out with details, costs, justifications, and consideration of how you create your recording and the supplementary and auxiliary products, is an absolute necessity. It will organize, optimize, and allow you to build all your products, helping you execute the plan to reach the sales and the success you are looking for. Plan for all the elements: the music, the written content, the branding, and the marketing of every product and every piece of merchandise. In turn, you will have a much better chance of seeing the project, the dream, and the expectations go according to plan.

7

IN THE RECORDING STUDIO

OPENING THOUGHT

Being in the studio to record your songs, your EP, your album, or whatever you are creating can be an amazing process. Many artists live for the studio, the recording, the production, the overdubs, recording vocals, the mixing, and that moment when you know you got what you were looking for. Others—especially the perfectionists—are happy but always have that sense that something else could have been done.

Some use the studio as a writing and creative tool, taking advantage of a producer and/or engineer to work out parts, write and arrange tunes in the studio, or test numerous options. Others hate the studio. They know the finished recording is crucial, but they would prefer to record live and only focus on performances.

Love it or hate it, thrive in it or still getting the hang of it, the recording studio is the place where your main product is going to be captured, recorded, mixed, and created. You need a clear plan from preproduction to the schedule, tracking to the overdubs, vocals to the final mix. The best-laid studio planning will save you the most money and greatly reduce stress. Allow every song you record every possible option, opportunity, and avenue of revenue in order to make the experience and the end results that much better, more effective, and more profitable.

FROM PRE- TO POSTPRODUCTION

The studio is the epicenter—ground zero—of everything that will allow you to do *all* the things you want to do for your recording. This is where you create the primary product that will be the base of your marketing and promotion for your gigs and all other products. The root of your marketing is your music. It's the foundational element that will connect you to the most revenue streams possible. You will build tours around your recordings and use them to create press packs for the media. You will use the recording to assist you with your promotion, your shows, your branding, and your sound.

Since the recording is at the root of what you're about as an artist, it's not a place to half-ass or shortcut. Taking the initial steps to preproduce creates the foundation of an effective recording and studio experience. Prepare your plan for the best results. Prep your charting, your preproduction, your lyrics, your arrangements, your writing, and all basic decisions before you go into the studio. In doing so, you'll save time and money for the things that need to happen during the recording sessions. Of course things will change when you get in there, and ideas can come about that are not what you initially planned for, but if you have a game plan to work from, you'll be much more effective than if you go in and have to deal with everything on the fly.

You need to answer some questions:

- What kind of studio do I need? What is the job description of a producer?
- What producer should I use or whom should I coproduce with?
- What should be set up in advance musically? Financially?
- Will a session player or players be needed?

Think these questions through beforehand so that the actual sessions can be more fun, less stressful, and more affordable.

NAME DROPPINGS . . . AND OTHER SMELLS

Booking the right studio and the right producer are two key preparation steps. Unfortunately, this is also a stage where many musicians get taken for a ride either because of excessive hype from a producer or unrealistic expectations based on results someone else got at the studio.

How many times have you read a résumé or bio from a studio, an engineer, or a producer and encountered a strange list of subcategorized names and references? "I worked with this person who worked with that person." While this impresses a few fans and friends, it actually can make you look worse to the industry. Name-dropping doesn't fool anyone—especially the people who matter.

I see studios promoting themselves based on so-and-so recording there twenty years ago or Big Artist who recorded a song ten years ago. So what if the biggest record labels recorded here over thirty years ago? Should that really be something that compels someone to want to use that studio today? Was it the same engineer, the same producer, the same budget, or the same session players?

This is sort of like someone saying, "Hey, I pitched two innings at Fenway Park for a Little League game." Sure, it's cool to be on the same mound, but that is not equal to being in the rotation for the Red Sox. (Pipe down, Yankees fans—2012 wasn't so great for the BoSox, but we'll always have 2004 and 2007! Not to mention they went 97–65 in 2013!

Instead of being impressed by the hype, get the *current* info. Listen to the most recent recordings from that studio. Find out who is engineering there now. Ask what the budget was for the recordings and demos you hear.

Before I was a music consultant, I put together a lot of overproduced and excessively budgeted albums; I have not used these as references for years. Instead, I play people recording samples from the studios I use now, with the teams I work with now and the budgets that I work with *today*. After all, what good does it do you to hear a $250,000 recording when you've got a budget that is 10 percent of that, or less? If you've got a budget for a no-options Chevy, why would you test-drive a Lamborghini? Would you really test-drive the Lamborghini and think that the Chevy would be anywhere close? Hell, no. You'd find a salesman who actually listened to what you wanted and what you could afford. Replace the soft BS with the hard facts. Make calls, check references, send emails, ask questions, and make sure you know what you are getting into before you invest your hard-earned cash. Do the research! Make sure you are recording at the right place for you with the right people and at the budget that you can handle.

Wouldn't it be interesting if artists treated their dreams and goals like a child—a living, breathing baby in need of attention, support, and love? I wonder, then, if we would see that usual laziness replaced with commitment. That passive, waiting-for-it-to-happen mindset replaced with assertive action. That shortcutting replaced with total attention to detail. That tiring workload that keeps getting put off replaced with a no-choice, must-do-now approach.

Step up for your dream. Respect your dream. Respect yourself. And respect the work it will take to get there. Treat it like a living, breathing, growing, and needy child. Be a good parent to your career! Or just give your dream up for adoption and do something else.

The choice is yours.

STUDIO MAGIC: DON'T EXPECT IT WITHOUT A BUNNY

Not trying to give away any secrets, but if magicians do not have their props, toys, sets, and effects, most of them are not going to be able to deliver the large-scale magic you want to see. Magicians, like the rest of us, have to work with what they've got, and the super-wild, disappearing, smoke-filled, exploding, limbs-chopped-off magic tricks require a certain amount of investment and infrastructure. Otherwise, you're pretty much looking at card tricks.

But some musicians set these crazy expectations for the studio. When you're deciding where you're going to record, don't expect big-budget studio magic unless you can afford the investment that makes it possible. You need to make sure that producer or engineer can work with you under the confines of the time, the budget, and the players you have available. So what if someone produced a million-dollar recording that took ten months in a studio that cost thousands a day? What can they do when you take away the parts of the scenario that you can't afford? Some of my favorite producers have blown my mind not only with what they can do over time and with big budgets but also what they can do with next to no budget, a limited amount of time, and a smaller studio.

So, when you investigate a producer, don't just look at the résumé. Check to make sure that if you take away the production elements you can't pay for, you can still get what you need in your recording.

On the other hand, don't tie their hands and put them in a box. When a producer or engineer asks for certain things such as a certain amount of time to mix or a certain amount of money to bring in certain musicians or players, understand that he or she is trying to create the best product possible. Compromise and work together to get the highest caliber project at the lowest possible budget. When they ask to record drums or vocals in a larger or nicer studio, see if it's possible to do the other tracks in a smaller, less expensive place. They're trying to pull a rabbit out of the hat—don't take away the rabbit!

Let's say you're working with a genius mixer, and you hand in ten songs with, let's say, thirty tracks per song (you are covering all the microphones for all the instruments, including overdubs, different vocal takes, and all the fixings). Then you decide that you are going to allow a single day to mix the whole thing. Do you really think you are going to get the best representation of the mixer's ability? You are now losing the benefit of the person you chose to mix your project by giving unrealistic limitations—while still expecting the bunny to pop out of the hat.

There are some amazing producers, studios, and engineers out there with incredible skill sets and the ability to record and mix under time pressures while still giving you the best possible product. But you may need to look past the biggest names to find the people who can give you the best product for the smallest price and under the tightest time constraints.

Think about what you are doing, whom you are hiring, what you are budgeting for, and all the expensive details that might have gone into the creation of one of your favorite songs, albums, or bands. Then, think both creatively and intelligently about what it will take to get the best production, recording, album, or song by planning, researching, problem solving, and budgeting for the project that is specifically organized for you, your music, your situation, and your resources. You will end up with a much better result.

HIRING A PRODUCER, COPRODUCING, OR PRODUCING IT YOURSELF

Successful artists and bands get their sound out to the fans with the best recording possible. The process starts before they go into the studio and can last a good while after the final mix comes back and before the recording is released. There is much more to an album than just the recording. You need someone to guide you through the process in order to do it the right way and also save the most money with the least hassle.

As we've already discussed, you need a solid music business plan with a well-prepared recording budget and a team that can get you what you are looking for. The first step is to find and hire a producer who will take responsibility for every step of your recording process, from preproduction to recording through postproduction.

Whether you hire a producer for the full album or just to organize and help you plan, I can't stress enough that you need to have an experienced producer involved in some way. The right producer can help you meet your goals and at the same time show you how to achieve some steps on your own. A producer does more than "make beats." Below is the spectrum of services a real music producer should provide. This starts from the preproduction and budget phases and goes all the way to the end of the recording. Remember though: Even if your producer is only covering some of these elements, you need to make sure you are handling the rest or have the right people in place to handle it.

Spectrum of Services: Your Producer's Job Description

Before you hire anyone as a producer or coproducer, you must be certain that each of the following areas is being handled by someone with the expertise to make sure it's done right:

Accountant—Designating the funds for a recording based on information given by the artist and making sure the money stays on track. Setting up your budget in preproduction is step one!

Hires for the project—Session players help to fill in and enhance any artist or band. Your producer will assist you in finding and hiring additional artists to help complete your sound. Players suggested by the artist or band should be reviewed, but final choices should be the responsibility of your producer.

Creative force—As needed, will add ideas, arrangements, lyrics, and alternate and additional parts to preexisting songs to improve flow.

Time manager—Runs the schedule for recording and calls the session when point of no return is reached (more on this later).

Shrink / peacemaker—Recording is emotionally and physically exhausting. A good producer encourages the artist, manages conflicts and emotions, and keeps tensions to a minimum. The producer is also the middleman between investors, other parties involved, and the artist, allowing the artist to focus on creativity during the sessions.

Objective listener—Hearing the sound from a third-person point of view. Someone who is not focused on a single instrument, idea, or style. This is a role that most artists in a band have trouble with. After a take, you are trying to listen as a whole, but most artists' ears slide back to focusing on what they just played instead of the track in its entirety.

Quality control—Your producer will listen for intricate lines and pitches and will also make decisions on the best takes. This is an area that needs to be discussed in advance with the band or artist. Know exactly what you are looking for and concentrate on creating it so that the producer can make those calls according to what you want. If you're looking for perfection, you must have the planning, practice, and budget to back it up. Your producer will work with you to get the best takes while staying on schedule and budget.

Director / boss / Mr. Big / head honcho—This role can be adjusted and discussed, but when it's decided, it needs to be locked down. Someone must make the call when there are differences to be settled or decisions to be made. Ground rules—visitors allowed or not, for example—aid the process, the schedule, and the budget, and the producer's job is to be the enforcer. This also avoids time wasted by disagreements and wishy-washy decisions.

Vocal performance—The vocals are the top layer and usually the tracks that are worked the hardest. Having the producer concentrate on the best performance and the best schedule for the vocals is paramount.

Mixer / mix advisor—The producer will take all the sounds and find the right mix and levels with the artist, also working with the mixing engineer (if the producer is not mixing) to create the best mix possible.

Assisting engineer—The producer will work hand in hand with the engineer (if they are separate people) to get the sounds the artist is looking for. It's a good idea to spend the time to get strong sounds right from the start, so that the mix goes faster.

When the project is complete, the right music producer will have successfully set the artist or band in place as a well-oiled, professional product that is ready to move to the next phase of postproduction for release preparation, marketing, branding, and promotional elements. To have the best chance for success, artists should leave the studio with a top-notch, professional, and versatile product.

Whether you are working with a particular producer, combining producers, or self-producing, your desired end result is a strong and organized product showing professionalism and drive. Instead of going to a label, investors, or agents saying, "We need a studio," "We need a producer," or "We need money," you'll come to the table with a product already in the can that has the best chances for the most revenues. This makes you less of a risk and presents you as someone the industry will take a chance on.

In the end, a lot of people call themselves producers who aren't capable of doing half of what you need. At the same time, there are other producers who focus only on certain areas and can do them incredibly well and for a good price.

RECORDING STUDIO ENDURANCE: TRAIN FOR THE SESSIONS!

A lot of attention is centered on music and production preparation when an artist is heading into the studio. Certainly, it is a lot to deal with: the songs, the budget, the schedule, the overdubs, the timeline, and everything else. Still, something that's often overlooked is studio endurance.

The studio is a different beast than playing live shows, yet bands often approach it as the same thing, only with more repetition. It goes so much deeper than that. Artists need to prepare physically and mentally just as much as they should prepare musically.

I ask artists I'm producing to take a day off from work—or at least have an easy day—before coming into the studio. Getting a good night's rest the night before is always smart. The biggest misconception that people have about the studio is that it's a laid-back environment. Recording will wear on you, and even when you are having a good time, it is draining.

> If you are dating someone or you're married, have a good night of sex before going into the studio. I am serious! I have seen a major difference between the artists who got laid before a session and those who haven't—somewhere between confidence and release.

Recording *can* be laid back, but it can also be a very stressful place if you have to play a high number of takes on a song or if you run into trouble that you didn't anticipate. Listening to a song over and over can be tiring as well, and don't forget that a lot of bands do some pretty high-intensity arguing in the studio. Realize that the hours are going to be tiring, and get the proper rest so that you can be at your most productive.

> Forget the housewives of this city or that city. I have months' worth of material for a reality TV show called *Bands in the Studio*. From miscommunication arguments, to egos, to differing expectations, and everything in between, I have watched bands self-destruct while tracking only the third song of an album.

It's also a good idea to stay away from loud music the night before a session. Your ears can take a beating at a venue or a show, and even with earplugs, you're putting your ears in danger for the next day. Keep the day before the session a quiet one, and you'll have stronger ears for the session.

Everyone knows the old rule about avoiding dairy before you sing, and it's a good rule to live by. Dairy produces an excess of phlegm. Most people don't go too much further, though, when it comes to food. I heavily advise that you stay away from heavy-smelling foods like garlic. Sometimes you'll be recording in a smaller isolation booth, or your group may all be together in the control room. By making the room a more pleasant-smelling environment, it makes it easier to stay in that room for longer. The same goes for heavy-smelling perfumes or colognes. And it should go without saying, but I'll say it anyway: Leave the fart contests for the garage or outside.

These ideas are all designed to make the studio a place you can stay in for long periods of time. Also, having food, coffee, and magazines around can keep the nourishment level up and the boredom level down when you are not working or tracking. Remember, the goal is to try to get the best results out of each day with the fewest interruptions. What do you feel you could use in the studio? If it's reasonable, then bring it with you.

Wear comfortable clothes. I know it sounds crazy, but wear layers. As you're playing, you might get hot, and then as you're sitting around, you might get cold. For the more active players, bring along a towel and an extra shirt to change into if you're sweating heavily.

Take breaks to give your ears a rest. Oftentimes I will kick everyone out of the control room for ten minutes or send everyone out for fresh air. Sometimes going too long between breaks can kill the effectiveness of the band toward the latter part of the day.

Look at it like this: A band who can go four straight hours but begins to slow down and fade after a long break may require more frequent breaks as the day goes on and could eventually be completely ineffective for the latter part of the day. This does not make for an effective use of your studio time. Breaking for five or ten minutes every hour to hour-and-a-half, in addition to a dinner break, can keep the effectiveness and endurance of the band up and make the time used much more effective.

Get up at a good hour and be outside for a bit before you go into the studio. You're going to be inside for a lot of hours, and many studios don't have the best lighting, so spend some time outdoors before the session; go for a walk, take in the sun.

Personally, I don't like guests in the studio all that often, but sometimes, if it brings up confidence or helps an artist, it can be a good idea. If a guest is not talking too much and serves as an energizer for the session or the band, then by all means get that person in the studio. This is a personal thing, though. While some artists do well with others around, it can negatively affect others.

Keep the endurance up and plan for the day to be long. Think about what can help you, what you need in order to be at your most productive for the longest amount of time. Ask yourself what helps you maintain endurance in other circumstances. What did you do when you were able to be effective, playing your instrument, doing your job, or paying attention to detail? Once you figure it out, apply it to your studio time.

THE DEMO SESSION: A GREAT WAY TO PREPARE FOR THE FULL RECORDING

When an artist is preparing to record an album with me as a producer, there's often a good amount of time in preproduction and preparation before the recording is made. Even after, there's a lot of work that goes into preparing the release and putting out the album the right way. But you need to continue to book and play in the meantime. Most musicians can't close themselves in the studio until they have the top-notch product. You need something to use for booking and promoting your group. That's why it's important to have a demo that will represent you well.

In fact, wouldn't it be great to have a hint of the studio you are going to be recording in before you do the full album? Wouldn't it be nice to be able to familiarize yourself with the feel of the room, the engineer, and the producer? Getting in a pre-session to get more comfortable with the room and the people, as well as to generate some inspiration for the album, can really get an artist or band pumped up about the project. At the same time, it can also help with preproduction and give you some new demos to work with.

This is why I recommend what I call the Speedy Gonzales, or demo session, for recording the best demo. The artist comes into the studio where he or she is eventually going to record the full album and spends a day recording a demo. It's a fast-paced day and not for the weary. Most if not all of the tracks are recorded live with the setup time and recording taking a little less than half a day. You leave the other half of the day for a quick mixdown, giving the engineer and producer half a day to knock out a solid mix. You'll leave with a really solid demo that you can use for booking shows, putting up new samples, or playing for people who might donate or invest in the full project. You'll also get excited about the full-album session. You'll have a greater sense of the studio, the personnel, and how things will go when you record the full-length, as well as a greater level of comfort once recordings begin.

Remember, you're recording a *demo*. The more time you take to record, the more time is taken away from the mix down. The goal is to split the day in half. Budget your time to do the recording in the first half and the mixing in the second half. It will be a rough mix, not even close to the full album, but it's crucial to get the best rough mix you can. If you continually try to redo, retake, or overdub, you're only making it harder to get the best mix possible in the shortest amount of time.

Once the recording is mixed, a basic mastering can be put on it and you leave with a product that you can be proud of. Using the day for marketing material is also smart. Bring a camera and a video camera or shoot from your phone; give people a look at the place where you are going to be recording your full album. This can really help with fund-raising if you are trying to crowd-fund or bring in investors. Take notes as you see things that you want to understand better and make sure to set up a meeting after the session to discuss your questions and your observations with your producer.

Doing a speed demo helps in so many different ways. Most of all, though, a great pre-production session can help you save time and money once you reach the actual, full-album recording. The more comfort you have with the environment in which you'll be working intensely for a number of days, the faster and better things will go. It may cost a day of studio time, but it could save you a lot more on the back end when you do the full recording.

YOU DON'T NEED TO KNOW EVERYTHING IN THE STUDIO, SO DON'T PRETEND TO

When you are working with a studio, an engineer, or a producer, you are paying them for their knowledge and experience. So stop trying to act cool and use terms that are over your head; don't nod your head when you don't get it. People who nod their head or continually say "yeah, yeah, yeah" while someone is talking to them are often neither listening nor "getting it." Ask the questions when you need to, and stop pretending to know what you don't. It only hurts you. And if you feel like you have to come off cool in front of girlfriends, boyfriends, or buddies, then don't bring them into the studio.

I prefer artists who say things like "I like the sounds of the drums in this song by this band" or "I love the tone of that guitar in that song." You do not have to try to impress with fancy technical terminology. Most studios, producers, and engineers would love to hear what you want in the simplest terms so they can give it to you that much faster. Bring in samples if there is something you like—from a mix of a favorite song to a vocal effect, and everywhere in between.

The more you ask, the more you detail your vision for the song or songs in the best ways you can, the better chances you have of getting the desired sound. You are paying the producer or engineer—you don't have to impress them. It only wastes time and ends up costing you more money.

PAY PER SONG? THE PROS AND CONS

This is another area that comes down to getting it in writing. I have noticed a lot of music producers who take the charge-by-song approach, and it can be a legitimate model. But a lot of people screw this concept up with lack of definition, clarity, and expectations. Bottom line: Does the cost of charging per song cover the goals for the recording of that song? What happens when a producer says a song is done and the artist says it isn't? If it's not in writing, you now have a serious issue.

As a music producer, I prefer to charge by the hour or day. I like to have a music business plan, production plan, or recording plan that sets some basic timelines, and I give the artist a schedule with a crystal-clear budget. If we start taking too much time on a song or a part, I can bring up the fact that we will either need to take time from somewhere else we have scheduled for it (like another song or another part of the song being recorded), move on, or potentially need to plan for higher costs. This method keeps things aligned with the artist's expectations and the budget.

> Get it in writing. Do not try to put expectations, assumptions, and percentages down on paper after you have recorded or worked with someone.
>
> Do not go into a studio that says they will track you for free with nothing in writing before you go in.
>
> Not putting it on paper first and trying to figure out how things are going to work after something has been created sets the artist up, more often than not, for disappointment and a legal hell.

It really comes down to whom you are working with, what you are expecting, and what you have in writing. How much time is going to be spent on the tracking, the overdubs, the mix? How many times does the artist get to make edit notes or ask for changes? Since the producer or studio is getting a flat fee, what is the bare minimum they will put in and what is the most, before they would ask to charge you for more time? Will you have a time sheet from the producer that shows you both the amount of time they have been working and where they can justify that it might have to cost more? All these questions are reasons why you should figure out whether the pay-per-song scenario will work for you and your music.

Address these issues and get them in writing if you are working with a music producer who is charging by the song or track. Make sure you know what that charge entails, what you deserve and get for the money, and when you may have to pay more. I know truckloads of solid producers who will be happy to put all that in writing. So, before you go the pay-per-song route, make sure you know what you deserve for what you are paying.

PRACTICE BLIND TO SEE AND HEAR THINGS YOU MIGHT NOT BE AWARE OF

One of the best tips for going into the recording studio with your band is to practice your music without seeing each other. This is also a great rehearsal tip. Have everyone turn around and practice without seeing each other. In the studio, views may be blocked, and when tracking separately or overdubbing, you might not have a visual connection.

When I coach bands in the preproduction phase, I try to find the ways that each band or artist can best deliver a song to the recording medium. In other words, it's not only a question of writing or performing a song, but also how to best record a song to get the track you are looking for. Playing blind will not only help in the studio, but also with your live playing. It can highlight parts that may be troublesome and identify things that you need to work on.

Try it in your next rehearsal, whether prepping for the studio, a show, or just rehearsing. Turn around or blindfold yourself. Then listen to what happens when you only have your ears to work with.

ORGANIZE AND OPTIMIZE YOUR PREPRODUCTION

I'm a big fan of preproduction sheets. There are a million ways to set them up, and many producers and engineers have their favorite and personalized ways. For the albums that I produce, I prefer a great deal of preproduction before going into the studio. It's a balance of creativity and having ideas in place so that things can move at the best pace. I don't try to create the album in a very strict format that is carved in stone before the sessions. I prefer to have blueprints that allow plenty of space for creativity and inspiration, while still working in a smart and time-effective environment.

I suggest breaking up each song for any recording into a series of four sheets:

- Preproduction

- Tracking

- Lyric

- Chord chart

The preproduction sheet is usually the first one I start. It's useful for outlining and hinting at ideas that an artist may want but doesn't know how to express.

Preproduction Sheet

Your preproduction sheet should contain the following elements:

- **Artist name**—So as to not mix it up with other sheets.

- **Song title**—Kind of obvious.

- **Time signature**—Again, kind of obvious.

- **Key**—Ditto.

- **Tempo**—Where is the song currently tempo-wise, and what has the artist been playing around with?

- **Time**—How long is the song in its current form?

- **Songwriter info**—Who wrote it, and how is it being credited across the band or writing team?

- **Description and inspiration of the song**—Artists and bands should talk about where the song came from, who and what it's about—almost like a bio for the song. This helps me as a producer see where they have taken it and where it might go while still keeping the essence of what the artist is looking for. I can bring up ideas and create thoughts around what could be removed, added, embellished, or complemented. It's a way to see the song from another angle.

- **Style of the Song**—I find it interesting to ask bands or artists the style of a song or where they see the song, as a single linear element, being placed. It might be a hard rock band, but if it's a slow ballad or Latin-ish bossa nova that they have in mind, I would rather get that wording out of them. Then I'm able to attack the idea and the layout of how we can bring the song to the best place musically and production-wise.

- **Songs This Sounds Similar to**—What songs do the artists hear in their minds that would come close to this song? It might not even be the song itself, but more of the idea of a guitar solo that sounds like this song, or a drum sound like the drums from that song. This helps the producer get a little more into the heads of artists and find what they're hearing that they might not be able to explain. It also helps in postproduction, when it comes to the mix that the artists want to hear for that particular song.

- **Keywords for the Song**—A lot of my preproduction ideas feed off the keywords for the song. This allows artists to use words they feel instead of thinking musically or technically. Artists oftentimes talk about not being able to say what is in their heads, and this section really helps to get some of that out in the open. At the same time, it also allows me to bring the end product closer to their vision.

- **Instrumentation**—What instruments do the artist or band have in mind, and what instruments would they potentially like to add, and why? This gives me a tonal idea about what people are thinking, what they would like to hear, and where they want to hear it. It also gives me a better sense of what ideas I could bring to the table that

One band I worked with kept referencing the word "revving" for a song. They wanted a particular section to be revving, like an engine. We had a little fun with the idea, and I ended up putting a microphone on a Jeep and capturing its "rev up." Later, the engineer and I added a slow fade Auto-Tune to the sample, which made the rev slowly come into the root pitch of the next chorus. Then we added a delayed guitar a little backed up, and in the end we had what sounded like a car starting and morphing into a guitar. The section literally revved up.

I may have come up with the idea and the production of it, but the band had the vision and the concept of what they wanted. Since they filled out the preproduction sheet in detail, I was able to be more effective for them, even if they weren't sure exactly what they were looking for or how to ask for it.

they might like. This is also where I ask artists what they can't stand or would never want on a song and where they draw the line.

- **Special notes**—I leave this section very open. It really allows the artists to say anything they are thinking. Some random thoughts about the song, about a section of the song, or about how a single instrument should sound can give me a deeper view of where the artist is coming from.

- **Specific vision or ideas**—This is sometimes what I see as a continuation of the previous section, but for certain bands and artists who feel a song has a very direct image, they are able to describe it here. They can bring to light any last thoughts or ideas, and it has proved to be very helpful to me in approaching the song.

- **Marketing 101 for the Song**—This is more of a concept for postproduction and other opportunities, but I like to ask the artist to write down who they think would perform this track if it wasn't them. Also, where do they think they see this track in a commercial or in a movie scene? These ideas can help not only give a sense of what the artist might not be able to explain, but also offer some of the initial marketing content for potential licensing or insertion opportunities.

Once the artist has filled out this sheet, we go over every section and every idea in the preproduction meetings. This helps the communication, understanding, and creative flow and connects me to the artist and the song. Being able to talk outside of the studio about ideas and initial feedback while the studio clock is not running also saves a fortune over having these meetings during the sessions.

You can also use this sheet internally with the band. If you are in a group where everyone is writing together, try this cool little trick: Have everyone fill out the sheet separately for a song. While the basic structure of the tune will be similar, it can be wild to see how each member sees the intricacies and the creative elements differently.

Tracking Sheets

In addition to having a preproduction sheet for each song, I advise musicians and bands to go into the studio with a tracking sheet for each song as well. Just like the preproduction sheet, you can have a lot of different formats and go after different information.

Tracking sheets lay out the song in an easy-to-follow recording format by showing how many tracks you have for that song and what each track is. By having a tracking sheet laid out and even emailed to the studio in advance of the session, you can save time and money, because the engineer or studio will know in advance what needs to be set up. It also allows them to set up their digital files and name tracks in advance.

The tracking sheet provides a blueprint for the engineer to know at least the following:

- How many tracks to set up for each song and for the session as a whole
- The basic information, such as song name, tempo, key, and time signature
- How many microphones are going to be needed and for what
- What kind of effects to plan for
- How to physically place musicians in the studio for the recording

My tracking sheet has seven sections. Again, there are many ways to set up a tracking sheet in different basic categories; this is the one I use, because I feel it gives the most options and the most information.

Section 1—Basic info—On the top of the tracking sheet, list:

- Band name
- Song name
- Time signature
- Key
- Tempo
- Song length (or basic estimate, if you know it)
- Intro
- Outro

Section 2—T#—The actual track number. This is kind of obvious, but it's good for review to know just how many tracks there are on the song.

Section 3—Track—Each individual track is listed and named in this section. You want to list drums as a track, but you don't want to list every drum and every cymbal. You want to list the microphones here and what they are covering. List the track for each instrument. If the track is prerecorded, use the file name that has been previously cut. This is crucial for loops, samples, and prerecorded sections. Make life easier on your engineer!

Section 4—Microphone type or specified sound—If you have a certain microphone you'd like to use on this particular track, this is where it can be added. The same goes for a specific type of sound. Listing different words here, even if they're not technical, can give the producer and engineer ideas for how to capture the sound you're looking for on that specific track. If it is a sample or an already existing track, this is the place to note what you are thinking of using it for in production.

More often than not, this section is mostly left blank, but those small details can help you get the sounds you desire. It is something the engineer can fill in with his or her thoughts.

Section 5—Tracked—This is a checklist to make sure you recorded everything you had originally planned on laying down. Each section that was marked off and tracks that were added during recording need to be noted. This tracking sheet is as much for you as it is for the engineer and producer. It will often change, with additions and subtractions, during your recording. Still, by tracking what has been recorded, you'll have an easier time when you reach mixing, since you can look down at the sheet and see everything that was done. I know it's up on the monitor, but having that paper right in front of you can make a real difference. Often during the final mix, while talking to artists who do not use tracking sheets, I will hear about how this track or that overdub was forgotten about, left on mute, or ignored by accident. Using the tracking sheet and checking off each track ensures that everything you recorded is addressed and that what you leave out is by choice.

Name the track on the tracking sheet the same name as you have it on the prerecorded tracks to avoid confusion or problems that can arise from one item being named ten different things. This is a problem I've seen more often than I care to say. For example, if you record a keyboard sample in advance of the session and the engineer is importing that in on a track, make sure it has the same name on the import file as it does on the tracking sheet. This will make things move smoother and faster. All too often, the engineer or producer has to look up and ask what file "34543-dub" is. Name your tracks and organize them, always!

Section 6—Mix notes—As the track is being laid, this is the place to make specific notes for later. Also, listening to technical mixes and making notes on the tracking sheet can help communication during mixing flow a lot faster and smoother.

Section 7—Issues—This is for any additional thoughts or if you need more room beyond mix notes. You can list what you don't like about a track that you are on the fence about keeping, or mention the repairs that you feel need to be done on a specific part of a track.

You can fill out a copy of the tracking sheet while you're in the studio as part of a studio diary. You can take down what kinds of microphones were used and what kinds of effects were added. It also can be interesting to see just how many tracks were recorded and which ones were later removed from the mix.

Knowing all of the above information will also be helpful if it's a fade-in or fade-out. If a certain instrument starts the song, knowing what key the tune is in will be helpful so that if Auto-Tuning is needed, it's a simple add. You should know what tempo to set the click track at and the most basic element—the name of the song.

That's the layout I use for my tracking sheets. For the engineer, the producer, and you, it forces attention to detail, down to the single microphone or single track. The more aware you are of the sounds you're creating and the more you can reference them, the better the mix will be in the end, and the easier it will be to identify and correct issues along the way. Think of it as a road map to lead your song all the way to final mix.

THE LYRIC SHEET AND CHORD CHART: GPS FOR YOUR SONGS

The last two sheets I like to see prepared for the studio in preproduction are the lyric sheets and chord chart. I don't care if the entire band knows the song or if you're a hip-hop artist who has a non-chord-based song that's mostly a simple loop, having the chord chart will allow you to make sure that the band, the engineer, and the producer are on the same page—and the same chord.

It will also allow for easier changes. If you've been playing a song one way for a very long time and decide in the studio to do a slight change or adapt something in a different way, it is much easier to mark a chord chart and have that reminder right in front of you for reference. For instance, if you do not have a sax player or backup singers and you decide on the fly that you want to add them, you have a chart that will be easy to read—and professional, to boot. This will also make the eventual mixing much easier.

The same goes for lyric sheets. Being able to mark a word or phrase where you might want to add a harmony, recut, or edit can make listening back to the mixes a lot more productive than having to listen over and over to catch all your notes. With all the changes that can happen to a song in the studio, having the foundation of the chord chart and the lyric sheet will give you the basic blueprint to be able to track, edit, subtract, or add while keeping everyone on the same page—literally. With everyone having a copy of the lyric sheet, it will make vocal takes go worlds faster. If the engineer and producer know where you are, they can be that much more helpful instead of flying blind. Print out the lyrics! Print out the chords!

Make both the chord chart and lyric sheets easy to follow. Clearly print them in a large, bold font or write them clearly, so that anyone can catch onto your form and any musicians you bring in will have a shot at getting it on the first pass instead of sitting with a pen and clarifying or fixing errors.

To recap: The song production packet I prefer when producing includes the preproduction sheet, the tracking sheet, the lyric sheet, and the chord chart. I've been told I'm anal retentive about asking for these four items for every song early on, but it becomes very apparent in the studio that by covering all the bases, you can be much more effective and creative, ending up with the best studio recording possible. I have never heard an artist say, "Wow, that was a waste of time"; usually the opposite occurs, when artists see how much time is saved.

Beyond that, filling out all these sheets and laying them in front of you or pinning them up on the wall can give you four more views of the song you already know and have been so close to, which can lead to new ideas and creative elements that might not have been there before. It may also make you think about where there might be too many similarities between certain songs and differences you might not like between others.

These sheets can also serve as marketing items. You can give away or even post online the history of the song to show your fans how it was laid out. It can add another facet, letting your public see your music from another side. Even if you're a skeptic, try it with your next song and see how it goes.

EXPECTATIONS AND GROUND RULES IN THE RECORDING STUDIO

Be organized in the studio and make sure that things are running smoothly. So many sessions get out of control, from budget problems to time problems to internal fights and everything else. By setting up the basic ground rules and expectations in advance of a session, it can help to reduce and eliminate issues, especially with those who are less familiar with being in the studio. The following ground rules are used by many of my producer and engineer friends at numerous recording studios. These basics can keep the hours down and the productivity up. I advise anyone with a studio to have a basic set of requirements and ground rules for the artists who come into the studio. It not only aids productivity but also increases respect for the studio's time, gear, and space.

1. **Arrive at your set call time.** Allow sufficient time to get to the studio, find parking, and load in. If the call time is noon, you should be parked and ready to start loading in through the studio doors at noon.

2. **Turn cell phones off. Not on buzz and not turned down.** You are working and do not want interruptions or additional sounds on the takes. I have noticed more people recently with charts on their iPads or laptops, but the electronics that are not part of a session should be off.

3. **Yakkity yak . . . Be aware of the talkback.** If the engineer or producer is talking over the talkback to one of the musicians, the other musicians should remain quiet and not play their instruments.

4. **Have your gear ready and in top-notch condition.** Make sure to have your instruments ready upon arrival. Change strings and drum heads before the session. Bring extra batteries, strings, and cables, just in case. Make sure your instrument is properly intonated.

5. **Be physically and mentally prepared.** Be in the state of mind to work. Do not be drunk or hung over for the session date, and do not bring any alcohol or drugs to the session.

6. **When concentrating on a sound, don't add others.** If the engineer is moving a microphone around the kick drum or a loud amp, that's not the time to do the drum solo from "In-A-Gadda-Da-Vida" or your Slash guitar solo tribute!

7. **Bring in samples.** If the band is going for a specific sound, bring some CDs into show what you like. This works for tracking and mixing. No sense going for a John Bonham drum sound when the band likes the Steely Dan snare drum sound in "Peg."

8. **Start with drums.** Drummers, have your drums ready for the session. Make sure you have the sticks you need and a backup snare head and duct tape with you. More often than not, the engineer or producer is going to start with the drums. If you are in a band and showing up together, help get the drummer set up first; often, he or she will take the longest.

9. **Don't bring guests.** Try to bring only yourself. If you have assistance for loading in, ask them to come back at the end of the session. This allows for the control room and environment to be as conducive to working as possible. This also keeps people working on the music and not trying to impress guys, girls, family, and whoever else.

10. **Respect the engineer and the studio.** Watch for cords and do not step on them. If a take is playing and the engineer and producer are listening, remain quiet and do not interrupt. If you have thoughts or ideas for the mix or things you feel should be mentioned, note them and deliver them when the take has stopped.

11. **Shhhhhh!** Don't talk, play, or move for a count of eight after you finish a take. Wait for the last notes to die away completely; allow everything to die out

naturally. You may do a fast fade-in mix, but allow for the take to organically fade out without any extra noises that would need to be taken out.

12. **Be open to change.** You may have to alter your normal amp settings to get a better sound on tape. Sometimes your stage settings don't work in the studio, and the studio may have to experiment to get your sound back—even to the point of switching amps or going directly into the board.

13. **Never start with a ballad.** For energy levels, for sound levels, for everything on all levels, plan on the first song being something up-tempo or mid-tempo that showcases the higher side of the dynamics in order to make things go easier and faster.

14. **Watch where you are.** Never walk into a room without seeing if recording is going on inside. Believe it or not, people often walk right into an isolation room or main room where someone is tracking.

15. **Lose the extra percussion.** Take off any clingy or noisy jewelry that could affect a take. This goes for everybody. If you have something on your drum set or instrument that rattles, make sure you have done what you can with duct tape to silence it.

16. **Stink with consideration.** The studio is a small and closed-in environment. Avoid heavy colognes and perfumes during session days. Bathe and do not have an excess of body odor.

Enjoy yourself; make the experience a fun one. The ideas for basic ground rules are not to make it a strict session, but more to cover the issues that could turn problematic. Have fun, take it all in, and enjoy it. At the same time, the more prepared you are, the more work that can be done and the more money that can be saved in the process. Applying these simple steps can make everything move smoother and keep everyone's endurance and confidence levels high. Recording is about the music, but it is also about mental state. If you can keep the vibe in the best place, you can deliver the best results in the most comfortable atmosphere while having the best time.

SESSION PLAYERS

Session players can really help an album sound its best. When you're a solo artist or even a band bringing in a session musician to play an extra part or an overdub, that professionalism and skill will support the song, and the playing will be executed in a fast and top-notch manner.

"But my friend is really good . . ." I've heard this hundreds of times. I understand that people want to bring their friends into play on their recordings. "It will save money, because Billy will play the horn part for free!" Does Billy have a professional tone? Does Billy know how to perform in the studio? Can Billy adapt or adjust very easily or be able to quickly change a part or improvise a section?

Usually when friends come into play, it costs more. Even though Billy is playing for free, with his lack of studio experience, he adds a lot more time in the studio—time you're paying the studio, the engineer, and the producer for. Every take that Billy doesn't get adds to the end price tag. I'm not trying to be rude about your friends, but if you're on a budget and a timeline, it's best to bring in a top-notch studio player to deliver the part you are looking for quickly and professionally. Studio and session players may cost more than friends, but they will deliver fast, saving you money in the long run.

Decide in preproduction what you're going to need beyond the core of the band, and book your session players early. The really good players are often booked well in advance. If you've followed my format, you can send these players a chord chart, lyric sheet, preproduction sheet, and scratch MP3 demo, all by email. This will give the player more than enough information to be able to come in and knock out exactly what you need.

Be realistic about your abilities to execute parts in the studio as opposed to hiring session players who can really keep the quality at its best. For instance, you may have a great drummer. He grooves well and is solid with the click; she has great feel and hits the drums right. However, he or she might not be a percussionist. Yes, there really is a difference between a drummer and a percussionist. Amazing drumming on the recording could be pulled down by uneven shaker patterns or beginner-style conga playing.

If the drummer is not up to par and unable to track precise percussion parts, I'll advise the group to bring in a professional session percussionist to play the parts. It may seem as if it's an insignificant difference, but listen to albums where there are top-level percussionists. Even the small things like the tambourines and shakers are placed just right and played with the continuity and accuracy that makes the groove that much stronger.

The idea is not to replace you or your members as secondary part players. If you've already made the decision that your group will play all the instruments, that's fine, but for songs that have the best and most opportunities for success, you want to have all the instruments sound as if they're being played just the way they should. If you play guitar for the group and your guitar part is top-notch and you want to add a part with an instrument that you play at a beginner level, bring in that session artist to play that part or instrument while you play the guitar. This will keep the sound at its best.

What Is a Session Player Anyway?

Today there's a broader definition of what a session musician is compared to what it used to be. In all honesty, I find the new definition disappointing, as do many true session players. Here's what I look for when I hire session players or studio musicians:

- Musicians who truly have professional, technical, and tasteful control, skill and prowess on their instruments, and the ability to execute in numerous genres, time signatures, keys, feels, and improvisational concepts.

- Musicians who know their keys, their modes, the best way to draw the best sounds from their instruments, and are able to listen briefly to a song and know what should be played to fit the song.

- Musicians who can take direction and criticism and who possess the ability to alter parts easily and without hassle.

- Musicians who have the best-sounding gear and a spectrum of options for different sounds, tones, and embellishments. They keep their instruments studio-ready and in top shape.

- Musicians who can get through chord charts and challenging reading charts. I prefer players who can sight-read, but if you have all the elements listed above and you are not the fastest sight-reader note by note when it comes to certain genres, it's fine.

- Musicians who are always on time and ready to work until the job gets done—players who have the physical and mental endurance to go a full day without a problem.

- Musicians who show up with everything they need and all the problem-solving tools for any issues that might arise. They should be ready with extra strings, sticks, backup equipment, oil, clamps, duct tape, and whatever might be required of their instruments.

- Musicians who have hundreds or thousands of hours of studio experience, working in studios of all sizes. They know how to play to a room, to the microphone, and for the song. I prefer a player with a minimum of twenty recording credits, from top-echelon studios to smaller, independent studios and everything in between, as well as references from other engineers, producers, labels, musicians, and studios.

These attributes, in my mind, define true session players or studio players. I'm not knocking those players who are building up their résumés and working toward becoming professional session players, but I have a really hard time when I hear people who do not possess those qualities call themselves studio players. Don't make yourself out to be more than you are. It doesn't take away from your growing and learning, but remember, if you sell yourself too high as a player and get fired from a session, you're starting your reputation with a bad taste in the mouth of the producer, engineer, or studio.

A Session Player for One of Your Players?

This is a topic that is talked about in small and careful circles. The idea of replacing certain band members with session players on certain songs in order to get them done quickly or up to snuff is a hard pill for some people to swallow. Still, it is a reality in the industry in certain circumstances and has been for a very long time. Ghost players have been on the recording scene for years. Very often they're the drummers and bass players who will come in and fix or play a part and be paid a little extra not to take the credit. I've spent a great part of my session career doing ghosting sessions. I enjoyed it and it was fulfilling, even though I didn't get the credit directly.

The Three Choices

Now, what if you're in a situation where something is not happening with a core member? There are three choices at this point, and they all have pluses and minuses.

1. Keep trying to get the track with the band as is, or cut the session and go practice the crap out of the song. Then come back and try to nail it. This can waste time in the studio and add another day or extra time that you might not have budgeted for. If you're under a contract with a larger-scale label, the producer will often make the call to pull in the session player to finish it. It's a daily occurrence in the majors and even high-level independents.

2. Call in the session player. It can be something of a blow to the ego, but it will get the track done, and the player being replaced can work to get that part down afterward. Good session players will not play far above the skill set of the player they're replacing. Many times they'll listen to what the replaced player sounds like and play a part that works, is solid, and is something that, with brief practice, the replaced player could quickly achieve. Anytime I replaced a drummer, I tried to bring his flavor into the track or tracks I was brought in

for. I would reproduce any signature fills or consistencies, and then I would just tighten up what was not working.

3. Call in the ghost session player. This is not as common anymore, but if it is important for you to have your name on it, it is a route you can take. If you want to bring in a guy or girl to play the part, but leave the band member's name on the track for continuity, ego, or whatever, call for the ghost player. The way it most commonly works is that the label, producer, or management will contact a session player who is familiar with and has done ghost sessions, after which a payment will be arranged as well as a nondisclosure agreement (NDA). This will be a contract with the ghost player to keep this session a secret. You'll be paying a little more to hire someone who's not going to be receiving direct credit, so be prepared for the pricing difference.

Using session or ghost players to replace parts on songs or even full tracks can be a hard decision. Look at all the angles and make the decision based on what's best for the band and the recording, but also be careful to read recording contracts. Inside many larger-scale contracts, there are stipulations that allow the label or producer to make that decision for you.

The best approach is to be prepared. Practice, practice, and practice some more. With luck, the only session players you will need are those who will embellish the sound if the tune calls for it.

TIPS FOR ASPIRING SESSION PLAYERS

When I record in a new city or in a place where I don't know the local players, I often have to ask who the session players are. Many people talk the talk but most can't walk the walk. If you're honest about your abilities, you are more likely to land a job with a producer who understands where you are, as opposed to selling yourself above your level and not being able to cut it. Even if you're a great player, be totally honest about your playing. Humility will help you grow a résumé that will give you the right to call yourself a session player.

I did my first ten albums on drums for free. I put up posters around four studios in Boston and the Berklee College of Music studios. The poster simply said, "New drummer looking for studio experience. I WILL PLAY FOR FREE!!! Use me and abuse me. I have a great drum kit, no ego, and I will give you the best I've got." That got me a truckload of sessions; I was recording almost every other day. Some were just demos and some were preproduction tracks, but with all the experience, I got my name on ten albums, too. I also began to build a reputation with the studios around Boston. I got some very nice compliments, but at an honest level for where I was at. I would hear feedback like, "Not the greatest guy, needs more chops, only fluent in certain styles, but works his ass off, takes criticism well, and doesn't complain."

> Do not expect to get paid or get top fees right out of the gate. Sometimes proving yourself for free can open up more paying options down the line.

I was used by many of these studios for the free work, but at the same time I gained experience and got to work with some amazing musicians who helped get me gigs, shows, and more studio work. That experience helped me improve and grow into a session player.

I remember one session where I could not get the track. I was easily the youngest guy there, seventeen at the time. As I kept screwing up take after take, the other players who were worlds above me gave me the evil eye. They had another drummer called in from a session in the studio down the hall. He was in the control room when I was called in and told the news. I knew it: I was fired.

As the other drummer was getting ready to bring his drums in the studio and the engineer was heading out to strip my kit and send me packing, I swallowed my pride and offered my kit to the other drummer. The evil eyes around the room lifted. Everyone was amazed that even after being pretty much ridiculed, I offered up my kit.

Honestly, the kit was much better than I was. It was tuned up right and already covered with microphones. The drummer sat down and nailed the track in just two takes. That stung. He finished out the other tracks so fast and with such precision. I sat in the corner and watched him with tears welling in my eyes. Yeah, I felt humiliated, but I was trying to save face and learn something.

After the session was done, I quietly packed up the kit and loaded out as fast as I could. Just as I got home, the producer of the session called. He offered to take me out to dinner. I still remember sitting in a D'Angelo eating a steak and cheese hoagie, washed down with my pride. He told me that what I did was probably the best thing I could have done and that he wanted to work with me on things that he knew I'd be able to handle. He also turned me on to some other styles and a few teachers, but best of all, I got to be a fly on the wall at a whole bunch of his future sessions. A number of years later, I got to work with him again. It was a kick; all the players were top notch, and the session was a blast. Of course, he had to tell that damn firing story to everyone during a break . . . but whatever.

The point is that you can't just go calling yourself a session or studio player. That's a prestigious term that should only be associated with years of practice and experience. You have to build up the chops, the knowledge, and the experience over time. After all, you don't start karate and then become a black belt overnight. You are honest, you tell people what belt you are and what your experience level is, and you earn the belt to prove it. Maybe session players should get a belt system, like karate.

> Balance your self-hype with self-respect. If you have the work ethic that an artist in the music industry of today needs, other people will see that, and it gives you a much better chance for success.
>
> Too many put the time into the verbal delivery, but never back it up with the work, the efforts, the strategies, or the plans to make it a reality.

I'm not saying you shouldn't promote yourself, but do it based on your *current* ability and experiences, not on where you want to be. You can get there, and you can earn that reputation, but put in the time. Study the art of the session musician, because it's an entirely different world than the average musician or the touring musician. Don't put on the black belt if you don't have the experience; otherwise you might be in for an ass-kicking and you are marking yourself with a bad reputation right out of the gate.

For session teams like the Funk Brothers or the Wrecking Crew, and with session drummers like Vinnie Colaiuta, Questlove, Hal Blaine, and Jim Keltner, being a session player is lucrative—but out of the spotlight. These are the guys and girls who have been on more hits than you could ever imagine, but the average person cannot even recognize them on the street. A perfect example is Hal Blaine. This session drummer has been on over eight thousand tracks, more number-one hits that any other drummer ever. If you turn on an oldies station, it's hard to go ten minutes without hearing Hal.

But how do you jump in and become a session player? What do you charge? How do you get your name out there, and how do you develop a solid, sustainable career or set up a supplemental career as a session player to balance out touring or live performing that you may already be doing?

Be Versatile; Be Good; Be Able to Listen

First, it takes a strong musician to be a session player. Jumping right in is not realistic. Know your instrument, know how to make it sound good, and have a strong mixture of the technical and the creative when it comes to your abilities. You also need excellent communication skills, a great deal of patience, and the ability to keep the energy and concentration up, even after a series of takes in which you might have played it the same way four different times, but the artist or producer is asking for a fifth.

A good session player is a musician's musician who knows many different styles and is aware of numerous genres, players, and sounds. If the player doesn't know that style or song, he or she has the drive to find out quickly what needs to be known. A great ear is a crucial element to being a great session player. It also helps when a player can listen for what the song needs and what will work, not just what he or she can do. In a band setting, you might want to play a really wild and full line to showcase yourself, but as a session player, you want to play whatever will showcase the song. As the session player, you are the sideman, the supplement to the song, the support for the tune; unless the chart or song calls for you to go wild, it's your responsibility to understand what should be played and, even more important, what shouldn't. A good session player is as professional in his or her chops as he or she is in the upkeep of his or her gear. It involves more than being a good player; it requires an array of skills that make you the go-to guy or girl when a player is needed—whatever the situation.

Show Me the Money: How Much to Get Paid

The questions I get asked most are "How much do I charge?" and "How much should I pay for a session player?"

Unfortunately, there's no simple answer. For a while, it was routine to pay a session player a certain amount plus a performance royalty later. While this can work in your favor on high-budget recordings, it really doesn't do you all that much good on smaller recordings, and it can only hurt the artist as more pieces of the pie are being distributed before the album is even done.

My preference as a session player and as a producer is an agreed-upon, one-time fee. Deciding a fee based on either a full day, by the song, or by the full project can work out well. Make sure that the fee fits the project and you as a player. My first sessions, I didn't charge at all because I wanted referrals and reviews. As I built a solid reputation with my playing and my professionalism, attention to detail, and patience, I got more calls, and, in turn, the price tag went up.

Find the Balance in the Fee

Obviously, you shouldn't do freebies for every session, but it's not about charging top dollar every time, either. Find a happy medium in marketing yourself while taking into consideration what a session could do to get you future work. Take the focus off yourself for a moment; think about how a studio, a producer, an engineer, or an artist would feel about hiring you. You may know what you're worth or what you think you are worth, but how does it appear to someone else? Building up the resume with recordings, reviews, and references can help your initial presentation, but keep in mind how you're selling yourself to people who probably already have a crew that they prefer. Think of how you're being viewed by a producer, engineer, studio, or artist. Are you bringing not only your musicianship to the project but also the professionalism, the patience, the ability to change, and the willingness to adapt?

The Best Option: Pay per Day or per Song

Make a decision based on the work and time that's going into the session. As a session player, I preferred to be paid for the day. If it was a half-day session or even less, I would set a basic minimum so that if the session was done fast, it was still worth the time, travel, setup, and so forth.

Try to get a sense of what is being planned for the session. If it's some band that's still in the writing phase and you are recording for hours on the same song, being paid by the song is not the best bet. But if an artist is running off a truckload of charts for some kind of licensing opportunity, you are able to make a fortune per song, and you are recording with some solid players, payment by the song can work.

Sometimes you may be offered a payment along with performance royalties. This isn't bad for the session player, but these days, with sales drastically down and most recording on a more independent level, I advise artists against it. Artists need to maintain as much ownership as possible, so I recommend finding the budget to pay the session musicians as independent contractors so the artist can keep the bulk of the percentages.

Amounts

Consider the economy and the session you're working. In recent years, even the top names I have hired as producers have asked me what the budget for the recording is, understanding that no one is making what he or she used to. Top session cats from LA and NYC are working in general business and cover bands these days, too. So don't get cocky when setting a price tag or referring to what someone was making a number of years back. The average rates were never that average, and the standard doesn't really exist anymore. In my experience, everyone has a different rate system. I do know that if I'm hiring someone for the first time, he or she is making less than my usual crew until I can get a sense of the player. At the same time, the guys and girls who I know are going to bring everything I need to a session will always get more.

In the end, taking the occasional free session to get involved with a studio, other producers, engineers, or musicians can help build you up even more than word of mouth, but when it comes down to the actual price tag or what you should charge, it should stay open for negotiation until you have truly established yourself. Don't short yourself, but make sure you understand the situation you're going into and charge accordingly. Ask questions: Will meals be covered? Is there parking? For drummers or key players, will there be equipment at the studio already? All these elements can make you decide about your costs and what to charge.

In the end, knowing exactly what to charge or what to offer for a session can be tricky. Consider all the elements and decide accordingly. Decide based on specific situations and individual budgets. That, plus the ability to compromise and having a clear understanding of what is expected, can help you come up with the best fee.

FOOD AND NOURISHMENT IN THE STUDIO

In my album budgets, I always allot a cost line for food in the studio. This is one of the most overlooked items in a recording budget, but it can cause large amounts of wasted time as people leave the studio to pick up food or eat out. That's not to say that you should be locked in the studio for an entire ten-hour session with no breaks, but you should take breaks that are real breaks, not leaving to pick up food and then having to get right back to work.

Think about the number of the days you are in the studio and how many people will be in there each day. By planning a basic menu of snacks and main courses, you'll know what is needed up front. Some band members prepare meals each day to bring in. Others will set up a shopping list and go shopping to pick up bulk supplies at a cheaper rate than buying these items in convenience stores each day. Bottled water, coffee, soda, and other basic snacks can really add up if they are purchased on a day-to-day basis.

Coffee . . . by the Numbers

Think about coffee purchases alone. I produced a record at a studio in Los Angeles—which will remain unnamed—for a label that will also remain unnamed. This state-of-the-art facility in Hollywood had all the bells, whistles, and toys you could imagine: two-inch tape, Pro Tools, isolation rooms galore, and a main room that had a very, very high ceiling. Yet with all the incredible toys, gadgets, effects, outboard, and plug-ins, it was missing something basic: a coffee maker.

An engineer who was often hired at this studio told me that there were five coffee shops in walking distance; any time we needed coffee, one of the interns would go out and fetch it. This was fine with us, because it was not on our tab; our coffee would be billed to the budget of the band that we were working with. But then I started to do the numbers . . .

Let's say a band is in the studio for ten days. Assume that there are ten people in the studio:

- 6 people in the band
- 1 engineer
- 1 producer
- 1 assistant
- 1 intern

Let's then say the sessions are ten hours or more, and, using a low average, we will say there are three coffee runs taking place each day. Again, I'm being very sparse here; I remember days of five to six runs. Next, let's average out each drink to three dollars. Some will want tea, which might be less; some might want the frilly, high-maintenance drinks, which will be more; and some might want a bottled water or Odwalla juice drink, cookie, whatever. Anyway, say three dollars a person per run.

Basic math: three coffee runs a day for ten people at three dollars a drink. Now multiply that by ten days, the length of the session. This is also assuming that the entire crew is in the studio for every day, but you get the idea. That's thirty dollars for every run, not including tips, which is ninety dollars each day for coffee. And the grand total: nine hundred dollars, just for the coffee for that series of sessions!

Yes, folks, and it gets more expensive, because that nine hundred dollars is now owed back to the label or investor with an interest rate, and this is just one of the places where waste and abuse occurs in the industry. When you plan and organize your budget, you can save a fortune on coffee, food, or anything else you want or need to have while you're in the studio.

With my budgets, we would look at a ten-day session with ten people and see how we could make it as affordable as possible. I like to have a coffeemaker in the studio. Elliott Bay Recording Company in Seattle, Washington, has a great coffee maker, by the way. Just let Scott make the coffee if you are in a session with me; I always make it way too strong. Jason Rubal has a state-of-the-art coffee maker in Steelton, Pennsylvania, too, if you are on the East Coast . . . man, I could sure use a good cup of coffee right now.

Next, prior to the session, I have someone go out and buy a couple of those mega bags of coffee, filters, sugar, creamer, milk, soy milk, honey, and assorted teas (for you non-coffee people). All of those combined can cost thirty dollars, more or less, depending on your coffee choices or if you need soy milk, rice milk, or whatever your condiment fancy is. Now balance it out: Nine hundred dollars plus interest to a label, plus wasted time on trips to a coffee shop, or thirty dollars. That's a pretty big savings as well as smart budgeting. Unless you're Dave Grohl and you need your "Fresh pots!" Rumor has it that he has cut back, but who knows?

This is the basic idea for all the food, regardless of whether it's a snack or a main meal. Say you want sandwiches for three days for ten people. Instead of going to Subway, purchase a meat plate and all the condiments. You will save money and have it available anytime someone wants to eat, which makes for an easier and more productive use of everyone's time.

Think realistically about how many you have to feed, what people eat, and what you would like to have on hand. Also consider effective food to have in the studio. Try to stay away from heavy meals and too much junk food. Have fruit and water available; make sure it's not all candy bars and Doritos. When you eat crap over and over again, you will feel like crap and potentially deliver a worse performance in the studio.

It's also okay to plan into the budget a night where everyone eats out. Sometimes at the end of recording or during a mixing day, getting everyone out together to eat somewhere can be a good stress reliever, and if you plan for it, it will be something you can realistically do.

Finally, plan what food is going to be picked up and when. If the sessions are on top of each other, this aspect is easier, but if you're booking over a couple of months or longer, remember to figure in the bulk purchases that can be made plus the weekly buys. Organize the shopping list and make purchases accordingly. If that means that before you lock in the budget you head down to a local Costco or supermarket, then do that.

If you're recording a well-budgeted album, the food and nourishment budget is one more place to show how organized every piece is. When everything is prepared for, from recording down to coffee, it can dramatically increase the level of confidence in those potential donors, investors, and backers for your project.

STUDIO WELLNESS: MASSAGE, PER DIEMS, AND STRESS REDUCTION

Wellness in the studio is crucial to ensure the level of performance, endurance, and patience necessary to handle the long hours of a recording session. If you're not well, you're not going to be at your best to represent your music in your performance for the recording. Wellness of body and mind makes for the best sessions.

When you're not worrying about things and you're feeling relaxed and able to work, you'll get the finest work done. The best plan is preparation and practice. Having the preproduction sheets available and all the preliminary elements in place is essential, but that is only one part. What about the worries around money and the stress of the studio on your body? To counter this, I add per diems and some type of massage to the music business plans I create.

First, the per diems. When a group is doing a long run in the studio, I like to make sure that the budget includes money for the artists to be able to take time off from work if possible.

It's more effective to have the artists concentrating on the music and not on their finances while they're in the studio. It's also not as effective to have a musician put in a full day of work and then come into the studio and have to put in another day's worth of work that night. This is especially problematic when it has to happen many nights in a row.

Preplanning a fair and realistic per diem for the artists allows them to feel less worried about time taken away from work. I have noticed a drastic difference in the patience, endurance, and energy level of bands who either raised funds or found investors to cover this part of the budget. Being able to write a couple of checks to each member of the group before entering the studio gives everyone peace of mind. They can settle basic financial issues before going in for a long run of sessions, so the group can focus on the music and not on the work they might be missing or the money they aren't making. Basically, work to remove all the parameters of outside stress, and the creativity, performance, and abilities will be dramatically better.

This may seem unrealistic. Still, this is one of those places in a budget that might seem excessive and unaffordable on the front end, but on the back end of extra hours and additional sessions needed, it ends up being less expensive. Exhaustion, long days, and stress can mean that many more tracks and that much more time to get it right, and it will cost that much more.

Along that same line, let's think about massage . . . yes, massage.

In many of the music business plans I have created for artists or for other producers, I have added in the services of a massage therapist, a chiropractor, or even an acupuncturist. Not all in one session, though! I've had a lot of people laugh at this initially and then either add it to the budget or wish that they had. A massage, chiropractic adjustment, or acupuncture treatment can be very helpful. Again, although they can appear to be an unnecessary expense, they can be a money saver in the end.

The basic concept is that you are in the studio and working hard; and after a lot of hard takes or long hours, your body can tire out and energy can be lost. A massage, which is definitely the most popular of the three, can be relaxing, invigorating, and energizing. It can help tired arms that have been playing for long hours and shoulders that are holding up basses, guitars, or the straps attached to some big, old tenor saxophone. In a lot of cases, a massage therapist can come in for a bulk rate and give fifteen-minute massages to each member on a portable table in a room not being used for recording. You can also set up in a different location before the session to have everyone relaxed at the start of a recording day.

Sure, it's optional, but when you think about sessions in which you get really tired or burned out early, a massage is the thing to keep you playing at the best level possible. That massage might also be the difference between getting a keeper take later in that long day and having to push it off for another expensive day of studio time.

> Budget for your dreams. Is it more important for you to have that overpriced Kate Spade purse or to put some of that cash to promotion, recording, or marketing?
>
> All too often we claim we don't have the money to do the things we want, but we spend on items we don't actually need.
>
> It's your choice. If you really want it, you will make the changes in your life and lifestyle to make it happen.

Know your body and your fatigue levels. When do you find yourself getting most tired in a day? When, during a practice or gig, do you start to feel exhaustion set in? What songs are the hardest and bring the most tension? This might just be the time to bring in a massage therapist, chiropractor, or acupuncturist to give that extra boost of energy. Just as you tune your instrument and make sure it's able to sound just right, the same can be said for your body and your mind. Think about how using per diems or massages to relax the mind and body might play helpful roles in the recording process. What might seem like additional expenses may end up saving a lot of money later.

VIDEO AND PHOTOGRAPHY IN THE RECORDING STUDIO: CAPTURING THE PROCESS

When you're recording, there's a lot going on, and your concentration should be on the music, but remember that everything you do to be effective can have a ripple effect. Let's say you're in a recording session and you have a friend, or even a professional photographer or videographer, in the studio to capture some of the recording time. This can be very useful for marketing and promoting the recording and the band.

Bring in the cameras at the low stress times, like while you're setting up. I usually tell people to avoid bringing the video cameras during vocals. When the stress is high, having cameras there can be a bad idea, but if you can find someone who can be a fly on the wall, you can capture some great moments for your website, social networking sites, and other marketing and promo materials.

Being able to document with photos and video can be a good learning tool as well. How were the drums set up and with what microphones? What were the settings on different amps? Sometimes a quick picture of certain setups can help you discover how things might have sounded better on your rig when you were recording. Also, what if the band as a whole becomes famous or a member goes on to a band that becomes very well known? People pay a lot for video these days. Who knows? The simple footage you take of the guitar player in a local bar band could be footage that you sell in ten years when he is a major draw.

This footage could be edited into shorts that you can put up on YouTube, some of your networking sites, or any other video website that can help get your music and your band out to more people. These videos can also be the start of a documentary you could do on the band, from being in the studio to doing shows, touring, and beyond. Try to think about the different times to shoot montages or themed footage to showcase the creation of a song or the album.

By the same token, the more photographs you can get, the more you can put up online and have more visual items to optimize on the Internet. You can post to your Pinterest, Flickr, any other online photo accounts, as well as any of your normal social media sites. It's great to be found online with your name and your music, but these days the more people that can search and find your images, the better. Current research indicates that video and visual elements are what get attention for your site; many are seeing you before they hear you. Post pictures frequently with the right keywords and content to be found and seen that much more.

Think of video and photography in the studio as one more element to help from the educational, marketing, promotional, and documentary standpoints. Of course, you should make sure that everyone feels comfortable and is not distracted by someone taking photos or video. The person taking pictures or video must understand the environment of the studio; he or she must understand that you are working and you have to concentrate. Sometimes it can be better to hire a professional photographer who knows how to fade into the background quietly to capture the best shots of the band.

With all the video capability on smart phones, you can grab a series of amazing captures and combine these elements. With the new iPhone 5 iMovie app, you can even edit down some of the footage right on your phone while you are taking a break during the session.

Photography and video in the studio can capture a group in ways that the fans may have great interest in seeing but rarely get to witness. The behind-the-scenes stuff can do well for a group and bring more exposure and marketing to a release. Bring in the cameras, have fun with them—but don't let them distract you. Capture another side of you: something to share with your fans, your friends, your family, and the world.

PRODUCTION: TRACKING DAY OR THE FIRST FEW TRACKING DAYS

My favorite days in the studio are right toward the end of mix, when everything is being pulled, nudged, tweaked, and adjusted right to where the artists wants it. This is when you make the song into what it's going to be. I also love the looks on the artists' faces as they hear the final mix. My other favorite day is the first day or couple of days of tracking. That's when the energy is at its highest, when everyone is running around, and when the most music is usually being laid down at the same time.

I'm completely jacked up and on fire on the first day. Running between the control room, the main room, and the isolation booths; answering a billion questions coming from a billion directions; conducting the cacophony that is tracking—this is what I live for. Don't get me wrong; I enjoy vocal tracking, overdubs, and the other days, but hands down, the first day and the initial tracking days just rock. They can be chaos in a good way. So much is happening at the same time and in so many different ways, but the mayhem can be organized to work in your favor. On the other hand, an unorganized and unprepared tracking day can be downright brutal and take forever.

In the production segment of the music business plans I set up for artists, all have the four preproduction sheets prepared. As we discussed earlier, walking in on day one with a tracking sheet, lyric sheet, chord chart, and preproduction sheet for each song can make your life infinitely easier and will allow for things to move at a faster pace with everyone on the same page.

The schedule and direction sheets are two more elements that I use and implement with a production plan. Most studios and labels will send them out as well. These act as call sheets, so people know when they're supposed to arrive and how to get there. Along the same lines, calling and confirming the crew and the people the day before they are supposed to be there is a small detail that will avoid confusion and stress on that day.

It's almost impossible to schedule the day the way you want, but laying out a ballpark schedule and a checklist of what you are looking to do and timelines you'd like to do it in is an effective approach. Also, on the first day, bringing people in as you need them can make things run smoother. You don't always need everybody at the same time. You're most likely going to be in for a long day on the first tracking day. Why not show up when you're needed and not have to hang out longer than you need to? In my opinion, that can maintain a higher energy level.

Under most circumstances, for me and many people I know, we are going to go after the drum setup first, so planning for the drummer to load in, get tuned up, miked up, and ready can be done by the drummer, the engineer, and the producer alone. The band needs to be as smart as possible with the time they have. If the guitar player wants to set up guitars and doesn't disrupt the drumming setup, great! He can help the drummer with the load-in. (Yes, I said it: Guitarists, you can help your drummers with loading in—hint, hint!) On the other hand, if the guitarist and a couple of friends are just in the way and making noise while the drums are being prepped, then none of them need to be there.

Things can move faster if you obey the engineer. When the engineer asks for certain sounds or certain instruments, don't embellish with other players or other instruments; play what you are being asked to play. So much time is wasted at this stage by people screwing around. Listen to the engineer, give what he or she is asking for, and don't play if you are not asked to.

The tracking days on which the most time is wasted are the ones that find the musicians just screwing around. Cut down on the messing around—cut it out altogether—and things will move exponentially faster. You can have fun and be funny, but stay aware of the clock and the budget.

Now you're underway; you got the headphone levels and a basic mix that works, and it's time to hit the first song. Make sure it's neither a ballad nor something that is all-out, crazy intense. Find that middle-of-the-road tune, the one to get the energy moving and the band flowing. Pick the tune that is almost like a solid warmup, something where work is getting done and a song is being tracked, but it's also loosening you up for the other songs.

You want to make every moment as effective as possible to have the best first day of tracking. Ask questions as you have them, and be aware of things around you. If you hear something that's off and it's one of the foundational things being tracked, call to stop the take. On the same note, don't stop if you're in a flow and you hear a scratch instrument do something wrong. Most times, unless you're tracking the entire song live, the focus is going to be on the drums, the bass, and maybe rhythm guitar. So that scratch instrument track that you didn't like isn't even going to be in the mix, but you stopped the take and lost a great drum and bass track. Don't do that!

Grab several takes of a song before listening. It's a serious waste of time to listen to a track after every take. Be aware of the energy in the room; if things are really in a flow, just keep tracking. When the natural live energy is moving and the sound is coming, don't stop. If you have cut three takes of one song and feel as if you have a keeper in there, but you're in the flow to play another song, go right to recording that next song.

Have fun with the first days of tracking; they can be a blast. If you have all your ducks in a row and everything ready, you will be able to relax more, play better, and have a really great time with it, too. The more prepared you are, the easier it can be to deliver the songs the way you intended.

SEPARATE THE TRACKS FOR ISOLATION AND EASIER MIXING IN POSTPRODUCTION

Sometimes separation is a good thing, especially when it comes to recording and you're looking for the highest quality takes with the least troublesome mix. The more you can separate sounds, instruments, and voices, the easier it will be to address each component individually when you mix the track down.

I'm all about recording together and the vibe and connections that can occur. If this is something you want and you're prepared to have the mix reflect that, then it is an option. If you're looking to record with fewer microphones and grab a more live feel, recording with instruments in the same room and musicians in close proximity is something you can do. However, if you want to be able to make the most of a mix in consideration of all its possible incarnations and uses, the more you can separate the tracks, the sounds, the instruments, and the voices, the more control you will have when you're mixing, and the easier it will be to give attention to each element.

Isolation is a key factor. If you can put an amp in one room and a drummer in another, you can avoid the bleeding of sounds into other microphones. This can allow you to track together while separating the sounds at the same time. A second way is to record guitars directly into the board and record the amplified version later in the room where your drummer recorded earlier, if you are looking for that big, live-room guitar sound.

Any sound can be picked up in the microphones meant for other instruments, which can make the mix of the specific track difficult. This goes for digital tracks as well; when recording drum machine patterns, loops, and more complex samples, they should be separated to different tracks for the different sounds.

A perfect example: A bass drum is a large, full, round sound, whether as a sample or a real drum. It's a deeper, darker, low tone most of the time. It also has some resonance and low-frequency hum to it. Of course it can have other tones, but that's the essence of a kick drum or kick sound. Now a snare drum is a smaller, tighter drum with a much higher pitch. It has a resonance that's at a much higher frequency, with a crack and sharp sustain. This tone is higher, shorter in resonance, and lighter. Most of the time, when a drum set is recorded, you pick up a little of the bass drum in the snare microphone, but it's barely noticeable because usually the drums are closely miked and don't really get in the way of each other. You can still get a great amount of separation between kick and snare in the mix, and you have a lot of options in creating the best sounds for both the bass drum and the snare drum separately or together. But if you have a loud guitar amp in the room, you're now infecting the drum microphones and may not only pick up the guitar in the drum tracks but much worse: You may pick up the bass drum or the snare drum in the guitar track.

Let's keep going to the worst-case scenario: The drummer was off on a few hits and you have to move the drums digitally to put the drummer in time with the rest of the song. A problem now arises, because you have drums that are off in the background of the guitar track, and that may tie the hands of the engineer or mixer who might want to add this effect or mix a certain way that he or she now can't because it will highlight the drums in the background as heard through the guitar amp microphone. What might be a small adjustment to really make the guitar sound exactly as you hoped can't be done because it will highlight an offbeat drum in the background. So now the mix is being adjusted for problem solving instead of creativity. Many engineers are very skilled at flying in other similar parts to fix this type of issue, but you are still forcing time for solving problems that didn't need to be there in the first place.

Furthermore, if a drum loop is recorded and the snare and bass drums are on the exact same track, which commonly happens, you now have two very different sounds that will have to be mixed the very same way. If you want extra highs on the snare, those same highs are now going to be on the bass drum sound as well. If you add any extra reverb to the snare, it will be heard on the bass drum, too. No separation means fewer options.

The bottom line is that if you have the tracks, use them. Separate the sounds so you can have as much isolation and control over them at mix time. And keep a well-marked tracking sheet so you know what's on every track, including small things that you might forget about otherwise, only to remember them after you have finished the record.

The easier it is to isolate tracks, the easier and faster the mix can go. It will also allow you to mix more creatively and not worry about problem solving and making mixing and effects decisions that are being chosen to fix and repair instead of for the creativity and the tune. The more separation you have, the easier it will be to remix or make fast changes. So add more tracks and more isolation for fewer hassles in the end.

In home studios with a single room, going direct and overdubbing can work very effectively. Yes, you might lose some of the playing-together element, but, in turn, you will be able to create a better mix with an array of options if everything is separated.

CLICK TRACKS, STAYING IN TIME, AND YOU: THE HATED METRONOME DEBATE

Click tracks and metronomes are hated by a lot of musicians—or maybe only the ones who never learned to use them or got past the "honeymoon of hate." The argument about feel, grooving, and moving the time often just comes off as an excuse for someone who can't play to a click. Click tracks suck to get used to, but any musician should know how to not only play in time but also be in control of the rushing, the dragging, and the overall array of the pocket.

I remember the scrapes and dents that ended up on my metronomes when I used to practice with them for hours on end. (Yes, I said "metronomes," plural. Many were destroyed in fits of beat-per-minute frustration). My metronomes would occasionally take flight and impact the wall at tremendous speeds. Still, they're necessary tools for practicing and learning your instrument. Good timing is an absolute requirement if you want to work in the studio or with top-notch producers and engineers.

I see beat replacement used these days; I see the effects to fix the time, which drives me nuts. I see the older style of recording a pattern to just get the loop for copying and pasting throughout the track. I also see drummers that can't hack it in the studio replaced by drum machines altogether, and then when they play live, their wavering is not the type that is done on purpose.

Energy levels can fluctuate; tempos can change drastically, both live and in the studio. Listen back to some of the songs that were recorded prior to click tracks being used, and you can hear it. A really drastic example is "Canary in a Coalmine" by the Police. The intro and outro of the song are drastically different. I am a big Police and Stewart Copeland fan, but Stewart was known to heavily and radically fluctuate tempos. In a lot of the Police and Sting biographies, it was said he often wanted it faster and Sting would want it slower. So you have not only a drummer pushing the time, but a bassist pulling back on the time. In some ways, that tension did work well for them—but I wouldn't make that part of the plan for most bands.

Practicing with a metronome or a click track can help you zero in on the tempo of a song and learn how to play patterns with precision and total rhythmic accuracy. It may drive you crazy, but it'll help your technical and groove abilities.

Some say the click (playing a certain number of beats per minute) is robotic, but it's more about accuracy (beat placement by the player), the time and speed being played in a lined-up fashion. It's up to the musician to set a feel that's comfortable, locked-in, and relaxed while still playing in solid time. You do not have to play exactly on the click. You can move with it, sit on the back or front of it, or even move around it. I have had sessions where I would take the click back to a half note to let the musicians feel a little more freedom. In other cases with intricate and exact parts, I would sometimes bring it up to the eighth note.

> For the melody players who sometimes get a little thrown by the click track, just feed the click to the rhythm section. This can help the other players focus on the drums and the bass without feeling overwhelmed by the click. Bassists and drummers, get to the point where you own any click at any tempo and do not feel overwhelmed.

I've never thought that the groove was the beat; I always saw it as the space between the beats. I believe that's where the phrase "in the pocket" originated. In the same approach, think of the click track as your foundation for the beats, while still having the freedom to work with it and create the grooves or the pockets for a tune.

On the production and business side of things, a click is essential these days. If you want a song with the best opportunity for success, it absolutely, hands down *must* be performed to a click track. This makes songs easier to rearrange, since every part of the tune is in the same tempo and locked into a click. If the song needs to be shortened, lengthened, or altered, it will be much easier to make those adjustments for a remix when an engineer can very easily cut and paste sections together that are not wavering.

The click track can be hard and very frustrating at first, but it can increase the opportunities and avenues for your songs. To be successful, a song needs to be prepared for TV, movies, commercials, insertions, international licensing, video games, etc. Working on and recording your songs with a click will make your music tighter and stronger as a whole while giving it more opportunities for revenue. I'm not saying that a click track must be used for every song, but it can make a difference in the possibilities of success in today's industry. Talk with your bandmates or your producer about using a click. If you own a smart phone, you have a metronome. I have seen great metronome apps on the iPhone, the Droid, the Galaxy, and on a number of other smart phones, tablets, and laptops. So really, you have no excuse about increasing your skills as you work on decreasing your rushing and dragging, all while learning to lock in with solid time.

Finally, practice with metronomes if you aren't used to them. Don't make the assumption that because you've been playing a song at a certain tempo you'll be able to lock it right into the click in the studio. Prepare yourself in advance; practice with the click and make it line up. Don't go into the studio only to be surprised that certain sections are rushing or dragging. You'll end up needing a lot more studio time and wasting a lot more money.

REAL DRUMS AND DRUM MACHINES: ONE OR THE OTHER, OR MIXING THEM TOGETHER

I remember getting a call on a session where there were already some drum machine tracks put down on a number of songs. Before I even heard them, I was critically biased, coming from the view that all drums should be played by a real drummer. I had heard a lot of drum machine and electronic drum sequences that sucked, and I made my stand—a weak one—based on my views and beliefs.

After finishing the few tracks for which I played live drums, the producer asked if I wanted to hear a couple of the other tracks and help with some manual fades that were going into mixing (yes, for the younger crew, there were boards where you needed to actually move the sliders to get the dynamic effects you were looking for, and it took more than just the engineer). As I was pushing the faders I was assigned, I heard something I had never heard before: a really cool, tasteful, and musical electronic drum loop. I liked the tones that the producer and engineer had gotten and I liked how it layered into the song. Right then, I became a convert . . . with stipulations.

I believe drum machines can be programmed tastefully, and I believe drum loops can work well for a song. At the same time, they can just as easily be used poorly. There are certain tones and loops that I have tried to mimic from a drum machine while playing live drums. So yes, I have joined the electronic nation for certain types of tunes. (Drummers like Questlove of the Roots and Swiss Chris kill at this; they are groove machines.) I don't, however, believe in using a drum machine when you want real drummer sounds. I know that the advances in technology allow for amazing sounds, but a strong ear can hear the difference. If you are using a drum machine, program the loop or sample in a tasteful, creative, and musical format. You can also get help from a drummer or producer. Some of those guys that "make beats" (I still hate that term) actually have some pretty solid skills.

There are many different ways to use electronic drums and drum machines in an exclusive way, but there are also ways of mixing them with live drums and percussion. One option that I like is to add in a live percussionist to play conga, shaker, or tambourine parts over the drum machine track. It can bring together a very interesting mix of digital perfection and human imperfection. A shaker that is played with a little pull on the backside of the beat going over a perfectly timed drum machine loop can deliver a very cool feel. The same can go the other way: Have a live drummer play a solid groove over a percussion bed from a drum machine. If you feel more comfortable as a drummer playing over a percussion bed or programmed percussion parts instead of a click, try that with a few songs. It can help your feel and time if you are grooving to patterns with sounds that you like, versus a click that is just on the quarter note.

For many years some drummers were hired to play simple, short patterns for sections of songs that were looped, copied, and pasted together to create the track, with a drum machine pattern running under it. Again, I'm suggesting a mix of the real drummer and the machine working together. I like the creativity. I enjoy the hip-hop and funk techniques of mixing live and electronic voices. For instance, I have cut a drummer playing a groove without a snare drum. He played the hi-hat, the bass drum, and the rest of the kit but stayed off the snare. I kept a solid click going for the drummer and then later laid a snare drum sample from a drum machine. The mixture of the two really embellished the feel. Or, when you're setting up a click track, you can program an interesting pattern or feel with sounds or voices from a drum machine that can serve as both a click and a foundational bed underneath the live instruments.

As mentioned before, Questlove, the drummer from the Roots and the musical director for Jimmy Fallon's house band, is one of those guys who just burns on the mixture of live drumming, drum machine programming, and playing over loops. Love that dude. Some of the drum and bass cats like Swiss Chris, Jojo Mayer, and Johnny Rabb also have these awesome blast-beat grooves that sound incredible and, at times, drum machine–like.

Explore and expand your horizons. There are a lot of options where both the drummer and the drum machine can work together instead of fight each other. When you can see the drum machines as an additional tool or a supplemental voice, you can create new sounds and arrangements of percussion that can work well together and complement each other. If you are only using drum machines or loop patterns, put in the time to be tasteful and musical when adding them into your songs.

I am a drummer and I always will be. I love the sound of a live drummer more than anything, but there is a compromise and a creativity that I have found as a drummer and even more so as a producer that has allowed me to see the possibilities and expansiveness in a situation where the drummer and the drum machine don't fight. They can work together and create even wilder ideas than just one or the other alone.

PERCUSSION AS EMBELLISHMENTS FOR YOUR SONGS

Anyone who has worked with me on a recording knows I got a thing for percussion. Maybe it's because I'm a drummer, or maybe it's because percussion, *real percussion*, always just amazed me. I remember listening to *The Rhythm of the Saints* by Paul Simon when I was thirteen and just being blown away by the album because of its percussion. I also started paying attention to Sting and Peter Gabriel, not just for the songs but also for the percussion. I started to listen to more Latin and Cuban music as well as West African and Turkish music. I got really deep into Trilok Gurtu, Airto Moreira, Ed Mann, Tito Puente, Lionel Hampton, and other drum-set players who were much more percussion minded. I loved Max Roach's approaches and views on percussion, along with guys like El Negro, Joey Heredia, and so many more. If you're not familiar with some of the names above, go check them out when you can.

I found percussion and drum set, though in the same family, to be two very, very different jobs. Learning about the history of percussion helped my drum-set playing, but in the end, I had a greater understanding that I was a drummer. I have applied many percussion techniques to the drum set, but I'm not a percussionist by far. I've studied basic percussion and can perform at a basic level in the studio, but, again, I am not a percussionist. In my opinion, a percussionist is a musician with the technical ability, and the understanding and education, for numerous percussion instruments. A percussionist has a steady hand and can play the most complex pattern in solid time for a long song, while also being able to play a simple quarter-note pattern on the cowbell for ten minutes without deviation: hitting that same sweet spot at the same dynamic, over and over again.

A lot of drummers who say they don't need percussionists in the studio find themselves to be very mistaken once the take starts. As crazy as it sounds, drum set and percussion can be two different worlds. To be able to play solid parts, especially in more modern music such as rock, funk, blues, country, and pop, requires top-notch precision that many don't have because they simply aren't trained in it. Studio percussionists like Don Alias, Luis Conte, Jorge Bezerra, Cyro Baptista, Robby Ameen, Johnny Conga and many more have blazing percussion chops and this amazing sense of exactly how to put the right piece in the right place. These are the cats that can also sit in front of a microphone, holding that percussive item in the same place, and deliver a precision and groove that is nothing short of amazing.

If you're a great drummer but not a great percussionist, hire a percussionist. It's not a personal attack, but bad percussion will take away from your good drumming and the song. Don't take away from what you already have down; let percussion embellish it and let it be played as well as you played the drums for that track. In the studio, you want someone who can get the job done fast and support your songs as much as possible. That's a big reason why I will try to block a good couple of hours, if not more, for percussion overdubs and percussion time with a pro that will add to the song while not taking away from it or wasting time and money in the studio. It's not about filling the song with too much, but laying a good amount of percussion allows you more options to play with in the mix of the song. Just because you track it doesn't mean you have to keep it. But if you don't track it and then end up wanting it, you have to do it again.

Keep these things in mind when you have a percussionist come in. Think about every possible piece of percussion you have ever thought about having on the given song. Talk to your producer or the engineer about ideas he or she may have. Talk to people who have more experience and a different set of ears. Work out in advance what you absolutely know you want and what you may consider for a track, so you can save time.

So now you're in the studio, you have blocked the time for a percussionist, you have a basic idea about a shaker part, and that's all you hear. It leaves you with two options. Is this a simple tune that you don't want anything more on? Or do you want to play? If you're happy, leave it be. If you want to play, then there are a couple of different approaches.

First is the conceptual arrangement idea. This is where you have a picture of how you want to see layers run across each other and how the different parts could work together. This brings up accent and looping-type ideas that you might want to have in one voice or across a number of voices. As an example, you could have a single accent occurring on a tambourine in a pattern that lasts two bars and then repeats, or you could have the accent pattern be the same and move across the tambourine, a shaker, a bell, and a bongo.

Second is the bulk concept. If you're only putting tambourine and congas in one section of the song, and if you have the time, add it to the whole tune or add it to the section before and after where you want it so you can play with transitional ideas when it comes to mixing. The more you have, the more you can play with.

Another really good trick is to go to the end of the track, past the end of the song, and get a series of samples of each percussion item alone. Have the percussionist play either a basic part or a basic sound to the click after the track, and then if you want to add or play some more in the mixing stage, you have some easy samples to pull from.

With the overdubs, have fun and be creative. On most tunes, I will usually lay at least a conga, cowbell, shaker, and tambourine part. In a mix, many parts are often ejected or simplified to fit the tune. Sometimes, as with guitar, you can double parts or play around with different percussion instruments phased or panned differently in the mix. Play percussive lines on items that are not always used for percussion, like pipes, tires, and other items you would not usually hear. You also can create loops and electronic samples of these parts mixed together to create a percussion bed loop underneath the song.

In the end, there is a world of opportunities and options with percussion; I haven't even scratched the surface. Think of where rhythm could supplement or complement a song, or where a layer or pad could be added that would embellish or highlight the song or its motion. Listen closely to some of your favorite albums and pull out the percussion in your head. You'll be surprised by how much you'll hear, even in more contemporary songs. It's there; see if you can find it. Some of the simplest percussion parts taken out of a song you know would be missed by the average ear and possible yours. It's not always obvious, like the cowbell at the beginning of "Low Rider"; don't you think the beginning of "Livin' on a Prayer" by Bon Jovi would feel a little empty if those finger cymbals weren't there? Play with some extra percussion while you're tracking and give yourself an array of sounds and layers to play with and mix around. If you have the time during the mix, layer and play with volumes, tones, and sounds of the percussion. Try to create beds of supplemental rhythms to drive some of the songs that need that extra push.

Hire a percussionist to explore and play for a few hours by tracking ideas across all your songs; this can give you a layering option that is easy to take away in mix but more expensive to add later. Allow a percussionist to deliver a bed of various sounds and ideas to play with. More often than not, you will find an element that gives you a touch, a tone, or a supplemental piece that can really bring something to the track you were always looking for but didn't know how to make happen. The simplest clave or shaker can bring an extra touch or a little more motion and punch to a song.

Not all tunes need percussion, but take a listen, or just think of your tunes from a more percussive standpoint. Could something be added? Maybe it's not another guitar or vocal that it needs; maybe it's percussion. Take some time to listen to some of your favorite music and see if you can hear the percussion you might have missed before. You might be surprised at how percussion and a professional percussionist could work for you and your songs.

OVERPRODUCTION IN EARLY TRACKING

How much production is too much? Where do you draw the line between supplemental sounds and embellishments and having way too much going on? Even in the takes or sounds you might not be using, the same questions can be asked. How many vocal takes should you work from? How many solos should be recorded? How many basic tracking takes should you have for each song?

This is an area that's very hard to define but where opinions abound. Some view it as a money and time issue. If you have the money and time to do all that tracking, why not track the hell out of each song, overdub, and vocal? In response to that approach, I wonder how bored the musicians might get and how lackluster the takes would eventually become.

There's a fire and an attitude in early takes; there's an energy before the monotony sets in. The excitement and newness of a song or a take can really shine through, especially in those first few takes. Even on the largest budget recordings that I have been a part of, we would really try to get the tune in no more than six takes. If we were going past five or six and the energy was still there and the vibe was good, I would sometimes continue to try to capture the basic track, but most often I would move on to another tune and return to the song later in the session or even on another day.

Gauging an artist or a band can really help to decide what you need to go after and how many takes you might need. What is the mood of the band? What is the mood of the songs? What songs cause the most problems for the band as a whole or for specific members? Taking all the elements of technique, personality, and confidence into account can help you plan how to approach tracking and overdubs. Who has the shortest attention span? Who hates to redo things over and over again? This all has to be taken into account when you are deciding how many takes you are going after.

I personally feel that if you have to go over six takes, you should step away. I prefer to find that one take to move forward with as opposed to having a number of different keepers, unless it's an album or a song that doesn't have many overdubs, if any, and we're just trying out differ-ent feelings at different times. I prefer a commitment to looking for the right take and not a series of takes to choose from. I find that most artists work that much harder when going for a solid take versus those who see it as just a couple different attempts.

For artists who are not overdubbing, a jazz recording approach I like to take is to record the series of songs for a record like a live set. Have them run straight through the set a couple of times in a row. Then take a listening break, see if anything stands out or anything needs to be addressed. Play another couple of sets, listen once more, and call it a day. I like to bring back the jazz or non-overdub groups to do the same thing on a second day, but mix up the order of the sets. Then at the end of day two, send them away for a week with a rough mix, listening to the eight to ten sets they have recorded so they can pull and grab each song from those dif-ferent sets. I've found it to be a very productive approach, but it is also an approach that works best for stronger artists with a good sense of their sound.

However, I don't take this approach with styles that are going to require mass overdubs. I take the time with the jazz groups or the non-overdub groups, because it will capture a certain energy and those days are covering all the tracking. With other styles, I prefer to work a num-ber of takes and search for the foundation and the single keeper take. This makes life easier and it reduces stress for the players.

Having a producer listen to the take while the group is playing can save time and money. I can stop when I see the energy getting low or I know it's the right time to bring in everyone to see if each approves of a take. This saves time, takes, and money. I was pretty blown away when I read up on the Michael Jackson "Thriller" sessions and how many keeper takes they had to sift through, and also how they pushed Michael for more than seventy vocal takes. Today? No way! Who could afford that, even on the largest scale?

TRACKING AND LAYERING GUITARS

Layering guitars in the studio is an art in and of itself. When you listen to tracks—from Pink Floyd and U2 to Led Zeppelin, the Who, and too many more to mention—you can hear amazing guitar tones that just don't compare to anything else. Whether as a comp or a lead part, the tone itself blows you away; add a great guitar player, and you have a real winner.

For example, the tone of the guitar solo in Pink Floyd's "Comfortably Numb" was one of those experiences that made me want to learn more about sound. The texture, the tone, the ambience, and how it related to everything else in the song was a game changer for me. I remember being more interested in learning how to get that sound than wanting to be able to play that part.

Yes, first and foremost you're going to want to have a great guitar tone before you go in the studio; then you'll want to take some time to play with microphones, preamps, and amp placements to find that perfect tone you want. But what is that last step in the recording that seems to make some guitars stand out and have a richer, broader, and warmer sound? While a lot of that comes directly from the guitarist, a great deal can also come from guitar layering in production.

You have to decide what and how much you want to put into a given guitar sound. I have no problems with laying a single guitar track for a song, and some songs call for just that, but I do tend to have a great deal of fun when we can play with different layers and tones to bring out something a little different.

The first tool I use is basic: simple, secondary layering. The guitarist doubles or sometimes even quadruples the part that he or she has played; then you simply spread the guitars across the mix, opening up the sound and the tone.

A variation of this idea is to double or quadruple certain sections to beef up a chorus, a transition, or a change that is felt more spatially than in volume. Sometimes the panning and fading of sections coming in and out of a primary part can draw the ear to hear something that it might not be able to actually define, only feel.

Move the amps around and change them out, play with microphones and even play different guitars for the double. For example, if you play one guitar track with an amp in a very large room and the microphones are a little bit backed up, and then try the double with the amp baffled tightly with a rug over it. This will create a different type of tone and allow for the double to bring a different type of texture.

Another variation of that concept is to just double the double. That is where you're just looking to thicken out the tone and use more of a panning production approach while you go after a double or a quadruple of the exact tones and the exact layering that sounds the same. The double itself, spread out, will give a nearly choral effect.

I'm also a fan of doing a second run of the original guitar with an acoustic on some songs or playing a double with no effects at all. This can bring some punchiness and draw some higher and tighter tones that can really sound great, depending on the tune. One alteration that I use is having the acoustic guitar double for part of a repeating phrase, or only double the acoustic on the lower notes of an electric guitar arpeggio line to beef up the lows, but not double on the highs.

A third variation is to double with other instruments buried under the guitar line, like a banjo or a medium-to large-string instrument. Sometimes running a small horn line such as an oboe, a cornet, or a soprano sax, or even defined keyboard sounds can subtly accent a line that seems like it is guitar alone. Sometimes transitioning from a voice into a guitar or a guitar into another voice is a great trick. Slowly crossfade one instrument into a guitar, or vice versa.

You can sing as a double, too. Double a guitar line, sing a doubled part of that guitar line with a voice, then pan the four tracks with the singing a little more buried. Remember "On Broadway" from George Benson? He does a very cool singing part, doubling his guitar line. And who can forget "Do you feel . . ." with Peter Frampton adding that flange part to his voice? This concept and both these elements used by Benson and Frampton and many others allow for a breathy (literally) foundation for the guitar. One cool thing I liked to do with a song that had a dissonant but resolving guitar line was to have a piano or even a sax just play on the dominant and the root of the line far in the background and low in the mix to add a cool texture.

Note that you can make some cool sounds by singing in unison with the guitar (Benson), singing a harmony line to it (Stephen Stills), or even using other instruments to play specific notes or parts. But if you're not making the guitar primary and mixing the additional tones to supplement the guitar track, it will not sound as if it is part of the guitar. Not that it's a bad thing; just something to keep in mind before getting carried away.

If you have the time to experiment in the studio or even at home, play with guitar layering. It can help you create a more individualized tone and a different sound presence in the mix of the song. Try amps in different rooms with different microphones as well. Take that extra time to experiment and create your own sounds for your songs instead of just plugging in and going.

SINGING AND VOCAL TRACKING

Vocal production and tracking can often be the toughest part of a session. It is taxing, repetitive, annoying, and exciting all at the same time. Some of those little things that can occasionally get passed over in the tracking of other instruments can stand out like a sore thumb when it comes to vocals. It's an absolute necessity to approach vocals and the production of vocals with the fullest attention to detail and top-notch preparation.

I really don't think you need to get seventy-plus takes on a single song; I don't care how big your budget is. I find that to be a complete waste of time and money. I personally believe that getting three to four solid takes of vocal tracks for a song gives you plenty to sift through. I like to try to get a full take or two of the song and grab a couple of takes of each section of the tune by going backward. For example, if a song has three verses and three choruses, in the best-case scenario, I look for the singer to run the tune front to back, twice straight through. Then I will have him or her do a take or two of each section and then stop for a small break between each verse and chorus. Then, and only if needed, I have the singer do the sections backward to add new energy to the backside of the song and see how that affects the takes.

I look for solid keepers or takes with great performances that need little to no pitch adjustment. I find that this is an effective approach—without overproduction—to getting a series of vocals to choose from without going over the top, Michael Jackson–style. There was a lot of money behind "Thriller," and I would bet the house that the average artist is not working in the same universe. Remember: All those extra takes you want to record need to be reviewed. Think about that when it comes to time management and costs.

When it comes to overdubs and solos, I like to capture two to three solos to choose from and also do a take or two where the soloist just does runs and embellishments throughout the entire tune. These might not even be used, but it provides some extra textures to play with in the mix and does not take much time to get. Occasionally, if I hear a take that is dead-on, I might go after one more just to have it, but I won't go further than that. Some people have told me I overproduce in these phases, but I think there's a fine balance between too little and too much. I want some solid things to choose from, but I don't want to have someone track a song fifty ways from Saturday, where listening takes hours and hours.

This approach has worked well for me and the artists I have worked with and has saved a great deal of time. In the end, it's best to decide your plan of attack in preproduction. Basically, the more you track, the more there is to be reviewed, the more there is to be mixed, and the more time and cost you are adding in the studio. If you designate a plan of attack and go after a preset number of takes and keepers, you will save time and money. But these decisions and choices are best made before you start recording instead of when you are in the thick of it.

Having said all that, there are many different ways to approach vocal recording. I like to split up the concepts into "before" and "during" for the recording session. I have found these methods and ideas to be the most effective to get the best vocals and the best performance.

Before

You're going to record an album? Be ready! Practice; work on strengthening your voice and your chops to be able to sing the songs, but also work on the endurance to be able to sing those songs over and over. You will need to be able to work for a long time through many takes.

"I can get these vocals in one run . . ." I cannot tell you how many times I've heard this from singers, and it has never, I repeat, *never* happened. Practice the songs, work on your voice with exercises, and prepare as best you can, even when your voice is at its best.

If you don't have a vocal coach or teacher, get one. Think about it: Before you go on a really long trip, you do an overhaul of your vehicle, right? You change the oil, check the tires, and get an overall tuneup if needed. You do preventative maintenance so that the vehicle will run well and potential problems will not arise. Why not take a couple of lessons with an experienced, top-notch vocal coach as a tuneup and preventive maintenance? Having a vocal coach go over your songs with you will help you be as strong as possible. This person can give you exercises and helpful hints to prepare well in advance, which will make things go much smoother and faster in the studio. They can catch and focus on areas where you might not be as strong. Often when I recommend this, singers turn it down, saying it's too expensive or they don't need it. In the end, the time spent on having to go over tracks and lay extra vocals can be more expensive than hiring a vocal coach. Vocal coaching is an investment that will save you money and time on the other side and prepare you in a way that is vocally healthy. Many vocal coaches are also available to come in the studio to help you during tracking as well. While it might seem like an extra expense, it always saves time and money.

Also, take care of your voice—your instrument. Maintain it with the right food and activities to help you be the most effective. Have your body in shape to make sure your lungs are healthy. During the sessions or just prior, stay away from phlegm-inducing foods and drinks; go for the teas and water.

I prefer to cut vocals in larger or more open rooms. I really don't like the hip-hop boxes or the miniature vocal booths that, to me, deaden the vocals. They are the easiest rooms to repair vocals, but if someone can belt and deliver, wouldn't you want to get the fullness and richness of the room's acoustics in there as well, instead of only processing the voice with effects and digital enhancers?

During

A basic checklist can simplify your vocal sessions. By mixing vocal preparation with problem solving, you'll make the workload move fast and flow better.

First, a studio administrative word: Don't grab the microphone, especially if it's one of those three-thousand-dollar jobs that's on a top-notch stand. It doesn't want to be touched. If it's too high or too low, let the engineer or producer make the adjustment. You don't want to try to adjust a microphone the wrong way and end up dropping it. This is a surefire way to make things much more expensive for you.

Also, don't put the headphones down on the microphone stand. That stand is balanced out for the microphone; don't add weight or throw off the balance; this may send the microphone falling to the floor. I have seen this happen way too much. And don't put the headphones on the floor!

Watch for the cables around your feet and avoid stepping on them. Those are some nice cables, and they don't need shoes—especially high heels—breaking through them. And honestly, ladies, do you really want to track vocals in high heels? I have told more women to take off high heels and gotten better vocal takes so much faster. You are in the studio, not on stage. Be comfortable, be balanced, and stand with good singing posture.

Navigate your position to the microphone when you sing. Look at your body position relative to the microphone. You are going to want to keep that same spacing. You want to stand in the same place, but also be aware of your posture and where you're leaning. Try to find the most consistent position to get the best vocal takes and allow for easier overdubs and mixing.

If a producer or engineer makes a comment about your sound or your dynamic being great; freeze! Look at where you are, where you are standing, how you are standing, and other elements of your body and your position. If you found the sweet spot or angle, make sure you know how to get back into it for each take.

Be aware of the dynamics. While you do want to lock your hips, your lips, and your body in a single, consistent location relative to the microphone, you'll want to back away at the times when you're hitting louder, heavier dynamics. When you're hitting a dynamically loud word with a very enunciated "T," "P," or "K" sound, you may want to slightly turn your head. This will keep the natural performance at its strongest and require less editing, saving more time in mix.

Watch your posture. Make sure you're singing and breathing in the best form. Practice in front of a mirror. When you're slouching, you're constricting airflow. That said, I like to work with certain forced constraints if artists are having problems. I will try to either open them up or constrict them to get certain notes or phrases—everything from crossing their arms to condensing their chest to holding their hands clasped together behind their back to open up the lungs a little more. Sometimes I use what I call the "hostage position," where the singer puts both hands together clasped behind their head. Try singing troublesome parts while moving your body around in different ways to see what may work and be a quick fix for the studio.

Other times, when singers are not hitting a pitch or are going flat or sharp, I'll have them take off one headphone to help them hear themselves in a different way. Still, whatever changes you make, they need to be made for you in a personalized and customized way. Don't be a diva, copying how this star or that celebrity sings in the video. In most cases that is a pose, and in even more cases they have been Auto-Tuned to hell.

Think about where you're singing from. Feel your body, your lungs, and how you're positioned. Wear comfortable shoes and balance your body. This is different than posture; it's allowing the notes to come from you in a strong way. If I see that someone's posture is strong but we are still having problems, I will have the singer lightly bend the knees and concentrate on the chest or stomach to remedy the issue.

Not everyone has to be in the studio staring at the vocalist. It can be a great strain, especially for the vocalists, and it's very different from being on stage. Try to keep the number of people around the control room down during vocal days. I've found that the fewer people around, the faster the vocals go.

I prefer to get a single song in one day rather than breaking up tunes across a series of days. Voices can change. Temperature, humidity, and a thousand other variables can make small changes in tone and sound. As far as harmonies, those can be done on other days, in my opinion, since they will be a different part. I prefer to get all leads and any type of double from a single voice on the same day.

Understand the PONR (Point of No Return—more later) and respect it when it's called. If your voice is about to reach that point and you're going to be singing the next day, *listen* when the producer calls the session. Stop singing! Small tremors in the voice or exhaustion can be heard by a vocal coach or a solid producer, and if he or she calls the session, it's not a doubt of your abilities; it's your producer making sure that you will be fresh and able to sing well for the next session. Trust the professionals who are there to help you get the best work in the shortest amount of time.

After you're done, take the time to listen to the tracks and the different versions if time allows, but take them home to listen. If you feel you need to take the time to pick and choose sections and phrases, then ask the engineer to burn the rough mix copy or MP3 with the different vocal takes, and you can go through them outside the studio, where the clock is not running.

If you want to go right to choosing the tracks in the studio, it can be much faster and more effective right after all the takes are done. Then you can listen to them, one after another. This also allows for small corrections if one of the tracks or sections needs to be redone.

Work smarter, not harder. Prepare for your session with the mindset of being tuned up but also armed with tricks and skills that give you preventative maintenance for problems that can arise. Do this, and you will get the best and most effective takes in the shortest amount of time with the least hassle.

POINT OF NO RETURN (PONR)

There is a point in the studio where people will hit PONR, or, as I like to pronounce it, "ponner": the point of no return. You know what I am talking about: that point where you've been recording for hours and hours on end and the quality is slowly beginning to diminish, as are the technical capabilities, the listening, and the overall ability to make decisions and play at the level you want to. Hey, we're all human; everyone hits a wall at some point.

It's a really, *really* good idea to actually recognize this and not push beyond it. I'm not saying you shouldn't do your best and try to do things a number of times to get them right. I'm just stating that it's important to recognize when PONR is reached and to call it a day at that point. There's a major difference between takes that are worsening and those where you know that you have the adrenaline to carry you to what you're looking for. There's also a magic in some takes being done when you're a little fatigued.

Preproduction decisions impact these considerations. The song order and the overdub order should be considered when you're scheduling, so you don't just jump around from song to song. What's the vibe or the difficulty of a song? Which song gives a certain player a lot of confidence that can lead into doing a harder song that the particular player may not be as sure about? All this information can help you or your producer construct a strong recording plan. And that doesn't mean that if someone suddenly feels the energy to do a specific song you shouldn't go track it that very moment. Still, having the blueprint is going to help you.

But when PONR is reached, it's time to stop for the day. If it's on a specific song earlier in the day, it's time to move on. As a producer, I will *never* let an artist track more than six takes in a row of the same song.

This is not an ego thing; it's not about saying that you can't do it. It's about being effective for the track you are working on, for the next track, or for the next day. If it's time to move on, *move on!* When you hit the point of no return, it's not just that energy and ability are lost; it's that frustration, anger, fatigue, and a pissy, negative mood begin to set in, which will hurt the song you're working on and have a bad effect on the rest of the day. If it's early in the day, it can have an effect on other songs, and if it's at the end of a day, it can actually screw with the next day.

Early Tracking PONR

If a song is just not going right early on or an overdub is not happening early in the day and you're advised to move on, then move on. Go to an easier track and rebuild the energy and confidence to go back and hit the one you're having problems with. Sometimes you may find that doing another song will warm you up or loosen you up to be able to do that problem song much better than where you started. When you have the feeling of excitement mixed with achievement, your performance vibe will reflect it. Confidence begets confidence; on the other hand, feeling like you suck can make you suck.

If you need some air, get outside. If you're thirsty, get some water. Think about the different elements that might be making the take go bad. Problem-solve as best you can, but once you can't think of any more options, it's time to move on. If you continue to push on that track, the stress and the frustration can hurt the song and haunt you the rest of the day. You may also affect the mood of the other band members, which will make the day, as a whole, less effective than it could be. Accepting that you've reached a point of no return will help you return to the track sooner and get it faster without affecting other tracks in a negative way.

End of the Day PONR

Some people feel that if they book a certain number of hours in the studio, they have to be able to perform for all of them. But sometimes when a studio day is booked for ten or eleven hours, a burnout point or PONR can be reached at hour nine. Now, in the smart, effective, and productive world, it's time to either call the session, move on to some backups, or maybe have the producer or engineer do some work on basic mixing or preparation of other tunes in order to make use of those hours. That is an effective use of time. If an exhaustion point has been reached after a long day and you push to either track or continue to try to overdub, you might get angrier and not get the take that night. Plus, you leave the studio stewing about how crappy the end of the session was, which can easily carry over to the next session. When you listen back to what you might have thought you got (when you reached PONR) only to realize with refreshed ears that it's pretty much crap and you have to cut it again, that sets a real good tone for the beginning of a day, doesn't it?

No bands that I've seen go past PONR and continue to track has ever gotten that last take as a keeper. They all come back and need or want to fix something. They are pissed off, since they thought they got that magic take but now with rested ears find out it was not so delicious. This inevitably hurts the confidence for the new day.

I explain to every band I produce that I have the right to call PONR and stop the session or move on. I give a ten-minute, get-out-of-jail-free card for one fight against my call; then if I call it again, the session or that track is over for now. I ask if they want to start with that song the next day, or if we're going to try another angle or another song and then come back to that trouble spot later.

That makes the next song or the next day feel much better. The end of the session ends on an up note. People leave the studio knowing there is more work to do but are left realizing all the great work that was done that day and not focusing on the song or the point where the energy fizzled.

If you don't have a producer, keep on the lookout for the signs of PONR, and realize that sometimes the most effective thing you can do for a song is to stop playing it.

I always watch out for tones of voice, sighs, change in posture, continued sloppiness, or loss of technique in a performance. I also watch for people not playing together or not playing for the song. For example, if the guitarist was hitting juicy solos all day that transitioned well, padded the form of the tune, and had strong definition from their beginning to end, and I hear a total change that's not fitting, that's a real sign.

Also watch for overall energy levels. Do the breaks taken throughout the day have to be longer and longer to get the most effective takes? Is there a plan in place for some of the easiest songs to be laid first if certain members have the ability to go longer on those less troublesome tracks? Let's say the drummer hits PONR first. Then you can have the guitarist do his or her guitar overdubs when you call PONR for the tracking of drums that the day.

Think of the session from many different angles. It's not just about laying it down; it's about having everyone in the best space mentally, physically, and technically to achieve what you're going after.

A mentor of mine in Massachusetts had scribbled on the corner wall of his studio, "The later it gets, the better that take sounds." It couldn't be truer; the ears fade and the mind goes as well. Be aware enough to make the PONR call or, when a producer calls it, listen! Remember that it's not about that moment or the very end of that day; it's about making the best recording and the best songs you possibly can. If you need to call the session for the day, call it. Make sure you're not wasting studio time, going well past the point of no return, and only creating a frustrating environment that may carry over into future sessions. When you hit the point of no return, *stop!*

OVERPRODUCTION REVISITED AND RECAPPED

The idea and execution of production is a very individualized thing. Oftentimes it is based on what the artist is looking for in a song. Other elements can include whether the song is being produced for the recording or for the performance. Should this be a product that can be reproduced live on stage with the basic group, or should it be a richer and fuller production that would take a pretty big stage to allow for a crazy number of instrumentalists?

There are a dozen angles to take when it comes to production and they are all correct in different ways. The one universal approach toward songs where the artist is open to production ideas is figuring out how best to represent the song. If a song is very deep, heartfelt, and has nice melodic flow and harmonic motion, then in my opinion it can go with a simple arrangement, even just a voice and a guitar. In other cases in which the song might not have as strong a motion or arrangement in naked form, such as one with repetitive chord progressions, not the strongest transitions, or simpler melodies, the addition of production and richer arrangements can be a support system for the song.

It's not that the song is bad, but you're trying to move it into a place where it will have the best chance at success. Discussing ideas and ways to layer, whether throughout the whole song, only in sections, or just in transitions, will help you designate the arrangement and production of the song. Are there deeper or lower parts of the song that could be supplemented with some high sounds or voices? Is there a rhythm that could be complemented or supported by being played on another instrument? Take the time to create, listen, and feel what could add to the song and what might belong in the song without overwhelming it.

POSTPRODUCTION: GET OUT THE WHISK AND START MIXING IT ALL DOWN

Artists, engineers, producers, and everyone else often argue about the time it should take to mix a project. They all have different opinions and again, they are all correct in different ways. A key element for many musicians is the money. The band or artist has tracked for a series of days and has added all the overdubs, vocals, and whatever else. Now comes the point where the flaws in the budget appear, and the money left for mixing is minimal. At this point the engineer is often asked to mix down a ton of songs with only a few hours to do it in. You have now taken the song and the track that you worked so hard to lay down and are finalizing it with a shortcut mix that's not going to allow the engineer or person mixing to take the right amount of time to address the mix in the best way possible for the song.

Think about what you're doing in order to have an effective mix and final product. If you have a song with a lot of overdubs, horn parts, vocals, or backing vocals, then budget for the engineer to have the time to really address that mix in the right way. Don't just budget a certain amount of time for each song; figure out what you're tracking. The more instruments, overdubs, and vocals, the more time you'll need in the mixing phase. Tunes that are just vocals and guitar are going to take a lot less time.

Other factors to consider are the basic edits as well as Auto-Tuning, if needed. Cleaning up fades, lining up notes, and doing crossfades between different takes or fixes are all things that need to be considered as well.

You'll hurt the work you've already done by forcing it to be mixed too fast. There are some amazing engineers out there who can mix very fast and still deliver an amazing product, but they all have their methods and ways of pulling different sounds together. Ask the engineer or producer you're working with how much time he or she will need to mix the song or songs to the best of his or her abilities. Discuss in advance what you're thinking about doing when it comes to overdubs and additional tracks for each song. You're taking the time and the effort and spending the money to get the right take, so make sure you're getting the right mix to present the work you've done.

How Many Mixes for a Song?

Let's say the band is coming around the corner as far as a song is concerned. The overall mix is just about there: All the levels are right, all the instruments are balanced, and the song is basically done. Is it time to save that mix and move on to the next song?

Not if you want to get the most out of your work. There are all sorts of different profit routes to take with your music. Investing that time in the songs now, while you're still in the studio, has the potential to reap big rewards in the future by creating the most products for the most avenues of income from a single song.

Artists and bands need to take the time to create the most opportunities for each song. Analyze every conceivable scenario for promoting and soliciting a song. Though these opportunities will occur out of the studio and after the song or album is completed, you should plan for them before you even set foot in the studio (see my chapter on the music business plan).

How many mixes should a group have for each song? I like to have at least five different cuts and a consolidated version of the track as a whole.

While a song is being mixed down, the concentration and bulk of time should go to the song as a whole. Make sure all the levels are balanced, everything is equalized, all volumes are right, and the tune sounds the right way. Once you get to that point, though, take a few steps back and get the extra mixes, too.

Mix 1—The Full Song

This is the track that will go on the album and the track that will be available for download. This is the full version of the song, the mix that everyone always gets.

Mixes 2 and 3—Two fifteen- to twenty-five-Second Samples of the Song

Find two segments of the song that you want to showcase. While you're in the studio, you'll be able to cut or fade in / fade out of the sample you want to have. These can easily go on demos that you will send out for the album or put up online as additional marketing tools.

Many artists pull samples off a CD or an MP3 that has already been compressed, but compressed tracks are of lower quality than getting them right out of the track in the studio. These uncompressed samples will be at a higher fidelity and you can very quickly set a place to fade in and fade out that sounds top notch and much more professional than most.

In the samples you set up, make sure every sample is not the same. For example, do not set up every sample from the beginning of the song to twenty or twenty-five seconds in. Showcase all the different elements of the song. One sample can be an intro, another can be a bridge into a chorus, and another can be a final chorus into an outro. Taking it a step further, if you can fade out the sample right before a transition or change, such as on a dominant that hasn't resolved or a section that is about to go somewhere else, you leave the listener wanting more—sort of like a mini-cliffhanger.

Having a second disc or digital sample set of just the samples of your album can be a great marketing move, too. If you send out a disc or links to an online streaming sample to industry people and there are twelve tracks that are each twenty seconds or so, there is a much greater chance someone will take the time to listen to them all. Remember, time is expensive. An industry professional is more likely to invest four minutes in a sample demo disc or streaming download than an hour or more listening to a full album.

If you are posting songs, make sure they are only in sample form. Anyone can easily rip and steal full songs. Post samples for free, or if you post a full song online through any of the streaming channels, make sure you are giving it away for free, because basically you are—whether you intend to or not.

Tease with the samples. Fade in at a strong point and fade out right before a chorus or a hook. Leave them wanting more, and maybe they will go to listen to the full song or album.

Mix 4—No Lead Vocal Tracks with Backing Vocals Still In

Have a mix with everything except the lead vocals. This track can be used for potential television or live radio shows as a supporting track. It can also be used when you perform but do not have a backup band or the ability to support a full group.

Having this track ready can open other opportunities for performances that may not be able to occur otherwise. If you make the industry aware that you have these tracks available, it will in turn make you available for more performance opportunities than most other artists.

Mix 5—The No-Vocal Track

When you're mixing, create a version of the song without vocals or backing vocals but with all of the instrumentation. This may be used for licensing opportunities in certain TV shows, movies, commercials, and other media outlets. Having a version ready to go with no vocals will not only showcase your professionalism but also prove that you're prepared to meet the needs of the industry. Many times artists are unprepared when asked if they have a version of a song with no vocals. They scurry around to get the files and find someone to mix it down without the vocals. Remove the stress and replace it with opportunity by having that no-vocal mix ready to go for anyone who might request it.

The no-vocal track that is well recorded can also be used by other artists for different opportunities. This allows for the chances to sell or license the song to a label or an artist to perform or record his or her vocals over your music. There are many ways you can use a no-vocal track to your benefit and profit, so make certain you have a mix of it done.

Other Mixes?

If you are an artist who doesn't have a band, you can go a step further and do a few minus-one mixes. These are mixes that are mixed down without a certain instrument, like the guitar or the drums. These can be given to potential touring players or new players you are considering bringing into the group. Minus-one mixes can also be sold to fans who might want to play along with your songs. You could even hold a contest and have people record themselves and send it into your website or post on social media sites like Fandalism. Call it the "Guest Guitarist Contest" or something along those lines. As always, do something a little different that might drum up some media attention and excitement.

The Backups

Now you have all of the mixes and you're ready to take these songs to the industry in as many ways possible. Take the final step to make sure you have your backups organized. Make copies and save them in different locations. Make hard copies and keep them in a different physical location, like your parents' house or your Aunt Dorothy's guest room closet. That way, if anything were to happen to your hardware and your copies, you still have a backup somewhere else. I also recommend having downloads available on private pages or password-protected pages of your website so that if something is requested, it can immediately be sent.

Having backups of the album as a whole and of each song can make things much faster if you receive requests for the studio tracks. That means having a separate backup for each song so you can send the discs or the files for just that song. If you really want to be prepared and you have a good amount of space on your website, have a compressed file of the song so that someone could download it after an agreement is made for licensing. At the very least, have the tracks ready for FTP. When you show how professional and prepared you are with all these different mixes and then can top that off by delivering immediately, you're setting yourself apart.

SONG TITLES

Oftentimes all the little things make the big things work better. Many of the details that are often ignored can add up to a heavy weight that will hold you back from going as far as you want to go.

One of those small things is the song title. As you finish and release your album, EP, or song, make sure the name of the song is always the same. This will help with search optimization around the web, uniformity of the song names, and better recognition both from a fan and marketing standpoint. It will also keep things clear around copyrights and publishing.

A common mistake is to list songs in abbreviated ways, such as only the first two words of the title or some kind of acronym. These songs may have been written years ago and have been with you for what feels like forever, but for most they're brand new. Just as you need to brand your music and your band, you also need to brand the songs.

If you have a song called "Off the Counter Jazz," make sure it's written out correctly everywhere it's listed. From the download to the CD to the website to the posters, make sure it's always complete and full. Don't abbreviate in blogs or anywhere else you're writing about the song. Even if you're posting samples in places, make sure to use the full name. Don't use "Off," "Counter," "Off Jazz," or any other alteration.

Try to keep your song titles under seventy characters as an SEO strategy for having the title picked up easier in the search engines. If you have samples, a video, a blog, or a photo that is titled with that song name and has all the keywords and content written well, it will optimize much faster than a song with a longer title.

The more the song is seen correctly and written out fully, the more it will optimize online and be recognized by fans, potential licensing groups, and other profitable avenues. If the name is the same across the board, there is a lower chance of issues arising around legal matters, royalties, or even plagiarism. It's a small thing, but it's one more task that can help you in the long run. Decide the names of the songs and stick to them.

TRACK ORDER: CREATING THE BEST FLOW AND MOTION FOR THE FINISHED SONGS

Have you ever listened to a song on the radio and as soon as it's done, you can't help but hear the next track in your head? Do you ever have to play an album all the way through because anything short just wouldn't be right? Can you hear that beginning or ending of those songs and know, almost to the second, the space between the songs? That's the sign not only of a great band and great songs but also of a great compilation and formation of the songs on an album.

In our world of digital downloads, EPs, single releases, and demos, we've lost a lot of the beauty and structure of an album. It's more than just the songs; it's how they're laid out. This is the last step before you master the recording.

When you choose and go to record your songs for an album, even after all the basic song preparation and preproduction, there's still a world of things to go over and review before, during, and after the recording. You need to address the marketing and promotion of the recording and the songs themselves. This is what I call internal music marketing: the layout of the album, EP, or compilation, which includes the actual order of the songs and how each song ends and leads into the beginning of the next one.

The goal is to draw in listeners and keep them listening. Pulling the listener into hearing the album, EP, or compilation of songs all the way through brings him or her closer to you and your body of work as a whole, which is rare these days with attention spans being shorter than ever.

The best approach is to create a blueprint before recording. Make sure that you have a variety of keys, motion in the tempos, and feels, as well as a number of different intros and outros to make sure that everything does not sound the same. This goes for the smallest EP or the longest album. If you are releasing small runs of three to four songs every few months, see if you can give a flow and order to them that can lead in and out of each release.

Intros and Outros

Make sure that each of the intros has its own touch and originality. While some intros may sound close to each other, make sure there is something about each of them that distinguishes the intro to each particular song. The body of the song will speak for itself, but it's about making those decisions on how to lead the ear in and out of them.

Don't let the first five seconds and the last five seconds of every song sound exactly the same. Listen to the beginnings of every track as you skim across a CD or your iTunes. Make sure that if someone other than you listens to only the first five seconds, they do not think that every song starts or ends the same.

Fade-ins, drum fills, hook lines, selective instruments playing before the rest of the band joins, accent patterns, samples, and loops are just a handful of ideas to try. The same goes for outros. You can do the fade-outs, ending accents, whatever you want.

The Final Order and Heading off to Mastering

Jump a couple of steps forward: You have your album recorded, you're in final mix, and you're getting to the decisions about the actual order of the songs. This is where it gets fun. Don't shortcut this part or just toss out a list. As I mentioned before, the order and the layout can help keep the ear listening throughout.

First, think of the creative element. Is there a storyline inside the album? Is there a method or motion that you started with or developed through the recording? Look at those songs and how they move.

Second, think technically. Make a list on a whiteboard of each song. List the following:

- Song name
- Intro
- Outro
- Key
- Tempo
- Feel/groove/style

Seeing this list in front of you can put things in a different perspective and help you make decisions.

Also, get the producer or engineer to make you a recording of the first fifteen seconds in and the last fifteen seconds out of each song. Take home that disc or fifteen-second digital in-and-out cuts and load it on your computer or smartphone, then move the order around to see what feels the best. This way you can spend a lot more time on playing with the order options outside of the studio, which will give you the time to make decisions and play around without spending studio time and money.

There are many approaches for deciding where the strongest song should go in a record. Some say track two, some say track three, and some say track one. There are a lot of ideas on how you should kickstart the recording and how you should close it. You can research online about different approaches. This is a very personalized and customized stage. It is not about learning the best way, but rather taking options into consideration and seeing what feels best for you and your group.

The obvious bullet points are to draw the ear in fast, so I don't think the first song should be a long one. It should be a grabber, something that will make people want to hear more. In the same way, with the last song, sometimes a long fade or a long song that carries the ear away can be effective. It all comes down to making the decisions that give the album the motion and personalized touch you want.

While I prefer back-to-back songs to have different keys, some tunes work well moving from one song to another in the same key. Take the time to set up the recording in the order you want it and play around with it to see what flows the best.

Finally, have fun with the order. Have some friends who are completely outside of the recording come over to listen and give their thoughts on the order. Take some time and treat it like a puzzle. See what kind of picture the different orders can create for you; then choose the order and head to mastering.

PATIENCE IN THE POSTPRODUCTION PHASE: PREPARING FOR THE BEST RELEASE

One of the hardest points in any recording is the postproduction and release phase. How do you actually choose the release date? When is everything ready, and how will you release? Do you have a plan to make the release work for you and your group in order to gain quickly the highest amount of visibility? Oftentimes none of these questions is answered or even considered; that failure can drastically hurt the potential of the release, initial sales, and marketing.

Most commonly, I see bands get the discs back from the duplicators, and whatever day that is becomes the release day. Another example is that as soon as iTunes or TuneCore has the songs available, that is release day. CDs start going out, you are live on iTunes, maybe a CD release party occurs, but it's not much more than a normal show, and the only additional element is that it's called a CD release party.

The most effective releases have a plan behind them. Just as you prepared to record your album and worked on the tracking and mixing with a great attention to detail, you have to finish the project with the same level of focus and commitment. I often see the great work ethic of an artist through the preproduction and recording process dissolve as soon as the recording is completed. Laziness sets in, and sometimes an ego builds with expectations that the recording is so good it will get out there and sell without any marketing, promotion, or branding. The music will just sell itself!

Actually, the postproduction, release, and continued push of marketing, branding, and promotion is the most intense and the longest phase of an album. This is where you have to balance out normal life, playing, practicing, touring, relationships, and everything else while keeping a consistent level of marketing.

Is your promotional package ready? Do you have a press release that can go out nationally? Do you have digital and online sales systems ready to launch on the day of your release? Do you have a special or discount for the release day or a sale for the first so many physical copies, secondary merchandise pieces, or downloads sold? Do you have a basic marketing and advertising plan to hit different markets around the country, even if it's just a couple of ads or social media posts? If you have money to buy small ads or basic insertions for certain websites or social media sites, great; but have you set up an advertising plan to be as effective as possible with your budget over a series of months? Do you have a daily plan for postings and updates on the web across your website, social media pages, and other music sites around the Internet? Are they organized for different cities, colleges, and music genres and for music reviewers, bloggers, and other music media? Do you have your secondary merchandise, such as hats, shirts, and stickers, ready for sale?

If you have not answered yes to all these questions, take a step back. Of course there's a certain amount of money that's required, but the marketing and advertising plan does not have to be over the top. The press release should be national if you want a realistic amount of respect and attention from the media. You should have all your ducks in a row for the most effective release.

> One of the biggest differences I see in artists who succeed over the artists who fail is that when faced with a massive, time-taking, pain-in-the-ass task or challenge, the ones who suck it up, drive ahead, and get right to work are the ones who seem to achieve success, as opposed to the ones who try to find ten ways to make it easier, spend time bitching, or try to modify the challenge.
>
> The ones who procrastinate, complain, wish things weren't a certain way, or put energy into blame end up getting nowhere. In the end, they waste time and effort, and most lose the end result of the desired success.
>
> When you got shit to do, do it. Don't go on to Facebook or grab a drink and bitch about what has to be done; just do it.

Tens of thousands of albums were released last year on a larger scale; this does not include all the independent releases put out under the radar. So how are you going to stand out? How can you be seen in the sea of music?

The answer is actually simpler than you think. Be patient. Think of the postproduction and release with the same mindset that you thought about the recordings. Pull together everything for promotional and marketing support to give the release the best chance to shine and be seen in the strongest way possible. Find a way to stand out, be seen, and, even more important, be purchased.

Releasing a disc or a set of downloads that doesn't have support in marketing, branding, and promotion is a bit like releasing a song that's not fully tracked or is unmixed and unmastered. You wouldn't rush through one of your songs to just to get it out, would you? So why rush the process that will get the same song out to the most people, the most reviewers, and the most media possible?

Get it all in order and then release. People are used to seeing another band releasing another disc or another collection of downloads; it happens every single day. Take the steps to make yours memorable and recognizable on a scale that will help build and grow your popularity and your sales while helping to create a long-term buzz that will reach more and more people over time.

> Ignorance, arrogance, fear, and laziness are the biggest hurdles to success. From what I have seen in my twenty-plus years in the business, those who continue to learn, watch for the changes and trends, never get too cocky, push through with courage, and truly commit to their goals always succeed.
>
> This went for me as well. Every time I failed, one of those first four elements played a role in it.

COMPLACENCY RIGHT BEFORE AND AFTER THE RELEASE: AVOID IT!

You have created a recording and the support materials to promote, market, brand, and advertise the release and the group. You have taken the right steps to set up all the supplemental contracts and distribution. Your solicitation materials are organized and prepared to push your music to international markets, television, advertising, video games, and potential movie licensing and placement. Let's also say you're now ready to solicit to higher-level distributors, touring agents, managers, and labels who could help push you forward. This is a great place to be and a lot of hard work has been done to get to that place. Unfortunately this is where so many artists begin to make the mistakes that can jeopardize and ruin a career.

Even though artists do things the right way to create the right product or music, an unfortunate trend can still occur: Laziness, complacency, and arrogance can set in. Once the CD comes back from pressing and the release date nears, or even as early as basic postproduction, things can change for the worse.

> There are many paths to success and many people out there telling you to go this way or that way. Trying to listen to everyone or not committing to a path will keep you from ever leaving your front door.
>
> Research, study, plan, and choose a strategy. Then do it! You can make changes along the way, but if you do not have a plan of your own to follow, you will never create a solid foundation.
>
> Picture an architect who has a great set of blueprints. Some changes can be made, even after the building has started, with little to no problem, but if that same architect has no plan and a hundred people telling him a hundred different things, the structure will never be built.
>
> Commit to your goals. Make a plan. Execute!

The problem is that the postproduction phase needs to be treated with the same effort, the same attention to detail, and the same kind of problem solving that made the earlier phases work so well. I've discussed different methods of promoting, booking, advertising, and marketing. These are all elements that have to receive the same attention and effort as the recording and the music. This, unfortunately, is where many artists decide to take the short-cuts. They stop following the budget set in place in the business plan. Some of these artists become a little arrogant, figuring that "it will happen" or "this is going to break through." This complacency sets up the project for failure in the long run. This is also why labels and managers drop artists even when they're handling a great deal of the media and marketing.

Just as you need to practice to learn and maintain your abilities on your instrument, you need to practice and perform in postproduction and the release phase. You have to continue to work or you will lose your proficiency. Don't put together the best package you can and then just relax. This is actually where the most work begins. It's true that having a product of industry caliber will give you an exponentially greater chance of success, but it takes that last step of making sure you're doing every single thing you can do.

Just think of an amazing band that pops out of nowhere. You get into them and pick up all their older materials. You wonder how they could have become such an overnight success and yet have been around for so long. It really is simple: The best bands, the best packages, and the best look can't be seen if they're not being brought to the public in all the proper ways. Today there's less money being put into artists, and there are excessive numbers of artists doing it the wrong way. However, doors open for artists who are showcasing themselves in the best way possible.

It's your responsibility to apply all of the skills you have developed in getting the recording and project this far: professionalism, work ethic, and intensity. You need to continue and apply them to through postproduction and ongoing efforts after the release. Even with success, you will have to maintain your career.

Be prepared, be patient, and be ready financially, technically, creatively, and emotionally, and you will make the most out of every studio session. Look down the road to what the release of the album can do, and prepare all the supplemental elements of secondary revenues such as licensing, no-vocal versions, and backing vocal or karaoke versions. Think about what you can bring from the studio experience—pictures, stories, and videos—to the promotion and marketing of the recording.

Those whose mindset embraces the widest array of possibilities will get the most results, from both the music and the marketing, to make the sales and get the gigs. Those who think in this way will save a lot more money and have a lot more to work with. Those who don't will need to spend more money backtracking to get second no-vocal mixes, shoot additional footage, and whatnot. The more you can get out of every session, the farther you can take it.

The reality is that the postproduction and release will be the most expensive phase of the project. Make sure you have either saved up the cash or are using the product to find the funding from investors or crowd funding to be able to release the end product with the attention it deserves. The final stage of getting back the master and getting ready to release it to the world is the place where the most artists fail. Don't be one of them.

CLOSING THOUGHT

Are you sure you are done? Along the journey of the recording, make sure you are capturing all the elements that you might not be directly using for the album.

Don't get rid of the bloopers: They can be used as marketing content, just as pictures in the studio or video can. While you are recording "the album" or "the product," make sure you are taking advantage of all the marketing and promotional content that can be created in the process. From studio journals to fun stories and whatever, you have so much more to work with to promote and to sell than just the full album, EP, or individual songs. Make sure to schedule time for those non-vocal versions; cut the nice fade-ins and fade-outs for samples while you are there. Burn the best demo and sample cuts for promotional and booking use.

Those artists who take all those considerations to heart in the recording studio process leave the studio with an array of products with the best chance in an industry that is giving fewer and fewer chances every day.

Preparation in preproduction leads to the best studio experience. This ends in having the recording that you are proud of, which then needs to be followed by the most productive steps to release that recording the right way, which includes the necessary funding.

You gave your all to the recording; make sure you give your all to getting that recording to everyone you possibly can with the most possible options for success.

8

FUNDRAISING AND INVESTORS

OPENING THOUGHT

Can you afford to bootstrap your plans for success by yourself, without investors? Probably not, without a solid fan base, a marketing structure, and branding in place.

Even with crowd funding, you have to budget past the recording; you need that initial tour budget in place to get out on the road.

You can make the choice to not borrow and try fundraising on a much more grassroots level. But again, you must be aware of all your needs, especially if you are trying to begin a career. It's like opening your own small business; most need a small business loan to start.

To increase your chances for funding, you must organize your branding and have a solid music business plan.

Artists who have nothing prepared, nothing organized, and need all sorts of support from the label or management group usually end up signing contracts that leave them with very little control over their own destinies—those lucky few who are offered contracts in the first place, that is. On the other side of the coin, the more prepared you are and the more you work to stay in primary control, the less of a risk you will be for a label, manager, or investor, and the better the chance that you will get the support you need while being able to achieve a profit point where everyone benefits.

FROM CROWD FUNDING TO MUSIC BUSINESS LOANS

Gone are the days when you could put out a demo, get signed, and then have someone else do everything for you. That's not really bad news, though; to be in control, maintaining your own rights to your work, is a much smarter way to go. The more you can prepare in advance before going to representation, the less percentages you will to have to give up. The smaller a risk you are to a label or industry organization, the better your chances of getting a more favorable deal.

However, this does require you to set up a thorough budget, one that includes not only getting the album done, but getting it released in the best way. You must also think not only about success for you and your album but also about the return on investment for your funders. Nickel-and-dime budgets that overlook sales, promotion, marketing, and maximized revenue potential are the biggest mistake most musicians make.

We covered music business plans in chapter six; this all-important first product provides the blueprint for building your success. Now we're ready talk about the actual nourishment for your plan, the sustenance that will prevent it from withering on the vine before it can grow: finding the actual funding.

You may have heard the saying: "It is easier to get a loan for $250,000 than it is to get one for $25,000." You probably thought, "That is absurd," right?

Wrong.

Those who go after the smaller money often have an improperly budgeted plan that doesn't take into consideration all the elements or address all the risks the bank or the investors will have. This also goes for the crowd-funding artists who say they only need $10,000 for an album, not taking into consideration the much larger amounts needed to ensure success, return on investment, and profit for a project.

Can you do an album for ten thousand or less? Sure. Can you market, promote, distribute, tour, and advertise an album for that? Highly doubtful. All these other very necessary steps to success can still cost upwards of a quarter-million dollars in today's business.

Let's look at another angle. Say you put together an effective music business plan and are looking to find an investor, investment firm, record label, or management group to launch you and a recording. As a conservative estimate, let's say we set up a two-year budget of $400,000. Yeah, it costs that much—even scaled back.

You create the music business plan for the recording, the marketing, the release, and the launch of this artist, taking all line items into consideration while still being conservative.

The next step is crucial. Put yourself in the shoes and the mindset of the investor. If a band or artist was coming to *you* and asking for this kind of money, what would you want to know to feel secure and safe in your investment? You'd want to know things such as:

- Who you are investing in and who will control the investment and accounting?

- When you are going to get your money back?

- What is the marketing and sales plan for the band to pay back the investment and ensure the profit?

- Where do all the elements currently stand for production, promotion, marketing, and branding? Does this artist need additional development first?

- Why is this a good investment, and why will this have the best chance at success?

- How much profit will you see, for how long, and how many other people have their hands in this project?

That $400,000 music business plan—with all the elements laid out, including an intense focus on the marketing and financial success of the project—gives you as an investor a bit more comfort, doesn't it? If you consider your concerns and the risk of the investment, your chances of recouping that money you invested, and the likelihood for the success of the project, it's nice to see a budget that has taken everything into consideration, even if it comes with a pretty considerable price tag.

Now, by comparison, let's go back to our earlier theme and assume you're being asked for only $10,000 to finish and put out an album. Ask yourself the same questions as above, but now looking at a $10,000 budget. How is this $10,000 album going to be released, marketed, distributed, or promoted? If none of these things happen, how will you get back your money? What kind of profit could you reasonably expect from an album with no marketing, promotional, or touring support?

To be very clear: Most artists who try to "bootstrap" too much of their budget are not going to reach a sustainable or successful level with their release. Though many artists are convinced that the "once they hear it" scenario will allow success, they seem to forget that it takes marketing for people to hear it. If you record the greatest album in the world, spending a fortune on the studio, the producer, the overdubs, and the mix, but leave no funds to release, market, and promote the album, how will people find it?

A record label has the team, the investors, and the marketing staff to create the music business plan, hire the people from the start to finish for the recording, and then spend the bulk of the time, effort, and money to get the band and the product out to the world and become profitable. A record label's goal is to get back all the money they put into the project plus a very high percentage of profit so they can build up their coffers for more projects and more profit. That is the business model of the larger scale labels, and it has been that way for decades.

Many bypass that model, taking a more independent road, but they still need to take care of all the things that a record label would be doing. I certainly believe in the do-it-yourself approach, but even if you are doing it yourself, you will still need people who have to be paid. There really is no such thing as a completely independent artist—unless, of course, you are already wealthy.

However, if you're doing a project that includes a full music business plan, it's very possible to acquire all capital needed from investors. It may be a little more challenging to fully finance through crowd funding, because the number is going to be larger. However, to have part of a budget set for crowd funding can still work very well.

Is it possible to do it on less? Is there a chance that you can be heard and either launch your own product or achieve backing from a label, management, or investors to bring your product to market on the scale you want with no money out of your own pocket? Yes, but the chances are about like those of a high school athlete who expects to get rich by turning pro, and it often doesn't have anything to do with how good you are. As I mentioned at the beginning of the book, if your plan is for magic to happen—to have others swoop you up in a helicopter to the top of the mountain, funding your project or putting you out on the road instantly—you'd better be prepared to see what life is like behind the curtain. The Great and Powerful Oz of the music industry tends to be not so great and far from powerful.

And remember: The "fast track" to cash or funding through a label, manager, or private investor will also be the most costly in percentages and rights. Many of those who took the quick route lost everything they gained, and many have gone bankrupt. Others are still being sued by their labels, managers, and investors.

So, do a 180: Look from an investor's or donor's point of view. In fact, let's take a closer look at what that potential investor is thinking about while you're making your pitch for capital.

1. **Does the artist have a music business plan?** A funder wants to see that the artist is organized, professional, and paying attention to detail with a plan that shows how the project can be executed correctly and come to fruition. The numbers may be bigger, but they take into consideration the requirements for the marketing necessary in today's music business. When an investor sees an artist who has realistic numbers instead of bootstrapping at every level, his or her feeling of risk is reduced and the funder's confidence in the project is reinforced.

2. **Does the artist have a clear solicitation strategy for investors and fundraising?** Savvy artists work with a consultant or a development team to learn the most effective, productive, and protective ways to obtain capital without losing the hefty percentages normally associated with recordings and the older models. With the organization, preparation, and plan in place for how to solicit in the most effective ways, the artist will have the confidence to achieve the budget without being taken advantage of.

3. **Is the artist working to raise capital from the fewest sources?** Artists need to be empowered to stay in control and not be abused by the industry. With a plan that includes budgets to buy out services such as the studio, the producer, the photographer, the videographer, the graphic designer, and other expenses that are often reduced by percentages, the artist retains a larger percentage of ownership of the project.

4. **Does the artist have the full spectrum of sales, licensing, and performance built into the plan?** This point is important for sales, crowd funding, or donations. It shows that many more avenues and options are available to make profits than just sales of the download or the disc itself. This also highlights how an investor may see a faster return.

5. **Does the artist possess a reasonable foundation of industry knowledge and the problem-solving skills needed to make responsible career decisions?** Donors and investors want to be involved with a project that is organized and optimized for the widest array of choices and ideas to create success. They want to see that the artist has been educated on potential situations that can arise and how to handle them in the best and most responsible ways possible.

6. **Is the recording and all related marketing, branding, and promotional material being created simultaneously?** A recording being made with all supporting materials prepared gives a potential investor or donor the faith that the right steps are being taken to improve the chances of success. This also shortens the final mix-to-release stage, meaning that everyone can start seeing money faster. This is opposite of the groups who wait till the recording is done and then begin to rush through marketing and, all too often, put out the release prematurely.

And these questions are just the start. We haven't even scratched the surface of justifications as to why someone should donate or invest in your project. It all starts with reading through your plan and pulling out the points that strike you as the strongest. It's up to you, the artist, to solicit and raise funds. You must find the right way to explain the concept to each person, business, or contact you approach. The same can be said if you decide to go to a label.

Each potential donor or investor should be approached in a personal way that addresses him or her specifically. Don't try to create a cookie-cutter template of a letter, a pitch, or an approach; customize for the specific contact.

I won't tell you that it's easy to obtain funds; it's a great challenge. However, if you have the attention to detail, the drive, and the ability to problem-solve, adapt, and try things that are not always the most comfortable, you will succeed. Actually, all those traits are needed to succeed in music anyway, so this a great stepping-stone toward creating the product you need as it prepares you for an industry in which you will have to apply all the above traits over and over again. Why not start now?

> The key steps to problem solving any issue in music: honor, realism, drive, patience, and commitment. If you can say and live the following, you will fix any hurdle. In facing a problem, I am
>
> - honorable enough to admit there is a problem;
>
> - realistic enough to realize that if I don't make changes, it won't go away;
>
> - driven enough to get organized so it won't get any worse;
>
> - patient enough to know that some problems will require a lot of time to fix; and
>
> - committed enough to give every ounce of effort to correcting, fixing, repairing, or solving the issue.

CROWD AND FAN FUNDING: FINDING YOUR BUDGET THROUGH FANS

It's funny, great, and sad all at once how fan funding and crowd funding websites have progressed in the past few years. I started using the process of fan funding with some of my clients as far back as 2002, and it was an easier sell, because very few were doing it. Now, with websites such as Kickstarter and PledgeMusic, as well as different ways to donate directly, fan funding has taken center stage. Still, it presents serious problems due to the popularization of social networks and the hundreds of thousands of bands who are now taking this approach.

There are also some misconceptions with crowd funding that need to be addressed. The recent success of Amanda Palmer is a case in point. People went wild when she raised over a million dollars for her "independent record" through Kickstarter. Social media lit up as everyone proclaimed that "we have arrived" at fan funding.

But Amanda Palmer had already been part of a major label group. In the past ten years, Amanda Palmer has amassed and developed an incredible fan base. She has had songs in the charts, played in front of millions, and, by the scale of most musicians, had already made it big. (Many of those same bloggers attacked her when she was asking for musicians to play for free, but that is a whole different story.)

The point is that when Palmer reached out for fan funding, she had a very large audience to tap, and she made her goal. Please understand, I am thrilled for her and for her album, which she will retain control over. She is going to do very well with that. But some bloggers out there are yelling about Amanda being an "independent" artist and how great it is for independent artists to start their careers like this. All the new artists with relatively small fan bases who think they can copy Amanda Palmer's model and expect the same results need a serious reality check. Apples and oranges don't compare well.

Another problem is that artists often seem to be throwing small, unrealistic numbers at dart boards and telling fans that's all they need to make the album that will bring them to the masses and give them fame and fortune. Usually, the number is way under what is really required, and many of these projects don't get funded and either fail to see the light of day or fall apart right out of the gate.

Some artists are just trying to make a recording for a smaller fan base on a shoestring budget or are creating a product for the fun of it. If it is a hobby or a release on a local level, this approach is fine. Yet it can cause issues when artists are pushing for a bigger project and a larger level of success. The music business is a crapshoot, but whether you are taking the fan-funding route or you are a fan who is funding an artist, the devil is in the details—or in the lack of details.

From the Fan Standpoint

So you've received a request to help out a band or an artist. First off, if you are not doing it out of the kindness of your heart or as a friend, you might want to reconsider doing it at all. Most fan-funded projects are underbudgeted and lack the organization to attain sustainable success levels, leaving many donors wondering what happened. Also, a new problem has arisen in which some of these sites will pay out what is raised even if the goal is not met, taking the money and the project into a very gray area.

It is fine to help out as a friend or a fan, but have a realistic view. Watch out for promises that might seem over the top. And if someone tells you they are going to give you a tax write-off for a donation, make sure they actually have a 501(c)(3) nonprofit associated with the project. Many artists are painting much larger pictures and trying to come off more organized than they actually are. This can come back to bite you in the end. So, if you are a funder, find out the information you need to know; if you are a friend who is just there to help, then be that friend.

For the Artists Looking for Cash

A lot of you out there want the same thing. So how are you standing out? I get at least four fan-funding requests a day. Most of them consist of very simple emails or messages through Facebook or Twitter with no details and all-too-common phrases:

- "Help me finish my recording so I can take it to the top."
- "Donate to my Kickstarter."
- "Give to my Kickstarter."
- "Help me finish the album."
- "PLZ donate 2 the band."

These are oversaturated, overused phrases that everyone is putting out there. Google "donate to my Kickstarter" and you will find over a million different results, all saying the same thing. Add some details if you want to get the dollars!

The bulk of these come as mass emails—practically spam. Seriously, people? I'm not even a fan or, for that matter, friends with the bulk of these artists on any social media networking site. I also find it interesting how the goal is always an even and round number. This brings up suspicions as well, especially when no budget or details are attached or offered. These artists usually explain how all they need is this or that amount and their careers will just take off. As I hope you understand by now, it takes much more than just finishing an album or a "guestimate" number to find the funds you will need. Unless, of course, you have very, very rich friends.

So what do you do? Take a more personalized approach. Set yourself apart by, for example, giving something back: not just a prize or an album for the donor, but maybe a percentage of the project and merchandise to a charity or nonprofit. Use a philanthropic approach: A percentage of every sale of the product goes to a charitable organization. This can entice donors to give to your project. It is good to give back *and* it's good marketing as well.

Successful fan funding is all about the details, the organization, the preparation, and the execution of what you are going to do with the money and not just asking for a number that you think will cover it all. Create a letter describing a well-planned budget, or give the bullet points out of your music business plan: what you have already done and are doing prior to funding in order to move things forward. Personalizing your solicitation or pitch letter shows a rare attention to detail. Of course on your Kickstarter page, Indiegogo, or your own website, you will have to create the sample and template pitch for the web. Still, the more personalized the letter to those you are reaching out to, the better your chance of getting some kind of donation for the project.

Kickstarter

Do you really think that as soon as you put out an album and have a CD release party that every person showing up is going to buy a copy and then run to the Internet to market it to every single person in the world? Even if you have friends or local fans who decide to share your iTunes link, like your band page, or copy a post about your recording, do you not realize it is being lost in the sea of social media oversaturation of so many other bands doing the exact same thing?

So, just going onto Kickstarter and asking for enough to finish the album or enough to make a certain number of copies is not the most effective route to go. If you are not taking into consideration the promotional costs to get the word out about the recording, you are tying your hands and not reaching the audiences that can make this product sell. Note that larger organizations budget albums on a 20 to 80 ratio: 20 percent to make the album, 80 percent to market it.

For Kickstarter or any of the fan-funding sites, I advise allocating one piece of your budget rather than the whole number needed. For example, what if you did a fan-funding campaign to fund online ads for three months? Or for the basic budget to get a tour started? What about Kickstarting your merchandise line or pressing a certain number of discs, buying so many download cards, or hiring a publicist for a one- or two-month period?

In other words, view Kickstarter or any of the fan-funding sites as a kick-start approach to a *part* of your whole budget. Rather than presenting yourself as needing ten thousand dollars and you are on your way, set up a campaign for one section and one requirement. This will enhance confidence in things being completed and, while more money will need to be found down the line, at least you are taking positive steps to get there.

THINKING OUT OF THE BOX FOR OTHER WAYS TO PUT CASH IN THE BOX

While fan funding and investors are the most common approaches, there are other avenues to bring in money, push sales, and create interest in your project. Fundraising events, raffles, and even garage sales can be innovative approaches. Look around online and in your town or city: How are sports teams, high schools, and other groups approaching the idea of raising capital? Also, visit http://fundraising.com/ and look at all the creative resources and all the various products you could be selling to raise money for your project. Imagine the band selling chocolates; how often have you seen that? Remember, the more you stand out, the deeper you research, and the more creative you get in fundraising, the better your chances for achieving your goal.

Bartering: Trading Your Services for What You Need

In this economy, many people are finding their bank accounts, wallets, and savings a lot leaner lately. If money makes the world go round, the earth has been turning a lot slower lately for most folks.

Unfortunately, waiting until the recession ends or for the economy to right itself is a passive and ineffective approach for aspiring professional musicians. You still need to find ways to move forward. Bartering can help professional musicians find other ways to help each other get the word out despite lean times. Instead of sitting back in a dark place thinking about all the money you need to pay for the things you need, why not think about what skills, abilities, or services you could potentially barter with someone who may have some of the skills, abilities, or services you need? Bartering is an excellent way to work directly with other individuals, to build community, and to create networking ties—while still accomplishing the things you need.

It's all about supply and demand. Sit down and think about what you can do and what it's worth. Take the time to write down and review what you know and think about people who may have a need for those services. Make sure those people have a service or services that you need yourself. Does your band need a website, and you happen to know another band with a member who designs websites? Maybe someone in your group is a plumber by day and you know the house another band lives in is having plumbing problems. This is a perfect fit where both parties can help each other and save money at the same time.

Offer and Ask

Reach out to other bands, fans, and friends. Talk about what you need: web work, flyers, recording, mastering, editing . . . or car repair. It does not have to be a trade for two entertainment or music services; it can be anything, just as long as both parties feel there is a fair and well-defined understanding of what is being traded for what. Sit down with the band and brainstorm a list of what you can do and send it to friends, other bands, and people whom you feel might have services you could use in return. Added bonus: This can lead to extensive networking that can help you longterm.

Be Considerate

Be careful about how you ask and how you offer. Some people just don't barter and may be offended at the offer. Just because it may make sense to you doesn't mean it is going to make sense to everybody.

Ask first if they would consider an exchange or trade for services. Would they be open to having a discussion about bartering? Is there something they need or are looking for? Be assertive but not aggressive and make sure that what you are offering is truly worth what you are looking for in return. For example, if you are a beginner web designer and you are asking a professional mastering engineer to barter for services, show some class and offer a lot more time and extra design time to make it balance fairly. Consider the experience and reputation of the person you are hoping to barter with and make sure that the barter for both sides is equivalent; if not, make sure you are supplementing fairly, either by doing a little more work or even paying a very small fee to make it feel like a fair and even trade.

Get It in Writing

Let's say you reach an agreement with someone to barter and trade services that both of you need. You are getting something you need without the cost of paying for it and the other party is receiving the same. Make sure to put it in clear and concise writing. Many relationships, personal and professional, have ended due to lack of communication, clarification, and under-standing of the other's expectations. Consider your actions, the service, and formalize your agreement on the invoice. While no money is being exchanged, you are still being paid. Make sure to clearly identify what services are being exchanged and the extent of those services. Cover the circumstances of potential "overtime." Clearly describe and make sure you know the expected outcomes. Make absolutely certain to get all of this in writing in order to avoid conflict and maintain the relationship.

Just because the economy is in a hole doesn't mean you have to skimp on the things you need. Network! Communicate with people and businesses you know and those you don't. Be prepared for rejections, because there will be many. But those rejections will also open the doors for acceptances. Do not be offended and do not try to sell or push people. If someone says they do not barter or do not need any of your services, ask them if they know anyone who does. Get the word out about what you have to offer and what you need. Keep moving your career forward; reach out to find those whom you can help while they in turn help you. And hey, if you think you have something I could use or a service you think I would benefit from, drop me a note. I am open to bartering, too.

Raffles: Getting Fans and Strangers Involved Using Prizes

Many different types of organizations and individuals use raffles for fundraising. Collecting items to raffle is often a very good start to a fundraising campaign, since it can be easier to obtain physical items than a cash donation. It can also be easier to ask people to purchase raffle tickets, which give them the potential to win prizes, whereas a straight donation does not offer any direct return.

Many artists who use the crowd-funding approach find the raffle concept a good place to begin. Throughout a fundraising campaign, you can conduct a number of different raffles. The raffles can build confidence in the fundraising process and your solicitations down the road.

Raffles work especially well with people or businesses who want to know, "What's in it for me?" Some people you approach may see value in your project; however, there are people who want to get something, even if it's only a chance of return. These are the people who will buy raffle tickets.

Think of someone you might want to ask for a hundred dollar donation. This person might easily have the money to give but may not be inclined to simply donate it. But when you present your plan, that person might purchase a hundred dollars in raffle tickets with the hope of winning something, when he or she might have otherwise said no to a straight-up donation.

Raffles can be an effective way to achieve part of your budget goal with an indirect ask for money from those you do not feel comfortable asking directly.

So how do you get the prizes for a raffle? Anyone who has done raffles can tell you; it's a lot easier to ask for items instead of cash. It can also help you build your approach and hone your skills for when you approach investors or ask for cash donations.

Delivering a well-organized music business plan portrays it as a sound investment and increases your chances of receiving a service, item, or gift certificate. This does not cost the donor anything in cash, and many businesses are already set up to give away certain products and/or services to charities, raffles, and benefits.

When looking for items for the raffle, make a quick pitch. Call ahead or email and ask if you can speak with the manager or owner. Ask if it's a convenient time to speak. If you're looking for a gift certificate from a restaurant, walking in on a Friday evening and asking for the chef or owner, well . . . let's just say that would not be smart or respectful.

Schedule a time, be brief, and cover what you're doing, why you're doing it, how you're doing it, and how a donation of a service or product could help you out. Sell yourself and the concept.

Bring a copy of a fundraising letter or press release with you (you should have both of these already if you are raising funds) a copy of your current music, a one-sheet flyer on the band, and maybe a T-shirt or some other kind of merchandise to give them as a thank-you if they are interested and want to help. Point out the cross-marketing that the company will get; tell your contact how you will advertise his or her company. Explain how the business will be mentioned on your website, your social media pages, on posters for the drawing show (if you have one), and in press releases. When an organization sees that you're thinking about how you can bring attention to it in return for its gift to you, you will see a greater response and a better chance at a larger donation or gift. If someone were coming to you with the same pitch, would it draw you in and make you want to help?

Look for services and products in numerous arenas. Restaurant gift certificates are always very popular. Oil changes, even a couple if you can get them, are great. Items where people can choose their prize is also effective, such as are gift cards from any store. Paintings, trinkets, toys, CDs, tools from a hardware store, coffee cards from a local coffee shop . . . Just think of things you'd like.

Services are great, too. Cleaning service, a maid-for-a-day (or a month) service, or car detailing are other good ones. Go to a personal assistant company and see if they will donate a personal assistant for a day. Just brainstorm and the ideas will come. Be creative and you'll find success.

Think about services that the band or you could raffle off. I've seen bands offer themselves as maids for a day. This is a great idea and it's good cross-marketing for the band. Imagine the band cleaning someone's house in maid outfits, calling the local media to talk about the raffle, and having the local newspaper take pictures of the winner and the band cleaning the house or apartment. Raffle off dates with each of the members. My favorite raffle of all time was one where the guitarist of a San Francisco band raffled himself off as the soundtrack guy for a day. He followed the winner around for an entire day with one of those backpacker guitars and provided the soundtrack for a lawyer, who bought fifty dollars' worth of tickets. It was hilarious, it got media attention, and the band was featured in the Arts and Lifestyles section of the local music rag the following week.

You can easily do a series of raffles with different themes. One could be seasonally based, and another could have a music theme. Do a raffle that's all about clothing; raffle off some gift certificates to different clothing stores. Or pitch a number of different restaurants; see if you can get more than one gift certificate. I have a raffle item I tell artists to try to organize called "Eat Out for the Week." This entails a single raffle gift, usually first prize or the solo prize, where the winner receives seven gift certificates to seven different restaurants in town. Since the prize is bigger, you can charge more for those tickets.

Put the prizes together in different raffles and different levels. One raffle could be of a higher level or quantity. More expensive items might be set up as a "VIP Hollywood Raffle." Another can be more affordable items. Before you start, decide when the drawing is going to be or how you are spreading out numerous drawings. Do you want to make it during a show where people will have a final chance to buy tickets and you'll announce the winners there? Do you want to just make an announcement, or do you want to hold it at one of the stores or establishments that has donated? Think creatively of how you will bring the most awareness to your raffles and at the same time get the most tickets purchased. Make sure that when you draw, anyone who purchased has a chance to win. Do not require the winner to be present. It will turn people away and you'll sell fewer tickets. Just make sure you get contact information on each ticket.

Get your friends to help sell the tickets. You can even give them a percentage of sales. For example, if someone sells ten tickets at five dollars, maybe give him or her 10 percent. This can help with getting other people involved in helping you sell the most tickets. Some of the businesses involved in the raffles may also sell tickets at their establishment. Take advantage of every avenue you can find.

Very important: Check the local and state rules regarding raffles. Some states will require that you call it something else, and certain states even consider raffles to be gambling.

Raffles are just one more approach to help you raise the money for your budget. They'll also help you get more comfortable with the basics of fundraising and presenting your pitch.

Garage and Online Sales: One Person's Junk Is Another's Treasure

If raffles won't work for you for whatever reason, sales of donated items through eBay or a garage sale can help you raise cash for part of your recording or postproduction budget. This leans toward the more passive approach but is often very effective in the early stages while you're getting up the confidence to ask for money. Going to friends, family, and various stores to get donated items can help you make the cash you need.

Start with your own stuff. What could you get rid of? Talk to friends; some may not be able to give you money, but they may have old items or things that they were going to get rid of or sell that they might donate to you. It all comes down to how you market the sale of the items.

Hold a musical garage sale, where your band plays while you sell. Try to think up creative concepts that will make your garage sale—or as they call it in New England, a tag sale—stand out in the best way possible. The more creative you are, the more people will come by to check it out. Oh, and by the way, postering telephone poles in a four-block radius is not exactly creative. Be different, be original, be you!

The same goes for online. Post items for sale on your website or on social networks. Put up pictures of the items on Pinterest or take a cool shot of an item and post it on Instagram to make it look that much hipper. Talk about the project and about how the proceeds are going to your recording project. See if you can get some fans to bid for something like an old action figure or toy on eBay. It might even be something that's not worth all that much, but perhaps you can offer the winner something crazy—maybe something involving the album credits. "Thanks to Phil Gent for buying my younger brother's old Lego set." It's a little obscure, but in the end, it might be something that brings a little more media interest your way, which could, in turn, draw in potential investors or donors who were unaware of you before.

What item do you have that you could put a sticker of your band on? Think of different ways to structure the sale and bidding for items. The more original it is, the more attention the items can get and the higher the price they can sell for.

Think about how you want to price things. Setting exact prices can get you just that: exact prices. If you list items with minimum price tags, it allows for the purchaser to buy it but also to potentially donate a little more. List some items as a "you-pick-it price." They can choose the price and they may go a little higher to help you out.

CONVINCING VS. COMMITTING

It takes a driven person, someone almost animalistic, primal, goal oriented, and dedicated to make the dream happen. If you want to be successful today in music or any other business, you must be all these things.

Still, it is interesting how those who claim all the above seem to be putting more of the blood, sweat, and tears into *convincing* people they are, instead of actually *doing what they need to do* to win the prize.

Those who are truly committed to the goal commit all of their energy to the work and the execution of the plan instead of spending too much time, energy, and effort telling everyone just how bad they want it. Commit to being a champion.

THE PASSIVE/SUBMISSIVE APPROACH TO THE ASK FOR CASH

Many artists who fundraise have little or no prior experience in asking for money. With the passive or submissive approach, you can learn how to talk about the project and solicit donations. The idea is to refine your pitch and delivery. Create effective and personalized approaches to discuss the project. When you reach the point of asking for the donation, you take the passive/submissive approach and ask the person you're talking to if he or she knows anyone who would be interested in getting involved. This approach can help get you ready for taking the direct or assertive approach. If your pitch is refined and ready, you'll find that some of the people you approach in this format may want to get involved or donate to the project themselves.

You can also ask for opinions of your pitch and your delivery. This empowers the person you're speaking with. Many times people who are being asked for money feel backed into a corner and uncomfortable, but by asking them what they think of your delivery and how you could improve it, you're allowing them to give their two cents and to feel that they have helped you make your pitch better. Those unwilling or unable to donate get to feel they are still helping you. Regardless of whether you disagree or agree with their critiques or criticism, be respectful and attentive to every idea that they share with you and thank them for their feedback.

Analyze people in order to individualize your pitch. At the same time, take notes and ideas from those who offer feedback. You can refine and hone your pitch for when you're asking others in a more direct and assertive way.

Test your approach. Think about when you feel strongest and when you feel weakest. What reactions from listeners give you an extra boost of confidence? On the other hand, when you felt that they were losing interest, what were you saying and how were you saying it? It's just like music: Every part has to fit together. It has to flow, transition well, and keep the listener's attention. Though it's possible that some of these listeners may give to the project, don't count on it and don't look for it. Take the approach that you're simply asking for their opinions and for suggestions of people who they think might want to be involved.

You're testing the waters. You're talking directly to people about what you're doing and letting them know that you're looking for the money to do it. Think about the marketing points and don't drag it out. Review your plan and work the pitch. Think about how to address each individual. Each person will be different and therefore each approach should be a little different. This is a great chance to build your confidence as you effectively use your time to search out potential donors. Make a list of people you could talk to who would take the time to hear your pitch and see your materials. Again, it's all good training and preparation for the more direct, assertive approaches.

THE ASSERTIVE/CONFIDENT APPROACH IN ASKING FOR MONEY—OR ANYTHING

The assertive/confident approach is the best but also the hardest approach to use when going after money. This is also known as the direct sale. It requires you to be direct, assertive, and confident. As much as people talk about having confidence, security, assertiveness, and overall fortitude, when it comes to asking for money, many find out exactly how little they actually have.

Remember the major selling points of the pitch. You are doing more than asking for money to make an album; you are asking for money to help your project have the best chance of success in the music business. You are taking organized and concise steps with a solid plan of action to see it through to completion.

Read through your music business plan. Gain an understanding of what you're doing from a number of different angles. This will help you to create and refine your pitch. As you practice and individualize your approach, you'll gain the confidence you need to come off as assertive and strong. Believe in yourself, your career path, and the plan you are following. Use strong body language when you're talking to people. Speak in a tone that shows you care about what you're doing without being overbearing. Don't be too loud; that can display a cockiness that will push people away. Conversely, don't speak too softly or mumble and stumble on your words. This will make you seem more nervous and less confident.

Whether asking for money or anything else you need, you should present yourself in the most confident, respectful, assertive, and professional manner possible. Don't talk too fast; don't fidget. Make direct eye contact and be prepared to handle the nos. The confidence you exude will make the potential donor that much more confident in you.

If you're speaking with someone who used to be in the music industry and got screwed over, bring up the points of how you are working to prevent that for your project and your band. If you are talking with an accountant, focus more on the numbers. Focusing on the points likely to draw the most interest from that specific person is more effective than some sort of template.

Give an overview of your plan that hits the marketing points as much as it touches on the business elements. Allow for questions, and write them down in order to have those answers prepared in advance for the next person who may ask them. If people give you a doubtful look and don't know what to say, offer your confidence to them. Ask what they have questions about or what they feel is not clear or well addressed. Regardless of a no or a yes, treat them both like a yes. If people say no, thank them for their time, never losing the confidence in yourself or your ability to achieve the budget for the project. Many times these nos will watch you from a distance and donate later.

Go to any of the numerous fundraising websites. Research tips, quotes, and approaches shared by professional fundraisers. Simply search "fundraising" and you'll see hundreds of websites come up that may be helpful. After each pitch, think about whether it went well or didn't go as you hoped. By treating each pitch not only as a potential donor or investor but also an opportunity to learn, you'll be able to develop stronger pitches.

Visit Kickstarter and other crowd funding sites and do some research on independent artists who are on track to raise their budget. What is something in their pitch that could also work for you? Stick with smaller, independent artists' ideas; trying to copy an established artist's formula can, more often than not, hurt your approach.

If you're sitting down with a number of people, casually address points to each person; don't try to focus on only one person. Dress well, but don't go over the top. If you're a more casual type, wear something that shows you care about yourself and your appearance. Review your music business plan with a prospective investor without spending too long on any one section.

Most of all, deliver your pitch as if you're talking to people who are helping to make your dreams come true, because they are! You're looking for people to help fund your recording, your release, and the necessary materials to make your project successful. Let your dream be fuel for your confidence, assertiveness, and delivery.

Remember, you've played onstage to people who didn't like your music, but that didn't stop you. You kept playing because you knew you could reach new fans, and the more you played, the better the band and the songs got. Fundraising is the same thing. Some people might not give or might not like the plan, but if you view it as a chance to make your pitch that much better, to be able to deliver it in a stronger fashion to someone else who will donate or invest, then you win, whether it's a no or a yes. Be assertive and confident. If you're not naturally that way, learn and practice the skills to gain those traits. It will not only help you in the fundraising, but it will also give you the tools to handle many other aspects of the industry that you will be faced with down the road.

LINE ITEM OR SECTIONAL FUNDRAISING APPROACH: ONE COST AT A TIME

Line item and sectional fundraising can be a smart and more centralized approach for some people. It also depends on the type of person you're approaching for help. Instead of looking for a certain number or monetary amount, the basic idea is to approach potential donors or investors as sponsors, asking them to take care of a section or line item laid out in the budget, pinpointing a direct need instead of going after the larger picture.

For instance, if you had a record that was being recorded in eleven sessions at a studio that costs five hundred dollars a day, you could ask someone to cover one day or a couple of days. You could even go a little further in detail and ask him or her to donate for just the tracking sessions or the vocal sessions. This specified and detailed approach can bring more confidence to potential donors, because not only do you have the big plan and all the large-scale information together but you also have a solid grasp on the costs and an understanding of the small stuff.

Smaller donations could also apply to gas and tolls or food costs for the session. Perhaps you have someone who might pay the session bass player because he's a big fan of the bass. Take a different view of your budget, looking at everything as an individual item that needs to be paid for. You can also offer credit on the recording. For example, I had one artist who had a donor pay my entire fee as the producer for the project. In turn, he ended up getting listed as one of the executive producers on the recording. He was thrilled and even has the album hanging on his wall. The band was thrilled—a chunk of the cost was out of their way, and hey, I was thrilled: I got paid.

This approach can get people more involved in your project and allow friends to team up together to help you. If a group of three people decided to donate the food budget, they could be given the list that is planned for the sessions and either pick up the food and deliver it or even cook certain meals for different days or nights and bring it down to the studio. This way it allows those donors to give financially and also to feel like a part of the project.

Some people may be wary about donating a large amount to be put in a bank account maintained by the artist or band. The concern is the money will be spent prior to the sessions on items not in the budget. In this situation, by going after a specific donation and having the donor pay that exact amount to the person supplying the given service, it can make the donor feel more secure about where that donation is going. Having a money manager for the project can also instill a greater sense of overall confidence in the budget. The money manager handles, tracks, and distributes all the funds—and keeps the money out of the band's hands.

What parts of your budget might appeal more to certain people you know? Who could you go to and ask for help on specific items? What kind of fundraisers could you set up that would directly affect specific parts of the budget?

RALLYING THE TROOPS

When you create an album, you're not doing it alone. It takes a number of people to help you put the pieces together to bring a project to fruition. The same is true for fundraising. You don't have to do it alone, and when you don't, it can be worlds easier. Whether you're in a band and have a group of people to fundraise or you're a solo artist raising funds on your own, bringing in a team of people can help you reach your budget faster. Friends, family members, and even fans can all play a part in what I like to call rallying the troops.

What's in It for Them?

Close friends and family will generally be supportive, especially if you are organized and have the details in place. Those closest to you will do what they can to help; that's what makes them friends and family. However, getting the help of others may require some kind of incentive. It doesn't necessarily make them selfish; it just means that time and resources are often hard to come by and they would be more driven to work on things that offer them some direct benefit.

I advise people to offer a percentage to those assisting with fundraisers. Talk to friends and family about the project and about what you're trying to do. Then tell them that you will give them a particular percentage (of your choosing) for whatever they help raise. Most give 10 percent to friends and occasionally will give larger percentages to individuals who may have access to potential donors who could bring in larger sums. Ten percent is not a lot to give away considering that you are, in a sense, hiring a fundraiser. If a friend were able to take some of your materials and bring it to even two people who both donated $250 dollars, you would end up with $500. Then after giving $50 to the person who found those two donors, you walk away with $450 for your budget. That's $450 that was not there before, raised outside of your networking channels.

Bringing in a team of people you know can speak and communicate well, people who believe in you and understand your goals, can give you a wider spectrum of options and ideas. Just as they can help get the word out to donors, they can also give you ideas for whom to talk to. This larger circle can help transform a cold call into a warm call: someone with whom you have a connection based on common acquaintance.

Sometimes fundraisers who are working for a percentage can get you in the door for a sit-down with a potential donor. Remember, even though you end up making the pitch, the contact was made through someone else, and that person should still receive your chosen percentage.

You can set goals to inspire your helpers. If they raise a certain amount, then the percentage they receive can go up. For example, if someone goes out and finds a thousand dollars total for you over a period of time, you can up his or her percentage as a sign of both gratitude and inspiration.

Certain goals can be set as benchmarks for fundraisers. These could qualify them for certain album credits or titles on the recording. For instance, if someone were to raise a sixth or more of your budget, you could list that person as a coexecutive producer. Some people love the credit and will want to be involved to get the bragging rights. These people can be a great asset to you as you help them live out some of their vicarious music industry dreams.

Remember, the more people you involve, the more resources, names, and contacts are available to you to achieve your budget. The bigger your network, the easier it becomes to spread the word about benefits, raffles, and fundraising shows. The more the word gets out, the more press and marketing will come your way. The more people you have spreading your info to their friends, the more those friends may in turn tell others. It's about building a major network to gain the most contacts to find the donors and investors you need.

Realize that these are the exact concepts and methods you'll need to implement when marketing and promoting your recording once it's completed and released. Reaching out to people to raise money is much harder than reaching out to people to sell and promote your band and product. This funding period will give you a better understanding of how to market and promote more effectively once you release your recording.

KNOW WHEN TO HOLD 'EM AND KNOW WHEN TO FOLD 'EM

Finding donations and investors can be tricky. Still, in today's music business, it takes money to do it right, and most people do not have the budget to correctly take care of the business that an effective release requires. This doesn't mean you need to come up with hundreds of thousands like the bigger labels, but not having a basic budget to cover the items you need can dramatically hurt your chances. You don't need a BMW, but driving a car with only two wheels is going to be a challenge.

Emails, beating the streets, reaching your fans, asking for donations by handing out a CD or download card on the street—you have to put your all into it, but you have to keep it respectful.

For example, while walking down the street a few months ago, a rap duo approached me, and one of the guys had a pitch that was sharp. They were working toward winning a contest and getting out on the road to be on a tour. They were giving out CDs for donations to be able to support themselves out there. I like that: beating the street and pushing for the goal. I explained that I was not in the place right now to help with anything financially, and then he hit me with the second pitch. This wasn't bad; it worked well and he was swift about it. "We aren't looking to get you to pay full price for this; I mean, even five dollars would be great."

That was cool, and I reiterated that I appreciated the pitch and what they were doing. I said, "Look, I can't give you any cash right now, but I do have something you might like." In my laptop bag I had a copy of my book, *The Artist's Guide to Success in the Music Business,* First Edition, and

I asked if they would be interested in a free copy. I told them that I knew it wasn't cash, but they could consider it a twenty-dollar-equivalent donation; I felt this would help those guys some.

The point is that if you put potential funders in an uncomfortable position, you set yourself up for a bad reputation. Show respect, appreciation, and understanding for whom you are talking to. Thank someone if they do something for you, whether giving you a book, saying they are going to push your "ask" on their social network, or passing your request along to someone else. A lot of people might be in a tight spot like you; imagine how you would like to be approached and try to keep that in mind when you are approaching others. Otherwise you are going to burn a potential contact, relationship, or networking opportunity that could have brought you a few steps closer to your goal.

SMALL CASH, PAYPAL, AND ONLINE DONATIONS OR PRESALES

Small donations in cash and through PayPal can amount to much more than you realize. Yes, it's amazing when someone comes at you with $1,000 or even $500. Still, unless you have some very rich friends and relatives, a great deal of your budget will more than likely be raised in very small amounts.

Having a PayPal donation link on your site and your other social networking pages is a great step to getting those small amounts to come in easily. While $5 might not seem like much, fifty donations of $5 amount to $250. In a lot of budgets, that could cover half a day in the studio, a percentage of the food budget, or even a session player to do some tracking or overdubs. You need to look at the big picture and not lock into the concept of trying to raise only large amounts. The most effective fundraising occurs when you're looking at every angle across the board, both small and large.

You can also get the merchant sliders for your smart phones, allowing for someone to swipe a credit card or ATM card on your phone or iPad. If the donation element is an issue, you can also view these transactions as presales, but make sure you are tracking who bought what and what you are responsible for down the line.

Be creative in your approach for small donations. Think about percentages of your budget or parts of it. For example, if the engineer and studio costs a total of $5,000, think about asking people to play a role in studio-time donations of $5. The donors, in turn, can feel as if they're being involved in a direct part of the project. True, it's only one-thousandth of the time, but it adds up. You can also cut it down to closer numbers. For instance, if a studio costs $500 for the day, go after a fundraising campaign for "one-percenters" to be involved in a single day of the recording. It's a small amount, but it can be a lot easier to go after very small amounts from a lot of people than it would be going after only a few people for very large amounts. Yes, we are playing a bit of a pun on the one-percent idea. Laugh, already!

Many have heard about the ad campaigns launched years back where some web designers sold a pixel for $1 and filled up a site with one million little ads and made $1,000,000. This really happened. It was a wild marketing idea and people bought from $1 to $100 in pixels to do their ads. In the span of a year, a number of these sites were filled and the creators made a killing.

What could you sell online for small prices? What can you come up with to do something a little different to capture the donating audience? A woman in Colorado wanted to get out of debt and go back to school; she figured she needed $100,000. With a truckload of work going through chat groups, forums, and anything and everything online, she raised all the money, got out of debt, and went back to school. This was back when social media was still new, but the creativity of her approach is what brought her the donations.

It comes back to the creative marketing approach and looking at things from different angles. The small amounts you raise are just like the small steps you take on the preproduction, production, and postproduction that you have to do every day. These smaller amounts will add up and help to supplement the funding of your budget so you can achieve the goal you have set. Every dollar truly counts, and since it's easier to get one dollar than it is to get a thousand through the smaller channels, you should pay good attention and put good amounts of time into raising the small amounts to achieve your budget and your goal. Just make sure to put it away, save it, and only spend it on the expenses related to the budget for your project.

THE POSTPRODUCTION BLAST: FINAL FUNDING PHASE FOR THE BEST RELEASE

Many artists who fundraise their budgets find it easiest and most manageable to break it down into four segments. This is based on the idea discussed earlier about raising funds through line items.

Segment One: Preproduction

This includes all the costs to get your specific recording plan underway, including the costs for the music business plan and consulting, the fundraising setup, and the beginning of preproduction.

Segment Two: The Recording

This includes all the costs around the recording, from the tracking to the mastering.

Segment Three: The Postproduction

This includes the branding, preparation, and creation of all marketing and promotional materials.

Segment Four: Duplication, Press Release, Promotion, Marketing, Advertising, and Launch

This includes the duplication phase through releasing the recording to the media and the masses. The artists who have completed the first two segments now have a great recording on hand. Oftentimes, they have raised the money to get them to the point of finishing segment two. The masters are in hand, and now the postproduction needs to happen. As we discussed in the previous chapter, the problem at this point is patience. Shortcuts happen all too often here; artists get excited to release quickly, they don't release in the right way, and the chances of success are cut down exponentially.

Just as much effort needs to be applied to the postproduction segments; the money you have set into the plan needs to be raised to make this step happen appropriately. In the postproduction phase, you still have the plan, but you also have the product. You have the recording you made; you have proof that you were able to stay within budget. You have shown that you're well past the 75 percent mark of doing exactly what you set out to do.

This fact alone can be a major help in finding the final backing you require. Take the approaches you used before and add the element of an actual recording that a potential investor or donor can hear.

With the business plan and the recording, you can show what you've done and how you've reached the mark. This will bring a higher level of confidence than earlier in fundraising, because you've already executed a majority of the plan and now have a product. Some investors and donors feel safer about being involved in a project that's almost done, as opposed to giving in the early phases. When you show that you're looking for the exact funds to put out the release properly, including marketing, promoting, and advertising, you show that your ducks aren't only in a row, but they're already quacking away.

The money you're asking for now is to put out the recording that you've already completed. Investors and donors who wanted to see progress first now can see that you're almost there. You still have to apply the different elements of the various fundraising approaches mentioned earlier, and it's still going to be a challenge, but now you have a great deal of extra ammunition to go after the final capital that will bring the whole project to fruition.

This can also position you to go to a label or an agent who may cover those costs and sign you to a deal. With a product in hand, you have reduced risk, time, and effort needed to get that product out of the gate. On the other side of things, think about how hard you have worked to this point. Why would you want to shortcut now? Hold your horses, plan for the final stages, and make the release worthy of the product you have created.

> Check the names you are using. Whether it is a name for your band, an album, a tour, or whatever you are going to put out there to market yourself, see who else is using it and where it is showing up first.
>
> Times have changed; of course you want to stay creative and have fun with the music, but when you are picking titles and names that bring up everything else in the search engines except you, it is going to be that much harder for people to find you, your music, and your information.
>
> The Internet has become oversaturated with many phrases and words. When you are choosing names and titles, take that into consideration. It will give you a much better chance of not ending up at the bottom of the search results and never being found.

YOU ARE GOING TO HAVE TO LEARN HOW TO ASK SOMETIME; WHY NOT NOW?

Learn the techniques to pitch and solicit; then you'll be able to execute, act, and react better once your project releases and goes live. A good deal of your career will be similar to fundraising and finding investors, though in different forms. The skills you acquire from fundraising and finding investors can help you get distributed, get booked, and solicit for representation or potential deals. Remember: For every task that you don't want to do, there are others out there willing to do it for you. But they are going to make sure they not only get paid for it but also have a percentage of anything you make. So suck it up and learn these skills now while you maintain a majority control of your recording and your career. You can hand off certain elements, but if you stay aware and maintain a part of the business side, you will know what is going on. In turn, you will be able to see early signs of when things might be going bad and be able to nip it in the bud.

To really build a business, you need to have all the elements and budgetary considerations in place to market, promote, distribute, and get your music and your band to a level of success that can carry you past the project you are creating. All the while, you are paying back investors and taking care of key responsibilities. This allows you to keep the majority of control of your career and your music. I see too many artists who shortcut to get to completion or fruition. It is going to cost more than you think, especially if you think you can cover it with ten thousand dollars.

The more detailed the plan, the more realistic the budget, and the more elements taken into consideration, better your chances to crowd-fund, fundraise, or find the investors you are seeking. Justify, rationalize, and explain the who, what, where, when, why, and how of your plan and your budget to answer the questions before they are asked.

Your plan is the map for the pathway of your vision; it needs clarity for a potential investor. Remember: What you do is a business, you are an entrepreneur, and your business is music.

A DIFFERENT TAKE ON FUNDING: A PROPRIETARY INVESTMENT STRATEGY PLAN

In my career I have been exposed to some of the most extensive and expensive budgets for both TV and music projects and have watched investors recoup their investments in the briefest of times, while others were waiting for a check in the mail that would never come. The successful ones were the bands that had a long-term plan, usually two to four years at least.

The old ways of funding music ventures usually came in one of two methods. In the first, the investor committed the money to a project (a band) and then sent the funds directly to the band or paid to the various invoices that needed to be covered. The second way was that other projects were fully funded up front: The whole budget came in all at once and was placed into an account that was overseen by a money manager; this account manager would then distribute the funds as they were needed. The big problem with the second model was that it often led to a worst-case scenario: labels and management groups funding a series of different projects and different groups having their monies placed into the same bank account. In this scenario, you were not in control of your own destiny or budget.

From the smallest of music projects to the largest music investment ventures, no monies should ever be comingled or pooled with personal, business, or other projects' accounts. Make sure it is in a single account that is separated from everyone and everything else.

Because of these risks and the high probability that new bands and music ventures will fail, there is a solution that will eliminate any risk you pose as a newbie musician or group.

What if you were able to approach a potential investor, backer, or label with a detailed music business plan and an investment strategy that would virtually eliminate their risk in investing in you and begin to return their investment in as little as ninety days?

This mountain has been conquered by what I call the proprietary investment strategy.

The Future of Music Business Funding

LEGAL DISCLOSURE

Neither the information nor any opinions expressed in this book, this chapter, or this section constitute an offer to buy or sell any securities or financial instruments or provide any investment advice or service.

All investments involve risk. There can be no guarantee that the strategies, tactics, and methods discussed here will be successful. Shares may be more or less valuable than purchase price at any time in the future.

I have never made a broad statement by saying that this or that is the future of anything. I have made some pretty spot-on calls about what I was observing and then watched it happen. For example, while I was producing back in 2003, I wrote some articles—right as iTunes was being launched—that were slammed for agreeing with Steve Jobs's "outrageous claims" of what iTunes was going to do to the music industry. How could I, as a music industry person, agree with him? Still, it did happen. I have kept my finger on the pulse of change in the industry; I have always tried to take a very clear stance without making sensational statements.

Throughout this book I do my best to state an issue or a problem and then address how to handle it. I do my best to deliver the reasons, concepts, and proof of why I see the industry the way I see it. But in this case I am going to take a little more aggressive approach with a much more assertive statement.

I believe this proprietary investment strategy, with its moderate risk and high liquidity, will provide investors the security and risk protection that will allow more artists, labels, and managers to get the funding they need. All investing does comes with risk. Still, we have been able to remove nearly all risk using the proprietary investment strategy, while maintaining the same rate of return that is usually required for this level of venture or investment.

Think I am talking over your head? Listen, I am not a finance guy or even a college graduate. I dropped out of Berklee College of Music at the beginning of my second year. I am a musician, music producer, and music consultant with more than twenty years of experience in the industry. I am not going to go too deep into this strategy, and you will want to research this for yourself or reach out to the right people, but I want to give you an outline of the proprietary investment strategy that you can apply to your music business plan and funding. Brandon Powers came up with this plan. He is a good friend of mine and can explain the exact details and structure of this proprietary investment strategy concept. Brandon is in the investment risk-management business and handles a great deal of money for private investors. From real estate investments to private lending and investments in the S&P, Russell 2000, and Forex markets, he has investments in many different asset classes: He comes from a very experienced background. As we connected some time back, I got to learn a great deal about what he does, and he was interested in learning about the music business. In a number of discussions we found some very interesting parallels between both of our worlds and how musicians, labels, and investors could benefit from using this strategy.

You will need to discuss your personal plan in detail with Brandon Powers or someone else qualified for this style of investment strategy. You can obtain a prospectus and the necessary legal documents from Mr. Powers if you want to invest. This is an amazing system, but it is one that needs to be laid out correctly, legally, and in detail. While you can manage certain aspects of your music career by yourself, this aspect should not be one of them! Okay, here goes . . .

Let's say that a band has put together a top-notch plan that includes the release of a recording that is just about complete. The investor brings the needed $400,000 to the table. $200,000 is used by the artist or is allocated to the artist by a money manager or someone who is controlling the account and reporting to the investor. The other $200,000 is invested in a proprietary investment strategy that utilizes compounding, modest risk, or leverage to generate substantial returns.

The band has finished the project with their own funds and some crowd-funding resources. The plan they have now consists of a twenty-four-month strategy to distribute, market, and promote to get the band out on the road for an initial tour. They create a music business plan with all the I's dotted and all the T's crossed. An investor funds the project with $400,000, and the budget for twenty-four months is presented. It shows how the band has hefty expenses in the first few months, but from months nine to twenty-four, that money is not going to need to be touched.

Here is where the investment strategy comes into play. Instead of getting the money on a monthly basis from the investors or investment group, or getting the bulk of it and locking it up in a low-interest account where the money is just sitting there doing next to nothing, the money goes into the "strategy" plan. The $200K that is not needed for six-plus months is invested in a low-risk, high-liquidity proprietary investment strategy that uses compounding to create high rates of return. This is not a traditional investment method such as stocks, bonds, or CDs. It is an investment vehicle using proprietary strategies in highly liquid markets. Compounding creates massive rates of returns in a system of moderate to low risk.

This is not a miraculous get-rich-quick scheme. It is compounding that allows the strategy of the system to provide part or all of the money that is being invested in an artist, label, project, or even film. For example, if the money is left alone for one year, the model suggests that the return will be one hundred percent or greater—a hedge. The use of this strategy will begin the process of creating a return on investment for the investors or investment group.

Investment Strategy

- $400K starting capital

- $200K set aside for band's initial use pertaining to the standing budget

- $200K put into investment account as described before

- $35K of investment capital used as working capital

- $160K remains in T-bill / money market account until investment strategy shows positive return

- $5K used as at-risk capital

Five thousand of the investment capital is initially at risk. Additional funds will be utilized as investment returns increase, to take advantage of the compounding strategy, while the probability of a loss of the initial 5 percent is under 10 percent. That means if the investor is unhappy or things go bad in the first year and the second year's money is cut off, that investor can walk away with the $200K that is in the "Strategy" account, plus the $200K that it has earned in compounding. They may not have made any money, but they didn't lose a dime.

On the other hand, if the project is on course, the investor can give the second $200K to the artist as designated in the plan, grab the $200K that was earned in compounding, and already be halfway back to the return of his investment. The best plan would be to keep that money growing and let it earn more, but those are personal decisions to be made for each project. The other consideration is the agreement between the artist and the investor as to what percentages are considered payment to the investor. The percentage will be added to the initial investment as well as what is expected by the artist and any rights the investor has to pull out at a designated time if need be.

I know this sounds very complex, but it is actually much simpler than you can even realize. Doing the work on the front end by planning, budgeting, and organizing, then presenting investors with a plan that takes their worries, the risk factors, and their money into consideration will allow you a wider audience with wider options to obtain the capital you need to bring your music, your band, and your success to where you want.

When you address and reduce the risk while reinforcing the security of the investment in the band and the project, you protect the investor while empowering the artist. This is a style of funding that supports and protects everyone in a way that has not been seen before in the music business.

CLOSING THOUGHT

When it comes to money, you really need to look at the whole picture and make the wisest decisions with the best-laid plans. Hell, look at *American Idol.* Look at the hundreds of contestants over the years who threw all caution to the wind to go to Hollywood—only to be cut. Do you think the artist who made it for four weeks in Hollywood was having his or her bills paid at home? How many of them lost their jobs, went into debt, or took bankruptcy? That teary reaction of getting to go to Hollywood for fifteen minutes of fame in most cases ended up delivering years of fiscal damage.

It is crucial to not only have the right plan and the right budget but also the organization of how you will achieve that budget. Whether you choose to go the route of a label, investors, fan funding, or some mixture thereof, your funding needs to be addressed. The more prepared you are to approach investors, donors, and fans for the funds needed to launch your project, the easier it will be, once that project is released, to market, promote, and advertise yourself.

As I've indicated, it's a more costly journey than you may think. But if you address all the parts of a budget and all funding needs while working to achieve the capital required, it will end up costing you less in the long run and allow you to make success a reality.

9

YOUR BAND IS THE BRAND

OPENING THOUGHT

You are the marketing and promotional catalyst that will draw people into your music and your merchandise. However, with the changes in the music industry, there is an oversaturation of bands online. In other words, the things you are requesting from friends and fans are the same things so many others are requesting at the same time and in the same way.

I told one artist to take an approach that mixed *Mad Men*'s Don Draper with one of those infomercial guys. Creative and effective people draw in the customer with short samples and quick pitches; links on the screen invite viewers to call, email, or visit the website to buy direct. A new, creative approach to your branding is necessary.

You have to draw them in with interest, recognition, continuity, and uniformity, and in many cases this has to happen before they even listen to you. Your tagline, the one-liner that goes a little deeper, the full bio that sparks interest—all must be uniform. The logo and font need to be legible and consistent whether they appear on the website, the CD, the T-shirt, the social media site, or any other marketing and promotional item, down to the front of the bass drum. It is unfortunate that your music can't just stand by itself and that branding is so crucial; it shouldn't be that way, but it is. Brand the band, then add the "call to action," and you will draw their interest, taking them where you really want them to go.

YOUR BRANDING MUST BE ORGANIZED

With the oversaturation of media and information online and off, it is now more important than ever to work on branding the band and realizing that your band *is* the brand! As much as you might hate it, people are going to see you before they hear you in most cases. Whether it's a poster, album cover, product, piece of merchandise, or stage banner, brand recognition is key. Dunkin' Donuts has it right: They have one of the most recognizable brands, and they have it everywhere. From coffee cups to donut boxes, you recognize the name and you know the logo and the tagline, "America runs on Dunkin'." To some, just saying that phrase automatically makes you hear John Goodman's voice in the commercial.

That same approach can and should be used to brand you and your band. The more you are recognized, even by those who might not have heard you or looked you up the first time they came across you, the more you will become familiar, the more you will be remembered, and soon, the better chances you will have of someone checking out your music, your show, and your products. Those who are recognizable, familiar, and have a sense of continuity and uniformity are going to attract a larger audience over time.

For a moment, pretend that you're deaf. Think of how many bands have the same look, the same vibe on stage, and the same performance moves. Imagine what it would be like if you couldn't be heard. That's exactly how important your logo, your images, and your branding are.

Some, including industry professionals, may make decisions based on your appearance and content before they hear you—if they hear you at all. These days, the package has to shine and the band has to display itself professionally before anything else. Don't you want to come across as professional and polished as possible? Don't you want them to go right for your CD or the link to your music on a computer? The band is the brand, so you need to be seen and stand out. Of course it's about the music in the end, but the band has to be the brand to bring the people and the professionals to your music, or you chance never even being heard.

UNIFORM CONTENT FOR MARKETING AND PROMOTING CREATE THE BEST RESULTS

Uniform—it's not just what you wear to work. While the music you make and the elements of your performance and appearance can be nuanced, embellished, and improvised, assuring the consistency of your marketing content and images is key. This will help people recognize the brand and the concept that is you. It will also give a clear view of the elements in your music, which may be more diverse and ever changing.

By creating a uniform branded base, people will recognize you in the best and the most repetitive ways possible. Leave the change and improvisation for the music on a performance level. Decide on and lock in your brand on the following:

- Logo
- Font (for your name)
- Tagline
- One-liner
- Full bio, including the short, medium, and long versions
- Basic color scheme

These are the basics of branding that you will apply across all of the following elements. As much as you may not want to stay locked in a box, if you don't properly define the identity and basic images of what you are, you will find it much harder to grab the extended audience. It's a proven fact: The majority of people are affected by branding whether they are aware of it or not. Look at Coke! Coca-Cola has had their famous logo and font since 1888 and their signature bottle design since 1915. When people see a font, color, logo, image, and content that is constant or uniform, it draws them to a product or artist.

This goes for your . . .

- Posters, flyers, and postcards
- Website and social networking sites
- All posted content
- Entire promo package (physical and digital)
- Merchandise: from the music to the T-shirts

Don't confuse uniform with boring. You can still have wild and creative designs for your flyers; just make sure your name is always in the font that you use on all your other items. You can showcase your creativity with your website design, but allow the branding to be present and to cross over to your social networking sites in order to bring both the new and regular viewer a sense of recognition. That will bring people back more often.

Think about the Beatles; there is a specific Beatles font on everything. The Who—same thing. It's just like Coca-Cola or Frosted Flakes: It's how people make their products memorable and recognizable. You're an artist and you're creating all types of different songs and improvising on stage and yes, the metamorphosis and continual development of your craft is essential, but the most successful artists have the best and most consistent branding at the base of it all.

"WELL, SO-AND-SO ISN'T DOING IT"

In recent years a lot of bands have somewhat stepped away from the type of branding I'm talking about. The branding is still there; it just comes in the form of hefty marketing budgets that allow the bands to be played, seen, or advertised everywhere; it's still branding.

But if you don't have a half-million-dollar marketing budget, I highly recommend that you work on uniform layouts and the basic branding that costs less. You're an artist, but to move your music and merchandise and increase and strengthen your fan base, you need to be uniform in your branding, marketing, and promoting.

These same branding elements need to be applied to your tagline, one-liner, and bio. The branded content becomes your signature on your posts, your website, and all your social media sites. The more you use that same content, text, wording, and copy, the more it will help to get you promoted, marketed, and optimized across the web. It will also help industry professionals get a sense that you have a well-crafted marketing base and a direct vision.

If you post a really funny video on YouTube that gets a whole bunch of views but has no links or information about you, your music, or your online store, you just wasted a free marketing opportunity. By branding your content with your signature, which includes your short bio or tagline, links to you, and a "call to action" for people to find out more, you make every post—blogs, videos, photos, and so on—into valuable, branded content that will give you the best chance to gain more exposure and build a larger fan base.

> Sometimes you need to know when to take a break: Take care of yourself mentally or physically outside of your work, your goals, or your dreams. The vacation at the finish line is a wonderful thought, but the music business continues to go on after the goals and numerous steps, making it a very long run. Make sure to stop, rest, and recover now and then.

LOGOS

Creating a logo can be simple. However, creating an effective logo is a much larger challenge, usually involving a lot of people weighing in with ideas on what a logo should be. Some feel it should be really artistic, others think it should be very simple, and still others feel a logo is unnecessary and want to switch up designs for every show, every poster, and every album.

Your logo is one of the most important elements of your band outside of the music. It's your visual calling card. It connotes your music symbolically. A logo, many times, is even more important than the photo of the group. It can fit into a lot more places than a photo and plays an even larger role in branding the band across different types of media and products.

Your logo has to be legible. Here's a good check: If you put up a poster on a light pole on the side of the road, you should be able to drive by and make out the logo and its smaller elements. If you can't, it's not the most effective logo. Your logo should look good, whether it's the profile picture on a social media site or on a seven-foot banner on the stage.

So when you're creating a logo, ask yourself, can it stand alone? Does it need assisting elements to make it clear? Are all the elements in place to be effective on a hat, a poster, an album cover, the web, a newspaper, a bumper sticker, or any other type of merchandise? The logo that you create needs to work in all these mediums, or it's not an effective logo.

Make Your Graphics Clear, Easy to Read, and Uniform!

The logo, the font, and the graphics have to line up. All too often bands will connect with a graphic designer who makes all sorts of wonderful images, great graphics, and dozens of artistic variations. But there's one small problem: no branding whatsoever! Continuity attracts all those people who have not heard you but have seen your posters around town.

Remember: On every corner of every city there are truckloads of posters stuck up by tons of bands who change their visual imagery too often and make themselves forgettable.

A logo is made up of four elements:

1. **The Logo Itself.** This should be a design that can stand alone and has an artistic and pleasing quality to it, oftentimes some kind of image or graphic that's not necessarily the name of the artist and may not even have words.

2. **The Name Font.** This is the name of the artist or band in a font that will go with the logo. This font should always be used after it is decided upon. The font you choose should be on every poster, every album, and every piece of promotional material—*everything*.

3. **The Tagline.** The tagline defines the band. Have the tagline in a uniform font that can be used as a variation with the logo.

4. **The Website Address.** This is your website in a uniform font that can be applied and used with the logo.

Below is an explanation of the different aspects of a logo set, using the example of Michael McFarland, an artist I worked with. To reference these explanations and examples visually, visit http://michaelmcfarlandmusic.com/logo-identity-graphics/

The Michael McFarland Logo Set

1. The logo = The coat of arms (but the main logo is his emblem)
2. The font = The lettering for his name
3. The tagline = Writer, Rocker, Biker, Geek
4. The website address = http://michaelmcfarlandmusic.com/

Once you have these items in place, you create your full logo set. Use your logo to create twelve different combinations of the above four elements; you'll be able to apply them across the board for any possible situation in which you'll need branding. Don't see it as stifling creativity; you can still create many images, posters, and photo ideas, but always apply the logo set that you've designed to brand your band.

Here are the five variations with the elements of each:

- Branding logo set 1: **Logo**
- Branding logo set 2: **Font**
- Branding logo set 3: **Tagline**
- Branding logo set 4: **Logo—Font—Tagline**
- Branding logo set 5: **Logo—Font—Tagline—Website**

Once these were in place for the artist, high- and low-resolution versions in both color and black and white were created. Then they were made available in JPG, PNG, and EPS formats for easy use in any type of promotion needed.

In the end you'll have a series of different images that can be copied and pasted into anything you need. It may seem like overkill, but having all these versions available on the web for download will make life a lot easier on people who need to use a variation of your logo for promotion or marketing purposes. Industry folks, fans, and others can easily access your images to help promote your band. Have you ever received a call saying, "We need an image to go to press with right now?" Or have you ever been asked if you have something with your font without the logo? If you haven't, you will, and this is a great solution.

Are you starting to get it? All of these logos give you the most variety for the most placement and use for your brand. Once you have the basic design, font choice, tagline, and website set up, you can pretty much shuffle things around with your designer and set these twelve in place. This will go a lot faster if you have the separate elements already designed and agreed on.

Make it simple to share your images. Post them on Flickr and Pinterest, and put up washed-out variations on Instagram. Upload them to a collection on your Facebook page. Get those images out everywhere!

Logo sets will make it easier to create T-shirts, stickers, flyers, posters, web designs and graphics for web use, magazine and newspaper ads, and millions of other marketing and promotional elements. Having both high- and low-resolution versions will allow people to place your logos on their websites or use your images to help advertise a show. Of course, you'll have a third version of these that are of the highest resolution for use on products like T-shirts, merchandise, and swag that you will control and not share.

When you brand and define the image, the name, and the group, you will bring a new level of recognition and potentially a new group of fans who would not have found you before. Just as you define your music, define the images and the logo elements that will bring people to your music. Get this done early on, and it will save a major amount of time and cash in the long run.

FONTS AND TYPESETTING: CONTROLLING THE APPEARANCE OF THE NAME AND LETTERING YOU USE

What is your font for your artist name or band name? How often are you using it to promote your band? Just as you decided on your artist or band name, the way that name appears needs to be branded, and the first step of branding your name is your font.

Build visual recognition that doesn't depend on your face, your image, or your music. Make it yours. Make it readable and clear, whether it is shrunk down small or blown up large. The more you can define your branding with your font, the more people will associate you with it.

> When it comes to your name/font/typesetting . . .
> • make it legible,
> • make it clean,
> • make it yours, and
> • make sure it is everywhere and on everything.

You can still get crazy with posters and other promotional items, but make sure that font is the same across the board to reinforce your brand with existing fans and to introduce your brand to new ones.

Buy and own your logo, font, and designs. Regardless of whether you are getting a logo created, a font designed, a website layout, a CD cover, a T-shirt design, photos, or a video, make sure you have the exclusive rights to it.

There are many unfortunate stories about artists who called in a favor or got something for free, at a discount, or for a reduction, only to have the photographer, producer, designer, or web designer come back to look for compensation when the artist started to make money. Put it all on paper, even if it means that you will have to pay extra down the road for ownership. The more you have exclusive or majority control over all the aspects of your branding, from photos to designs, products to recordings, and everywhere in between, the more it will allow you to profit in the long run.

CREATING KEYWORD PHRASES AND DESCRIPTORS TO DRAW PEOPLE IN

Much of my consulting on promotional content starts with the bio. Let's face it: Writing a bio is a pain, and writing a good one is even worse.

There are a few basic rules for the strongest keywords, comparisons, and bullet points to attract the media to you. The foundation comes from continuity in the proper phrases, tagline, one-liner, bio, and branding to stand out across the board, on paper or on a screen. I often advise bands to come up with a series of keywords about themselves and their music and then add some influences and comparisons to have a list of words to work with and shape into the different elements for a bio. Reading the tagline, the bio, the one-liner, or the description out loud and recording it and listening back to it help refine, define, and align the words you want. And those are the key elements you want when it comes to your promotional and marketing content.

1. Refine it.

2. Define it.

3. Align it.

4. And repeat it . . . over and over.

What would you say if you were in front of the following people?

1. A new, young fan who doesn't play an instrument

2. An older fan who might have a good musical ear

3. Another musician of the same caliber as you

4. One of your favorite musicians of all time whom you most look up to, respect, and admire

A lot of people tailor what they say to whom they are talking. Individualization can be good, but when it comes to defining you or your band as a brand and really locking down the promotional groundwork, it is best to say the same thing every time. Say exactly the same things when it comes to your core marketing and overall description of yourself. You can go into additional details afterward, but give them that fast, secure, and confident delivery that is strong and assertive without being over the top.

One of the biggest ways to make sure to keep yourself in check (unless you are an arrogant prick) is to ask yourself what you would say in front of your favorite musician, biggest inspiration, or major influence. Would you really go off on one of those rants telling how you put everyone else to shame? How you are the hottest thing in years? How you are worlds better than this artist or that band? How you are breaking the mold, changing the face of music, redefining your genre, or some other ego-driven, bullshit, hype statement? I hope not.

Craft the lines, phrases, and descriptions to attract someone that you hold in the highest regard. Then apply them to those that might not know you at all; you will find wording that is respectful, assertive, and confident without being too exaggerated. That uniformity will help to optimize you online and with fans. The more you maintain a solid and branded basic tagline, one-liner, and bio, the more you can go into much deeper, personalized, and individualized descriptions, depending on who you are talking to. Your goal is to draw people to your music and your shows. Stand out by being consistent at all times to optimize faster.

PRETENDING TO BE MORE THAN YOU REALLY ARE: BRANDING LIKE A FOOL

Too many bands are trying to paint a picture they can't live up to; this is hurting much more than helping. Presentation is certainly key, but fake representations just don't balance out.

Find the middle ground. Some artists brag about the cars, jewelry, money, and fame before they make it. They have major labels or investors giving them all of the things that they are bragging about. These are the minorities in the music industry! When you talk about your "ride" being the best but you are sporting a broken-down Toyota, this sends a negative message. An artist who has backing from a label or investor can totally live up to the hype. But when you are copying that model on a zero budget, you are failing miserably.

Don't try to copycat upper-level branding. It's all been done and it's too much. Try to stand out by stepping out of the same old shit. Appear professional while showing your own personality to an industry that is full of copycats and liars.

> Seriously?
>
> Are you are taking a promotional shot with your phone in your hand?
>
> Do you need to hold a wad of cash in your other hand for the picture?
>
> Can a picture of you giving a gang sign or holding a gun really make you look pro?

Do you really . . . want to take your promo shots with your phone? Come on! How many poseurs take shots of themselves on their phone, looking like they are doing business while trying to pull off a cool pose at the same time? I don't care if you are an artist, a manager, a label rep, or anyone else, taking a picture of yourself on a phone is overused, overdone, and not as cool as you think.

Instead: What about shots of you on a typewriter, with a bullhorn, giving off the town crier vibe, or something a little more original that might give off that cool business sense you are trying for while adding a touch of something different?

Do you really . . . want to be that asshole with the excessive bling? The jewelry shots? That is so original—*not*. At one point it was impressive, but now it's gone completely over the top.

Instead: Go minimal. Try something like augmenting your stage clothing with interesting accessories. Make your picture look like your own and not a carbon copy of a hundred thousand others.

Do you really . . . want to be the guys surrounded by the scantily clad girls—like everyone does? Because again, no one has ever seen thousands of these pictures, right?

Instead: Have your picture, image, or ideas stand out from the bland and repetitive. Try a shot with a bunch of old men around you. I know, a little weird, but *different*.

Do you really . . . want to brag, to put down others while talking shit? "I am the best!" "No one can touch me!" "We don't sound like anyone." "All the girls want to be with me; all the guys want to be me." So very unoriginal and so very annoying. Do you really want to do that?

Instead: Try coming across confident and assertive without being arrogant. That would be a serious breath of fresh air in today's music business. Show your ability through your performance and not through trash talking, overhyping, or putting other people down.

Do you really . . . want to be the liar with the fake music business entity? There are too many people out there claiming to run a record label or management group or to be an agency when they actually aren't. People are calling themselves CEOs who don't even have an incorporated business; to the industry, they look like morons. People who imply that they have organizations looking to sign artists or have contacts to all the major labels hoist red flags for real industry professionals. Don't hurt your reputation and your chances.

Instead: Tell the truth! Start an LLC, a small company, or a sole proprietorship. Make it legal. Match your words to the facts to look like a true pro, regardless of where you are in your career. The Internet makes it easy for people to check up on you; make sure you are checking out.

Sometimes what we *think* is making us look really good or professional is actually doing the exact opposite. Stand out as professionally and creatively as you can. Use the ideas that work, but add your personal touch to them. In an industry where it has all been done and seen before, the more you can alter, edit, adapt, and add to everything to make it a bit different than others, the more you stand out.

TAGLINES: THE SHORT, FAST PHRASE THAT SUMMARIZES AND OPTIMIZES YOU

Just as your sound and name have to be recognized, so do the other elements of your branding, of which a tagline is key. While your name represents your band and your creativity, your tagline should be that short quip that gives a persuasive overview and description of you as an artist. Usually the artist's or band's name is not a descriptor; it is a creative title. The tagline will give people a simple summary that gives them a little more information. Hands down, taglines are a requirement today. With so many musicians and bands competing, the tagline is one more element that will allow you to stand out.

What Exactly Is a Tagline?

- A simple, poignant phrase used to set off a logo or ad.

- A phrase or short sentence placed directly below a website's masthead. The tagline functions to quickly identify the artist past the name and logo. It may be a subtitle, an organizational motto, or a vision or purpose statement.

- A short statement describing the artist's or company's position or purpose.

- A phrase used repeatedly in communications and advertising that, through repetition, eventually comes to identify the brand.

Taglines are used for everything from food products to cars, companies to computers. From simple, broad promo types like "Fly the friendly skies" to ego types like Frosted Flakes' "They're great!" taglines add another marketing element to help draw in fans.

Maybe you're thinking, "I don't hear about bands I know having taglines, so why do I need one?" But have you ever referred to Ozzy Osbourne as "The Prince of Darkness"? What about Sammy Hagar, "The Red Rocker"? Or Springsteen—"The Boss"? Understand that all bands have taglines; many aren't released, but they are still part of the music business and marketing plans for bigger artists. When the plan is presented and funded, the marketing and advertising money comes into play and taglines are not required as much, because overall exposure plays a bigger part of the branding role.

Take your time coming up with a tagline, and make sure it best represents you in the simplest form. Be proud of it. When someone asks what your band is about or sounds like, the tagline should address that question simply and quickly.

To help give a basic sense of how some taglines are created, I want to share two of my favorites, which I worked on with a couple artists, and how the artist and I came up with them.

I worked with an older artist named Jeremiah. His tagline was "A Gentleman of Soul." Jeremiah was an R&B and soul artist. We wanted to find something that would help define him but not get him lost in the shuffle. Many R&B artists just list themselves as that: R&B. We knew we had to use the words "soul" or "R&B." As we brainstormed, we thought about "The King of Pop," "The Godfather of Soul," and various phrases that had been used by others. We presented Jeremiah with a clean cut, smooth, and clear image, which brought us to the word "gentleman." From there, we decided to stay away from ego, and instead of "The Gentleman of Soul," we thought something more *gentleman*-like and less arrogant would be "A Gentleman of Soul." That ended up being his tagline and an effective one at that.

Remember, a tagline is not intended for the audience who knows you: It is intended to draw in those who know nothing of you or your music.

Das Vibenbass was an amazing jazz group. However, "jazz" is a terrible descriptive word, because it's way too vague. Das Vibenbass crossed the spectrums of jazz, fusion, Latin, bebop, swing, cool, big band, stomp, rock, and blues. The borders of jazz have been coming down and changing in recent years, thereby creating opportunities for different sounds and approaches to the genre as a whole. The group took some time with their styles and what had been happening in jazz and came back with "Crushing the Borders of Jazz." I loved it. To me, it was a great way to come at the jazz idiom while showing the depth and diversity of the group in a nice, tight little tagline.

Remember to stay away from the ego and avoid the arrogant words like "innovative," "different," "original," "revolutionary," and "new." These take away from the tagline's effectiveness, putting you in an oversaturated category where so many others are saying the exact same thing. Instead, be original without using the word "original"! Be innovative, but find another term! Be revolutionary by finding a word more descriptive and not as overused!

Working on your wording, from your taglines to your one-liners, with the consideration of presentation, optimization, and avoiding oversaturation will give you the phrases that will stand out and be found by more fans. Take a marketing stand on your sound and your professionalism, not a cheesy arrogance that will end up hurting you in the long run. Ask friends; post a survey online; find out some of the keywords and phrases that your existing fans associate you with.

As you work on creating taglines, don't throw anything away. Zero in on the tagline, but don't be surprised if you end up using some of those phrases, bullet points, or sentences for your one-liner, your bio, and for other content and branding items. Creating the tagline is the best first step of building the beast that is your bio.

Start with the who, what, where, why, and how of your band or yourself as an artist. Imagine this tagline on a T-shirt, a coffee cup, the back of a hat, all over your website and social media, and in the listings at venues you are playing. Imagine you only had a few seconds to summarize yourself for someone, and avoid those overused words. What you have left will be your tagline.

> "Everyone says they are going to be the next hot thing. Truth be told, most hot young things don't have anything good to say."—Unknown
>
> *So very, very true.* I am not taking away from the root talent of these younger, newer stars. I think that there is a firm base of quality in some of them. However, I don't really give a crap about some of these interviews and opinions of very young, overly protected, and heavily spoiled stars. I know that is not true for all of them, but it is for many.
>
> There are way too many people talking too much and not saying anything.

THE BIO AND NOTHING BUT THE BIO: THE SHORT, MEDIUM, AND LONG OF IT

Creating an effective bio can be as challenging as creating the tagline. To sum up your group in a way that will draw people to your band is sometimes harder than making the music itself. The problem with bios is that all too often they are either poorly constructed or soaked with excessive ego statements. Your biography has to shine and envelop your band, your sound, and your marketing.

The bio also needs to be formatted for the business side of things so that it's easier for reviewers and media professionals to use for potential stories, interviews, and reviews. In a lot of ways, it's like a press release: When you deliver a bio that's easy for the media to access, they will use it more than one with no content. Just like the tagline, logo, and images, stay uniform with your bio. You can, of course, use different sections of your bio and alter the length, but stay consistent. Keep people aware of what you're about, and as they recognize the same words, phrases, images, and sounds coming from you, they'll be more compelled to follow you—even the toughest crowds.

Below is the breakdown of a full bio I worked on with one of my clients. We are going to open with his old bio first.

Note that the client, Michael McFarland, is a great sport, a great client, and a talented graphic designer. He approved the use of his before-and-after bio as an example. He said, "I'm 100 percent okay with you ripping everything to shreds and pointing out everything I was doing wrong!"

Here was the one he was using:

MICHAEL MCFARLAND'S OLD BIO

Garnering comparisons ranging from modern-rock radio successes such as Rob Thomas, the Goo Goo Dolls, and the Fray to venerable singer-songwriters such as Willie Nelson and Elton John, Michael McFarland's songs have a universal appeal. Ignoring genre lines and musical expectations, McFarland's autobiographical lyrics have found their way into the hearts of fans with diverse musical tastes and a wide range of ages, from preteens to pensioners.

A born performer raised in Kent, Ohio, McFarland spent much of his teenage years and early twenties playing in rock bands, touring the country, and developing his skills as a songwriter, producer, and audio engineer. When he decided to set out on a solo career in the fall of 2010, he locked himself in his home recording studio and emerged four days later with his six-song debut EP, "Made a Mess," which he not only engineered, produced, mixed, and mastered, but on which he also performed all instrumental parts. McFarland put this same DIY ethic to use on his first full-length album, *Waking Up Is a Letdown*, released August 26, 2011.

This gives some comparisons but says nothing about Michael and his overall vibe. In talking with him, I learned about his love for motorcycles and so many other interesting parts of his life. I worked with Michael to define him more effectively, using some existing elements outside of music to create interest in him and get rid of the extraneous and older information that would not push him in the here and now.

The original opening sentence is very long, and his name is not mentioned for some time. We discussed omitting the dates and creating sentences that work together but that can also be pulled out individually to be used as press pieces or bullet points for reviews, solicitation, etc. As we began the process together, we cut the bio up into five sections. The third section would be used as a signature and a marketing call-to-action element outside of the bio itself.

These are the five sections:

1. **Tagline**

   We already covered this earlier in the chapter. After Michael initially wrote out a series of keywords and phrases that best described him, we went into further detail to find the best phrases that were not overly used or overly saturated. We then looked at some of the various search engine optimization rankings of the phrases to allow for the best optimization online for the tagline and other parts of the bio. Michael's tagline:

   Writer, Rocker, Biker, Geek.

The tagline appears in this format at the end of the short bio and the end of the first paragraph of the full bio. Inside the bio itself, the tagline has a lead-in:

   Michael McFarland in the simplest summary?
   Writer, Rocker, Biker, Geek.

The focal point is still *Writer, Rocker, Biker, Geek.* That is what will be going on the merchandise, on the website, and in the graphics.

2. **One-Liner**

   Here's what we came up with:

   Unleaded rhythmic alt-pop fuels singer-songwriter and two-wheel
   troubadour Michael McFarland's engine.

This is the first sentence of the bio. It's the first thing that the reader sees, and it can stand completely on its own. It's a full-sentence version of the tagline, or, in some ways, the extended tagline with more detail. It covers the basic information, including the name of the artist, with a couple of the keyword phrases that give a sense of the artist, his overall genre, and his approach.

Here you get the information about Michael through the following keyword phrases:

- Rhythmic alt-pop
- Singer-songwriter
- Troubadour
- Michael McFarland
- (And the sense that this guy must be into bikes)

3. Signature

The one-liner should have an effective flow into the tagline. The two most prominent branding statements can piggyback each other, followed by the addition of a call to action, like so:

MMF

Unleaded rhythmic alt-pop fuels singer-songwriter and two-wheel troubadour Michael McFarland's engine. Michael McFarland in the simplest summary? Writer, Rocker, Biker, Geek.

For Michael's music, CDs, downloads, merchandise, live show schedule, music blogs, music videos, and everything else you want to know about McFarland, visit the Michael McFarland website at http://michaelmcfmusic.com/

This signature, which can now be used at the end of every post, picture, video, song sample, and social media site, delivers the one-liner followed by the tagline and then a call to action for the person that is listening, watching, or reading to know where to get more information about Michael. For Michael, we added his initials and a small line on top as a literal autograph signature of sorts.

> Always have a call to action with everything you are putting up online!

Let's jump back to the body of the bio. Next up:

4. Short Bio

Unleaded rhythmic alt-pop fuels singer-songwriter and two-wheel troubadour Michael McFarland's engine. Garnering comparisons ranging from
modern rock groups such as Matchbox 20 and the Fray to classic singer-
songwriters such as Paul Simon and Elton John, the Asheville, NC–based
performer mixes an intensity with a sensitivity wrapped in effective contradictions. Astride his motorcycle with a guitar strapped to his back, making
references to quantum mechanics or science fiction, McFarland embraces and
explores his wide spectrum of knowledge, interests, experience, and hobbies in
his music and writing. Michael McFarland in the simplest summary? Writer,
Rocker, Biker, Geek.

This is the complete short bio and also the first paragraph of the full bio. Notice how the
one-liner is the lead of the short bio. Each part of the bio (when you add the medium and
long) should start with the previous section. This is how you maintain uniformity while adding elements for the best ways to optimize the bio and the keyword phrases online.

In the short bio, you continue off of the one-liner's information about your style by adding
some of the influences, which can help you by giving a ballpark definition of your sound to
those who don't know you and haven't heard you yet. Adding some fun facts outside of music
can also be a great marketing approach to bring into the short and the long bio versions. Close
the short bio effectively by ending it with your tagline. This is the bio that will often get used
in shorter stories and reviews.

5. Medium Bio

Unleaded rhythmic alt-pop fuels singer-songwriter and two-wheel troubadour
Michael McFarland's engine. Garnering comparisons ranging from modern
rock groups such as Matchbox 20 and the Fray to classic singer-songwriters
such as Paul Simon and Elton John, the Asheville, NC–based performer mixes
an intensity with a sensitivity wrapped in effective contradictions. Astride his
motorcycle with a guitar strapped to his back, making references to quantum
mechanics or science fiction, McFarland embraces and explores his wide spectrum of knowledge, interests, experience, and hobbies in his music and writing.
Michael McFarland in the simplest summary? Writer, Rocker, Biker, Geek.

The self-deprecating humorist who makes a solo intimate acoustic performance with just his voice and a guitar sound like an arena show with all the

volume, the lights, and the smoke, McFarland entertains the smallest crowds on the largest scale. Raised in Kent, Ohio (where students get shot and rivers catch on fire), McFarland is a self-professed "proud kindergarten dropout" after escaping the public school system to be homeschooled. Coming from a family of scientists, his father being a nuclear physicist and mother a former biologist, Michael grew up strongly embracing the arts and the sciences in a simultaneous harmony that allowed him to thrive. McFarland believes that his fondness of motorcycles may be a genetic condition: His branch of Clan MacFarlane was run out of Scotland in 1805 for being horse thieves. When it comes to saddling up, however, McFarland prefers two wheels to four legs. "Motorcycles are easier to keep fed," he says, "and much more pleasant to clean up after."

This bio, following the piggyback format, starts with the one-liner, adds the short bio, and adds another paragraph to become the medium bio. This second paragraph adds even more detail about the sound of the artist, from a deeper description of the influences to some basic marketing plugs, all delivered with confidence and assertiveness without being too cocky. It also closes with something sharp, humorous, or relevant that can be pulled by writers to be used in reviews.

Finally . . .

MICHAEL MCFARLAND'S NEW BIO (FULL/LONG VERSION)

Unleaded rhythmic alt-pop fuels singer-songwriter and two-wheel troubadour Michael McFarland's engine. Garnering comparisons ranging from modern rock groups such as Matchbox 20 and the Fray to classic singer-songwriters such as Paul Simon and Elton John, the Asheville, NC–based performer mixes an intensity with a sensitivity wrapped in effective contradictions. Astride his motorcycle with a guitar strapped to his back, making references to quantum mechanics or science fiction, McFarland embraces and explores his wide spectrum of knowledge, interests, experiences, and hobbies in his music and writing. Michael McFarland in the simplest summary? Writer, Rocker, Biker, Geek.

The self-deprecating humorist who makes a solo intimate acoustic performance with just his voice and a guitar sound like an arena show with all the volume, the lights, and the smoke, McFarland entertains the smallest crowds on the largest scale. Raised in Kent, Ohio (where students get shot and rivers catch on fire), McFarland is a self-professed "proud kindergarten dropout" after escaping the public school system to be homeschooled. Coming from a family of scientists, his father being a nuclear physicist and mother a former biologist, Michael grew up strongly embracing the arts and the sciences in a simultaneous harmony that allowed him to thrive. McFarland believes that his fondness of motorcycles may be a genetic condition: His branch of Clan MacFarlane was run out of Scotland in 1805 for being horse thieves. When it comes to saddling up, however, McFarland prefers two wheels to four legs. "Motorcycles are easier to keep fed," he says, "and much more pleasant to clean up after."

Michael McFarland spent much of his twenties playing in rock bands and developing his skills as a songwriter, performer, producer, and engineer. His first solo album was all Michael. From every instrument played, to the writing, production, engineering, mixing, and mastering, McFarland clearly reinforced the definition of the DIY album. From touring across America on the back of a motorcycle to reflecting and inserting the experiences of his life, loves found, loves lost, and his childhood, Michael McFarland sings his heartfelt, autobiographical songs, accompanied by only an acoustic guitar, a loop pedal, and a motorcycle waiting outside to bring him to the next show.

The full bio incorporates the one-liner, the short bio, the medium bio, and then finishes with the last paragraph. This paragraph, again, digs even deeper into the music, the artist, and hobbies and elements outside of the music.

Elements outside of music can be a great tool to initially connect with new fans. By allowing someone to relate to you, your life, your influences, and interests outside of your music, you have the best chance to draw them in on a much deeper level. They see a kinship, someone to relate to, and a familiarity that may make them find you and your music that much more enticing.

An effective bio will bring more people to your music and make it easier for the media to write about you. In a lot of ways, you want your bio to be geared toward industry professionals; it's those people and groups who will deliver information about you to others. The people you are trying to reel into noticing your band are accustomed to seeing horribly formatted, terribly written, vague biographies. Give them something different. Let your bio stand out, just like you. For the fans, this format will be just as effective. Instead of the long-winded ramblings that many fans are used to reading, you are delivering a well-written, sharp, and flowing bio to build interest.

This bio showcases Michael, what he brings to the table musically, what his interests are, and the various ways he can relate to a fan, industry professional, or reader. These sentences make it easier for someone doing a review or story or looking for a short phrase or sentence to use for a promotion.

Notice that in Michael's bio, he never tells the audience what they will feel, what they will do, or how they will react. He shows them respect by avoiding those elements and allowing readers to decide for themselves. It is assertive, professional, and solid while being humorous and interesting. This is the kind of bio that would make me want to take a listen. I am not just saying that because I wrote it with Michael; he is genuinely interesting, and this bio brings out who Michael is musically and who he is outside of music.

Bio . . . Biooo . . . Branding Come and Me Wanna Go Home

So make sure you have the tagline, the one-liner, the signature with the call to action, the short, medium, and long bio locked in. This puts you in the best position for content branding and makes it that much easier to send out, solicit, or cut and paste uniform information for online marketing.

Don't tell them how they will feel, how they will move, how they will need to buy your music, or that they must tell their friends. You don't know that. Those aggressive statements can set up a mental response like, "Don't tell me what to do—oh, hell no!" Instead, present a bio that you would happily share to draw interest from a fan, from someone in the music industry you are trying to connect with, or from your biggest hero. That's right: You want to be able to say your tagline, one-liner, or bio in front of your biggest inspiration or influence without feeling stupid. You need the sentences and statements you can present with confidence and assertiveness, regardless of the audience.

> Draw them in, share with them, intrigue them, relate to them, and offer them a way to connect with you and your music.

Finally, read it out loud! When you are writing the tagline, the one-liner, the bio, or anything, take the time to read it out loud. Get someone else to read it out loud for you, too! Listen to how it sounds. Does it flow? Does it drag? Does it sound like someone you would want to check out? The whole bio should be as powerful in spoken form as it is when written.

LETTERHEAD: CREATING A PROFESSIONAL TEMPLATE PAGE FOR MULTIPLE USES

Sometimes it's the little things that can bring people to the larger things you want them to see. When you're trying to get a booking agent, venue, promoter, manager, label, or anyone else to listen to your music, every step and every piece counts. It's also crucial to consider whom you are sending your music or promotional package to. The envelope, the package, and the basic presentation are what they see first before they slip the CD into a player, enter the number for your download card, or click on a link to hear your music. In such a scenario it's those little extra elements of professionalism that will bring that person to your music faster and create a greater focus on your request.

A letterhead for your band is very easy to create and adds a professional touch. This falls in line with the concepts of continuity and branding that I have been pounding into your brain in this chapter. When someone opens a package and sees a cover letter with a letterhead showing the band's name, logo, website, and contact information, they start off on the right foot.

When you create these documents in PDF form for the electronic kits, they should have the uniform letterhead as well. Do not assume they will come to a link and go to your contact page. Make it easy and streamlined, whether it is a physical package or a digital one.

Many bands send packages that don't even have a cover letter, or worse, send a blank piece of paper that is handwritten or terribly typed. Using your letterhead in all your mailings, physical or digital, will show that you understand the importance of professionalism and that you pay attention to all the details of your career.

This simple but effective letterhead can now be used for anything formal. It becomes the template for a number of your core promotional documents, allowing them to look as professional and to be as effective as possible. Your letterhead will allow people to know who you are and the numbers, site, addresses, and emails to contact you. You now have a blank template where you can instantly create any letter, solicitation, or request.

The best basic letterhead should have these elements:

- Band name
- Band logo
- Band tagline
- Band website
- Band primary social media page
- Contact person
- Contact email
- Contact phone
- Contact address

The little things can make the biggest difference in someone getting to your music and looking over your materials. For an example of a solid artist letterhead, visit http://tag2nd. com/letterhead.

POSTERING

Still a crucial part of your marketing and promotion, postering has been a mainstay for decades. Even with all the websites and social media promotion online, the physical poster still has a place in marketing. The same telephone poles that have posters on them advertising shows for tonight were advertising shows some sixty years ago. (By the way, some cities have made it illegal to post on telephone poles; check what the laws are for that city before you get arrested for marketing your show.)

Yes, there is the Internet, Facebook, all those event sites, and a ton of new ways to promote yourself, but you need to remember that some people don't search online, and you have to find a way to reach out to them. Postering accomplishes this. A person who knows nothing about you or about your show might become interested enough to find out more with the right poster in the right place.

The Poster Itself

Is it a good poster? Are you using your logo and branding? Is the information clear and catchy? Can someone drive by at a moderate speed and get the basic information? You probably want to be artsy and creative, but a poster is about advertising. The poster should attract people to the show you are advertising, or it should draw them to look you up online, find out more about you, and listen to your music. If your poster is too artsy and hard to read, you are not doing all you can to attract new fans. Remember, the poster should also be a reminder for people on your mailing lists, friends on your social networking sites, and everyone familiar with you. The key point of posters is to pull in new people and entice new audiences to create new fans—along with getting people out to that show, of course.

A good poster for a single show—even a past show—can still serve as a marketing and promoting tool until it is actually torn down. Yes, maybe someone didn't go to the show, but they continue to see your well laid out, creative, and informative posters around town; they might decide to look you up. It's not just about attracting the new fan with a single show, a post online, or a poster in a coffee shop. Some people want to see your name consistently before they decide to check you out. Keep that in mind as you promote online and offline.

The logo can be used in different sizes, just like the font of your band, but always—yes, I really mean it—*always use the same logo and font!*

You can get creative with the overall design, but maintain the uniformity of "the band is the brand." Let the date, the location, and the time shine. You are bringing in people who don't know you, so give them a sense of why they should come to see you, and don't forget that you are advertising the show. QR codes are great to use in the corner of a poster. This allows people to scan your poster with a smart phone and get information about the show or you as well; your poster becomes a gateway to your website!

Keep in mind that you want to present the information as clearly as possible. Do not assume anything when you are creating a poster:

- Do not assume they know where the venue is.

- Do not assume they know what day it is.

- Do not assume they know what time it is.

- Do not assume they will just look your band up on Google.

The less you assume on a poster and the more you clarify, the larger the audience you will reach and potentially bring to that show or a future one.

Where Do You Poster?

Where do you put up posters? Don't just hit the radius of the venue you are playing—a common mistake. Of course you want to work the general vicinity of the venue, but you have to stretch farther out to truly be effective. Hit the busy places: intersections, bus stops, high traffic areas, and places where people may stop and have time to look and read. Record shops are good, too, but don't waste too many little leaflets or mini-flyers in them. How many times have you gone into a record or music shop and seen dozens of handbills with expired dates?

Think of locations where people can't leave for some time. People are more apt to look at your poster or flier and read it while waiting in line: coffee shops, laundromats, the local independent movie theater, and community bulletin boards outside of supermarkets. Use your brain. Do not just print up a series of posters and hit the front and back side of every pole in a concentrated section of town right by the venue. Work to find different ideas and solutions where you can put up posters that will stay up.

Ask businesses that you frequent or that might be owned by people you know. Maybe even offer a small amount of cash to a centralized business if they will put up your flier in their window. This is advertising, period. Think of it as paying to get a poster in a place where you know it will not be taken down and will remain visible right up until the show. You will get a lot of nos, but you will get a number of yeses, too. There are tons of other places: local schools, colleges, different sections of a city, suburban areas, and places as far as a fifteen-mile radius from the gig.

Stay away from trees and other places where posters shouldn't be put up, aren't allowed, and don't belong. Don't get a bad rap as one of those obnoxious spam-poster people who cover up other time-relevant posters, or others will start to cover you up—and there are more of them than you. Be respectful of other bands and events, and check in with the local laws about postering and advertising.

When Do You Poster?

I know some bands that do one crazy session of postering, spending hours canvassing and then hoping for the best. Other bands will hire a poster service and not make any effort whatsoever. These are two methods, but there is a more effective in-between way.

Start about four weeks out, and increase what you put up as the show gets closer. This can be a great method, especially if it is in an area where you live or have close access. Then think of it like a daily task. How many times have you grabbed a cup of coffee at a café and wished you had a flier to put up? Do you have posters, fliers, or leaflets in your car or in your computer bag to drop off when you see a prime location? Make a list of the different sections of a city or town you can hit on different days.

> A great branding and recognition tip is to always put the name of your band and your logo in the same section of every poster. That way, you can be creative with the other art and information while ensuring that even from a distance, people know it's your band and some kind of gig for you.

This does not mean postering for hours a day; this means postering for minutes a day. While you're driving, pull over, put on the blinkers, and put up a poster or a flier. It will take two minutes and that time will aid your exposure and promotion. It will be much easier, and with the new posters going up, you will be seen a great deal more. If you do choose to use a postering service, view it as supplemental to the postering you do yourselves.

Of course, it is more of a challenge for out-of-town shows, but you can reach out to fans through the Internet. Ask them to download that show flier off your website. Offer prizes or some kind of contest or competition for these people to help you get the word out by putting your posters up. Hint: Have your posters available on your website for download both in color and black and white. Ask each fan to print out and put up five posters a week until the show. Make sure they are available in 8.5×11 so that anyone can print them out.

These are very effective methods and an easy way of getting fans involved—an especially great way to create a street team to help in the future.

The more consistently your posters are seen, the more fans you can draw in. You will increase the recognition and the profile of your band and brand. Stretch out the advertising campaign so that as many people as possible can be aware of you and the event. It can only aid you, your show, and your career.

> Make it a rule for yourself to return every email within forty-eight hours. If you don't have the time to address the email, write back and say you will respond at a later date (*mark that in your calendar so you actually do it*) or ask when it is convenient to reach them.
>
> Your strength in networking and professional connections will help you stand out. Show everyone professional respect; it is something they will all remember about you.

STAGE BANNERS: LET AUDIENCES HEAR YOUR MUSIC AND SEE YOUR BRANDING

The stage banner is your opportunity for additional branding of your name and logo *while* you're performing. I'm a big advocate of artists putting up a banner on the stage while they're playing; this provides another level of branding, marketing, and promotion that can help you find and keep more fans.

A banner that's placed behind a band during a show, with their name in the right font and the logo of the band, can help get that name and image into people's minds. When they visit any one of your networking pages or your website and see that logo again, it will remind them of your show. Even having the website on the banner can be helpful for those with cameras on their phones (which these days, is almost everyone) to take a snap shot and visit your website later.

Some places may give you trouble about putting up banners. Don't throw one up if they say no; work with them. Sometimes you might need to drape it over an amp, hang it off the drum riser, or have it on the side of the stage in a less visible place.

Bring along the items necessary to make your banner easier to hang and move. One group I played with had a banner with a really nice case, so it could roll up, which kept it looking nice. These guys had scissors, clothesline rope, and duct tape with them at all times. This allowed the group to put up their banner in any situation that might arise and still have it look its best. Paper towels and Windex were included to keep it clean and looking sharp.

Every time you're seen or heard, you want to convert as many of those people as possible into fans who will come see you again, buy your music, and buy your merchandise. Having a stage banner or even a standing banner by your merchandise table can help to reinforce your name and promote your product. Stage banners can cost a couple hundred dollars but are well worth the investment for the additional branding that they bring to the band.

APPEARANCE: FROM GLOVES TO HATS TO CLOTHES TO ATTITUDES

In addition to all the branding items we've discussed, it's also very important to focus on your actual appearance. How do you physically present yourself? This goes for the pictures you take, the way you appear on stage, and the way you look and sound in interviews, promotional segments, and when talking to industry professionals and fans. Your appearance is a supplementary part of your branding.

This is an area where people get way too stupid. There are those who show up in whatever clothing they have on, without any thought given to their appearance or presentation. There are those who go way overboard with their look and their vibe. Fortunately, there's a happy medium. Look good, smell good, and present yourself well. From the standpoint of the stage appearance, the photos you take, and merchandise, think along the lines of defining a basic look. It doesn't mean you can't switch it up, but think of the effectiveness of Slash's top hat, Alicia Keys's bandana, Michael Jackson's glove, and a thousand other defined and refined elements that help brand an artist or a band with an aspect of their physical appearance.

Sticking with a certain item, color, or overall appearance for a while can help with this branding. Alicia Keys no longer wears the bandana, but it was part of her branding and marketing as she came up and helped to make her that much more recognizable.

Small apparel consistencies can be remembered. Think of the Mighty Mighty Bosstones with their Converse shoes (yeah, I'm dating myself a bit, but still love those guys). There are dozens of artists you can think of who have that one consistent accessory or piece of clothing. On the same note, watch out for copying a worn-out fad, like big jewelry or bling. It's been overdone; you'll just pigeonhole your look as a copycat.

It's true that larger artists will switch things up and change styles more frequently, but while you're growing and building up to that level, have consistency in your appearance and dress. This will help people remember you and help to brand your look and promote you beyond the music. Define your look, and if you need help, ask someone you know who has a sense of style or might have an idea of what you do or don't look good in.

Remember, while Nicki Minaj can have a thousand different looks, she also has a marketing campaign well over $100,000, commercials, and a very high level of exposure to allow her the freedom to express herself with a wider array of fashion and her appearance. Find that initial look and stick to it for a while as you grow your level of recognition. Give people and the industry a sense of a physical branding to your look and your appearance. As things grow with your fan base and your sales, you will be able to play a little more with various looks.

HONOR: THE LAST PART OF YOUR BRANDING FOR THE MUSIC INDUSTRY

All industries have liars, and the music industry is definitely no exception. Many people don't follow through on their word; many lack honor, consideration, and professionalism. It's unfortunate that those who do lack honor—who lie or skip out on promises—grow defensive about their lack of honor when called out on it. Instead of righting wrongs or taking steps to modify their actions, they offer excuses for why it's okay for them to be dishonorable.

In the arts, as in any other profession, you must have the professional abilities and skills; with so many artists going after the same jobs, tours, and recordings, it takes ability, professionalism, *and* honor for people to call on you and continue to call on you again and again. Your word—your honor—is the final element of your branding.

Communication and a clear mutual understanding between two or more people builds the best route to success in any venture. I don't expect . . .

- immediate action,
- instant perfection,
- total comprehension,
- complete implementation, or
- flawless execution.

I do expect the best communication and honest effort to create the best plans for the best results while being able to stay on the same page as much as possible. If that concept doesn't work for you, then you won't be working with me.

Brand your honor in the same way you brand everything else. Uniformity, consistency, and recognition of an artist or band with a good reputation stands out brightly in a world delivering the opposite. When you give your word, honor it and follow through with it. These simple (Captain Obvious) steps will give you a leg up with honor:

- You say you're going to be somewhere. Show up.
- You know that you are going to be delayed. Tell the person that is waiting on you.
- You say you're going to do something. Do it.
- You say you're going to pay someone. Pay them or make arrangements.

In today's music business you are going to want to brand yourself with the reputation of a skilled, competent professional whose playing lives up to your honor and dependability. Be one of those people known for making it happen, executing, and completing things—not the person only known for doing his or her best, trying, or "seeing what we can do." The difference between these two types of people is paramount.

Honor your commitments, your promises, and your own goals. If something goes wrong, do all you can to make it right. Regardless of the booking, the gig, the contract, or the promise, as long as you do what you say you're going to do or make every effort to resolve an emergency situation, then you truly are a professional with honor in every sense of the word.

CLOSING THOUGHT

Your band is the brand—you are the brand. Your brand needs to deliver consistent content that carries the uniformity of your message, description, reputation, links, and information to the person or persons looking at you or trying to find you. It is imperative that you never lose sight of this.

Do not assume that people are seeing you. The more you can clarify, optimize, and engage your fans and strangers with branded marketing and merchandise, the better chance you have of being seen and then heard. The bands who build the best fan bases out of complete strangers are the ones who brand their images, their logo, their message, and their tagline and bio, all while giving these strangers as much content as possible to pique their interest.

Post easy-to-follow links that allow potential fans and industry professionals to simply click through them to get where they want to go. It would be nice if you had the opportunity to just get to play in front of every single person. But since you probably don't have the marketing and touring budget to play every city in the world, to contact every media outlet, or to reach every industry professional, why not work on the root of the brand to draw in as many people as possible to your well branded, uniform, and recognizable information, music, and merchandise? That way, people who don't know you yet can see your brand and then click through to listen, watch, and connect with the music.

10

MUSIC MARKETING AND PROMOTIONS

OPENING THOUGHT

The final, continual step in a successful artist's career in music is the marketing and promotions phase. It doesn't matter whether you are Lady Gaga, with millions of dollars, or Baby Indie Artist, with a couple hundred to your name; marketing and promoting is what will allow you to do what you dream to do: make your living by playing music.

From your presence on stage to your presence online, from the print advertising to the advertising on your website, from the social media updating to the blogs you write, the videos you post, and the pictures you are tagged in, it all comes down to marketing yourself, marketing your music, marketing your shows, and marketing your merchandise. When the money starts to come in, this is the place where you have to reinvest to continue to grow and make even more money; your marketing and promotions budget needs to be fed like a growing child.

Sad but true: The worst product marketed the best way will still be successful. Anyone can survive with the right promotional push behind them, even if just for a little while. But with your great music, as you continue to write, perform, tour, and stay on top of the business *and* creative sides, you can have a rewarding career.

GETTING OUT THE WORD FOR THE RESULTS

After the album is finished, after the branding is in place, marketing and promotions constitute a series of steps you will continue to take to drive the sales of your music and get people to your shows and your merchandise. Budgeting for your marketing and promotions from the beginning of your music business plan will make life easier for you and the band once you release and are out there pushing that product. But you must plan *effectively for your marketing*.

Regardless of what size budget you are working with, the lion's share must be allocated for making people aware of you and your products. I'll say it again: The most common mistake is spending every dollar on a release without leaving a single penny to push it. The bulk of those projects fail, right out of the gate. A blended marketing approach has to consider the advertising and the marketing plan as well as cross-marketing, music marketing, and band promotion to connect you to the widest audience possible.

Be creative and think out of the box, but never forget that the longest part of your album journey is not the recording or the release; it is the marketing to move it to your fans and your continually growing base in an organized, money-saving, and productive way that creates revenues for a long time to come.

Marketing is the biggest part of your career outside the music itself; like it or not, marketing your music will sometimes overshadow the music. Have you ever seen a band and had no idea how they could score that particular gig or be selling so well? Maybe you even see yourself as better. Or perhaps you know of other bands that are just as good and have gone nowhere. The answer is marketing.

Once you've accepted this principle, you then must determine how and when you start marketing. The first three initial steps of core marketing include preproduction, production, and execution. Approaching these three steps with attention to detail, patience, and preparation will deliver the best results.

1. Preproduction—The pre-production step of your marketing approach involves the careful consideration of the materials you are preparing to market. This also applies to how you put together the foundation and the blueprint of your band, your brand, your sound, and your image. Creating the bio with the tagline and one-liner, making sure the logo works and can be copied and pasted across everything online and off, and organizing the key marketing elements of your content, your call to action, and the layout of your marketing plan will allow you to be uniform and prepared. Are you building the promotional items for the launch? Is your website designed for easy access and navigation?

Remember, you shouldn't wait until the album is done to start this stage! Artists who take care of this before the album help their releases happen faster and stronger than those who rush through the marketing after the album is done.

Do you have a plan for social networking sites, with branding and continuity across all platforms? Is your CD and download card being designed with your branding in mind? Do you have a content plan to continually build consistent, well branded, and uniform marketing pieces to go up online and out to press and media on a regular basis?

2. Production—Make sure you have all the items in place and a plan to handle the smallest online post to the most expensive advertising campaign. A sturdy, multitiered approach is essential; this includes the flyers you're going to be putting up, the contacts you're going to reach out to, the ads you're going to buy, the hands you're going to shake, and a prepared database of addresses and emails you're going to maintain. You should have a plan for reaching out to people that avoids spamming or bothering people; they'll just throw your mailings away or delete your emails, two things you want to avoid. Plan to do the most effective things on a daily, weekly, monthly, and yearly basis.

3. Execution/launch and release—If you build it right, the fans and sales will come. Just as you write songs or work a tune until it sounds the way you want it to, you should hone your marketing until it achieves the same level of perfectionism. You've created all the pieces and you've made the plan for the launch; now you're headed to the deep end of the pool. This has to be done relentlessly, diligently, and consistently with the plan and all the pieces you created in the first two stages.

Don't imagine that you'll magically have a team of marketing people who will do all this for you. You'll need to be the one to stand at the merchandise table instead of drinking right after a gig. You'll need to be the one who gets up a little earlier to update your social media with fresh content or add a few new friends on this or that platform before you head to your day job.

> By executing your marketing with the most effective methods on the smallest budget, you highlight to investors, labels, and managers that with a larger budget, you could achieve so much more.

Besides, even if you do make it big and have a marketing department behind you, you'll still spend hours of time every day on phone calls, in interviews, attending events you don't want to attend, and working on things other than music. The biggest names in the industry spend more of their day on marketing than they do on music. It sounds crazy, but it's true. Just open Yahoo or Google and click on the music or entertainment links; notice all those stories, blog posts, and tweets from musicians, actors, and others? Look at your Facebook news feed. Do you think that content got there by accident?

Too many bands are just buying up the latest music business directory and spamming everyone they can on Facebook, Twitter, YouTube, ReverbNation, iTunes, and other social media pages. That is not a marketing plan! Neither is trying to sell yourself and your music to new fans with the same tired pitches, or cutting corners with unbranded materials and no marketing plan whatsoever. Your marketing has to stand out. If it doesn't, you're just one in the millions getting lost in the mix.

SO YOU THINK YOU HAVE A BACKGROUND IN MARKETING AND PROMOTION?

I find it interesting that so many artists only think about the recording; when it's completed, they face the scary world after the release in a completely unorganized fashion. Now they have to back up and clean up before they can move forward effectively. Even when artists realize all the elements that need to be taken care of—the ones that they missed the first time around—they still cut corners. You didn't cut corners with the recording did you? So why cut corners on marketing the right way for the release? It's essential to create the right plan for your marketing. Many artists actually do have a sense of what it's going to take.

We've all grown up with marketing and branding; that's made us want Cocoa Puffs and Trix. The box was cool or the cartoon was neat. The cartoon characters, the tagline, the song, and the rest of it drew us in. It was consistent, well branded, and marketed to reach us. I remember telling my mom we needed to get StarKist Tuna because of Charlie the Tuna on the ads. And the concept of marketing affected us even if we didn't eat that cereal or brand of tuna.

Those same rules apply to music . . . mostly. People who say "Oh no, you don't have to worry about some specific marketing point or requirement" or "That can easily be accomplished on a grassroots level" don't understand how to market independent musicians. Many marketing or music industry pros who held high positions in multimillion-dollar companies—including some with résumés that include big-name artists—claim to be able to help independent artists. While some have transitioned and understand the differences, many only know how to market a project if they have the label contacts and the large budget to which they are accustomed. In other words, that person you hired because of the amazing résumé can't do anything for you unless he or she has skills and know-how for working on a grassroots budget.

The marketing items and approaches you create must be adjusted to the budget you actually have, not the budget of the bands you love. For example, let's say you love a group that has a very detailed logo. You need to understand how much that logo is being exposed and the cash required for such visibility. That group can afford to have a logo with a little more detail and even a font that might be a little harder to read because of the exposure their large marketing budget allows for. But an independent artist with a much smaller budget would be advised to go with a logo that's easier to read, whether it's on a pen or on a poster, since he or she doesn't have the money to put it everywhere they wish they could right off the bat.

I'm not saying that someone with a fancy résumé is lying when telling you that he or she knows how to market, but I am saying their knowledge and experience must fit your unique situation. Lo-fi and grassroots marketing approaches are still in the process of being created and honed. Pay attention to the person who's giving you advice. Make sure you move forward with people who can help you advance with plans that apply to you, your budget, and your career. By asking for examples or references for the work they have done *on your level*, you will protect yourself from involvement with someone who may have had a successful background in marketing but who does not have the knowledge, skills, or abilities to help you market your product in the industry of today with the budget that you currently have.

You know those people who tag you in shoe ads on Facebook? You know those emails you get through Twitter with a link where someone is supposedly saying something horrible about you? You know them: They are spam! And the ones that came from accounts of people you know indicate that they have had their accounts hacked.

Change your passwords every six months.

Ask your fans now and then if they have ever received some kind of spam from you. Stay on top of the applications you add, and double-check the small print for what you are allowing the apps to do.

The more proactive you are with spam and watching out for hackers, the less chance you will get hacked or come off like a spammer.

EXTENDING YOUR NETWORKING SPECTRUM: ONLINE MARKETING 101

How do you reach out and market to fans, industry professionals, and everyone else on the web? Most people think the answer is a website, a Facebook friend or fan account, maybe a blog, a YouTube page, a Pinterest account, some sales pages, and maybe a couple of other social networking sites.

But it takes a lot more than just having a website and being on some social networking pages to build an effective presence and reach new fans, create awareness and sales, and keep the existing fans engaged.

In order to have a persistent and effective web and social media presence, you have to show up on a number of these sites and deliver consistent, well-branded marketing content with a call to action that connects people with you, your music, and your products. This will give you the best results that will find you new fans, contacts, and opportunities.

The more places that you and your content can be optimized and discovered on the Internet, the larger the audiences you will be able to reach. Do not take the stubborn mindset of saying you only need to be on Facebook. Yes, it is the most popular website in the world—one billion accounts—but you might get skipped over or lost in the sea of other artists.

Whether you are a musician, an author, a business, a manager, an agent, or anyone else who is trying to reach a wider audience, it is your responsibility to be as accessible as possible. This allows the most options to be seen, brings in a new fan base, and raises your visibility. So when you think about it, just having a website, a Facebook page, and a YouTube channel really isn't the most effective approach to achieving the broadest recognition and awareness. Having a legion of networking sites updated on a regular basis will create continuity, activity, and awareness while helping to get your name, your band, and your brand optimized.

Don't get overwhelmed with the idea of being on a ton of these sites, either. With many of the site aggregators like HootSuite and the share options on YouTube, where you can simply click a share button to post your video on sites like LinkedIn, StumbleUpon, Tumblr, Blogger, and others, it makes it easier than ever to update more sites faster. Setting up these sites with basic content and logos and then connecting them to HootSuite or site aggregators like ShareThis will allow you to easily update and share links in seconds to blogs, videos, music samples, and pictures.

What Should I Have on These Sites?

Uniformity and consistency is key. Don't have five different sites with five different bios. That is neither good branding nor will it help to optimize you on the web. It doesn't display professionalism to the industry professionals or investors that you may be trying to attract, either. You want to display uniformity, branding, and show you have an understanding of the basic requirements of proper promotion and marketing. Use the marketing items you created in the production phase of your marketing plan. Here is the basic list of things to have on social media sites after you have set them up and connected them to your main page or site aggregator:

- **Bio.** Depending on what the site allows—one-liner, tagline, signature, short bio, etc.

- **Tagline.** Always have that tagline on every site!

- **Logo.** Your graphic image.

- **Photos.** A primary photo and at least five other photos that you can display. Some sites will allow for just one, and that primary photo will always be the same. On others (like the photo sites) you can put up nine or as many as you want.

- **Artist website and link to other social media sites.** Have ready to be added a list of the links from other sites where you can be found so that you can be cross-referenced as much as possible. Include places where people can buy your music, albums, and merchandise.

- **Video.** Have your videos ready for sites where you can add a video.

- **Songs and albums.** Upload your music samples so that people can hear you. Get more of your music out there where it is easy to obtain.

Keep track of it all your materials in one place. Create one master document for all your networking sites. Have a Word document, a text document, or spreadsheet where you can easily copy and paste each content element listed above as needed. Some sites make simple copy/paste rather difficult; have your text in a simple format (.txt) to avoid this annoyance. Certain sites will allow you to list all of your information, while other sites allow only limited amounts. One master document that can be consistently copied from will make signing up for each of these sites a breeze and dramatically reduce the setup time. This will, in turn, allow for marketing uniformity and better optimization all around.

On your master document, list your logins, user names, and passwords for each of your sites. Keep them all in one place to make tracking and updating easier. Add a column to note the last time you visited or updated the site. With site aggregators and sharing options, you may not log directly into a website for quite some time. For example, the Myspace page I have automatically updates my marketing content with a simple share button, but I haven't actually logged into Myspace in over six months. When you have a major change, you can visit these sites and update easily, while knowing when you were last there.

How Many Should I Be On?

How many fans do you want? There are limitless sites out there and new ones are popping up each day. Why not just keep signing up for different places to be seen, heard, and found? Don't think that a certain number is the right number. Think of it instead as creating more connections through more networks. At the same time, don't pull down a site because it is no longer popular. Myspace has not been too active for the past several years, but having your well-branded marketing content with simple and continual updates keeps the site effective for your overall optimization and branding. And as of this writing, Justin Timberlake has put in a great deal of money to help revive Myspace. So, while it isn't much right now, it does have the chance for a new resurgence.

The further you extend your online reach, the better. Be on numerous sites. With sharing and aggregation options, it only takes seconds to get your updates and marketing content to more sites easier and faster.

Your Posting Plan and the Most Effective Content for Online Marketing

Are you posting daily, and if so, are you only posting once a day? How many friends do you have who post way too often with stuff that you don't even care about? Do you want to be viewed that way? Or would it be a better approach to put up something strong and promotional that makes people want to go to your page daily to see what you posted or updated that didn't show up in their feed? That approach is simple, logical, and smart.

Did you put up a video? An audio sample? A blog entry? Maybe some of your lyrics? How about some pictures from a recent show? Did you take the extra steps to name them with the best keywords to optimize them? How about making a schedule for what you put up and when: blogs on Mondays, videos on Tuesdays and Thursdays, pictures on Wednesdays, and so forth. Give people a reason to visit your page and look for you instead of taking the passive approach that you will just show up in their feed.

Your website, Facebook page, Twitter, Pinterest, music sample sites, and other places that fans can find you should already have the static marketing and promotional content in order to be optimized. But the updating, the sharing, and the content that you post will maintain an older fan's interest while simultaneously adding new fans to the mix. Think about what is going to draw someone to your website, your products, and you. Unfortunately, too many artists think they can just post a single music video that will just draw all these fans, views, and interest. While adding a music video is a good idea, you should also be posting videos every week to keep fresh content updated on a regular basis.

Separate yourself from the pack! Millions of bands have millions of websites; besides the music, what is going to draw them to you? You can't put up a new song every day (and anyway, it should be a song sample, something they can't rip and steal). Mix it up and use a variety of media options. Think of both the fan who might visit your page every day looking for an update and the weekly visitor who wants to see a whole bunch of new stuff all at once. Your call to action is the cherry on top that draws these fans to your music, your products, and your shows.

Polyamorous Posting: Spread the Love (or at Least Spread It Out)

Don't be like those bands who throw all their updates and items up at once. That is oversaturation; it blasts out a whole bunch of new content and then there is nothing for a long time. Think for the long term, focusing on continuity and regularity. If you have five different items you can put up—a picture, a video, a blog, a demo or sample of a new song, and a news update about the coming gigs next month—then use a full five-day week to bring that information to the web. Take the time to find the right keywords to optimize every post and every update. Think of every update as constant marketing. A post that can work effectively for the day that you post it should also bring awareness of older updates. Make every post work for yesterday, today, and tomorrow.

Gain a reputation for presenting new content as often as possible and on a regular schedule. This will make hardcore fans come every day, and lower-level fans will know that if they have not been to the site in a while, they need to check in to see new content. Tease, play, and give people a reason to revisit.

You have more to say than you realize. Here is a simple list of some updates you can do:

- **Music samples.** Don't put up a whole bunch of new songs; stick with samples! Provide a different flow: maybe one a week or perhaps the changing versions of a song from preproduction to final mix. Maybe put a live sample next to the recorded material to showcase the comparison between the recording and a live performance. Even if the album is done, don't put the samples all up at once. If you are taking the time and scheduling the release right (hint!) it is going to be at least a couple months before you have your release party, your press release, and the promotional items in place. You can use the time between the completion of the recording and the release to put out little teasers and draw people into wanting to buy the recording.

- **Music videos.** Post a short video—again, samples! People have a short attention span and are viewing more brief videos than longer ones. These can include you playing in the studio, performing live, or even in rehearsal.

- **Nonmusic videos.** Interviews with the artist or the band on topics inside and outside music are a great way to engage fans, new and old. How about videos of the load-in or load-out—something a little different with a touch of your own personality? Video shorts that you capture with your smart phone a couple of times a week can be optimized properly to draw many more people to find your music versus posting a single music video that you spent way too much to make.

- **Blogs.** Update at least once a week. In a band, each member can take a different week to talk about where they came from, something personal, or perhaps their opinions on a particular topic: favorite musicians or songs . . . anything. These can draw people and create content about your band to get the name and links out on the web. Work the keywords and optimization while making sure that signature and call to action is bringing readers to you, your music, and your merchandise after they have seen the content.

- **Pictures.** Add pictures and, of course, put full captions on the pictures as well as tagging people, places, and so on. Try posting memes, too!

- **Merchandise items.** You can feature a merchandise item such as a hat, T-shirt, coffee mug, or anything that is selling less than other items. Make up a story about it; give it a special sale price. Do something to draw them to that item for that day or week.

- **Contests.** Try a monthly contest to draw people into participating on your site. You are trying to pull these people in and make them return, so pull out all the stops and give the viewer a number of reasons to click through and go to your main site.

- **Reviews.** Once a month put up a review about the band: a good review coming from somewhere credible, not just an iTunes user, ReverbNation, CD Baby, or fan review. If you have a series of new reviews, compact them to one link. Just remember, too many reviews covering the same album becomes redundant and annoying to existing fans.

- **References or referrals.** Occasionally link an update to another band or their song or video. This can help with cross-marketing while showing you in a good light with other artists. Talk about an artist you like, one that you opened for, or someone who opened for you. Often they will repay the favor.

Be a "Transformer": Optimize to the Prime (Get It?)

Mark every picture, every blog, every video, and everything else with keyword-significant titles, full descriptions, and as much information as you can add to every update, so that it optimizes as much as possible across the web. After time, these daily updates make you that much more searchable. Always close out all updates with your signature, the primary links, and your call to action (covered in the bio section in chapter nine). Update to market and bring the fans to you, your music, your shows, and your products: Never lose sight of that when posting.

Be a Squirrel: Store Nuts for Winter

You don't have to create your updates on the day they go up. If you are on a writing or a video spree, you can squirrel away updates for many days or weeks and post them over a longer period of time. When I am working in the studio or traveling for speaking, I always write my blogs and shoot my video blogs in advance so I can concentrate on the recording or the seminars and be able post them easily and quickly the day that I have scheduled to put them up. You can do the same, editing four or five videos or preparing the blog and picture updates well in advance. This way, during busier times or when you are on the road and have a little less time to do certain things, you have a backup that you can work from, and you are still putting up consistent, well-prepared marketing content and updates.

In fact, creating a backlog of extra content for your music marketing is a great way to get ahead of the game. It's hard to get into the daily routine of posting solid, optimized, and well-created content for marketing such as videos, blogs, and other materials for posting. It's also helpful for those days where you just don't have enough time.

WHAT ARE YOU RELEASING, AND HOW OFTEN?

To avoid having to constantly push the same product over and over again, think about not releasing everything at once. Why not go in the studio and cut twenty songs? Release two EPs six months apart with five songs on each, and then each month add a digital download online for sale. That gives you new music and products every single month.

Combine that with adding a different merchandising item, and you will be able to keep audiences interested as you market new elements that reinforce and invite people to look at the older ones. Much better than shoving "buy my album" down people's throats for twenty-four months!

It's simple: The more content you have, the more you are updating and the more media is being optimized across the web. That means more people will see, hear, search, and recognize you over time. You will keep the interest of old and new fans by constantly giving them more content to come back and view. Switch it up, make it interesting, and give yourself the opportunity to build a stronger base of existing fans while getting your name, music, videos, blogs, and whatever else out to new fans.

This also connects you on multiple levels with your old and new fans by engaging and networking with them to maintain and expand their interest in you. Posting regular, well-marketed, and optimized content will help in the moment and also will compound the information about you, making you easier to find online. Consistently putting up content will also help your reputation with investors, labels, managers, and other industry people by showcasing how you take every step you can to market, network, connect, engage, and build a larger fan base each day.

YouTube and the Most Effective Ways to Optimize Video Content

Musicians, artists, and people in and out of the music business need to think about how everything is going to be seen today, tomorrow, next week, next month, and next year. Branding online is crucial, content is crucial, marketing is crucial, and so is converting those views, listens, reads, shares, likes, pins, adds, and whatever else into fans who are going to buy your music and merchandise and come to see your shows. That is why you want to make sure everything you post and put online is converting to sales, new fans, and profit. Otherwise, you are just posting an online journal that will not have the staying power or the optimization for people to find you, learn about you, genuinely like you, and want to get more of you.

So how do you address this? As mentioned before, make sure you are adding your links, one-liner, tagline, and call to action about your songs, your EP, your album, and your merchandise. Ensure uniformity in the signature or attachment in your blogs, your videos, your photos, and the descriptions for song samples. Uniformity and the right keywords and phrases will allow your content to be found that much easier.

The most effective example of this in the past few years has been YouTube. According to YouTube press statistics (http://youtube.com/yt/press/statistics.html):

- More than 1 billion unique users visit YouTube each month.
- Over 6 billion hours of video are watched each month on YouTube.
- 100 hours of video are uploaded to YouTube every minute.
- 70 percent of YouTube traffic comes from outside the United States.

- In 2011 YouTube had more than 1 trillion views or around 140 views for every person on earth. And that stat is now two years old.

- 500 years of YouTube video are watched every day on Facebook, and over 700 videos are shared on Twitter each minute.

- 100 million people take a social action on YouTube (likes, shares, comments, etc.) every week.

Those are pretty amazing numbers and facts. So use them to your advantage! Right now YouTube is the place to have your videos. You should have a lot of them going up on a regular basis. Vimeo is gaining steam, and I advise artists to post in both places, but getting that content up on YouTube is key right now, and it places you in Google searches much faster. If you hone in on the best ways to post, you can achieve that branding goal in the short term and in the long term get the most out of your content and the conversion of that content to sales and fans.

The most effective videos are being put up with the correct content behind them. Content is king, and you want a lot of it, but you want to deliver the content so that it can be discovered by people who are not directly searching for you. In other words, if you only put up videos with your band name, the names of your songs, or the words that only you and your standard fans relate to, then those are the only views you are going to get. It is a much better idea to set that video up for the most views by having the best keywords, keyword phrases, and content listed under that video. This includes having the best copy and links to your websites and social media, and properly uploading that video for the highest rankings with the most ways for it to be found in searches.

So, here's the simple summary of YouTube effectiveness: Make sure that all your videos are formatted with correct titles, keyword phrases, and keywords for what the video is about. This way, more people who are looking for that sort of video will come upon it. For example, if you list a video as the title of your band, the name of the song, the date, and the venue, it will probably get lost among the millions of videos unless you are already famous. But, if you use Google AdWords or another keyword tool to find the best phrases at the lower competition levels mixed with the correct content, you will have a well-optimized video. This will also allow it to rank higher in the searches to allow for more views and a better chance at higher conversion-to-sales ratios.

After a friend of mine showed me some of the patterns of productivity on YouTube for achieving higher rankings, I started playing with YouTube videos. My original focus was on music consulting. I had put up a couple videos over 2011, but not all that many. They had my name in the title and the focus was very direct. The videos had good information, but the views were pretty scarce.

When I began to shoot videos at the beginning of 2012, I took that extra time to use Google AdWords and look at the global monthly searches and competition numbers. After a few weeks of posting, I was able to watch almost every single video track in the top ten for searches on the primary keyword phrase part of the title—almost immediately. In turn, I also saw the views go up. Very few people were searching for Loren Weisman, but lots of people were searching for music consultant, music coach, music marketing, music business plan, music consulting, music coaching, music mentor, college speaker, and other phrases that artists wanted to know about.

I formatted my videos with that consideration: When I thought about what people were looking for, I was able to draw more in for the searches by setting up, optimizing, and putting out the information that people wanted. Then in the video, I was able to share who I was, what I brought to the table, and more of the personal experience. This also made people more aware of my book and my services, which was the best way to advertise my approach, my views, and myself.

As of July 1, 2013, I had broken the four-million-view mark with 200 videos put up over 18 months. Eighty-five were showing up in the top spot and one hundred more were in the top ten on the first page of results. This was with no advertising campaign for the videos with YouTube.

Your videos do not need to be all music, and they do not need to be fully produced music videos. I shot most of my videos off my phone or my laptop. This is a place where quantity wins over quality. It is also free to shoot a video on a smart phone! You can make joke videos, bloopers, and videos about your influences, your rehearsal, your gear, or anything else. The point is that the more content you have going up that is fully optimized and uniform with all your branding, the more viewers, fans, and conversions you will achieve.

Make videos that will draw interest right now for some new people but also be part of the stack of videos that people can view later. At the same time, the well-optimized videos will work their way up in the searches and in Google.

What do you think is going to be more effective in drawing in more people more often for the longest amount of time: one really expensive music video that is thrown up with the hope of catching a viral wave or the attention of some label; or a whole bunch of videos about you, the music, the band, your influences, your background, jokes, bloopers, and other stuff? And remember that these videos are optimized for the highest rankings in YouTube and Google, building up better search capability, more visibility, and showcasing you as an artist or a group who puts up new and fresh content all the time.

Answer: Duh! Go with the second.

This is something you want to be doing, and I am the "proof of concept" example. Take the extra time to organize, optimize, and set up your content to allow you to get the most views by way of the most searches on the broadest scope to be able to funnel them toward you, your music, your merchandise, and your message.

Here are a few tips for posting the most effective search-engine-optimized and keyword-phrase-friendly videos to get your marketing, your music, and your band out there that much more effectively:

- Keep the title of the video under seventy characters. Google likes that!

- Find a primary keyword phrase using Google AdWords or another keyword tool that has low competition and is not too high in the monthly searches. Check that phrase in a YouTube search.

- Name the video with your primary keyword phrase. For example, instead of uploading vid18274h48.mov, upload musicmarketing.mov.

- In your title, try to capture a second and third keyword phrase that could help the video be found. Also, add five to seven more keywords—not in the title, but in the body of your description. Make it a keyword relating to the video or topic, and make sure it shows up in the description.

- On the top of your content area, add a web link or store link.

- Repeat the title of the video again in the body of the description.

- Give your video a subtitle that can go across a number of videos.

- Stay in the neighborhood of three hundred words—but not too much more—in the description.

- Repeat your primary keyword phrase and the second and third keyword phrases at least three times in the body of the description. This way . . .

  o the video is titled with the phrase;

  o the actual title has that keyword phrase;

  o that phrase shows up again in the title in the body; and

  o then it shows up three more times in the body.

- Add your signature, your call to action, and your links again at the bottom of the video.

This might seem like a lot of work, but it is very effective. For examples of this on YouTube, visit http://youtube.com/lorenweisman. I follow this method for every video I post; I recommend you do the same. These basic steps to building up keyword optimization and your search engine optimization can also be applied to your blogs, photos, music samples, and other content as well.

Blogging: Using the Written Word to Market the Music and the Band

Blogging is stronger than ever. Many people are out there complaining, commenting, and documenting their thoughts all the time. It's amazing that there are so many blogs, and yet in most cases, it's page after page of drivel. I'm not saying that bands and artists should always write a book's worth of blogs or try to adapt to a specific style of writing, but I do think that now more than ever, bands and artists should be blogging as part of promoting, marketing, and exposing themselves to the world. With the same formula for optimization as the videos, blogging on a regular basis can raise your presence and help you connect with your audience on so many different levels inside and outside of music.

Again, make sure you are getting that signature and call to action in there at the close of every blog post, just like the video. Tell them where they can find you and what you are about. Don't leave them to search for it; give it to them.

Never assume that someone will read a blog, see a photo, listen to a song, or watch a video and automatically go to Google and search you. Add links, your signature, and your call to action to make the next step of connecting a new fan to you as easy as possible.

Don't forget to switch it up among members (if you're a band), and remember that the blogs don't have to be long and complicated. Just keep updating your site and make sure new things are being posted on a regular basis. If something exciting is always happening, people will keep coming back for more. Consistent traffic should be a primary goal of your marketing plan to create the best conversion rates.

Start blogging! Say what you're thinking; share a little more of yourself with your audience. Of course, stay positive and don't fall victim to all that "woe is me" crap: There is enough of that out there. Give people something to read, something to click through that's fun or enjoyable, something that ties you to readers and will make them come back for more. Just as you share your music with your fans, share your thoughts and ideas outside of music, and maybe you will draw people in through other means.

You can grow an audience with your blogs and videos outside of music. Write about things that inspire you, other musicians you like, experiences, views on life, heartache, wine, and anything else. As long as you tie in your signature and call to action with the keyword optimization and marketing considerations in place, you are marketing your music in a great way.

If you really think when you put out a message or a request for a vote or a like that you will get 100 percent of your friends or followers to vote or click, you are either delusional or you have the most amazing Facebook network in the universe.

If you think tagging people who have nothing to do with your post or picture is really going to draw positive attention, you are off base.

If you continue to invite every single Facebook friend to every single gig, you're not doing it right.

Think about the best ways to reach the widest array of an audience with the best results without being annoying.

MARKET TIMING: THE WHEN OF POSTING

When is the best time to make posts and announcements? Let's say you have gotten to the point with your online music marketing where you are creating regular content that points people back to your website, your social media, and your store. This is all good stuff, but beyond the actual point in time when you post something, are you actually thinking about the timing and frequency of when you are putting up your posts? What marketing time or times are best for you? When you have your music marketing in place and your posts and announcements ready to go on a regular basis, take that last step to figure out the best times to post.

A lot of people have an overall answer about the best time to post, but it can be a very individualized thing. Think about the end result of the post that you are creating. Most are looking to get fans and to get those fans to share your music, your sites, and your appearances with others. Still, in the very end, isn't it about the conversions, the sales of the music, the merchandise, and the people coming out to the shows?

Only your biggest fans are reading every post and every announcement, so you have to think about what time of the day or week you are getting the most reads and how that is converting to sales. With both Google Analytics and Facebook reporting (right on the admin section of your Facebook pages) you can get a better sense of how many people are reading you or clicking through. Try a test: Pick a certain time of day for posting your items for one week. Then at the end of the week, look back. How were sales? How were the reads? How many people actually saw what you did? How much did you sell that week online?

For example, on my *Artist's Guide* Facebook page, I know the blog and the video for February 22, 2013, was seen by 742 people; the data is right there when you click "insights" on your Facebook page. Then for that week, I looked to see who filled out the consulting form. I found that when I posted certain things earlier or later in the day, more people were connecting or converting than at other times.

You can take the same approach. It may take a while, but find the marketing time that is most effective for you so you can reach as many people as possible and convert them to fans, buyers, and solid connections who will share your posts, your music, and your pages with even more people.

Sure, it is hard work to keep online content fresh, but it is necessary. You have to work hard to continue to update with new songs, new pictures, new blogs, and new material on a regular basis. When it comes to online marketing—or any type of marketing, for that matter—there are two key things you want to make happen and continue to happen:

1. Create a larger and wider fan base that is interested in you, paying attention to you, going to shows, and buying your music and merchandise.

2. Maintain the existing fan base by keeping them interested in you, keeping their long-term attention, and having them buy newer merchandise, keep going to shows, and referring you to potential fans.

Here's a very simple formula for maintaining and growing your fan base without being boring or confusing:

- **Think.** Before you update or post, think about what you are putting up there. Is it something that would draw in an older fan but still make sense to a potentially new one?

- **Keep it clean.** Your pages should be uncluttered and informative. Make sure that someone revisiting gets the idea of who you are just as much as someone coming to your page for the first time. Is the information about your sound clean and clear; are you communicating where to get to sites to buy your music or read about upcoming shows?

- **Get fresh.** Do not overpost things from the past or, at least, be very conservative about it. You do not want to repeatedly put up pictures or talk about events that happened months and years ago. Your fans have already seen it, and potential fans or industry people may view this as the only highlight you have to share. Though that might not be true, it can come off that way. If you have to put up older materials, try to put a new spin on it to keep everyone interested.

WHO DO YOU REPRESENT WHEN YOU PRESENT YOURSELF?

Who are you? Who can it be now? Who's fooling who? Okay, enough song quotes. Think about how you present yourself in front of people. Is it consistent? To maintain a good and consistent reputation, it is a good idea to ask the following:

- Who are you when you are in front of a fan?

- Who are you when you are in front of a booking agent?

- Who are you when you are in front of a *potential* manager or booking agent?

- Who are you when you are talking to someone from the press?

- Who are you when you are around your best friends or buddies?

- Who are you when you are in front of someone who can really help your career?

- Who are you when you are in front of someone who can do nothing for you at all?

- Who are you when presenting yourself online?

Do you change drastically or only slightly? You might want to think about how you are presenting yourself versus how you are being perceived across the board. Applying continuity to your presentation from a branding and marketing sense is important.

Remember that when you are in public, you never know who is in earshot. Standing by your convictions is the safest and easiest way to keep your message clear and avoid the worry of remembering what you told to one person and what you said differently to another. It will also ensure a good reputation in a business filled with two-faced and questionable people.

I have found that the most successful people in music and other businesses present themselves for who they are and what they stand for in a uniform manner, regardless of whom they are in front of. If you feel like you have something to say that you wouldn't say in front of another, maybe choosing to keep that private or shared in a limited circle is a good idea.

Personally, I stand on my convictions, my beliefs, and my experiences. If I am talking about you and have said something to someone else, I am going to say it to your face, if I haven't already. Some call it brash, but I see it as honest. I am the same person regardless of who I am in front of, and I prefer to surround myself with people who are the same way.

SOLICITING AND MARKETING YOURSELF, YOUR MESSAGE, AND YOUR PROMO PACKAGE

So you have the recording, the press and electronic package, a website, social network sites set up, and all your materials in order. You're ready to solicit. Whether it's for shows, management, labels, investors, talent buyers, agencies, booking agents, tours, or festivals, you want to make it complete and professional. Having the package prepared and all your materials, inside and out, in proper shape is extremely important and will allow for the most opportunities and callbacks.

You should have everything available as discussed earlier in the chapter on promotion, but you don't always want to send everything. Make sure you set up a specific packet for each individual recipient. In the intro letter, you can always mention that you have additional materials available for download. This allows immediate and instant access to whoever wants it.

For example, on the bottom of your cover letter or as a last page in the package you can say something like, "More information available upon request. Needed documents can be mailed, faxed, or downloaded at the following locations:

1. Stage Plot—located at http://tag2nd.com/stage-plot
2. Input List—located at http://tag2nd.com/input-list"

By having these links listed on your cover letter or a back page, your recipients have everything they might need or request without feeling overwhelmed.

Fast-forward a couple of steps. You have the marketing and solicitation materials, music, a professional layout, and a package specifically designed for the person to whom you are sending it. Now, how do you frame your package with the right cover letter?

A compelling cover letter is the primary element. This is where you make your case and where you will either stand out from the rest or blend in. This is also where too many bands and artists make mistakes. Arrogance, ego, and attitude are not what you want to portray here, unless you're aiming for an unsavory introduction and a bad reputation right out of the gate.

Below are the five worst things you can put in the cover letter. I compiled this list with help from some friends in the industry. We had a good chuckle emailing our favorites back and forth. The funniest part was that each of us, in all different parts of the industry, have heard all of these at one time or another.

1. We are totally new, unique, and different.
2. We are on the verge of blowing up, big time.
3. We are the next big thing.

4. We will deliver the best show you have ever seen.

5. We don't sound like anyone else.

Of course you want to be confident, and being assertive is good, but *always avoid the above phrases!* These are red flags for industry professionals. Instead, address your audience as if they were your heroes. Would you tell a person who booked one of your favorite shows of all time—some legendary act—that you are going to blow him or her away? Drop the cockiness while keeping up the confidence.

Below are some very professional opening ideas that are used in the industry. Make sure to think about these ideas from the other person's perspective.

- Offer yourself or your band as a service. Highlight in a brief outline how you can be a strong entity to book, sign, or hire.

- Show that you are easy to work with, professional, and business minded. You want to display that it would be a good business move for the person, company, or venue to bring you in.

- Soliciting is not a linear process; it is a parallel one. Just as you want a gig, manager, label, or tour, you have to show, in turn, that you have the best potential to make it a mutually positive arrangement.

- Explain your marketing; use your artist stat sheet to define your marketing and promotional abilities. Show them you are worth the investment and what you will do to market and promote the show.

- Ask nicely! Even when presented with rider and contract options, don't be selfish. Take what you need and don't be the rock star with over-the-top requests. When people are offered the world, honor and respect goes to those who take only what they truly need.

Soliciting doesn't have to be scary. Come off strong, assertive, confident, and professional. Edit your work. Make sure the cover letter and package are correctly put together for the person to whom you are sending it. This is the step where you reach out and pull the industry to you. Make sure everyone you reach sees the best picture possible.

THE ART OF THE EMAIL CONTACT: REACHING OUT THE RIGHT WAY

The ignorance, arrogance, and unprofessional nature of the solicitation emails I receive on a daily basis from artists or their management never cease to amaze me. I'm told these principals apply to basic email etiquette in every profession. Still, the lack of effort is jaw dropping. On any given day, I receive an average of forty emails that are completely out of left field. I mean, the wheel is turning, but the hamster is dead.

If you're soliciting an individual, think about what you're sending out and to whom you're sending it. Your lack of preparation, consideration, or professionalism can destroy that contact and get your email deleted. Worse yet, the person will never get to your music, which was the main point.

I asked some of the same friends in the industry to share their six worst emails, cover letters, or first-contact communications. Without further ado, let's dive into my favorites:

1. "Yo, I have the hottest thing ever. U gotta check this out. This is gonna blow and I will take you wit me." [A crappy social networking site address.] [A name.]

When you address someone as "Yo," it appears that you are mass emailing or spamming anyone who will listen to you. Second, when you state you are the hottest thing ever, you've set the bar pretty high for yourself. You're also using certain keywords that will automatically turn most people off.

The spelling and style are atrocious. The assumption that this person is going to be larger than life and deigns to carry me along is just flat-out rude.

Result: Trash the email. Skip the website. Move on. I'm not the only one; all the others I spoke to did so when they received that type of email.

Remedial action: Tone it down. Spell check. Pick up an English style guide; everyone needs one, not just grammar nerds! Use confidence, but use it carefully. An email oversaturated with confidence comes off as arrogant. Also, supply a little more information.

2. "My name is John Smith, I am the manager for John Doe. [Facebook link.] Thanks, John Smith."

Really? The first time I got an email like this, I was floored. I actually closed my email application and reloaded it, thinking the message was truncated or cut off somehow. When I asked my friends if they had ever received anything like this, they responded, "All. The. Time."

This is the, um, *less than bright* individual who has given you very limited information and seems to have these wild expectations that you will immediately race to the website, listen to the music, and make the magic happen overnight.

Result: Trash the email. Skip the page. Wonder just how foolish people can be.

Remedial action: Formulate a letter! If you are the management, introduce the artist. Make it snappy; summarize in a positive, professional tone. Then ask or request an action. Are you looking for guidance? Are you looking for a producer? Are you looking for a contact?

What is it that you want? Then sign that email with your name, your company if you have one, an email address, and a phone number. Maybe add a website or social networking link to your organization.

3. "Hello, I am the president and CEO of Blah Blah Blah Entertainment. [You know, that would actually be a pretty cool name for an entertainment company.] We represent X artist and are ready to sit down and discuss a plan to bring him over to your organization with us so we all can get rich. We have been waiting for the right moment and the time is now. Call us so we can begin to negotiate . . ."

Okay, these are actually kind of fun; they are very common. On the plus side, the writer does bring up the "we" element; this person is thinking of the reality that profit has to be realized by the artist *and* the companies or people who take an artist to another level. However, this is also a writer who comes off as someone who knows nothing about business yet tries to be the Donald Trump of the music industry. The arrogance implied by "bringing him to the company"—as opposed to confidently "submitting this artist for review or a signing inquiry"—doesn't usually earn many friends.

Result: This email is usually trashed. Sometimes there's a quick check to see if this CEO/president and company is real, but most of the time no one is going to ever hear that song.

Remedial action: Present yourself as accomplished, but don't lie; overconfidence reads as weakness. Remember that all anyone has to do to confirm your validity is search for your company's name in the secretary of state's online database. If you're looking to work with a producer, an agent, a label, or anyone else in the industry, you need to illustrate your business sense and your drive to learn instead of lying about your credentials.

4. Attachments in emails.

These are the emails where people send a song or even six. I've had massive emails come in with zip files of songs from artists that I have never even spoken to. They'll also attach many large picture files, which is unprofessional and rude.

Result: Not only trashing the email, but now you have really annoyed me and everyone else I talk to. Your email is flagged, if not blocked, at this point.

Remedial action: Do not send music files, pictures, posters, or any kind of attachment unless the file has been specifically requested. While some of the other annoying aspects of artists' emails may catch a person on a good day (so they let them fly), this is one that really upsets people. You're slowing up a computer with a large download and could potentially exceed the size limit of an inbox, taking up space and time that is not yours to take up!

On the other hand, placing direct links to streaming song files is a good idea. Let someone click on a link and get right to the song, not having to look through a page or find a button. Links that are directly set to streaming songs are very professional and get significant attention. The same goes for pictures. Place a link to a picture or two. Lastly, title the links; tell the person where they're heading to or being pointed to. For example:

TAG2nd 8 x 10 Promotional Picture: http://tag2nd.com/promo-photo

When I receive this in an email, I know exactly what the link is and where it is taking me. Try to rename the link as well so people know what they're clicking on instead of:

Band Pic @ http://www.tag2nd.com/473thecouchlooksbetteronfire748939383

You may also embed the link so that the text "TAG2nd 8 x 10 Promotional Picture" *is* the link to the picture. Keep in mind that old rule: "(Professional) actions speak louder than (arrogant) words (and sale tactics)."

A final, very important point: Check your damn links to make sure they actually work! Captain Obvious takes off again, but many screw this up and send the person to a wrong page, an empty page, or a 404 page.

5. Failure to follow instructions, of which there are too many email examples to list.

Many companies, producers, and agents have specific rules on what information to email and what information not to email. Some people ask you to fill out a form or they ask for specific information. Unfortunately, too many artists send mass email to the point of spamming, using static templates that do not follow instructions and, at the same time, telegraph that they're not personalizing their communications.

Result: Another trashed email and another contact lost.

Remedial Action: Individualize every email. If you are asked to supply a certain piece of information or present things in a certain way, make sure you do it right. Some of these professionals might actually be testing you; they want to see if you can follow instructions. So follow them and have a better shot at producers or agents not only reading your email but also actually listening to your music.

Take the time to craft an email. If you're trying to find a producer or investor, book a gig, solicit a label, or find a manager, you can draft a basic template letter. But take the time to individualize and format it so that it complies with the requests of the particular person or company receiving it.

Follow the instructions if they are supplied. If there aren't any, do your best to construct a precise, brief, businesslike email. I really recommend sending it first to friends who aren't in the music business. Let them help you edit to put together the best letters.

Have a clear-cut subject line. If you are looking for a review, then make that clear: "RE: Review Inquiry for Writer, Rocker, Biker, Geek—Michael McFarland." This is nice, clear, and to the point. I know someone is looking for a review, the name of the artist, and his tagline.

Tread very carefully on follow-up emails. Many times if you don't get a response, the person is not interested. Do not open up with "Why didn't you answer me?" My latest personal favorite is one that said, "You will be so sorry you didn't contact me, you are an idiot and I will show you." On one hand, I hope you do "show me." I genuinely want to see everyone succeed in the music business. On the other hand, when you tell me I'm an idiot, I absolutely do not want to talk or work with you. Also, if our paths were to cross down the line, you have now left a bad impression.

6. SENDING EMAILS IN ALL CAPS.

Avoid words in all capital letters in both headers and bodies of emails. It's annoying because the recipient feels as if you're yelling, and it makes you look stupid.

Every contact you make, every solicitation you send, every review you pursue is important. Display your professionalism in that first email to get the best results and hope that the reader will follow the link and hear your music to find out more about you. Remember that these people are already being contacted by tens of thousands of others. If you avoid the common mistakes, you will bring positive attention to your email.

> Be careful about direct contacts on sites like Facebook and Twitter. See if you can find a direct contact, and if it is a larger name, make sure you address the letter in a format that assumes someone else is reading it, because more likely than not, this is the case.

When people put effort into their communications with me, I want to return that effort and read the whole email, visit the links, and listen to the music. When they pay attention to the details, I will return the favor. Many people in the industry feel this same way.

Take the time to craft your emails. Show professionalism and demonstrate why your email should be read and why the recipient should listen to your music and consider your request. Be crystal clear in your communication, and your email will be read and considered, unlike those thousands of others who make common and foolish mistakes and end up in the trash.

THE ELEVATOR PITCH: COMMUNICATE YOUR POINT QUICKLY

People usually want plenty of time to explain themselves, their sound, their vision, their goals, and everything else that has to do with them. People like to share as much information as possible. They feel they need to explain everything when it comes to getting a fan or finding a label, a manager, an agent, etc. However, the fast pitch, the one-liner, or the quick explanation are often the most effective ways to present yourself. It shows consideration for the person you're pitching and it proves your overall organization and professionalism.

I get it: It has taken you years to hone your sound and develop your vision for your music, and all you're asking for is a lousy fifteen minutes of someone's time, right? But you need to remember that a lot of others are doing the same thing. The more professional and concise your presentation, the more you will be heard and the better impression you will leave.

Your Fast Pitch

This is your quick and descriptive summary. It's the pitch you make in the elevator when you only have a few seconds to present yourself or your idea. This same pitch should be in your soliciting materials. Make sure the one-liner or that first sentence of your bio is a grabber. It needs to be detailed, catchy, and quick.

The same goes for your tagline. Think of it as a shorter version of the first sentence of your bio. How can you sum up your band and sound in a brief and unique phrase? Stay away from "We are indescribable," "We don't sound like anyone else," "We are totally original, unique, and different," "You have never heard anything like us," or any of those stupid lines that will immediately cast you in an unoriginal light.

For both the written and spoken word, think highlights, think memorable, and think precision. Remember that other people are doing pitches along the same lines. So the faster, more precise, and more detailed you are, the more you will stand out.

Compel them to dig deeper, to ask for more. Go over the basics:

- Who are you?

- What do you want, and what do you bring to the table?

- When are you looking to do it?

- Where are you currently with sales and marketing?

- Why do you think this will work?

- How will this benefit the person you are talking to?

Make your answers quick and to the point. Don't drag on and don't waste time; you have no idea how many people will appreciate that. At the same time, when you are to the point, you will find an audience that will want to know more and ask you for it.

SportsCenter

Think of your pitch as a *SportsCenter* show, where two reporters give the highlights and details of a two-hour game in two minutes. Don't go into the longwinded story of how you were formed—it may not be an interesting marketing point. Instead, summarize your marketing points, your strengths, and any exciting elements to draw people's interest. Be quick, informative, and if you can, add some humor. Many salespeople will tell you it's all in the fast sell or the fast ask. The longer you go, the better the chance you will lose their attention and their interest.

The Tone of Your Voice and the Confidence of Your Delivery

Inflections, tempo, volume, phrasing, and embellishment can really make a difference in how your words are perceived by others. It's not unlike music: Sometimes it isn't the lyrics or the notes but the nuances, embellishments, and dynamic delivery that can make a song a hit. Whether you're speaking with a booking agent, a venue, a label, someone from the media, or anyone else in the industry, it's important to think about your tone of voice, the tempo of your delivery, and the sensitivity needed to communicate with specific individuals.

A couple of key elements can help you when you're talking to an individual or a group of people: Examine their angle and what they are used to hearing. Stand out by being respectful and understanding that you're not the only person who's made this call or contact. If you're speaking with a booking agent for the first time, consider all the calls and emails that this person probably receives and the common or overly used phrases that he or she has heard. Avoid those phrases.

A Few Simple Rules

Simple courtesies like "Thank you for your time" and "Let me get to the point" show respect for the person you are talking to. It also demonstrates an understanding that the world does not revolve around you.

It sounds stupid obvious, but make sure you're calling either from a place that has good cellular reception or from a landline. Make sure that you will not be disturbed and that there is not a lot of background noise. Turn off the music; make sure extra noises such as the hum of a dishwasher, washing machine, dryer, or conversation are eliminated. I also don't recommend doing first-time contact calls where the street noise is bad or when you're walking up a hill and might begin breathing heavily. Speak clearly and don't be too far away or too close to the mouthpiece.

I Sound Like That?

We don't usually think about how we sound to someone on the phone. So bring in the role-play. Not even kidding. Practice your pitches with someone else and record them. Listen back to see how you actually sound.

Now for the Call . . .

Think about what you're saying. Prepare your approach and your words. Talk at a steady pace but not too fast. People who speak too fast or too slow can often come off as annoying. In addition, speed can be associated with nervousness. You want to convey confidence and assertiveness without arrogance or weakness.

Breathe and Listen

Give room at the end of your sentences for questions, in the same way a comedian might insert a light pause for audience laughter. If you're not interrupted, keep going, but if you are interrupted, address whatever is said. This allows the person you're speaking with to address concerns or questions as they come up.

Red Flags

Confidence is key, both in your voice and delivery. Don't use those awful clichés that have been overheard, overused, and overdone. They can turn people off very quickly.

Give and Take

Whatever your reason for calling, make sure that you discuss the benefits for the person or organization you're speaking with. Many artists reach out in a linear way, thinking only of what they want, how they want it, and what it's going to do for them. Still go after what you want, but explain the benefits to the particular person you're speaking with; you will draw greater attention and be seen as a potentially safer investment, rather than as selfish or self-centered.

If you're talking to a venue about a booking, discuss how you will help to draw people and what you're willing to do to fill the venue so that everyone can make money. If you're talking to a management group or potential manager, talk about your planned efforts for promoting, marketing, branding, and booking your group. If you're talking to a newspaper, magazine, or media group, go over the extra marketing points about your group and how you have prepared materials or information to make the story a little different from others. Show that receiving what you're asking for will also be beneficial to whomever you're getting it from.

Speak Clearly

Speak with a full voice, don't mumble, and try to avoid "uhh" and "umm." Keep your voice steady if you're hit with a question for which you don't know the answer. Many people get quieter—some get louder—or their voice trembles if they feel backed into a corner. If you don't know an answer, simply say with confidence that you will either find it out or that you do not know.

The better you can present yourself when you're on the phone—your tone, your delivery and tempo, and the confidence in your voice—the better you can sell yourself and your group or product. Take that extra minute before the call to prepare and collect yourself to be as professional and confident as you can. Just as you warm up, stretch out, and make sure you're ready to play your music, use that same approach with phone calls. Confidence and professionalism, along with having all your physical materials well prepared and organized, can set you up for a solid one-two punch for whatever you're going after.

You can also apply many of these same rules in your email delivery. If your contact requests email first, do not jump the gun and call. Remember: Follow directions!

MARKETING ESSENTIALS: A PROMO PACKAGE THAT REALLY PROMOTES

I push very hard for artists to create the right promo pack. So many people have a view on exactly what a kit should be, but most of them are missing something or adding too much. The package I recommend is a complete inventory of what you should have at the ready, though it's not the package you will send to everyone.

Think of it as a set of necessary components that you can pull from for any given situation. The press pack for certain venues will differ from others; the kit you send to a label will differ from what you send to a talent buyer or agent. The truth is, with everything going electronic, it's really important to know what you are sending and to whom. Do the research: Make sure you know what forms to send to particular individuals. There was a time where every reviewer just wanted a free CD regardless of whether or not they wrote anything about you. Some no longer need that. These days, you can store this package in its separate forms online and then download the pieces needed to fulfill whatever pack you're making. This will reduce print costs and will also make it easier to set up your components for sites like ReverbNation or any of the booking websites you might be associated with. In fact, you may be able to send your promo pack electronically, circumventing print costs altogether. By adding your basic information on ReverbNation and then including web links back to your website to each of the pages in the pack, you allow potential persons of interest to pick and choose what they want to see without overwhelming them with too much or leaving them with too little. Remember, all materials can be set up with different passwords or private links online. You can send a link to a management firm with a login and password, saving everyone money and space.

> Change can be good, except when it isn't or when it is too much.
>
> I know that's a bit of a contradiction, but what I am getting at is that when an artist is making too many changes too often, it can be a bad thing.
>
> Artistically altering the creative content is a great thing, but from the business standpoint—logos, bios, fonts, taglines, and one-liners—change can bite you in the ass.
>
> With so many bands out there and so many changes made too often, your supposed "change for the better" may get you lost in the mix.
>
> Lock in, solidify, and create a strong presence with your key content and your logos to obtain the best branding that will optimize the fastest and get you seen the most.

Make sure every component is its own document with your logo, font, tagline, website, and all contact information. These should all be available online. As you are building your website, you will allow for a page dedicated to reviews that is available to anyone online.

I know: It's a lot of stuff. But this press/promotional kit covers all the bases and presents the artist in the most professional and polished way with materials that are organized, concise, and clear. It's also true that most bands don't have this pack together, but do you want to be like most bands? Organizing a packet like this will get you many more opportunities and make booking and solicitation much easier. Don't cut the corners that you see others cut; set a new mark and then watch the returns from your efforts. Again, you might not need all of it at any given time, but when it is asked for or someone wants to see all your materials, you will stand above and beyond most.

Having all these documents available for download as easy links to insert into an email will demonstrate your professionalism and the marketing you have in place. Start with the complete package and then send off what is requested.

FULL PRESS/PROMOTIONAL KIT ELEMENTS

- Press kit folder

- Compact disc, demo disc, and/or download card

- 8 X 10 promo shot

- One-sheet

- Review page

- Press release page

- Album information page

- Artist stat sheet

- Show poster

- Album poster

- Business card

- Postcard

- Quarter-page or handbill

- Sticker or bumper sticker

- DVD of live performance / press / demo video / download video cards

PRESS RELEASES AND ANNOUNCEMENTS: MARKETING CORRECTLY TO FANS AND MEDIA

The first step in promoting a show is the construction of a proper press release for the media. Flyers are not enough, and you can't simply count on your networking sites or mailing lists, either. This is especially important if you're playing a show in a new area. Announce it to the media at least four weeks before the show. The four-week window allows papers, TV, and radio stations to have an opportunity to list you and possibly do a story on you. Make sure your timeline for release doesn't put you in a position to miss the deadlines of local papers—that won't help you with any additional press. Email or fax the release to the venue, booking agent, and local media for that city.

If it's a larger show and you have the money, use a press release distribution company. I stand behind Chris Simmons at Send2Press (http://send2press.com/). I have known Chris for a number of years and love how he handles his business and the business of promoting others. Because he's a musician, he could relate to me, which made a difference early on. Send-2Press can help you write the release, and they have options for different locations and a plan of attack for where releases can go. Sometimes it's worth spending the money to invest in a proper release. A larger scale release is also a smart choice when you're putting out a recording; it will reach a much larger audience.

If you're sending the release yourself, research the locations where you're sending it. For each venue or city you're playing, keep this list of the newspapers, rags, radio, etc., and you'll have less to research in the future. If you're playing a number of shows in your hometown or in a twenty-five-mile radius, pick the show that should be the best one and forego the rest. Again, it's best play no more than one show in a twenty-five-mile radius in a six-week period; this gives crowds the sense that they need to see you.

As for where to send your press releases, research the cities you'll be playing in. Find the local TV stations, radio stations, Facebook groups for that area, bloggers, reviewers, newspapers, weekly entertainment papers, college media papers, and websites. Find out about local networking/promotional sites for that town. Find out who the music and entertainment writers are. You can dig in and find a good number of places to send this release; with the Internet, it's easy to do these things yourself. This will also create a very useful database for you to use and to trade with other bands who might be coming to that city. In turn, those bands may have information on another city that you can use. Work the collective and communal aspect; it will allow you to get more information more quickly.

The Best Content and Formatting for Your Event Press Release

A frequent problem I see in event or show press releases is lack of detail and the misconception that everyone is just going to come running once a simple statement is put out there. You need to give reasons why someone should check out this artist or show.

You have to reach out to those who may know who you are, but also make sure that you are enticing and exciting those who have never heard of you. The best music venues in any given city have read time and time again about how this band or that band is going to deliver a "must-see show" or a "can't-miss event," or they have heard the ever-famous and overused line, "You have never seen anyone this good live before." The truth is, they've seen it all. You need to prove yourself by your marketing.

First, make sure your release clearly covers the who, what, when, where, why, and how of the event. If those are not clear when you read through the release, you have work to do. Second, bring a twist to your show by offering up something interesting and different. Is there a way you can tie in a sponsor, giveaway, contest, or something else not part of the average show? Third, make sure you are hitting the correct people with a personalized touch on the grassroots level, especially if it is a local venue. Be aware of the requested deadlines for announcements and releases. With the right content, the standout marketing points, and the right distribution, you are going to see a better response.

The Body of Your Event Press Release

Fill in all the pertinent information in the body of your release. You need to be fast and precise, bringing a basic marketing element to your release. Every piece of information regarding the show and all its elements should be in there. Remember: who, what, when, where, why, and how.

The "why" is your marketing angle. Don't portray it as just another show. Bring something special to each night and find something that would make a newspaper, radio station, TV station, or website check you out and want to do an article. Think about it: The media receives dozens of releases daily. You need to make your release stand out.

The Parts and Pieces of Your Event Press Release

A release can be formatted in a number of ways. I've found this format to be the most conducive to getting stories and interviews:

- **For Immediate Release:** This lead differentiates yours from releases that are set for a later date.

- **Event, Date, Time, Location, and Ticket Prices:** Start right out with the what, when, where, and how (much).

- **Headline:** Draft a powerful headline about the show and the band.

- **Lead:** What city is the release being published in, what is the date of the release, and who is putting it out?

- **Lead Paragraph:** Sum up the show, the location, and the band. If there is a special element about the show or some kind of marketing touch, add it here.

- **Band Biography:** Use the short bio of the band.

- **Venue Biography:** Add a brief bio of the location. You can usually grab it from the venue's website. This optimizes and markets the venue, too. Venues like this!

- **For More Info:** Give the website and number for the venue and the website for your band. Add your most popular social networking site as well.

- **Contact Info:** Specify who the contact point is and how he or she can be reached for a potential interview.

- **Note to Editors:** Adding this note for potential reviews of the album you're pushing can help get requests for stories or reviews of the album.

There are other ways to format releases, but this is an effective template and it gets attention. Don't drag on in a release; keep it under four hundred words and remember that the person receiving your release is also receiving a great many more. Place this layout on your event invites on the social media sites as well! The more people you reach, the better the chance you'll be heard and your music will be passed along.

Give people the information they need in order to see you. Do not assume you are that well known, even if you are. You can always attract new fans, new customers, and a bigger audience. Remember, when the economy is bad, people are going out less or they are only going out to see their favorites. What can you add to your listing, announcement, or release to inspire a new fan to check you out?

Don't just list the venue, the address, a phone number, a website, and the band's homepage. Draw them in with information that intrigues.

Put up a new post on a new site each day for the gig. There are enough specialized and music sites out there to do it. Send the release or the event to the reviewers, bloggers, and other music sites. Just be careful to not post about the same event on the same pages too often.

Every step you take toward promoting on a wider scale will not only help the show that you're promoting but will also help you the next time you come back.

> It is not about wanting something bad enough. You think it really comes down to not wanting it bad enough for an athlete winning or losing a sporting event? Do you think a great quarterback is just sitting back all week working on how bad he wants to win?
>
> You can want, wish, and dream all day, but those that prepare, work, learn, practice, and problem-solve are the ones that find success in sports, business, music, or whatever.
>
> Back up what you want with doing the work it takes to get it.

ENDORSEMENTS: KNOWING HOW TO MARKET THEM AND BEING SURE YOU'RE READY

Free stuff! Reduced-price stuff! Everybody wants it. Getting free gear and being able to say "I endorse so and so" is a very cool feeling, but often people approach it from the wrong angle.

First of all, a lot of people talk the talk but don't walk the walk. People claim to endorse companies that have no idea who these musicians are. I find it completely foolish when people lie about their endorsements or advertise that they are endorsed but don't mention any of the elements involved in endorsing a product.

Simply put, whether you speak of endorsing a product or having a product or company endorsing you, you are talking about yourself as a marketing avenue connected to that product or company, an avenue from which it can gain exposure and revenue. It's the endorser's responsibility to use a given product exclusively, of course, but also to use it in a way that showcases the quality of that product and the quality of the player (you!) now associated with the product.

An ideal endorsement is more than the sum of its parts; both sides should gain marketing leverage from each other. Obviously, endorsers don't give free or discounted items to nobodies. As harsh as that sounds, if you are not signed, touring, teaching at a high level, or in a media spotlight that could influence others around you, you are not an attractive candidate for endorsements. Think about what you can do for the product and its company, not the exposure and "street cred" you get in return for having an endorsement. You must also be sure you have a clear definition of your endorsement.

That's why it is important to put out an upright, defined, and honest image. When someone claims to have an endorsement, this can be easily confirmed. If it doesn't check out, all the other information the artist supplied and all aspects of his or her presentation are called into question.

Therefore, even if you are in the process of getting an endorsement but are not quite there yet, don't advertise it. If you do mention it informally, give your contact point in the company, demonstrating that you know such things will be checked, and talk frankly about how it's coming to fruition.

How Do I Get an Endorsement?

All that being said, endorsements can help; that's no lie. It's additional marketing for you and it can open up opportunities with that company and others. As an endorsed/endorsing artist, you or your group may be approached to attend or perform at trade shows, conferences, and other corporate functions. An individual artist who has an endorsement may also lay the groundwork for other members of the group to gain endorsement status as well. Many larger companies will expect you to be on a major label or signed with a prominent management or publicity firm; these companies are not the place to start. Do not hound them with full promotional packages. That is wasted time, wasted materials, wasted postage, and wasted money.

Also, realize that most companies have different levels of endorsements; this can help your cause. If you were to ask for a free amplifier, for example, chances are you are not going to be taken as seriously as the artist who asks for a small discount on the same amplifier in a detailed letter that explains how he or she would like to start a relationship with the company.

Below are the top five things that you should never say or list when looking for an endorsement. I've asked reps from companies that I've endorsed in the past what their favorite lines were. These were the winners, with a few of the retorts:

1. "You need to endorse me; I am the next big thing and a lot better than a ton of people you already give free stuff to."

Most of these companies don't "need" to endorse anybody. You are coming out of the gate with an oversized ego and giving the impression that you might be difficult to work with.

2. "Your stuff is pretty good, but if you custom-made it my way, it would sell so much better."

Opening up with how they need to change their products to your specifications and design is an insult. Such rights are reserved for artists who have been with these companies for a long time or for top-echelon artists with extremely high visibility.

3. "My gear is from your company, but it's in really crappy shape, and it needs to be upgraded so I can sound the best I can; this will help your image as well."

In other words, you are already representing their product in a poor light and focusing on your needs while not defining how the company might benefit from developing a relationship with you. This gives the impression you're looking for a handout, which does *not* position you as a desirable endorser.

4. "You need to put my name on some stuff. It will really sell."

First off, if you want your name on stuff, there are numerous companies that will, for a fee, put your name on sticks, picks, and whatever else you might want. Named products are—and should be—reserved for the highest profile endorsers and clients of the company.

5. "I don't use your gear right now, but if you give me a rig, I will use you exclusively."

This is my favorite and one that I have personally heard bands use. Now, for a high profile artist who may not be using the company's gear, switching over may bring that company desirable attention from some of his or her fans. As a local, regional, or up-and-coming artist, however, it really is over the top to ask and, again, appears as though you're just requesting a handout.

Getting away from the negative side of it, ask yourself a few of the questions companies would want answers to if they were going to consider you for an endorsement:

- Who are you?

- Who is your fan base?

- What market would you reach that they are not already reaching?

- What market could you supplement that they are already reaching?

- When would you be touring or gigging consistently?

- When you be profiling their products?

- Where will you showcase their product, information, and logos online?

- Where will you showcase their products and logos on stage?

- Why are you effective as an endorser?

- Why are you supporting this product, outside of the deal?

- How do you deliver the image that the company would want to portray?

- How would your deal bring additional sales and more attention to their product?

When you can answer all these questions in detail, you'll improve your chances of receiving some kind of endorsement. Developing a relationship with a company and proving that your endorsement will help them is another good approach. So many artists are only looking out for themselves. Be different: Show the company that you understand its business.

Start small. Don't ask for a full rig or free stuff. Inquire about the different levels that are offered by the company, and ask if you can start at the bottom. Explain how you can prove that you are a quality endorser.

Believe in the product! Do not endorse something just because you can get the endorsement; it doesn't help the company or you. Artists who have a history with a product or company, especially in pictures or videos that clearly display the product and its label, show continuity and a long-standing relationship.

When I was first drumming, I used ProMark drumsticks, a model called the Simon Phillips 707. I am a big fan of Simon and loved the ball tips of those sticks. I tried a couple of different brands as a teen but always came back to ProMark and specifically to those sticks. Most drumming shots of me, from the time I was thirteen on, have me holding a pair of ProMark sticks. So, when I state that I have been playing ProMark since 1987, it rings true, and the proof is in the pictures.

It's also a lot easier to talk about why you like a product when you actually like it. To tell a company its product is great or "I don't play anything else" is not really much of a line unless you are a top-level client. I told ProMark honestly, "I found that your sticks have a great center balance, are well crafted, and have a touch that I can't find in other sticks."

I have used ProMark on the bulk of the recordings I've played on. I always have a couple of sets of the 5As, 5Bs, Elvin Jones Signature, Hotrods, 3ALs, and my old favorite 707s on hand in the studio for the drummers I produce to try to get different sounds and feels and to turn other drummers on to the sticks. This comes off a lot stronger than "They are good," and it also ties in the marketing element.

Figure out why you like a stick, a guitar, an effect pedal, or any other product. What has it done for your sound, your writing, and your performance? See what you can add to the marketing that other endorsers may not have.

You should cover a basic résumé about your playing and your career to date and projects you're involved in. Address these questions:

- What makes your band stand out (besides the music)?

- What makes you stand out as an individual player?

- Are you involved in charity work?

- Do you tour frequently?

- Do you teach?

Tell them what you would do for the company as an endorser. Talk about how you will do additional marketing for the business, and then show that it's being done. Explain that you will have the company's logo or mention on recordings that you endorse its product. You can also mention in early stages that you would be happy to put on the next release that you exclusively use the given product.

A few more questions:

- If you're the drummer, will you place the logo on the bass drum for shows?

- Will you wear a shirt or other item at least once a week, advertising the product?

- Will you reference it in your promo materials?

What other ideas can you come up with to justify the company standing behind you as you show how you will stand behind the company?

Finally, when connecting with the company, be respectful! Try to find out exactly whom you are supposed to contact. Do not send emails to every address at the company. I have heard too many stories about this.

Inquire respectfully. See if the company is currently looking to sign endorsers, and if not, ask if there is a good time of year or a better time than now to submit a letter or package. If a company has a form on a website, fill it out and send it to the appropriate contact. Just because you've heard that your favorite star works with Mr. X from your favorite company doesn't mean you should inundate X with your emails and calls.

If you don't hear back, don't continue to hound. Think! Is it during a convention or trade show period? This is not a good time to go after endorsements, and most likely, these guys and girls are not at their desks. Doing a ten-day follow-up by email is professional. If you don't hear back after that, leave them be. It's not that these companies are being disrespectful, but they are receiving thousands of emails with the same requests as yours; they can't possibly get back to each person. If you continue to hound, you will be flagged and possibly ignored as well as passed on for any future opportunities. In making contact, as I listed above, stand out in a good way: Explain why you want the endorsement and give the company a reason why it should want you to be affiliated with it and its products.

Take these steps in a respectful and professional manner. Look at the idea of endorsement from all angles. If you can honestly answer all the questions above and present yourself in a professional manner, then you may be ready to apply for an endorsement. If you cannot, wait awhile; get some more experience, street cred, or marketing elements under your belt before you make contact. Your responsibility, originality, creativity, and patience will portray you in the best possible light to a potential endorsee.

REVIEWS: GETTING THE MAXIMUM MARKETING

Reviews of the band's live performances, recordings, individual songs, and history are very helpful for marketing and promoting your group. They also fill up that review sheet you should have with your press package. Often, promo packages have either too many or too few reviews. I've also seen band posters and promo packs in which artists list numerous reviews from the same paper, the same websites, or even the same article. I've also seen artists list reviews from only a single area. For example, if you're in Philadelphia and you have a review from the *Philadelphia Weekly*, the *Philadelphia City Paper* and *Philly.com*, it reads that you are possibly too concentrated or localized. On the other hand, some bands stack their packets with cutout copies and sheet after sheet of text. I received a promo pack from an artist that had twenty pages of reviews: too much. They are not being read.

So how do you get the best reviews to include in your review section on your website or across your social media and promotional packages? It's actually easier than you think.

First, go after a review every day. I'm not talking about contacting the *New York Times* or *Rolling Stone*; start with the Internet. There are thousands of review sites out there where you don't even have to send full albums; you can actually send them digital samples, full MP3s, or password-protected links to streaming audio on SoundCloud, ReverbNation, or your own streaming page.

> Make sure your copyright and publishing are in order before you start sending any music out—especially complete tracks.

Then again, if you only have local reviews, how do you get someone to review you as a national act? The answer again is kind of simple, but it still seems to evade people: Go to the smaller local reviewers, but not just in your market. If you're from Boston, then email or contact the Los Angeles, Seattle, Chicago, Houston, Atlanta, San Diego, and Miami markets.

Next, do some research. How do certain magazines or music review sites actually review artists? Find out about their credentials and requirements for reviewing music. Make sure you're following the instructions; otherwise you chance being tossed in the trash. If they ask for electronic kits, send those links and don't waste the money or product by sending a physical package.

Think about it—how much cooler and more professional does it look to have reviews from all across the country, even if they're from smaller papers or websites, instead of a whole bunch of reviews from your hometown? Giving the sense that your music reaches further than the county line can make a big impression.

Go after legitimate reviews, though. Don't add reviews from places where you can potentially be called out for making it up yourself. For example, reviews from ReverbNation, CD Baby, and most social networking sites are good to have in your package. Yes, these are fans, and you don't want to take away from that, but using them gives the appearance that you're just trying to get any review you can, and it suggests your lack of ability to reach out for reviews. After all, anyone can write a review on ReverbNation, CD Baby, or any of these other sites. Make sure that your reviews are coming from professionals or writers. *They hold more water.*

One last note on reviews: Keep your sense of humor. One of my personal reviews that was on my producer and drummer promo sheets was "What a jerk; I never want to see him again," signed "Loren's Ex-Girlfriend." Whether or not there was truth to it—and in some cases there was—it's still funny. It also adds an element of humor and shows that you don't take yourself too seriously. In the world of huge music egos, this can fall in your favor.

An effective review sheet can have small fonts with the logo or name of the given paper or reviewer as well as either the date it was posted or the importance of who reviewed you. Cut out one-liners and short paragraphs from these reviews. Give the person seeing your review sheet a lot to see very fast that covers a very broad region containing a number of different media sources. Keep it down to a single sheet—two if you really feel the need. You can also supplement the review sheet by adding links at the bottom to a review page on your website, to a blog on your networking or blog site, or to the locations of the articles written about you. This is much better and is a much more professional way to streamline your reviews and get viewers to check out as much as they can.

As you get better reviews from larger papers or higher-echelon people, remove some that might be a little less recognizable instead of filling up too many pages. On the website, categorize the reviews by source. Provide a table of contents so readers can sift through the reviews at their leisure and not have to scroll down twenty pages, which I have seen—big no-no; don't do it.

A properly structured review sheet or two can be very refreshing to those who are used to seeing poorly constructed packets. Capture their attention with the streamlining and ease of scanning your reviews. It will lead you to better and more reviews and more opportunities.

The review page makes a difference. You should treat it as one of the most important parts of your package. Draw people in so they'll take the time to read each entry and make it apparent that they're from all over. You want viewers of your review page to see that they need to book you, sign you, invest in you, or review you.

Fan Reviews for Online Marketing and Social Media Exposure

Bands pushing a new release must continue to go after new music reviews on a regular basis. There are hundreds of music review sites and even more indie sites where you can very easily submit online for a review without spending a penny. If you have a couple members of the band doing this on a regular basis, you can really rack up a wider array of places where you can be found, a whole bunch of back links, and, of course, more reviewers!

Fan reviews are still a smart route to take. Though they should not be used in your promotional materials, fan reviews can do great things for your online and social media marketing. I suggest going after a whole bunch of fan reviews by putting it into a contest format. Try putting out a thirty-day contest for fans to do a video review online for you: Sixty seconds to say whatever they want.

Require a uniform title for the video and certain keywords and basic descriptions. (The point of this is to help place the videos higher in visibility and keywords.) Offer a prize of either cash or merchandise, and judge the videos at the end of a month based on views, shares, and likes. Announce a winner and maybe some runners-up as well.

Your end result? A whole bunch of videos loaded to YouTube and optimized in your favor. Since they want to be in the contest, they have to use your specified keywords and your band name and links. On top of all of that, you now have a slew of new music reviews being shared with lots of people who are talking about your music and your album and pushing your links and information.

Don't Worry about Hidden Critics and Bad Reviews

On any given day you can find a critic who is pushing his or her opinion online, making a loud, brash, and often harsh statement. In recent years, Facebook and Twitter have given a name or face to many of these critics, but you still see anonymous comments that are incredibly opinionated, usually rude, and brazenly offensive.

I notice that many of these secret commenters who make strong comments are not strong enough to stand behind them—they hide behind "anonymous."

Using anonymous posts and made-up screen names, these people will comment about anything from the music they hear on a site to a blog, from the look of your site to the look of your album cover.

In the movie *Jay and Silent Bob Strike Back*, Jason Lee's character has a hilarious monologue where he explains an Internet movie review site and how the anonymous reviewers who "live in their parents' basements" rip into anything with joy, since they can never be found out. It really hits the nail on the head when it comes to anonymous postings. Seriously, folks: Do you really want to get bent out of shape over someone who might be making fun of your music, your logo, your band, but who doesn't have the honor, the maturity, or the respect to at least identify himself or herself? In the end, it's a sad and passive-aggressive approach to come forward but not have a big enough pair to sign your own name and identify the source from which the review comes.

I have no problem with critiques or criticisms; I get them every week for the quotes, videos, blogs, and articles I write. I don't expect everyone to agree with what I talk about. Still, it is my opinion, and when I give it, I sign my name, give my website and access to my email, and am happy to hear other sides, viewpoints, and opinions. I welcome disagreements; it is how I learn about viewpoints I am not familiar with. When someone sends a harsh or attacking comment through a user name that does not have an email or real name, I just let it be. It isn't worth my time, and I have better things to do. Even if it comes through a Facebook page or account that is real, I do not fire back. No point.

Don't stoop to their level; grow a thicker skin. Will it do any good to respond to and argue with every anonymous or identified person making a comment that is harsh to you, your music, or something you are doing? Do you want to fight that fight, or should you put your energy elsewhere? Most often, I leave these comments up. I am not trying to make everything look perfect and pretty, nor do I think I have all the answers.

Don't waste time trying to justify yourself, your opinions, or where you stand, especially to a person who is too afraid to identify him- or herself.

Welcome to entertainment—or, for that matter, any business. Take it in stride. Be the better person and take the critique, the criticism, or the slam, and brush it off. It will only get worse and occur more often as you gain any kind of acclaim because, in the end, everyone is a critic.

Whether reviews come from a reputable magazine, newspaper, website, or other form of media, and whether they are positive or negative, just stock them up and store them away. Realize when you go after reviews that not everyone is going to like you.

I think of the Colin Powell quote: "Don't let your ego get too close to your position, so that if your position gets shot down, your ego doesn't go with it." Music is art, and art is opinion. Don't waste time trying to change someone else's. Instead, reach out to more people that might share positive opinions about you and your music.

> ## STREET TEAMS
>
> Don't abuse them! Make 'em feel special! Building that street team—the fan base or the venue that is pushing your marketing further—can be really amazing for your gig, social media, and marketing promotions.
>
> Still, you have to take care of them; make sure you are not using them and abusing them as many bands do.
>
> In return, making them feel a little more special will help them stay around and want to work that much harder for you.

INTERVIEWS: MARKETING YOURSELF IN THE MEDIA

Interviews and stories on you or your band are a must in the entertainment industry or any other business. They help to give exposure to your group and your music and support the press and media packages that you need to build online and in your physical press kits. Many artists don't like interviews, while other artists might like them a little too much. It can be a solid idea to have a spokesperson for the band who handles the bulk of the interviews; the person who is the most patient and the most well spoken might be the guy or girl for the job.

It's important to be prepared and to present yourself in a way that conveys what you're about with sound bites that will make you easy to write about. Send along an artist stat sheet in advance of the interview, or bring one with you. This is a bullet-pointed sheet with key marketing and promotional points about the band. Short, one-to two-sentence bullet points that are easy for the interviewer to insert into the story or review will improve the article and make it easier to write. Many upper-echelon acts and labels will send out a basic version of the stat sheet before appointments with high-profile interviewers.

Whether you're meeting at a show, your rehearsal space, or a coffee shop, make sure to be on time. It doesn't matter if the interviewer is late, but if they are, be professional and excuse the tardiness. These things will stand out in the mind of your interviewer. Remember, some of these people do this all day long. When you make their life easier, they will want to make your story or review better.

The first impressions that you give to an interviewer or reviewer often end up in the final article. Don't piss off a person who can launch a media attack. Or, as the old, predigital saying goes, never pick a fight with people who buy ink by the barrel.

Not every writer is perfect; many are far from it. Still, going into every interview as prepared as possible will, in turn, help get out the best story about you and your music. Treat the interviewer with respect, regardless of how small the paper, the radio station, or the website. When people feel respected, it makes them that much more interested.

Above all, don't pull a rock star attitude; these people have seen it more than enough from acts and artists much bigger than you. Differentiate yourself by being respectful and ready for any interview.

If you're at a café, offer to buy the interviewer a coffee. If you're at a bar, offer him or her a beer. This shows an appreciation for their time and the marketing that the interview or article might give you. These people deal with so many egocentric, over-the-top, and rude people; give them a break from that. Look at it from the standpoint that, though they're doing a job for someone else, they're likely helping you out in the end.

Be ready for the questions. You may not anticipate every question you'll be asked, but for questions that are directed toward the band, the more uniform and consistent you are on the key elements of the group, the better. Make sure to promote and repeat things throughout the interview, whether the interviewer is writing notes or recording you. Your tagline, website, album title, and the single you are promoting should all be brought up. Brand it into their minds; this will sink in and get into the story.

Speak slowly and clearly. Whether the interviewer has a recorder or is taking notes, try to speak so your words are easy to take down or easy to transcribe when played back. I'm not suggesting that you be all business; interviews can be an enjoyable experience, so have fun with them. But at the same time, if you feel something is off the record, don't bring it up. If you want to avoid a question, be smooth as you move your interviewer away from the subject. Anything is better than "no comment" or "next question."

Keep your delivery fresh while staying consistent and accurate. You may be asked the same question by fifty different people; it is tedious. You might get into a situation where you do a series of interviews in the same day and are asked almost identical questions over and over again. Keep in mind that these are separate interviewers and they are there for separate stories, so it's your responsibility to answer each question with the same fresh approach that you gave the first person. A response like a sigh or a grimace shows that you are tired or annoyed, which can put off an interviewer, and you may get things written about you that you don't want to see. Regardless of how tired you are, how spent you are, how many times you have heard the same question over and over and over again, be happy to be there. Remember, these people are creating a story to market and promote you. Always keep that in mind. On the other hand, don't go on and on when you're asked a question; try to stay brief.

Turn off the phone, or if you expect a crucial call, let the interviewer know at the beginning of the session. Don't be one of those people who plays diva and picks up every call, going on and on. This is the interviewer's time, too, and it has the potential to help you promote and market.

It doesn't matter whether it's a big media group or a small local radio station; your answers should hit the quick bullet points of your core message. Don't come off arrogant or cocky; make sure to thank the people who are seeing the shows, buying your music, and supporting you. With every interview, you have another piece of media for your press kit, your website, and possibly other links where you can be read about or searched for online. So make every one count, be respectful, and watch the results.

ONLINE AND OFFLINE ADVERTISING FOR MARKETING AND PROMOTION

So you've got a little bit of money and you want to do an ad campaign beyond postering or online posts. Now, I'm not undermining the importance of those elements; they're absolutely necessary. But if you can begin to build a budget that allows you to take advertising to another level, that is, as we say in the studio, "very all sorts of good."

When bands get an influx of funds for advertising, they often buy ads that are way too expensive and way too small. You don't need to advertise on the back page of *Rolling Stone* for a single month. For that amount of money, you can likely buy six larger and more eye-catching ads over six months in the smaller city magazines or online in very specified and chosen locations on Facebook or Google.

Research, analytics, and learning your market are core elements of advertising. Finding out the best places to advertise and the costs are important first steps. Even if you don't advertise online or in a magazine, newspaper, local rag, or trade paper, keep that information in order to build an advertising database later down the road. For that matter, you should be building databases for everything. Keep all that info; it might not apply right now, but it will be useful down the line.

There are many options in advertising, both print and web. Find out how long an ad can run. If it's on the web, look at click-throughs, impressions, and different locations within their publication or site. While some places will be crazy expensive, others will have great options and rates. It's best not to spend your entire advertising budget all at once in a whole bunch of locations. Spread it out!

First, figure out what you want to advertise. Do you want to advertise a new album or release? Do you want to promote a tour? Or are you just getting the word out on the band and its website? Way too many artists start up ads without a marketing or advertising plan.

Back to the ads: The basic dimensions for advertising are listed in most advertising sections of magazines, websites, newspapers, and other media formats. Find out what they require, what options are available, and the pricing.

Start off small. Buy a couple of web ads; see how they work. Research advertising in all kinds of mediums and markets. Move the ad around the country; if you place an ad in Seattle one month, try Atlanta the next. If you advertise in the UCLA student paper one week, try NYU the next. Bounce around, find your market, and reach people who might never have heard of you otherwise. This approach can help you connect with audiences on a much more effective and widespread level.

Remember, however, that for maximum effectiveness, you will need to find out where you were selling and where no one was interested. Buy a single ad for a week and see how it works for you. Does it bring in more fans? Do sales go up? Do you get more people added to your email list, your Facebook page, and your Twitter account when you buy an ad in some local music magazine or buy an online ad on their website? Either way, separate the ads by time and location so you can clearly tell the difference and be able to know your conversion from ads to sales or followers.

Plan your ad accordingly and figure out what audience you're going after. Think about what options might be most effective. Every ad doesn't have to be placed in a music magazine or an entertainment-based publication or site. Why not buy an ad in a magazine or website that is not focused on music yet somehow ties into you or your fan base? For example, I knew a Goth band who had a great deal of success advertising their website and new album in a clothing magazine. In fact, the sales went so well, they renewed the ad for another month. Remember what is not effective: If an ad doesn't work well for you in a certain publication or on a certain website, make note and keep that information. Track and study the results.

Also try small ads in obscure locations. See if there's a college newspaper that's either daily or weekly and try a week run for the album. You never know. There's not a set marketing plan that will guarantee success, but the more you can experiment, the better chance you'll have at a different type of exposure. These obscure locations can also be a great deal more affordable.

Look into Facebook ads for detailed and specific advertising. It is very cheap, and it can be a great resource to see who is clicking through, following you, adding you, and converting to sales. Facebook currently has the best online advertising system for breaking down where you are putting your ads and who is seeing them. I highly recommend investing in Facebook advertising campaigns each week, switching up and spreading out your marketing across locations, ages, likes, and favorites.

In the end, all advertising, whether online or in print, is about conversion to sales. Track your ads and track the reactions, interactions, social media ads, and sales to see what you are doing right and what you are doing wrong. Make sure your marketing and your branding is showing up in the ad with that call to action to get them to click through and bring them to where you want them to go.

FAN ENGAGEMENT AND OPINIONS HELP YOUR MARKETING AND ADVERTISING

Do you know exactly how and where your fan engagement came from? How did your fans and followers find you in the first place? Do you know what exactly drew them to you, or are you just glad they are there?

Ask your fans and followers how they became fans and followers. Musicians and bands need to connect their music marketing with an understanding of how they were able to gain a fan, create a buzz with someone, get that fan to tell others to buy your music, and keep them coming back. This knowledge can help you make the best decisions for where you advertise and how you market. It can also give you a different perspective on how you are being seen as opposed to how you want to be seen or think you are being seen.

Knowing all this helps you reach out to more fans in the same fashion. Think of it like the food samples at the grocery store. I tell bands to ask questions of their fan base—nothing wild, just a few easy questions. You can even turn it into a contest and offer a download or some kind of prize if you like. Ask them a couple simple questions like the following:

- Who told you about us?
- Who would you compare us to?
- What is your favorite song and why?
- What is your all-time favorite band (besides us)?
- What is your favorite thing about us?
- When did you see us?
- When did you buy a download, CD, or merchandise?
- Where did you see us (or find us online)?
- Why do you like us?

- How did you find us?

- How would you describe us to a friend?

These simple questions sent out to a fan base at different times can give you a wealth of knowledge on how others perceive you and react to you. In turn, this information can help you market to new fans, develop additional approaches, and reach a wider audience while creating better fan engagement. Make sure you look at age, sex, and location to see how you are perceived by women and men, teens and adults, and West Coast to East Coast.

Sometimes we are so close to something that we can't see another perspective, or we just assume everyone sees it the way we do. The responses from your fans can help you understand a number of different views that can help you reach the widest possible audience with the best marketing approaches while saving the most advertising money.

DO THE MATH: IS YOUR ADVERTISING BUDGET CREATING REAL OR FAKE NUMBERS?

Artists need to get a clue about the math, the advertising budgets, and the method behind social network site marketing. It has gone from ridiculous to completely freaking insane. For those of you who might not be aware, there are a number of artists out there who actually spend money on "marketing firms," "social media pros," and "number builders," as they have been calling themselves, to get more Facebook likes, Twitter followers, YouTube views, SoundCloud plays, and more. This is foolish and does nothing positive for these artists' careers.

In fact, it hurts them, since there is no conversion or any type of analytics, statistics, or tracking. A few people might think they look cool because they have thousands of likes on a fan page, but the industry as a whole is recognizing it for what it is: an artist wasting time trying to present a false fan base. You can spend the same money on a smaller Facebook regionalized campaign and potentially build an organic, interactive, and real fan base that has a chance to convert to sales—which, by the way, are real numbers that actually matter!

Yes, at one time lots of hits, friends, and play counts on sites like Myspace had a small level of promotional significance. These factors stood as something that people paid attention to a few years back when Myspace was the hip site and "add or play bots" did not exist. As Myspace was in the forefront and more artists were joining, there was a wide differentiation of who was being looked at and who was not.

These were contributing factors to some artists even receiving deals, *but only contributing factors.* No one—I repeat—no one has gotten a record deal or contract based solely on the amount of friends and plays they had on Myspace, and no one has gotten a deal on Facebook or YouTube data alone. Yes, the stories are out there, but at most it was only one factor that added to a number of other factors and justifications that got the artist a deal.

> We have 4,000 followers on Twitter. . . . We got 5,000 plays for this song. . . . This video got 2,000 views. . . . Our Facebook page has reached 6,000 likes. . . .
>
> So what?
>
> Those are analytics and not promotion. Share those numbers with the PR people, management, and agents while you use that information for tracking and analysis.
>
> Sharing these types of numbers comes off as bragging and it turns off your audience.

Getting a deal based on Facebook or YouTube stats sounds much cooler, though, doesn't it? Too bad it's not true. Think about it: Who with the money, the means, the understanding of the industry, and the resources would sign an artist based on those facts alone? I am going to go with . . . no one!

You want friends? Plays? Likes? Then build them organically, earn them, and learn to convert them into what is most important: fans and sales. Personally add a few people a day to your Facebook, Pinterest, YouTube, ReverbNation, etc. Add a message, and market yourself by reaching out to people and groups on these sites. Take the professional path to truly get people to read you, hear you, and connect with you. Then convert them to fans and buyers.

Sometimes—and those times are few and far between—these bots and programs can cause a few real people to find out about you and create new friends and download sales. Most of the time, however, instead of real fans, bots and programs play your songs, ping your site, and push to spam up your friend and number counts. Some of these spam additions are people who will just approve and never even check you out. That makes it a worthless contact.

Now, let's really do the math. A few months back I was on the YouTube page of a really shady artist who talked about wanting to work with me. This artist had 100,000 views on one video. His other videos averaged between 25 to 200 views—red flag! His Facebook link to his personal page had 300 friends, and his Twitter link had him at 43 followers. He claimed he did a marketing campaign for this song and the video.

It wasn't a marketing campaign. He paid for 100,000 views and got them, but nothing else. No sales, no solid fan base, and nothing to show for marketing growth or conversion. It's the worst expense: advertising that doesn't even make back the cost, much less any profit.

Furthermore, the industry is now completely aware of these bots and programs to add friends, views, and likes. At the end of September 2012, Facebook started pulling the fake bot likes off people's pages, and you could see these bands go from thousands of likes to hundreds.

Keep in mind that the people you want to listen to you often do not have that much time. So, when they immediately see evidence of someone faking popularity, instead of impressing you are immediately discrediting yourself. Think about this when writing the content for your press kits as well. Do not highlight friend counts, page visits, or song plays. Highlight the things that matter, like show attendance and sales. Highlight your logo, your professionalism, your music, and how you are ready to go to the next level based on your efforts and achievements, not your contrived appearance. Keep track of your actual sales instead of hits in order to show potential labels, managers, and talent buyers your viability and profitability. Keep track of your growth in fan numbers, balanced out by your conversion and sales numbers. Those two sets of numbers together are a lot more appealing to the industry than a video that has five thousand views.

You are an intelligent person; act like it. Spend your money on things that will actually help your career and not things that give the appearance that your career is more than it really is.

GIVE IT AWAY NOW AND THEN: SMART MARKETING AND PROMOTING

It's a good thing to give away CDs/downloads, T-shirts, download cards, and other merchandisc at shows or online. Free giveaways are the way! Do not look at every item as a singular product with a worth that is measured in dollars for just that item. Or in simpler terms, if you give away a T-shirt to a hot girl at a show who promises to wear it at the show and does, she is marketing and promoting your T-shirt for more people to see it and buy it!

Giveaways from the stage can be a great thing, too. You know how you sometimes have trouble getting people to move up closer to the stage early in the show? Tell the audience you are going to be giving away a CD/download, a T-shirt, a download card, or another piece of merchandise or swag—things you don't like to throw far. Maybe make another joke, saying the closer you are to us, the more you might get. Sure, it's cutesy and cheesy, but it's also effective marketing for others who might go to the merchandise table and buy the product you are giving away.

Offer discounts if they buy while you are playing a set as opposed to after the show. Raffle off merchandise. There are dozens, if not hundreds, of ways to stand out so much more than most. By giving some items away, you build up many more sales for the night or the show.

Free stuff helps to promote a band more than you know. When I build a music business plan with a larger budget or even one for a smaller artist, I always allocate a section for free merchandise. It is justified as promotion and a write-off, if you get to that point. Set up a certain number of items to be given away for free. Budget them over the month or across the shows you are playing. Make sure that when you are giving away it is enticing others to buy. Handing a T-shirt to the bartender who immediately puts it on for his shift while you're playing is much more effective than giving it to a guy who looks a little scary. Use common sense. Give it away and watch what comes back. One thing given away for free can create ten sales easily.

What kind of core product should you have and give away for free? How much should you charge for product? When should you discount or hold sales and when should you not? I'm never so amazed as when I hear how many different opinions people hold on these topics and, to be honest, how selfish people can get, staying way inside the box when thinking of free things and pricing.

First, do not look at the basic product as money you should make back. *That is the wrong approach!* I put that in italics for a reason—*wrong approach*. Thinking that you should make all of your money back on the initial disc pressings or product is an awful idea. Yes, you should make something on it, but the right mindset is that giving away a great deal of product is going to equal a greater marketing beginning. The more people who see your T-shirts or play your music for friends, the more new fans, new interest, and most of all, *new sales* you will get.

Set up a ratio of sales-to-giveaways for each week and each month. Remember, on this first batch you may not make as much as you'd like to, but the marketing elements will draw more sales down the road. Effectively branded merchandise and products mixed with a strong giveaway or discount plan means sales, fans, and conversions for the long run. So, as the Red Hot Chili Peppers say, "Give it away, give it away, give it away now" for marketing that will *get you paid, get you paid, get you paid* later!

THE YIN AND YANG OF THE BAND AND THE FAN

Not long ago I spoke to a band that was complaining that the people coming to their shows were bothering them too much afterward when they were tired and didn't want to socialize. I tried not to laugh as we sat in a coffee shop. I just looked at them and said, "You are either in the wrong business or you need to become songwriters, hired guns, or members of a backup band." It comes down to a simple fact: Your fans are your lifeline for the continuity and sustainability of your career. Period.

If you've chosen to be a performing and touring artist, you have a responsibility to your fans, not only to perform for them but also to solidify them in your fan base and to continue to cultivate and grow that base.

In a way, you can look at it like this: Your fans are your bosses. Elvis may have said it best: "I don't care if my fans tear the shirt off my back; they put it there."

If you grow a fan base that's sturdy enough, you'll be able to survive on the sales of your music, merchandise, and performances. The fans are the ones who are fronting that cash, though it's easy for musicians to lose sight of that.

It's true that larger scale artists are more private. They're not as approachable and not seen before or after a show unless the presenting organization sets up a meet and greet. Some of these artists do connect, but they have such a large fan base and such a rabid following that it allows them more privacy—but only because they hold a higher level of publicity with enough frequency to maintain that status. While they might not shake every hand at a show, they were most likely up at the crack of dawn doing morning radio spots, TV appearances, and numerous newspaper and magazine interviews.

So playing rock star by being elusive after a show is only going to hurt you when you're still a new act trying to solidify your fan base. Just as you give your fans a piece of you as you share the music in recordings, they are giving you their attention and their enthusiasm. This is not a one-on-one relationship. You are going to try to capture as many fans as possible while realizing that those fans probably have a thousand other bands that they like as well.

There is a yin and yang to the foundation that can be built between you and your fans. Every action has a reaction: As you solidify your base, they purchase your tickets and downloads and become walking billboards by wearing your merchandise. Think of every act committed by a fan. Have you ever received a letter? A friend request on a networking site? An email? Respond to all these things with a letter back or otherwise thank them for the request; do it in an honorable way. If someone added you and mentioned how much they think you're cool and like your music, respond with a thank-you and something personal. Don't just advertise yourself on their page to try to capture more fans. By making this kind of response, you connect on a more personal level and increase the possibility of those people sharing you with others.

Take time before and after the shows. Say hello to everyone. If some look like they want to say hi but seem shy, approach them. That goes for guys and girls. Make sure you're not just flirting; talk to everyone. Remember, they paid money for your show and took time from their day to support you. Many fans want a sense of connection with a band that they like, so give it to them. Think of ways where you can personalize your approach to fans as they have personalized an approach to you.

You will better understand what to do when you step back and see that there are two sides working together. Too many musicians get caught up in the above-it-all vibe—even unintentionally or mistakenly—and that is not what it's about. These people—these fans, these purchasers at shows and online—are giving you the ability to have a lifestyle of self-sufficiency in music. You have to recognize this. Once you do, you will connect more with your audience and your fans and promote a strong reciprocal connection. It's all a balancing act, and once you accept that angle, you can take the necessary steps to solidify your fan base and ensure its constant growth.

EMAIL LISTS, E-ZINES, AND ARTIST NEWSLETTERS: MARKETING FAN EXCLUSIVITY

Email has made elements of marketing much easier than it's ever been before. I kind of feel old when I explain to younger bands that a mailing list used to mean we actually printed out postcards, letters, or flyers and then addressed them and stamped them and put them in actual mailboxes. With the Internet, mailing lists have become much more green as well as much easier to do. It doesn't cost anything to send out an email, but artists need to think about the costs of too much emailing or posting, because it can have a negative effect on your fan base. For starters, plan an email newsletter that has consistency and regularity. This way it becomes something that people will want to read. You do not need to send out emails every single day, and if you do, you're going to lose the effect of your email newsletter and people's desire to read it. Put the attention into the daily updates with a weekly or, better yet, monthly email list newsletter and update.

I recommend a newsletter or e-letter or e-zine that has:

- **A show section.** Talking about the upcoming shows, festivals, and appearances.

- **A fan section.** Something about people at the shows, fans that you have connected with, or fan profiles, fan pictures, and other engaging approaches to connect with your fan base.

- **A contest section.** Some kind of contest or game just for people subscribed to the newsletter.

- **A story or article that the band writes.** Something exclusive that is not going up in any public place. Something from the band, exclusively for the fans.

- **A news section.** Recapping the public updates while hinting or sharing some news only for those subscribed to this letter.

- **A picture section.** A couple of pictures from recent shows meant specifically for the newsletter and not put on Facebook, Instagram, Pinterest, or Flickr.

- **Anything else you might like to add:** Again, this is something exclusive for the fans of the newsletter and not to be used as content for other places!

Think about it: If you are trying to attract a crowd to sign up to get one more email a day than they already receive from other bands, products, politicians, marketing groups, and so on, shouldn't it be exclusive content that they can't see anywhere else? If you do a giveaway or a contest once a month, it can also make your newsletter more popular and get people to sign up for it. Give people a reason to be on the list. If you're just putting up the basics from your site and your social networking sites, they don't need to be on a list.

Make sure every newsletter has information on how to unsubscribe. Sometimes people will want to get off a list because either they're receiving too many emails or maybe they just aren't interested in your band anymore. That is their right, and you should respect it. If someone asks to be unsubscribed, then do it and leave it at that. Don't get sensitive, and don't email back asking why. I've been on various lists that I did not even sign up for, and most of the time when I clicked unsubscribe or asked to be taken off, it wasn't a problem. I had one person email me, though, asking why I would want to be taken off, as well as telling me I don't know good music. I simply get too many emails and did not want to get the constant battery I was receiving from this artist, but after that email, he lost a fan forever.

Do not just add people to your lists or steal information from other lists and cold email. Do not buy email lists or buy those likes, adds, and so on, either! That's very unprofessional and annoying.

When you send out your e-letter, if it is not going through a social media or web channel, make sure to hide the email addresses in the BCC (blind carbon copy) section or send to a band email that distributes to everyone. When I sign up for any kind of email list, I do not want everyone on that list to get my email address, and many others feel the same. Respect the privacy of the email list that you grow and the people on it.

Keep copies of your own newsletter and use it as a template for the next one. Use the format and change out the information, the pictures, and the contest, but don't forget to keep the uniformity.

The newsletter, e-zine, email list, or whatever you want to call it is one more avenue to bring exclusive content to the fans you have engaged at shows or through Facebook, You-Tube, your website, or wherever else. Deliver content just for them in order to generate and maintain interest.

A FEW TIPS FOR BEING MORE RESPECTFUL
ON YOUR SOCIAL MEDIA SITES

Just as it is important to get the word out and do your marketing, promotion, and advertising on Facebook, Twitter, and your other social media pages, it is also important to be effective and respectful to get the kind of attention you want. Here are a few tips to consider applying to your Facebook or any other social media pages in order to be as effective and respectful as possible.

- If I don't want to be your fan or follow one of your pages, stop asking!

It is fine to ask people to join a page, but if they decide not to, then leave them be. Maybe they prefer to be on your personal page; maybe they don't sign up for fan pages or the particular site you are pushing; or maybe they just aren't a fan. Whatever the reason, constant requests to be a fan, to like this page, to subscribe, and all the other redundant requests has pissed many people off and can even get them to drop or block you.

- If you are effectively sharing your social media posts across your networks, stop asking fans or followers to follow you on your other pages. Why would someone want to see the same post over and over? Would you? If they are already following you at a site that is updating your information, stop asking them to double up.

Most musicians put the bulk of their updates on their personal pages as well. You can also easily add a link to your fan page so they can go there themselves if they want. Another tip is to leave the fan page public so people can check it out if they want. Don't spam for fans.

- Don't chase a dropped friend or unlike.

I have heard this from numerous people who have chosen to drop a friend from Facebook, Twitter, and LinkedIn and then later get an email or even a call asking why. Don't call! They have their reasons, and the last thing they want is a call asking why. Maybe you spam too much, maybe you overpost or overupdate. Maybe they are trying to limit friends or keep information a little more personal. Who knows, but let it be. On the other hand, if you feel someone is going to be to oversensitive and annoying and you want to drop them, then hide them so you don't have to see their posts. Just don't be that person who chases after someone who dropped you as a friend on Facebook, because when you think about it, that is pretty damn sad.

- Don't send flowers, gifts, dogs, farm animals, and all those other "app crap" items to people.

If you are trying to use Facebook to grab the attention of people or to connect with fans, new or old, use the information and updates that are yours, and don't send gifts, animals, flowers, and all that other game crap. Many people find it incredibly annoying, and it really isn't doing much for marketing your music or your shows. It will also make some people want to hide your updates, missing out on the real information and updates you want them to have. I even heard they are working on a *Honey Boo Boo* app game for Facebook—freaking scary.

- Don't post boring updates and news. That is pointless.

Trust me: Your public doesn't need to know that you just ate a sandwich or that I-90 is backed up. Nor do they need some quote that only you and a handful of people might get. Instead, post stuff you would want to read, watch, and view. I am not saying make it all business, but limit yourself with the mundane updates and you will have more people actually watching for your posts instead of skipping over them or worse: hiding them, hiding you, or blocking you altogether.

In the end, sometimes it is better to have different pages for you and your friends than for the world you are trying to reach. I know a number of people that preface their personal pages with a statement that says, "This is my personal page for friends and family. If you want more on my music or my band, join [fan page] as a fan or add me on that page."

Social networks have become important for reaching out to new fans, but it is crucial to make sure you are reaching out with the strongest voice possible. It is also important to make sure your message, music, and marketing is not getting lost in the noise of silly applications and excessive postings. Make sure the information in your posts contains the who, what, why, when, where, and how, along with your call to action.

Be respectful to your audience on Facebook and other social media sites. It can only take minutes a week to make an impact and gain new friends and connections who will convert, draw people to shows, buy merchandise and music, and help you build a fan base that wants to stay connected with you.

POSTING FOR POSTERITY: WHAT GOES UP MIGHT NOT COME DOWN

Have you posted stupid things online that you thought you deleted? Are you sure they're deleted? Because more than likely they are still up there—somewhere. Online and social media are still new and in the development phase. People are quick to put up personal aspects of their lives without a second thought; this sometimes includes words about someone else that are better left unsaid. A good reputation can be put at risk when you are attacking someone with harsh words. While it's great to have a footprint of different posts, links, blogs, songs, and other content out there and optimizing more and more, there is also the downside of having certain comments, rants, regretful posts, and even twunks (Twunk: the Twitter version of drunk dialing).

Many people have their social media and websites interconnected through site aggregators, feed-share sites, and other linking points that will keep a message, a post, a song, a video, or some other kind of media online and out there, even if you take it off the page where you first posted it.

So what do you do?

Think before you post!

Many of us have had situations where we've been taken advantage of, used, or ripped off, and we want to scream it out to the world. But is that the right thing to do online?

Mike Sinkula, a friend of mine in Seattle and a great web guru, told me a few years ago, "Post anything and everything you don't think could come back at you and hurt you in a court of law. Especially when you are angry, just be safe and don't post it at all."

My close friends know about a bad situation that occurred with me and someone in the industry a while back. I wanted to tear into this person online: really rip them a new one. It is not defamation of character if you are telling the truth, and the situation that occurred was flat out awful.

But I kept my mouth shut. It was not the right forum to say what I was thinking. Instead, I put energy into posting things I wanted to have out there. I put up blogs, pictures, videos, and audios about my productions, my book, the talks and seminars I have done, advice I give, or advice I follow. Before writing this section, I even scanned an RSS feed that doesn't delete anything and followed it back almost two years. I have not seen anything go up in the past that I would not mind someone reading today. Can you say the same?

Remember, you want to maintain old fans *and gain new ones*. If someone that didn't know you well read a series of posts where you're ripping this band or complaining about this person or that venue, do you think that is really going to nudge this prospective fan in your direction?

So think before you post. Think about the post and why you are doing it. Ask yourself:

Is this post good for . . .

- Promotion and marketing?

- Exposure?

- Branding?

- Building your fan base?

- Maintaining your existing fan base?

- Presenting the image and appearance that you want?

- Helping you reach new audiences?

- Helping you network and connect with others in the industry?

- Providing interesting content that could draw someone new to you and your music?

And is this post okay if someone reads it . . .

- Right now?

- Tomorrow?

- Next week?

- Next month?

- Next year?

- In court?

If the answer to more than one of these is no, take a breath and decide this is just something you are doing out of boredom, frustration, anger, or under the influence of alcohol. Of course you should stand by your beliefs, your convictions, and your ideals! Just make sure you can stand by these things you put out there if they were found a couple of weeks, months, or years down the line—by anyone.

Think how you can make your posts "timeless and time considerate." Of course, gigs and certain events are more about an exact date and time, but think of how you can put up things about the music, the band, or the history in an almost journalistic style that gives a clear idea of when a post was written. Even as things change with the group, the music industry, and the world, you can showcase and document how you handled it, changed with it, and experienced it. This can even make people interested in searching for more of your other posts.

And by the way, for all of you posting that little statement, "You don't have the right to share my information, pictures, music samples, blogs . . ." *It is not true.* Anything you post on Facebook, Twitter, and a number of other sites may be used in many ways. Go check the terms and conditions for Facebook or Twitter. Simply putting up a statement saying "No, you can't" does not change the terms you already agreed to. If you are concerned about something not being shared or used by someone else, *do not post it!*

Take a proactive but patient approach to what you put up. Realize that what you put up might not come down. Control the stupid stuff that you want to say in the moment but wish you hadn't said a day later. It's not like a fight with a bandmate or a face-to-face disagreement with a venue manager, where you can apologize for things said in a heated moment. It doesn't work the same for posts put up on the Internet.

SOCIAL NETWORK SITE HOUSEKEEPING: CLEAN UP YOUR &#@%!

You may not be able to make certain things go away on the Internet, but you should keep the primary pages of your website and your social media sites clean. These pages should be marketing you in the best fashion to old and new fans. So when is it time for housecleaning on Facebook, Twitter, or your website? When is it time for certain items to remain and others to go away? The answer is . . . right now!

Too many people do not realize that a good deal of what is posted by other people is unimportant, boring, and basically stupid. If you are just another face on Facebook, Twitter, or any of these sites, it doesn't really matter. However, if you are an artist, a band, or someone trying to promote and market, those little stupid updates can do more harm than help.

So what should stay up? What should go down?

Do some housecleaning now and then to make sure you are giving the information, the image, the marketing, and the promotion that will reach the most people in the best way. Be smart; stay in the mindset of the person visiting you for the first time, even if by accident. How far do they have to scroll down your Twitter feed or Facebook updates to really get a sense about you?

Thanks, but No Thanks for Your Dumbass Update

"I just had a coffee." "I just got a carwash." Well, this is me caring. . . . Wait! No, I really don't care, and as hard as it may be to take, just because you play in a band doesn't make a boring fact interesting. Leave the updates for interesting information that is about the band, the members, or places where you went. Tell us something interesting!

Purple Luggage / No Shirt

For example, a band on the road is staying in a lot of hotels. That is obvious, boring, and usual. Updating that you are in a Best Western in Richmond, Virginia, is not cool, hip, nor interesting.

But if you can spice it up with something different that you saw happening or take a picture of something out of the ordinary, then you are bringing something to the table. I saw an update where an artist said he walked out of his hotel room in a certain city and saw a man with no shirt on, dragging three purple suitcases. He took a picture and then posted it with the caption, "Just checked into [hotel] in [city] after [band name] played a fun show in [city]. Heading out for ice and we saw this [referring to the picture]. Is this normal for this city?"

That is a great post. First he mentions the city, the band name, and the fact that they did a show, and then he adds something different. He posed a question to get people to interact, tell their stories about this city, or mention where they might have seen something like it before. That is solid updating and network site marketing. Get the difference?

Housecleaning

Clean house now and then. Look through all the stuff that has been posted. Can some of it come down to bring up more important or better posts? It can be fun to put up funny videos, jokes, and stupid experiences or whatever, but it can be more effective to take that stuff down occasionally so people see the more pertinent stuff faster.

Even if you put up some stupid stuff, here is your chance to take it down. People may be breezing or scanning through your information for the first time. Is the information better for a new fan or a close personal friend? Clean out excess posts by other people on your pages, so that when people come to your page they can scroll and see most of your posts and what you are putting up instead of a couple posts and tons of other people putting in their two cents.

> Something to think about before you post anything on your band page or fan pages: Is it something that will retain the interest of an existing fan? Could it draw in the interest of a new fan? Does it say something that might get reposted, favorited, retweeted, or liked?
>
> If someone sees it that has no idea who you are, is there a clean link back to allow the viewer to find you easily? If not, rethink the post.
>
> Make the most out of your simple and free marketing online.

This page is about you! Sure, you want to get comments, but if some are more personal in nature or just spam, pull them off. The same goes for the schedule. I have seen many pages where you can scroll for a long time and only find schedules and show dates. If the date has passed, dump it and have some kind of well branded, strongly marketed post or update that will keep the older fans engaged and potentially catch the interest of a new visitor who knows nothing about you.

SHAMELESS PROMOTION AND LOOK-AT-ME POSTS: SHARING OR SHOWING OFF?

There is a fine line between shameless promotion, showing off, and publicizing certain facts and events versus promoting in a more positive, connecting, and relationship-building way.

Shameless Promotion

You have to think carefully about how you are promoting. Put out items that help you look strong, showcase your accomplishments, and draw in existing and new fans. Good promotion means impressing without trying to force something down someone's throat.

It is much more impressive to be recognized by someone else for an achievement than to show it off. You can still promote, market, brand, and get the word out without being a show-off. First, before sharing a post, ask yourself, "How would I feel if I were reading this from someone else?" Second, remember to use reviews, testimonials, and quotes from others to highlight yourself and your message. Get those review and testimonial pages up!

Another example: How do you feel about someone who posts, "Wow, I am so honored that I have a thousand 'likes' on my page! I am blown away, and you need to make sure to like this page and tell everyone to, also." This person seems to start off with a humble approach but it ends up reading as obnoxious. Besides, if someone is getting this message, don't they already like the page?

Instead, what if you posted something like this: "Thank-you to everyone who has liked my page. I hope you have been enjoying the content, the pictures, and the music. If you would pass it along to others whom you think will like my music and this page, it would be much appreciated." With a comment like that, I might actually pass this along.

Think before you post; read it out loud. How would that post come off to you if you were reading it on a friend's page or even on a page new to you? Would it make you want to read more? Would it push you away? Would it draw you in, or would it rub you the wrong way? Avoid the shameless promotion that turns people away instead of drawing them in.

SURPRISE YOUR SOCIAL MEDIA FANS AND FOLLOWERS: BE A PRUDE NOW AND THEN

In this day of oversaturation, overposting, oversharing, and telling the world everything the instant it happens, sometimes holding back and being a little prudish can be a great approach. Musicians and bands can get an explosive result, bigger conversions, and higher potential sales in holding back on an announcement rather than lighting the fuse too early.

One idea is to choose certain things that you are excited about—and bite your tongue. While it can be great to share the process of something, sometimes it's cool to surprise your audience, fan base, and social media followers with something you have said nothing about until, all of a sudden, it happens. This can also help you shine as someone who actually makes things happen. So many people talk so much, and a great deal of it does not come to fruition. If you have that big thing that you keep quiet about and then announce like an explosion, it can really help you stand out.

A few years ago at a Seattle performing arts school, the kids were told a few musicians were coming to perform for them and talk about the music industry. They were pretty surprised when Mike McCready from Pearl Jam, Duff McKagan from Guns N' Roses, and Velvet Revolver showed up—along with me on drums. (Yeah, most of the kids had no idea who I was, but it was all good. The drummer and the producers never get love . . .)

The point is, we were announced the morning of the event, and it had a cool shock value. At the same time, there was no crazy press or an excess of people at the school; it was all for the kids that were there. It was a blast. We did a few songs, talked about the music industry, and afterward those kids never had a clue who might be showing up or when. That was great marketing for the school.

This concept can also work for you and your fans. As much as preproduction is good for some songs, sometimes, just going for that raw take can deliver amazing results. Remember in promotion to occasionally go for that raw take. Don't tell in advance, keep it on the down low, and shut up; the results can be incredible for certain purposes.

Similarly, holding back on some posts to really hone them with the right words and the best layouts will make them all the more effective when you finally release them.

SEPARATING FACT AND FICTION: POSTS AND STORIES ON THE INTERNET

News flash: If it's posted on the net, it still may not be true.

We all read this and say "duh!" And yet so many people will run with stories upon first read. It's like everybody wants to be TMZ.com.

Take the time to look at the facts before you join the masses in some unverified announcement. Just as it can be smart to hold back on making certain announcements, it can also be a good idea to hold back on making certain judgments about things you read on the Internet or social media.

Be reputable in a world where lies run rampant. The less your posts prove to be contradictions or lies, the more people will trust you as a source. Some stories on the Internet are all about marketing, and when someone starts sharing them as fact, they are helping to dilute the truth or paint the desired picture for whatever company, website, label, artist, or other entity started the rumor. You need read deeper to see what is really going on. Don't put too much excitement, energy, or attention into chasing rumors that could be better spent on your career or your life.

A final piece of advice: In those cases where a celebrity has died and the fact has been verified, don't imitate the tabloids or the paparazzi. Be respectful. Share your thoughts—and your information, if you happen to have it—in an appropriate way, using an appropriate forum. Just don't overdo it.

MARKETING THE NAME: DOMAIN NAMES AND SOCIAL MEDIA SITE NAMES

How many domain names should you own? As inexpensive as domain names are these days and cheap as it is to point a domain name at a website, I recommend buying a new domain name every month.

Hear me out before you laugh this off! You have your primary site and primary domain name, but how many people are going to know the name of your site? Buying it as a .com, a .us, a .net, a .xxx, or whatever else can potentially drive more people to find you and keep other people from potentially branding themselves with your name. In turn, as the search engine spiders run over the different websites and domain names, you will become more searchable.

Next, how do you spell it? Do you have a name or a band name that could be confusing or misspelled? As a drummer and producer, I have more misspellings of my name on records than I do correct spellings. For example, my name is Loren Weisman but I have been credited as . . .

- Lauren
- Lorne
- Lorin
- Loran
- Lorrin
- Wiseman
- Weiztman
- Weismann
- Wiesman

- Wesman

- Weismin

- Weismen

That's five different misspellings of my first name and seven of my last. Combine the two names and you have even more mess ups. Now I only own the website domain of http://loren-weisman.com/. However, if I were a solo artist, trying to attract fans and sell my music, each month I would purchase a different misspelling and forward that link to my main page. This would work two ways: It would connect people who were misspelling my domain with the right domain site, and it would also optimize responses on the search engines—for instance, "Did you mean this?" or "We can search this spelling of the name as well."

Grabbing the right website name can be just as important as what you put on the sites. In the end it's about how easy you are to find. If you have a really long website name or Facebook extension, it can make it harder for you to be found, harder for you to advertise the site, and easier for someone to screw up when looking for you. If you have a site and your name is Trenton Ross Riley, it's a good idea to purchase the domain name http://trentonrossriley.com, which is your full name and can help people who are searching for you. At the same time, see if you can buy a shorter name, such as http://trriley.com/ or http://trentonrr.com/ or http://trriley.com/. It can make a positive difference.

For one thing, those latter names are shorter and less likely to be screwed up. Second, they're easier to use in advertising on flyers, postcards, and business cards. They can be a little larger in font and a little easier to remember. Finally, when it comes to email, it will be both easier (to remember the extension) and shorter (so it fits on promotional or marketing materials). A shorter email will get messages to you easier. For example, trentonrossriley@trentonrossriley.com is a damn long email address and would suck to fit on a card or even remember, while trr@trentonrr.com is worlds better and much easier to remember or add to a business card.

The same goes for your social networking sites, and it's almost more important there. If you're advertising your website and Twitter or WordPress together, like http://lorenweisman.com/and http://twitter.com/lorenweisman/, having them close in both name and size can make things more uniform and easier to read. Even more important, make sure you have consistency with your name across your networks. At the same time, again, it makes it easier to find and harder to screw up. Trying to find uniformity with the names you can choose while at the same time keeping them as brief as possible is going to help people find you that much faster on these social media sites.

The easier the site is to remember, the better it is for fitting onto promotional and marketing items, and the simpler it will be for people to get to you. If you can't find it in .com, go for .net. There are a lot of new extensions that you can buy, and you can buy a number of different web names and point them at the same site, but right now, people know .com and .net most, so go with those as the priority.

Uniformity in the name is key. For example, here are some of my basic page names:

- http://lorenweisman.com/
- http://facebook.com/lorenweisman/
- http://youtube.com/lorenweisman/
- http://twitter.com/lorenweisman/

Again, all are uniform and easy to connect. When you are branding yourself and setting up pages, open up the key pages in numerous windows to see if you can get a name across your core networks that is all the same.

If a name you want is already taken, being used, and has high traffic, getting that name is not going to happen and it's time to move on. Other names that offer buyouts from domain sites can cost a great deal. I wanted to buy a short domain name that was only three letters long, and when I filled out the request form for the price, they quoted me ten thousand dollars for one particular domain name. There are people and companies out there that just buy up domains and hope to turn around and sell them for profit to people who want them.

Think about the small elements; you may find that they can help the big elements. Something as simple as a domain name or a social networking site might lead people to you online; make sure these are the names that are on your promotional materials, your product, and your marketing items. Take the small steps early on in every area that will make for leaps down the line. It's a few dollars a month, and it's a small step toward closing the gap between people trying to find you and people coming upon you by accident who then become long-term fans. On top of that, you will have more words, sites, and tags pointing to you, your music, and your images. This is a good thing.

Do you have a single or a tagline that could also work as a domain name? Sometimes people might only know you by a song; let that song direct them to you. You don't have to renew these names unless you want to, but you can benefit from having a constant flow of different avenues to be discovered by new fans.

Finally, think about finding ways to brand your name for these different sites. Let's go back to Trent and say that for some obscure reason, the name "trentonrr" is taken on YouTube, Facebook, Pinterest, Twitter, and other sites. Try to keep the uniformity and continuity while being creative. For example, if the main website is http://trentonrr.com/ and none of the above are available, maybe you can try for something like this:

1. http://trentonrr.com/
2. http://facebook.com/trentonrrlikes/
3. http://youtube.com/trentonrrviews/
4. http://twitter.com/trentonrrtweets/
5. http://pinterest.com/trentonrrpins/

Again, it comes down to the continuity, the uniformity, and the consistency that help you market yourself and stay memorable. Keep the website and social media site addresses as close to the same as you can in order to stay as memorable as possible.

TRACKING YOUR MARKETING AND SALES: SOCIAL MEDIA AND WEB DATA

This is similar to tracking your merchandise, though it is not monetary; it can help you to see the critical data of your adds, friends, likes, pins, shares, views, tweets, listens, retweets, plays, and everything else. This also can give you a better idea of your online conversion rates from followers to those buying or seeing you live. Keeping a simple weekly and monthly tracking sheet is the best way to track the growth in your Alexa ranking (the ranking of how many people are actually visiting your website) for all your social media numbers.

For all those who claim they have thousands of visitors, anyone can use a Google Chrome app called SEO to see just how much a website is actually being visited. You don't need to be a web genius, and you can look up Alexa ranking online. I am not going too far into it here, but if you show a crazy high Alexa ranking on week one of some month and then show how that ranking drops down to a few million, then you are tracking and proving your growth for website visitors over that series of weeks and months. You can prove that more people are paying attention to you and your website.

The same goes for your Facebook friends, Facebook fan likes, Twitter followers, YouTube views, and all the other sites out there, from ReverbNation to SoundCloud, from Pinterest to Google+, and from every old social media site like Myspace to the newest ones just coming out as well.

"We have 4,000 followers!" So what? That doesn't tell me how long it took you to get them, the rate of growth by week or month, the conversion to sales, or anything more than just . . . "I've got 4,000 followers on Twitter."

To be effective and productive, keep track of your social media numbers each week and each month. How hard is it, really, to jump on Twitter and put into a document or spreadsheet the number of followers each week? Not at all! You don't need to do the analysis, but when you have weekly markings on your social media—your sales, your gigs, what you are growing, and what you are losing—you are tracking, compiling, and collecting all the data that real businesspeople can use to stand behind you, know how to help you, and know where to fund you.

I have a spreadsheet for my book and my social media, which I track every month. The list goes as follows:

- Alexa ranking (for my main website)
- Backlinks (for my main website)
- YouTube subscribers
- YouTube plays
- Facebook friend count
- Facebook fan page count
- Twitter followers count
- LinkedIn connections
- ReverbNation count
- Myspace count (yes, I still maintain one, and you should, too)
- Google+ numbers
- Book sales—paperback
- Book sales—e-book
- Book sales—download card
- Initial question sheet fill-outs
- Consulting sessions

Finally, I do a scan through the YouTube videos to track the views and the ranking of keywords. This type of tracking is simple, and when you are speaking to a potential investor, label, management group, or anyone, these numbers give me an understanding of what works and what doesn't.

Even if you are doing it on your own, by collecting this information you will begin to see patterns, recognize themes, and see what you should be doing for yourself. So whether your goal is to get that larger level of backing or to just back yourself up and do it alone, tracking is the route of understanding, giving you the best information to create the best moves for your career.

"BUT IT MAKES SENSE TO ME": UNFORTUNATELY YOU AREN'T MARKETING TO YOU

Many musicians and groups want to artistically stretch people's minds and make them think— to dive deep into the meanings of their songs, their name, their image, their marketing, and other elements. But when you confuse or actually deter people from listening to your music, that's a problem. Don't get me wrong: Adding elements of depth and creativity is a great thing, but think about it as a later or deeper step in your marketing instead of as a first impression. Make it something that confirmed fans dig for as opposed to something overly confusing for the new listener or first-time visitor.

Wild stories, confusing bios, and songs that make no sense or that tie into the more experimental side of you can be red lights. For example, if you're a grunge/industrial-type band with fast loops, dirty guitars, and in-your-face samples with brash harmonies and powerful hooks, you may lose potential fans right off the bat if song sample number one on your site is either least like your sound or one of your more experimental and, let's say, softer and more trancelike tunes.

Get over Yourself and Your Misconceptions of Marketing

The reality is that when new people are visiting your website or a site with your song samples, most are only going to be there for a few seconds unless they're drawn in. There are millions and millions of Facebook fan pages. People are being tossed links from spam emails, from friends, from strangers, and from third parties every day.

While every musician wants to think that people are spending a number of minutes listening to every sample, looking at every picture, and reading every piece of text, the truth is the majority are only spending seconds and moving on very quickly. We are a nation of ADD, AD/HD, and every other acronym that points to the bulk of us having less and less of an attention span every day. People have endless options, so it's up to you to grab them, wow them, and pull them in to want more. Just like having a fast pitch for industry professionals, you need to have a fast pitch to grab fans from the masses. Hint: This is the pitch you should have created in your preproduction marketing phase.

It's fine to go deep and to challenge your fans, but first get those fans through the door, interested in you, and wanting to be challenged. Make sure you have created a crystal-clear image that will demonstrate you, sell you, and entice them to want more.

Remember, just because it makes sense to you doesn't mean it will to other people. You're the artist. You're right smack in the middle of it all, and a big part of building the fan base is creating the right appearance and marketing to pull in the people who are sifting through thousands of sites, turning them into interested fans.

IT'S NEVER THE RIGHT TIME: SO MARKET AND PROMOTE—NOW!

How many times have you put off a challenge, a job, a plan, or an assignment and claimed you would get to it when the time was right? We all have, but a sad fact still remains: It's never the right time and it never will be. Do it anyway, even during the tough times. You will find the endurance, the drive, and the will to work under any circumstances that are occurring around you.

Right now, excuses for not working on what needs to be done is an epidemic in the creative and entertainment fields. With fears of the shaky economy, layoffs, escalating prices, and so on, putting things off has become a larger, more prevalent course of action than ever before.

The Problem

A strange equation seems to come into play when people are scared, overwhelmed, intimidated, or just plain tired. They justify not doing the things they know they should be in exchange for shortcutting or procrastinating. These people even convince themselves that procrastination is the way it has to be.

I hate the word "trying." I can't stand it when people say that they are trying. I think the word "trying" is turning into more of an excuse than an action. I don't think people have to be perfect, and I don't think everything you attempt must work, but if you are not doing your honest best while making things a little better than the last time, you're spinning your wheels and wasting time. And you certainly aren't trying.

When someone tells me "I'm trying," I dig deeper and find out what he's doing to complete his project or goal. What problem-solving measures are in play? What improvements, no matter how small, are being seen? Usually, people can't answer. They are using the word as an excuse, or they blame everything from the economy to not having enough hours in the day. I do not believe the real problem lies in saying "I'm trying," but in actually believing it.

The Reasoning

As a society, we have allowed ourselves to settle for less than what we dream, desire, and truly want. We have allowed ourselves to accept that everything happening around us is way too much for any person to deal with. We have justified why things are hard and why we can't achieve the dream. The blame, the excuses, and the reasons have allowed us to feel that it is okay to shortcut ourselves and dismiss our dreams.

> Calling for change and being part of making change are two very different things.
> Stop calling for change and be a part of making the change you want to see.

The Right Time?

The right time is never going to come. Money will always be an issue. Relationships will always be an issue. The problems around the music industry and every other industry will always be there. New problems will arise once old ones go away. This is not being negative; it is being honest.

Barring your Mega Millions lottery ticket coming in and taking away the bulk of your stresses, there will always be problems. Whether you are rich or poor, happy or sad, hard times do not discriminate; they just show up in different forms. This is ten times as true in the music industry or any artist-based career.

So . . . Quit Yer Bitchin'!

Complaining does not make things better. It doesn't get your marketing out faster, and it isn't drawing in new fans. Making excuses and assigning blame do not further your career. These actions only drain energy and time that you could be using to advance your dream. A number of years ago, I came across a great analogy in a book. The author said that the common person complaining and making excuses is like ten people standing in front of a burning house trying to figure out how the fire started instead of dousing the flames or calling the fire department. No one is trying to solve the problem at hand. Sound familiar?

Problem Solving

It is not going to get any easier, and if you continue to wait for that "right time," it could be years until you get underway. So why not get underway now? We all know things are going to be hard. We are stressed out and tired—and we always will be!

Simply put, the problem-solving action is to buck up, step up, and move forward, no matter how small the steps. This does not mean you must add extra hours to your schedule. But what if you can lay out an action plan that involves working toward your goal for only five or ten minutes a day? Most people can find ten minutes. After all, there are approximately fourteen minutes of commercials in the average hour-long television show. You can find ten minutes.

Organize your goal as if it is your full-time job. List the small steps; break the big things into manageable pieces. You may not be able to do it all at once, and it may have to be spread out over a period of months and even years, but if you are productively and effectively making progress each day, it may inspire you more on those days when it is a little bit harder. Plus, it becomes habitual. Don't take the shortcuts; they will make your work substandard. You have limited time, so use that time to do it right the first time.

Execution

If you can problem-solve, create realistic, daily plans, and refuse to shortcut, you can make it happen. If you can do this work in these hard times, it will make you stronger and give you the endurance, the patience, and the ability to handle all sorts of difficult situations in your career. Attention to detail is key; pay attention to all of the small elements that make up the whole. Time management is crucial. You need to know that you are getting the most out of the limited time you have and making it as effective as possible. Your success is founded on organization, adaption, learning, and keeping sight of your goal. Put these pieces in place and be aware that the directions that lead you to your dreams may change as the industry does. Those who grasp these elements will find a faster route to what they want.

I opened this book's previous edition with this statement: "It is going to be a harder road than you thought, and shortcutting will only shorten your career in the end. Step out, step up, and step forward. If you can't take those steps, you don't belong in music or the arts."

This may sound harsh, but it's true. In a world where so many have given up on their dreams and in an industry where people are shortcutting with excuses and blame, that quote stands true.

If you are not doing all you can in the hardest times, then you're getting nowhere fast. If you are shortcutting and skipping steps you know you shouldn't skip, they will catch up to you down the road. Stop making bad excuses. Doing it the right way and in the smallest steps doesn't mean it will not be hard, and it doesn't mean that success will show up fast. Still, if you are doing your best and working through the rough times while taking the correct steps, you have a greater chance of achieving those dreams and goals. You will also stand out, because it is a rare few that are actually following through the right way, right now. Be one of them, especially when it comes to marketing, because that is the task that never ends, regardless of where you go in a professional career in music.

MAINTAINING THE MOMENTUM OF YOUR MARKETING AND PROMOTION

Momentum creates a sense of accomplishment and provides a source of inspiration. Whether it's a feature of your band in a big magazine, a great tour booked and scheduled, or a song featured on a TV show, it's supplemental. It has to continue to grow and be maintained. It cannot take the place of your diligent daily output, though it can provide additional fuel to fire up your creativity and dedication. Enjoy the accomplishment, but don't stop doing the work.

When a wave of positive momentum begins to build, work it, rule it, and ride it. Don't stand there and let it wash over you. Now is the time to work harder. People often think that the event or events causing the momentum will automatically bring in new sales and new opportunities. This is partially right; a spike in any kind of promotion will hike sales, but only for that moment. By not exploiting that momentum, you will only get a single result for a short period of time. Instead, take action: Exploit new opportunities resulting from the new momentum to fuel more promotion, more sales, and more marketing.

Don't think that the results of this single momentum-inspiring promotional event will stick around forever. Use it for the moment; ride its momentum to create new opportunities. That is realistic and mature planning. Take joy in the accomplishment, but also use that momentum to build stronger and longer forward momentum.

Be creative. Did you have a TV or broadcast appearance? Can you get segments up on all the video sites or send out links to your fans? Can you use these segments to push other TV or broadcasting groups for more potential appearances or interviews? Can it be applied to your promotional materials?

Folks, this is not rocket science. Think about what has just occurred to help your momentum, and then think about the small steps you can take to exploit that momentum and continue it beyond the single action or occurrence.

Here are a few simple tips for creating forward motion from momentum.

- Keep the momentum while you are moving to guarantee additional motion and momentum. It's the law of physics for artists: "An artist with marketing in motion stays in motion. An artist resting on the laurels of an accomplishment stays at rest."

- While things are going well, push to continue to make them better.

- Plan as if the momentum is not going to last—because it won't.

- Reinforce and secure your momentum to sustain it for a little longer than just the action or event that is giving you momentum.

- Advertise, share, push, and create your ideas to make more people become aware of what other people already know about your music and your business.

- Research what other people have done, how they were effective, and what led them to other opportunities or other actions that allowed for more momentum—and then do those things, too.

These are basic but admittedly vague ideas on the concept of maintaining and exploiting your momentum. Every situation that pushes or creates momentum is different, but the basic concept about trying to keep it moving and creating more is the same. Research different options for how you can plan, exploit, and maximize the momentum that has been created. Then, formulate and implement ways you can sustain the momentum for more opportunities in your marketing. The equation comes down to four steps for every situation:

1. Research how others have made the most of a given situation, action, or occurrence that created good momentum. Look at the ways that you can best exploit and create a similar path to making it last. From being on a radio show to a TV show to appearing at a festival, what did other acts do to use that in the best ways to create more momentum?

2. Organize a plan before you start it. Figure out whom you are going to contact, how you are going to do it, and the methods you are going to implement in order to make things move forward.

3. Execute with consistency. Don't try a blowout for one day; make sure you are doing things every day to build uniformity, consistency, and support for what brought you into the limelight. Hopefully, this will keep you there a wee bit longer.

4. Repeat.

Momentum and the things that create momentum will climax and then either lessen or disappear entirely. Consistency, repetition, and continued, diligent efforts will build the foundation momentum requires to last. Always remember that it is about the long term. A one-time blast is great for that moment, but that will not help you a few months down the line. Look to the long term, and work to reinforce your sustainability and your effectiveness.

Do not get lazy or complacent. This is not the time, the economy, or the industry to rest on your laurels. It is time to use the momentum you have gained to responsibly and actively grow more of it to bring your promotions, marketing, and, most importantly, sales to a whole new level.

Marketing is challenging enough to bring to a state of forward motion and good momentum. Once something gives you that extra push, fuel, and options, make sure you are taking every step to reach every one you can to build on that momentum to make more and more and more.

CLOSING THOUGHT

From branding all the elements and aspects of the band, the recordings, and the performances to giving the best interviews, to going after reviews, to allotting the time to make sure you are consistently putting up the strongest marketing content that points back at you, your music, your schedule, and your merchandise, marketing is paramount in today's music business.

Put effort and attention toward what you are sharing with fans, when you share it, where and how you share it, and how you are being perceived. You can market constantly and continually without coming off as if you are spamming or selling. Deliver those consistent updates of videos, blogs, pictures, samples, reviews, and other content that engages the viewer while also pointing them back to your website, your store, your schedule, or your social media sites. Remember, marketing and promoting do not come down to the likes, the pins, the plus-ones, the followers, the fans, the friends, the views, or the plays online. They come down to the conversion rate of strangers to fans and the percentage of all the above that buys a download, purchase the album, order a T-shirt, tell a friend, come to a show, and help you get the word out.

It is your responsibility to market and promote to as many people as you can reach with the best marketing plan possible. It is your responsibility to deliver constant, branded content that is pointing back at you, your products, and your music. It is your responsibility to set up a marketing plan that will grow as you track your progress to see what is working and what isn't so that changes can be made. It is your responsibility to maintain that momentum.

Only when you have . . .

- created the music and the products that are all branded;

- set into play a marketing plan to reach more people to maintain the existing fan base's interest while sparking the interest of someone who has never heard of you;

- updated and continually posted well-branded content for marketing and promotion on a regular and uniform basis with a solid call to action with each posting; *and*

- engaged, built relationships, and networked with fans, media, and other bands . . .

. . . will you be able to create the marketing and promotions avalanche that will allow you to grow, solidify, and experience a successful music career for years to come.

11

YOUR CAREER IN THE MUSIC BUSINESS OF TODAY

OPENING THOUGHT

Most musicians want the same thing as Iggy Pop: "Success!" They want to sell records, tour, get rich, and buy all the toys. But the devil is in the details.

You need to think about how long you want to write, record, tour, be in a group, work as a solo artist, and whether you want to stay independent or sign with a label. You need to think about a realistic lifestyle. You need to think about how to manage money in both the short and long term. It's fine to go after the big dreams, but as you aim for the stars, make sure you're also looking at your feet and where you'll be tomorrow, next week, next month, next year, and five years after that.

How will you improve as a musician? Whom will you study with? How will you handle copyrights and publishing? How are you preparing yourself for the business details that go with a career in music?

You need a very realistic and detailed plan, not only for the short term but also for the long run. And you must bring the same attention to detail to your career planning that you bring to your music. Your plan should include the best-case scenario—being rich and famous—as well as taking into account the worst-case scenario—those periods of time when music has to be a part-time thing while you set your mind to getting and keeping that day job.

THE "WHO" OF YOUR CAREER IN
THE MUSIC BUSINESS OF TODAY: TELLING

Define the style, band, or sound with your tagline for business, marketing, and promoting. It can open the door for you to refine and further describe yourself, your sound, or your approach. Give people a quick taste, a fast summary, and an easy description. A tagline is not limiting: It provides a teaser into learning more about you.

Lots of people are out there, making lots of noise. They assume that everyone will come running to their websites, Facebook pages, and shows. Today's fans have many more choices; they can't possibly listen to every song they are asked to listen to.

So drop a hint, tease them, summarize, and tell them who you are. Start with the short tagline that carries them into the short bio, which can draw them in even more. Then when you have their attention and their interest, you can go all in with your long bio. Do not lose them in the details too early, or they will move on to another band, and it will be too late. Remember, we live in a world of faster, quicker, now!

Use your tagline, elevator pitch, and short statements to get them to listen to your music, come to your websites, and see you play. Make sure the "who" comes at them quick, clear, and fast. When you get right to the point, you will then have the option to expand, contrast, and go into detail on many other points.

THE "WHAT" OF YOUR CAREER IN
THE MUSIC BUSINESS OF TODAY: EXECUTING

What are you doing to reach new fans, maintain old fans, and sell your music, your merchandise, tickets for your shows, and licensing options? While creativity should thrive in both your music and your marketing, it has to be dialed in, uniform, and consistent in your presentation, marketing, advertising, and promotion. Make sure all your content, graphics, keywords, bullet points, and pitches are presenting a consistent picture of your professionalism, musicality, business abilities, and maturity in the industry.

Your logo, the font of your band name, your disc and album cover, download cards, website, social networks, posters, and merchandise should always be consistent and uniform. Brand your name, content, image, and appearance to increase recognition in those who may take a little time to come to you, your music, your shows, or your sites.

Keep in mind both the eager fans and those who need a little more convincing, a little more consistent marketing. The more people you can reach, the more you can easily familiarize fans, new and old, with your music, your content, your graphics, your branding, and what you are all about.

Your action plan should encompass the foundation of your marketing strategy, the way you execute it, and how you solicit gigs, investors, reviews, management, and everything else. Your efforts must be constant, consistent, and systematic to give you the best chances of getting you what you want.

THE "WHEN" OF YOUR CAREER IN THE MUSIC BUSINESS OF TODAY: TIMING

When is it the right time for the next step? When should you reach out for help, and what kind of help should you expect from the music industry? When is it time to contact a label, booking agent, investor, manager, producer, or consultant, and are you really ready to solicit at this point in your career? Often the answer is "No, it's a little premature."

You need to be as prepared and as polished as possible before you reach out to anyone in the industry. You must make an impactful first impression, as there are a great number of other people trying to contact the same person or company for the exact same reason. When you have completed every task to the best of your ability and have the right materials organized and prepared in order to stand out in the strongest and most professional manner, *that* is the time to send that email or make that call. Do your research before you pick up the phone or send that email. Find out what they are looking for and be prepared to showcase what you are bringing to the table in the way they ask to see it. Remember, just as you want a service from a company, they are going want something from you.

Working with a music consultant or a specialist who can help you build a great promotional, marketing, solicitation, or booking package can give you a leg up. Using that package will help you stand out by highlighting the organization and consistency of your materials.

The right package, built from the ground up, makes you a less risky investment. Remember, whatever you do not have in place in your planning, promo, and branding will need to be done *before* they can start helping you, push you, or fund you—at least with any reputable company or organization.

Don't rush to get a manager, an agent, or a label. Don't rush to pitch an investor for money or a producer for a recording. Take the time think about your needs; work to create the best package for presentation. Patience, professionalism, and organization are going to make you a safer bet. Prepare the materials you are going to use to present yourself. Pulling all those elements together will get the best results.

THE "WHERE" OF YOUR CAREER IN
THE MUSIC BUSINESS OF TODAY: EXTENDING

Where are you reaching out to promote? Where are you advertising? Are they all in your backyard, or are they all playing five hundred miles away? Do you really think the person who lives in Boston is going to drive to Virginia Beach to see you?

Build your databases and invites for a more localized campaign. Of course you can list the gigs in your schedule boxes and pages, but make the invite something a little more personalized, localized, and realistic. Many of the social networks have automatic ways to do this by distance, city, state, and region.

Set a very clear invite. Give the address, the cross streets, or other key landmarks, and add the venue's website. True, most people have GPS on their phones, but don't assume; give them every detail you can to bring them to the show. Deliver the *where* and provide *all* the information to draw the closest friend or the newest fan.

The same goes for advertising online. Go direct with the *where*. Pick one city per week to blast information, not just on the big social networks, but local classifieds, local music sites, and local bands' networking pages. You have the Internet; it's so much easier to do the research now more than ever. So do it.

Make the where of . . .

- your music reach well beyond the backyard of your local city;

- your band clearly defined so people know exactly how to find your gig;

- your advertising and promotion stretch beyond your backyard and set up concentrated blasts in different cities and countries; and

- your reviews broader and wider-based to give the appearance of an artist who is stretching out to the maximum audience and media reach possible.

This also goes for your home base: Are you able to reach as many cities, markets, and opportunities as possible?

THE "WHY" OF YOUR CAREER IN
THE MUSIC BUSINESS OF TODAY: ENTICING

Why should someone like you, buy your music, or come to a show? In a time when everyone is telling you to "like" their page, buy their music, go to their show, vote for a song, donate to a record or an album, buy a T-shirt, and everything else, you've got to answer the basic question: "Why?" I am so tired of being told to "like" a page! Give me a reason to like your page, some details as to why I might like you, why I might want to see you live, why I might want to become a fan. Tell me why!

Would you ever email a girl or guy and say "Like me"? No, you'd want to give them an idea of who you are, what you look like, what you are about, and a few details to entice them to like you or consider going on a date with you. Most women don't enjoy getting hit on by guys they don't know, but this is basically what you are doing online when you send a request that is empty, blank, and oversimplified.

Sometimes I get notes asking me if I would look at a page and see what the artist is about. Then, if I like what I see or hear, could I "like" them? One of the notes was personalized; it mentioned a post where I talked about how I liked a certain band. They added in their note that they were inspired by the same band and wanted to see what I thought.

That is more like it! They took a personalized, assertive, but respectful approach—and it worked.

Another person noticed that I "liked" this artist and that artist, mentioned having been compared to both, and asked me to check him out. I had a reason, and so I gave them a listen. Deliver a reason with your request if you want more interaction.

The same goes for that "can't miss" show or a "must have" CD or download: Why? Give your fans a reason why it is a "must see." And remember that lots of other bands are saying the same thing. Specify, individualize, personalize, and describe. Give them some history about the song or album you want them to buy: something beyond how "amazing" it is.

You need to stand out. Do a special giveaway; make something happen that is a little different and special. Deliver the *why*. When you make any statement about your music, band, sound, anything, back it up!

One of my favorite quotes, often attributed to Abraham Lincoln, is "Give me six hours to chop down a tree and I will spend the first four sharpening the ax."

The idea of focusing on carefully preparing the ax before going after the tree always stuck with me.

If you don't know your tendencies and can't analyze when you are most effective, then how can you get the most done in the least amount of time with the best results?

THE "HOW" OF YOUR CAREER IN THE MUSIC BUSINESS OF TODAY: ACTING

How are you doing it? When I first meet with artists, I often ask this simple question: What did you do for your career today and *how* did that work for you? By the time they talk to me, many feel overwhelmed and have already retreated into a mindset of excuses: "I only have so much time so it's not worth it"; "It's already late"; "I'm burnt out." But excuses don't help you at all.

That's not to say that feeling overwhelmed is unreasonable. The music business is intimidating once you begin to look at the business aspect and everything that you need to do to become self-sufficient, effective, and productive. But there's a little secret people don't know: The little stuff can be just as important as the big stuff. Forward motion can take place in the smallest snatches of free time. It's *how* you take the actions before you get money, before you get signed, before you release a recording.

How are you being as effective as possible in what you are doing to make the career you want happen? Whether you're waiting for someone else to do vocals on a recording before you mix or you're waiting on a tech guy or girl to set up your website, there's always stuff that can be done. All too often, many artists wait for something to be completed before they work on supplementary or secondary steps.

> Your ongoing affirmations, statements, and positive thoughts need the backup of actions, efforts, and endurance if you want to move forward in music or anything in life.
>
> You can read every damn self-help book you want, but if you are not taking the steps, putting in the time, and actually working toward the desired result, you are going to be shit out of luck.

How can you be as effective as possible every day, whether you have five hours or five minutes? Here's a simple checklist of what you can be doing at any given time:

- Updating a networking site with marketing content
- Practicing some of your songs
- Working on your instrument
- Adding friends to a networking site

- Researching new venues or contacting a new venue or talent buyer
- Researching new review sites or magazines and/or sending music to them
- Researching booking agents and/or contacting them
- Researching new management companies and/or contacting them
- Researching labels or investors or working on budgets for your recording or tour
- Researching hotels or places to stay for tours and adding them to your database
- Reviewing your set lists against shows and figuring out what song should go where
- Writing a blog and setting up the best keywords to optimize and post it
- Shooting a video blog and setting up the best keywords to optimize and post it
- Adding a photo to a photo site or networking site with optimized content
- Tagging a photo appropriately
- Liking a page that you want to be affiliated with
- Commenting on a page in a respectful, not-overly-self-promoting way
- Flyering for a local show or putting up stickers and other promo materials
- Contacting a new radio station or Internet radio site and sending out information to it (make sure to find out where they want things sent or if they want them sent)
- Sending out a press package to someone in the industry for reviews, production, record deals, licensing, or booking
- Emailing fans or people who leave messages for you
- Signing up for a new networking site for exposure
- Finding a new place where you can sell your music online
- Contacting a new record store and asking about consignment for a few recordings

- Following up with a venue you just played

- Making contact with a new band that is in your genre and with which you might be able to perform

- Researching licensing opportunities for your music or sending a query to a licensing site

- Giving away a free disc or free merchandise to someone

- Cleaning up a networking site of content that does not need to be up anymore

These are just a few things that don't take up much time but can help you to be incredibly effective and move forward in the right direction—the quickies that add up to large amounts of content, connections, optimization, and opportunities.

Sure, the big things matter, but small things can build into larger things. Yes, it's wonderful when you have five straight hours to dedicate to the business of music, but even if you're only dedicating five minutes a day—especially on those days when excuses creep in—you're moving farther than many others who simply do nothing at all. Just make sure that when you crawl into bed, you can respond to the question "What did you do for your career today?" with an answer that shows effective productivity, regardless of how little or how much.

To borrow a phrase from the Eagles, these small steps help you go the distance in the long run; make sure you take at least one or two each day. If it's truly your dream to make it in music, then it's going to come down to the continuity and the commitment to the big and the small on a regular basis. After all, that's how you learned your instrument, right? Just apply the same practice concept to the business side of your career.

The basic who, what, where, when, why, and how of your career are important to address in detail. Regardless of what you are doing, keep all the elements in mind, from the creation to the presentation, the music to the business, and the performance to the solicitation. When you can clearly and professionally address each element, you will get much farther than most in the music business of today.

NAME YOUR PRICE: HAVE CLEAR NUMBERS AND DEFINE YOUR COSTS

You don't have to be a Priceline Negotiator like William Shatner, but you do need to be professional, assertive, and confident enough to name the prices for your professional services.

Defining your costs with a rate sheet or price menu is the best way to go when it comes to building a good reputation with a potential customer. Revisit the who, what, when, where, why, and how concepts, focusing on how you get paid. Many problems, disputes, and arguments can be avoided when you agree in advance who is paying the band and how each person is paid.

Name a starting price before you negotiate. Prices can be adjusted, but do that *after* you have stated your expectations. For example, my hourly consulting and half-hour phone consulting costs have been locked in at $100/hour and $60/half hour for the past two years. But when I speak to musicians who may want to do a series of consults, a full music business plan, or another type of longer-term package, I offer discounts to make it work. Expectations and numbers are laid out and defined clearly first, then we can talk from there. Costs are defined on the front side and then negotiated on the backside. Name your price and then go from there.

Other People's Price Tags

Whether you are hiring a photographer, recording studio, music consultant, session player, mastering engineer, or whomever, make sure the price tag is clear and also followed up in writing. If you can't get a definite answer and it is not set in writing, then move on to the next person. Ignoring red flags like that in the initial stages can put you into problematic situations down the road. Understand the services to be delivered, and if you have negotiated some kind of special deal, make sure it is in writing before you pay a penny.

MUSIC BANKING: SETTING UP THE SYSTEM FOR YOUR CAREER

You should think about your finances just as you think about preproduction, production, and recording. Even if you don't have the money, plan for your needs and what you want before you quit your day job.

A system to project your short-term and long-term needs, as well as on a monthly, quarterly, and yearly basis, can keep you financially organized to make a well-prepared decision about when to quit the day job and go full-time with your music.

Also think about your future personal plans. Do you want to be married at some point? Do you want to have children? Do you have a goal to live somewhere specific? To own certain things? Take all these long-term ideas into consideration and set in place a functional, financially sound template for your future *while* organizing the present.

I'm not a financial advisor by any means, but I found it most effective to open up a series of different bank accounts to maintain money in separate places. There are five key accounts I recommend for the business side of things and three for your personal use. You may think this is overkill, but the level of organization it brings will simplify things drastically and make you more aware of the money you're earning and spending.

Business Accounts

First is your income account, specifically for the album, downloads, merchandise, and performance payments—mostly inbound or internally circulated money. Use it for tracking and tax purposes, and it will make things easier.

Second is your artist or band logistics account. You will transfer money from the income account to this account and use it to pay for logistical items such as gas, hotels, food for the road or the gigs, tolls, parking for shows, band purchases, and other necessary items. Having this as a separate account affords you an easier tracking system for the money being spent on your band as a business, thus making bookkeeping a breeze.

Third is the recording budget account. I advise artists not only to have an account specifically for their recording when they're creating a music business plan but also to have that same account used down the line for other recordings. You'll be able to track every dollar that goes into the recording process. Regardless of the demo, the album, the EP, or the single day in the studio, you can track expenses and decide what money will be shifted to this account. You may also shift funds from here into your touring account after a recording is done or keep this as an account that you slowly feed money into for the next recording.

Fourth is your promotional, marketing, and branding account. Unlike the first account, this is all outbound money. You'll transfer money to this account to pay for for posters, flyers, advertising, duplication, web work, and other promotional costs. This, just like the other accounts, will give you a full picture of how much is being spent and on what.

Fifth is the tax account. Don't get a bank card or a checkbook for this account; set it up strictly for deposits and withdrawals. To be safe, automatically deduct 25 percent from everything that you bring in from sales on anything and deposit it into this account. At the end of the year, after taxes are done, more often than not you will find that you will not have to pay any extra if you're diligent and constantly putting that 25 percent of everything away. Trust me, if you don't open up any of the other accounts I've mentioned, set up a tax account and drop 25 percent of everything into it. It will be one of the smartest decisions you make.

With your tracking, accounting, and receipt keeping, you will be able to write off many aspects of your profession. Still, put that cash away on the front side so you don't get kicked in the backside come tax time.

That, in my opinion, is the best way to handle band finances. You can set up budgets and designate what goes to where every time money comes in. Just as you designate the percentage for taxes, you can have a percentage going to promotions or a percentage going to the next recording. Then you can decide what everyone can get paid. This process will streamline and simplify things radically.

Personal Accounts

The first account is where your basic banking and living happens. This is where you deposit the checks you would write yourself from the business account as well as wherever else money is coming from. Use it for your spending money: rent, food, coffee, or whatever else your little heart desires.

The second account is a tax account—yes, you're going to get taxed both as a business and as an individual. Accountants can help you with this process and make things easier, but I would advise that for everything you deposit, you put that same 25 percent away for taxes and don't touch it.

Now remember, if you're tracking receipts both as a business entity and individual, a great many write-offs can occur, but let those write-offs be a wonderful surprise at the end of the tax season; put the money aside and do not assume the deduction. Be surprised at what you *don't* have to give to Uncle Sam instead of scrambling to keep the IRS off your back.

The third account is what I call the "far future account." This is money you slowly put away. Think of this account as the money you will retire on, that you will live on after you don't want to work anymore. This could also be the money you invest in CDs, stocks, mutual funds, and other vehicles to accrue money over time. Don't get a card for this account, and don't touch it.

When you make long-term investments, make sure you can't touch them. View it as money that's not yet yours but will be, years down the road. As discussed in chapter eight, you can also personally apply the proprietary investment concept with a money manager who can help make that money work for you with greater returns.

Every musician wants to bank on his or her career, but in order to have a career, a lifestyle, and long-term, sustainable success, you must organize, optimize, and prepare. Even if you open the accounts with only a couple of bucks, get into the necessary habit of saving. Many musicians just look to the stars and think they will be millionaires; they don't plan or prepare. Given all the opportunities—performing, licensing, sales, and insertions—it's possible, now more than ever, to maintain a realistic salary level. By preparing for the most avenues of success and sustainability and for your financial needs both now and in the future, you can achieve a long, successful, sustainable career with secure finances in place.

YOUR SECRET STASH: PERSONAL AND BUSINESS INFO

As you build up your stash of information and begin to collect websites, logins, passwords, usernames, and access codes, it's absolutely necessary that you track, maintain, and protect this information. In these days of cybercrime, it's not only important to protect and keep track of this information; it's also necessary to update and change passwords to keep security at the highest level possible.

Every band should have a secret stash or a safe document that is password protected on the computer and also printed out and stored with your most sensitive documents in a safe deposit box, a safe, or somewhere else that is fireproof and not easily accessible. It also can be updated and easily accessed every time you need information. I advise the following breakdown:

Personal Information

- Phone numbers

- Emails

- Emergency contacts

- Physical addresses

- Medical information *(blood type, allergies, etc.)*

  ○ This should include all of the medical information for every member of the band.

- Financial/business information *(the most important)*

- Bank account info

- PayPal

- iTunes, TuneCore, etc. *(distribution and sales accounts)*

- Duplicator, download cards *(primary merchandise accounts)*

- CafePress, Jakprints, Vistaprint *(secondary merchandise accounts)*

Basic Bills

- Phone/cell phone

- Internet

- Electric/water

- Rent or mortgage

- Car payment

- Credit cards

Does the band have a phone plan? Internet? Having all these elements in place and together will make life easier whenever passwords, addresses, or accounts change.

Basic Web and Networking Information

- Web hosting

- Merchant accounts

- Domain name information

- Emails

- Social networking sites, logins, and passwords

Your Lists of Primary Contacts for Shows

- Booking contacts, talent buyers, venue information

What is the login to your web hosting and domain name information? What if you need to make changes or hand off the information to a designer? All the more reason why you should have this well organized. Also, with all the different network sites, you should have different passwords and tracking of what you've got up and where you are.

I know so many people (including me) who have forgotten a password, a login, or even a membership to a particular site. Maintaining a backup sheet where you can track all your key information is a great solution for that problem, and it can make searching for information a piece of cake. Secure this information in a document that is password protected and store that password somewhere else! Also, have a printout available and accessible by someone you trust, in case something goes wrong with the computer and/or you're out on tour and not around.

Remember that in these times of hackers, spammers, and phishers, the more you secure your information, change up passwords, and secure your private information, the better the chances that it will stay private. Start your secret stash sheet today. Collect all your information, and store it safely and securely.

EFFECTIVE INFORMATION COLLECTION: TRACKING THE PEAKS AND VALLEYS

Organization and information tracking are central to most businesses and companies—and to bands as well. It takes a lot of work to set up websites, book shows, plan tours, implement advertising and marketing plans, and increase sales and fan numbers. It can be tedious and incredibly time consuming, which will require an attention to detail that you might not be used to.

But it has to be done if you want to be effective and productive. Most artists don't look past the project or task they're working on. But losing sight of the long-range objective won't help you succeed.

For example, let's say you're a Boston-based band and you're playing a festival just outside Atlanta this coming summer. Taking the opportunity to find shows on your way down and on your way back up might give you the opportunity for a small tour if the band has the time. This would allow you to reach new audiences in places you may not have played or haven't marketed to.

So far so good. Most bands will try to book shows that take them to a festival and back. Most bands will find accommodations, whether they're staying in hotels or trying to find a house they can use. But that's often where it stops. That is an ineffective use of travel, work, and band promotion time. Instead, think of every place you play and every town you go to as a place you will return to. You may not return to that venue specifically, but each stop should be viewed as a research-collection mission.

Let's say this Boston group goes west first and books its first night in Springfield, Massachusetts, on its way down to Georgia. Understand that the first time you play in a city you've never been to, it might not be the best show. All the more reason to collect information on bands that are already in that area and have a great draw. This is information you may want to keep in your records in a spreadsheet. What bands always draw a great crowd? Who is their contact person? How far out do they book? Who are the contact points for festivals, local music websites, or venues in that town, too? Keep this information for any city you hit and update it as things change.

When I was on tour with one group, Jack Dorin—a kick-ass road manager who is no longer with us, but his ideas still are—kept a ten-page Excel sheet with the following data:

- **Venues.** All the pertinent information—contact persons, addresses, phone numbers, fax numbers, capacities, the style of venue, and more

- **Hotels.** All the places to stay in a town and the best prices

- **Restaurants.** A basic layout of the best food places

- **Radio stations.** Every core radio station and its format

- **TV stations and newspapers.** Every one in the area. When he was a tech, Jack would pick up all the local papers in the mornings, copy the core information, and then leave the papers.

- **Major points of interest.** All the schools, colleges, major companies, etc.

- **Local band database.** The bands that are a really strong pull within the city limits

- **Sales.** Results in each city—not just the sales as a whole, but what was sold and where it was sold

- **Overall sales records.** All physical sales, downloads, and show payments. What was paid out and to whom?

Each city and each show was a research project, and if we had time, the backup band was sent out to find information about the town. We would dig up information that would help make the next trip there twice as successful.

To update the spreadsheet to the current day, I would add social media and website information. A database like this is not only great for your band, but it can also be used to barter and swap information with other bands in other cities.

Collecting information can be tedious, but the attention to detail and time spent on the front side can save hours and days on the backside. Your research will make you effective for that first stop and even more effective for the next time. You can even purchase databases that have been collected online, like college booking databases and press databases.

Create formats and templates so that each show and each piece of information is easy to add and use. You don't have to create a massive database overnight; taking small steps each day, adding information as you go, is just as effective, if not more so.

Keep the records for all your expenses, all your shows, all your web materials, everything easily accessible, and back it up on an external drive. Make sure there are also updated backup copies on discs somewhere safe. The more information you have collected and the easier it is to reference, the easier it will be to be more productive, more effective, and more efficient.

This level of tracking when it comes to the sales, audience attendance, and promotion can also be incredibly helpful if you are talking to investors, labels, or others that might be able to help back you.

THE "OH, SHIT! CARD" . . . WITH BENEFITS

Do you have an Oh, Shit! Card? It is a small business-card-sized card laminated with all the key information you might need if your computer or phone dies:

- Basic phone numbers of band members, managers, close friends, and people that would have the numbers you may not be able to access

- Email logins, especially if you have your own hosting and have a special site you need to log into

It's basically, all the stuff you can't recall—put those basics on a card, and keep that card in your wallet. It can be a lifesaver.

BACK UP YOUR MUSIC, YOUR INFO, AND YOUR DOCUMENTS: PLAN FOR THE WORST

Backups are always important; this is not a news flash. The horror stories about crashed computers and lost discs are everywhere. Are you taking steps to back up everything you need to? Is it properly marked? Are your old backups discarded safely?

A month before I finished the first book, my PC crashed; the motherboard went bad. I'm not really a techie, but I knew I was in trouble. Fortunately I had almost everything backed up, and I had a friend who was able to pull the last day that wasn't backed up off the drive. I'm now on a MacBook Air and have been taking some time to reorganize music files, documents, and plans. I went through discs and discs of crap as well as files that were backed up with different dates and different names. I have a lot of things well organized, but I don't think I was organized to the point I should've been until this minor catastrophe struck—minor only because I'd backed up. For artists, musicians, and everyone, it's incredibly important not only to back up your information but also to know where your information is.

In the studio, is your gear automatically backing up everything at certain intervals? After something amazing happens in a recording, is it being backed up? It seems secondary until you lose that file, that take, that song, that document. Don't let it happen: Back up—constantly.

Get rid of old demos, or at least catalog them as you burn them. Don't let music sit around unmarked or unnamed. I have spent hours going over old discs, trying to figure out what was what and marking it correctly. If you have a truckload of discs or tapes (yes, some of us still have old tapes), try to review one every day. It will feel less overwhelming and it keeps you moving toward organization.

Track your backups. I've begun naming folders with the date at the end of each name. As things change, I update or back up again. Discard or replace older backups, or date them and periodically discard outdated information.

And remember, a lot of the music or backup information that you are throwing away may still be stuff you don't want anyone else to hear or see. Make sure your music, business information, and personal information are not getting in the wrong hands. Don't just toss discs in the trash; break them in half or scratch across the disc a number of times. Or, my favorite: nuke 'em! Put a CD in a microwave for two seconds, maybe three max, and watch the light show. It's pretty cool and completely destroys the disc. I was going nuts with this the other day and fried twenty old backup discs. It's entertaining and I thought it was safe, but I was recently told it releases some nasty gases, but not at an excessive level. So, not completely safe . . . but still cool.

Make sure you have your ducks in a row. Back up that info stash, those databases, recordings, older music, and anything else important. With memory sticks and cloud backup sites, there is no excuse for losing your important information, even in a worst-case scenario.

MUSIC BUSINESS CAREER DETOURS: TOP FIVE REASONS YOUR CAREER WILL FAIL

Warning: Some of the following may come off a little harsh—because it is. Too many musicians put their energy into talking about why things have not happened or are not working for them. They have reasons, justifications, and rationale to explain why they are failing, yet these same artists do not take the steps to problem-solve, change direction, learn, educate, or empower themselves.

Like most artistic types, musicians need to exercise ego management. Add stubbornness and delusions of grandeur to ego and you get a failure trifecta. The music industry has changed dramatically in the last twenty-five—no, make that the last five years. The musician must learn the industry and its latest changes. You must have:

- Problem-solving skills
- The tools and patience to do the drudgework
- Awareness to watch for mistakes and missteps

Just as you watch for opportunities and new avenues, it is crucial to make corrections to keep yourself on the path to success to avoid the detours that lead to destruction for you and your career in music.

The following are the top five excuses for failure; I hear them all the time. Let's take a look at them, and I'll suggest ways to see them in a new light.

5. My friends tell me I am great. My fans love me and tell me I should be a star. Everybody loves me and I've got a ton of reviews, so I am headed in the right direction.

Congrats! Your friends like you and you have connected with some new fans. This is positive, but not something on which to base your business approach. When positive things are coming your way via comments, messages, and personal reviews, then work to find magazines, websites, media, and more reputable organizations to say the same thing. Keep in mind: When you have a whole bunch of comments on your website or your social networks, you are in the same boat as *everyone else*. Many artists get cocky at this point and think worldwide success is just around the corner because a song got ten thousand plays and some cute girl on Facebook commented that she loved it.

Instead, that is the time to work on getting ten thousand *sales* of that song. Go after reputable media to review your music or your band. In short, work even harder, and don't get cocky. This is how you capitalize on successes and differentiate yourself from the thousands of other bands who think they are on the brink of success. If you don't apply smart marketing to your new popularity, a year from now you'll still be working your day job.

4. I don't need to worry about the business. The songs will take care of themselves. I don't need to put the work into the business, because it is about me and the music. I just need a manager or a label to take care of everything.

Great attitude. Just sign away the rights to everything and let some manager or label do the work.

First, you've got to understand that a lot of labels have no idea what they are doing at all. By signing, you lose all sorts of percentages you are unaware of. Meanwhile, they own you without having to do anything. On the other hand, even if you get a fair deal, you are still giving up a great deal of ownership to other people; you could easily help with the work and retain more of a percentage.

Just remember: Whenever you sign contracts, you are giving other people rights to aspects of your musical presence: people who may or may not know what they're doing. You must know what they can accomplish if things go well, just as you should know what could happen if things go poorly. Whether you are independent or going to a label or manager, you need a crystal clear understanding of what is being done with your musical presence. Otherwise you *will* be screwed, every time!

3. [Name of my favorite artist] did it ten, twenty, thirty years ago. He/she didn't worry about this; why should I? These methods worked for them, so I am copying them, and I will have the same success.

In 1985 there was no Internet to speak of. The first MP3 tracks were distributed in 1999. In 2003, there was no Facebook. Why would you expect the same methods used years ago to work today? This is one of the most foolish ideas ever, but I hear it all the time. Whether you're talking about logos, recordings, or what it costs to put out an album, you cannot use the facts of the past to define the truth of the present. Certain aspects may apply, but you need to understand the changes in the industry and their effect on your career.

If you are so sure that what Duran Duran did with *Rio* is the shortcut to success, then you should have tens of thousands of cassettes made. Oh, wait . . . that's right, people don't use cassettes much these days. This also goes for marketing, recording, and soliciting. Things have changed. Has your thinking?

2. If I just had the money, the backing, the ears, or if this famous person heard the music . . .
You hear it at every bar, music venue, and music shop: "If things were different . . ." Well, you know what, if the world were flat, then it wouldn't be round. This attitude wastes time and energy that could be used to find investors or donors or work on a solicitation package for a manager, a label, or a talent buyer. Stop the excuses and get going after what you want.

It goes well beyond the song. You have to be the whole package and worth the investment. The upper-level executives, industry professionals, and investors receive thousands of packages; they need to be impressed enough by the package itself to open it up and listen. They see you before they hear you; keep that in mind.

Get real. Do you honestly think if a famous person hears you, you will suddenly be signed to a multi-album deal? Not gonna happen. He or she can recommend you and pass your materials along, but it's just one person. Would you rather have one person hear your music, or tons of industry professionals who might be willing to help you? Plan and research. Create lists of people who will look at your package, listen to your music, and have proven successful at doing what you need.

1. The industry is against me. I know how things work, and they just can't handle my sound and my image. They just don't understand, and that is why I am not where I want to be.
See response to #2. You can blame anyone, everyone, and everything, but when it comes down to it, it's about how you handle things. At times, you may even be right; things may really be against you. But if you just blame and agree, you are settling, giving up, and giving in.

Buck up, gear up, and fight for what you want. Learn different ways to present your sound, image, and goals. It might not always work, but it is a hell of a lot more effective than bitching. Plan, learn, grow, create, problem-solve and empower yourself—and then execute. Take those steps or quit. It's your choice—it really is that simple.

SCAM ALERT: WATCH OUT FOR SOME PUBLISHERS

Licensing your music is a great way to create different revenue streams and profits from your songs in ways well beyond just the song sales by download or CD. In addition, it can open up a series of connections for your music and your writing. Some have gone on to careers where they do all their work scoring, composing, or licensing older works to movie soundtracks, television shows, commercials, video games, and even corporate training videos.

Licensing and music-insertion opportunities have come a long way. Just as it has created revenue for the artists, it has also created revenues for various agencies, companies, and middlemen. Many of these are legitimate, but a great deal more are not. These scams play off a lack of understanding and the hopes that many artists have.

So how does this get fixed? Not by bitching or complaining. True, sharing your experiences with others is a good thing, and word of mouth will help your friends, but don't spend productive energy on a crusade. Instead, get busy finding a better licensing option or uploading your music somewhere else. Don't organize a rally, and don't spend time bashing them online every day. Put out the message: Post on some scam boards, the BBB, and any music-law watcher sites, and then get on with your life. Now, if you can nail them on a legal issue, then go for it. But the bulk of the time, they have a basic agreement that you signed, which should have made you fully aware of what you chose to give up by signing with them. If you signed the contract that allows them to get away with what they did, then in all honesty, buck up, Binky—it's on you.

Now let's talk about how to avoid getting screwed. Carefully read the sites you visit or the emails you receive. Most mistakes occur due to excitement and unclear thinking. If something seems too good to be true, it usually is. Hell, in the music business, it almost always is.

The Spam Email: Red Flag Number One

I hate to break it to you, but that tune they "heard" on YouTube, Facebook, or ReverbNation is usually no more than an excuse for a spam message. These outfits troll the Internet, looking for people who will sign up, pay into, or, sometimes, execute a contract for their song rights.

I get these emails on a daily basis: "I heard your song on Myspace"—yes, Myspace! In 2013!—"and think you should submit it to this licensing opportunity. It is only X amount per song . . ." Some are "free"; they ask you to sign a "simple" terms-and-conditions sheet that gives them exclusive publishing rights if anything happens. But, of course, that is the small print that you don't have to worry about, right?

Here's the thing: *I don't have any songs on Myspace.* My Facebook player, SoundCloud, and ReverbNation pages have a couple of my audio rants as MP3s, but I still get email saying how my "song" sounds like "something that could be in a movie." Check out who is contacting you and get the facts about the bridge they are trying to sell you.

So How Should You Do That?

First, if they have all these amazing contacts, check the contacts out. Ask for references. Make sure they show up online and mention being involved with the people soliciting you. Drop an email or give them a call. This is called basic research. Some scammers give references who are just other people involved in the scam; don't get nailed with that. Ask questions about the process, how it worked, if they got paid, and what they like or didn't like.

Watch for Fees: More Red Flags

These scammers charge per song, per full upload, and even per membership. They tell you they have the inside track to get you to the right people: the top names at the television companies and movie studios—the same people who are routinely blocking the spam emails they're getting from the people who are feeding you these lies. If you tie yourself, your music, and your name to someone in the industry that people see as a liar, a fake, or a scammer, it's not hard to figure out what happens to your reputation.

Now, some of the fee-based sites are reputable, such as TAXI and Sonicbids. I know many people have issues with both, but I think that both those organizations do great things. It is up to the individual artist to make them be as effective as possible. Artists who aren't fully utilizing TAXI the smart way, for example, typically blame TAXI for their own shortcomings. Ditto for Sonicbids. If you set up a half-assed page, don't organize a promo pack beyond their simple EPK, or show limited branding, marketing, or promotion, then why should a festival, venue, or tour choose you? Just because you paid a small fee, you aren't guaranteed success. The site only works as hard as you do.

Top Three Ways to Avoid Scams

1. **Ask questions, and make sure you understand the answers.** Get proof that this person or company actually does what is claimed.

2. **Try to stay nonexclusive.** Do not sign on for situations where only one person is allowed to push and license your catalog. If it is a scam, they are lazy, or don't know what they are doing, you are still signed into an agreement. If something happens down the road, they are getting a piece of your profits for doing nothing except talking you into signing a contract.

3. **Doubt, question, and raise every red flag you can.** This is your art; this may lead to new avenues of revenue to support future recordings, touring, and networking—or it may be a dead end. Treat your music and your art with the respect it deserves. Find sites where you can upload and post for free and that have nonexclusive, nonbinding agreements. There is a great list of sites at http://musiclibraryreport.com.

As with anything, when you apply patience, a serious attention to detail, research, and double checking, you will find yourself getting involved with more reputable, professional people and organizations who can actually help you with your career.

MANAGEMENT, LABEL DEAL, OR REPRESENTATION: ARE YOU REALLY READY?

You have completed the album and the promotional materials and set your branding and marketing in place, but you feel that you want to concentrate more on the music and less on the business. You understand that you will still need to be involved with the business, but maybe you feel it's time to turn over the booking, promoting, and marketing to another person.

When is the right time to get a manager? When is the right time to go after an agent? A label—and what kind? Should you work with a booking agent or a promoter? If and when you do, you need to understand the responsibility that's going to come with handing over certain aspects of your band, your music, and your business to someone else.

Finding a manager is easy—they're everywhere—but finding a good manager is a challenge. I've seen all kinds. It comes down to how the manager or management group is going to work for you and what they're actually going to do. Talk is cheap and actions are truly what matter. The same goes for indie labels, talent buyers, and booking agents. You have to decide whom you're going to go with, what you're going to get, and what you're going to have to give in return. You need to find someone who's organized, with a game plan and the experience to move you toward your goal. This manager, label, or agent needs to be able to keep you in the loop and explain every step along the way.

Interview managers as they interview you. Find out what they've done and what they believe; is it something that you believe in? How often do you meet? Will this person or group show you time logs and work charts? It's your right to know what's getting done and when. Clearly define who's responsible for doing what. Managers have many different fees and percentage plans with the different bands that they work with, based on the work that has to be done.

Think about what is being done for you, what is being said about you, and the professionalism of how you're being presented to others. You want to make sure you're getting reports about what's being booked, what's being sold, and basically what you're paying for. If someone is being paid or taking a percentage of everything from sales to bookings, along with time and hours logged, you should know what those hours are and what's happening during them. Many artists feel as if management or representation lifts a weight off them, freeing them to be "rock stars." Guess what? People and companies know this fact and take full advantage of it by taking larger percentages and doing less work than they promise.

Look at Billy Joel and what happened to him a number of years back. His ex-brother-in-law was handling his career, and Billy just let him run with it. Well, he ran with it until Billy realized he was almost broke and had to go back out on the road just to make money to support his lifestyle.

A warning sign is hesitation if you ask this person to report hours and activities or to meet with you to talk about what he or she is doing. This is information you have a right to, and an honorable organization or person should be willing to share with no delay whatsoever.

It's your responsibility to review and look for discrepancies. Ask for references; talk to other bands that have been involved with them. Research for yourself and not just from their press materials or website.

See if you can sign a preliminary deal or begin with a trial period. Set down some basic ideas for booking and promotion and see if it goes down the way it was discussed. As you read the fine print, make sure these questions are answered and are clearly defined in the fine print:

- Do they have exclusive rights to you?

- Can they profit from or get in the way of bigger deals?

- Will they have a percentage of profit if you achieve a certain profit level, even if you're no longer working with them?

- How will they market you?

- What tools will they use?

- What kind of money will they spend?

- Do they have effective and proven techniques that have worked in the past twelve months?

- What physical media will they use? How will they market online?

- What plans do they have for booking shows and properly promoting them?

- What plans do they have for booking tours?

There are dozens of other questions you can and should ask to find out what's going on and how it goes on with these potential suitors. A manager can make life easier for a band if he or she is working well with the band and presenting you in the best possible way. At the same time, managers have ruined deals, lost bookings, and ripped off bands due to poor planning, unprofessional execution, and lack of knowledge. I've seen management groups still using ten-year-old models, and you can guess the results; they just won't cut it anymore.

Finally, make sure you have an "out clause" in the contract. This is the biggest safety net if something's not working or the relationship is not benefiting your band. It should be stated somewhere in the contract that if the manager is not doing the things he or she agreed to do with no explanation for the lack of execution, you have the right to terminate your agreement and the manager will have no rights to your band or your work anymore. Remember, it's all about the details, and finding the right manager involves a truckload of details.

PRODUCTIVITY: KNOWING WHEN YOU ARE AT YOUR CREATIVE BEST—AND WORST

Have you ever put much thought into when you are at your best and most productive? When does your practicing seem most inspiring and self-fueling? On the other hand, when do you seem to be accomplishing less? When do you feel uninspired? When is rehearsal a drag? We all wish we could be operating at 100 percent all the time, but often it just doesn't happen that way. So instead of comparing your phenomenal productivity of yesterday to your lackluster results today, why not take a closer look at the patterns and factors that allow you to be your best and, alternately, bring out your worst?

The first thing to consider is your physical well-being. Are you getting too little sleep, the right amount, or too much? What about the food you eat? Those sayings about brain food—they apply to you personally. How do various foods affect your creativity? Your attention span? Eating junk food might help you practice better but eating healthily allows you to concentrate better when you're working on the business.

Another factor to consider is your emotional well-being. How does the stability of your relationships affect your productivity and creative output? How does a fight with a significant other affect these things? How does loneliness factor in?

Some people are more effective with certain tasks at certain times of the day. On a similar note, doing certain tasks before others can affect your productivity. For instance, if you're stressed out by accounting and then go to a less stressful task that still manages to upset you, it could be that the stress is being carried over from the previous task. Reorganizing the optimal order of odd jobs may help.

> All the excuses are valid; all your reasons for not starting, not following through, not stepping up are rational.
>
> If these valid, rational, and present truths are what you have subscribed to, why bother going after your dream, working harder than you ever have for anything in your life? Because the fact is that the excuses have become all that you are.
>
> *All the excuses are now truths. So just quit.*
>
> *On the other hand . . .*
>
> If you are ready to face the fears, take the steps, do the work, be more than you thought you ever could, and attack the dream, what is keeping you?
>
> Lose all the excuses and replace them with all the reasons for success. Be the change for yourself. Commit to the dream or quit. There really is no middle ground.

KNOWING WHEN IT'S TIME TO CHANGE THE PLAN AND DIRECTION FOR YOUR CAREER

Sometimes you need to change things up and find a more effective approach. Artists often have a very hard time shifting mindsets or accepting change when it comes to their careers. This only perpetuates the problems or lack of success.

You've heard that you shouldn't change horses in midstream. However, in my opinion, if the horse isn't going anywhere and you're sitting in a puddle of water, it's time to jump down, get your feet wet, and get to finding a better horse.

You need to look at your goals and figure out where you are at every step of the way. Don't look too far into the future, or you won't be able to see the path right at your feet. Yes, becoming a multimillion-dollar superstar is a great dream, but the dream itself can distract you from taking the basic steps to achieve basic self-sufficiency in music.

Some bands use the same formula for booking, promoting, recording, marketing, and soliciting: "If we keep doing what we have been doing, we will get _____." (Fill in the blank—noticed, seen, signed, rich, famous, successful, picked up, or whatever.) But think about people who go on diets to lose weight. If they don't see any results after a month, then isn't it time to take stock of what's wrong? Why are things not working?

When you track and analyze what you're doing, how it turned out, and what positives and negatives occurred, you'll be in the best frame of mind to move forward effectively. But to be able to track and analyze, you're going to have to keep and organize information so you can decide if what you're doing is the best thing possible.

- How many shows did you play in a month?

- How many people were at the shows?

- How much merchandise did you sell at the shows?

- How much merchandise did you sell online?

- How many downloads did you sell?

- How much did it cost for gas, advertising, equipment repair, etc.?

- How much money came in and where did it come from?

- How was that money distributed?

- Where did you market and how much did you market for shows, product, etc.?

- How many website hits / what is your Alexa ranking?

- How many views for your videos on YouTube by the month?

- How many plays for your songs on streaming music sites?

- How many "likes" on Facebook?

- How many retweets?

- How many shares?

- How many follows, networking, or friend-adds on different social networks?

When you have all the information, you can run it against—yes, you guessed it—more information! The conversion of all this information is the crucial part.

Where and when did you advertise and market? Answering this question can give you clues to surges in sales or profit. How much promoting did you do for the shows? If the biggest turnouts had a different amount of postering or marketing, then maybe apply that level for all shows.

You can then ask yourself a series of questions to see what is and is not working. This can also help you see if your manager or agent is doing his or her job correctly. If he or she doesn't have the information to the above questions, then that person may not be an organized or effective manager.

At the same time, if you're doing something that's only producing limited success, you need to make adjustments. If you're not moving forward, you're moving backward. It's crucial to take an educated, intelligent, and humble look at what's happening. Creating time frames and setting goals is also a very good idea. Whether it's a certain number of shows a month, a certain amount of sales a month, or a certain amount of solicitations or number of bookings a month, *set a goal and hit it*. If you don't make it in the first month, then aim for the next. If you don't make the next, then it's time to get some help or readjust the plan and the approach.

Many artists have used the consulting services I offer as a monthly checkup and as a way to see things from a different perspective. These are not artists I am producing; instead, these artists schedule a consult every few months in order to go over where they are and organize ideas to get to the next level.

Having someone with a fresh perspective review what you're doing can really make the difference. Make sure whoever you talk to is someone with an understanding of the industry as it is today.

There are stories out there about bands doing it one way and then being discovered, but those stories are right up there with the chances of winning the lottery. You need to give the same attention to the business of your music as you do to the music itself. If you're not clearly tracking what's happening around you and how it's happening, you won't gain the full understanding of what you're doing right and wrong.

SO NOW YOU GET IT—BUT DO YOU REALLY?
IS THIS THE CAREER FOR YOU?

It's a hard thing to admit when you're wrong. Whether it's in an argument at work or at play, it can be incredibly challenging to suck it up and admit that it's not someone or something else's fault, but your own. You know the people who have a thousand reasons for why they're not getting somewhere, and the reasons always have to do with all these other people and all these other things, but let's be honest: The world at large is seldom solely to blame.

Fortunately, the sentiment can have a motivational flip side: Admitting that you're wrong often means you're ready to change it. This is a great place to arrive at, but it's important to figure out exactly what you need to make it right so that you're not just putting a Band-Aid on the crack in the boat.

Realization Translating into Action

So you realize that something or some things are not working. It's time to identify and analyze what has happened and what hasn't. You haven't been getting that many shows; the places you play are not drawing. Maybe your sales are on the decline or you've never really sold that many downloads or CDs at all. You took an approach and it's clearly not working.

Don't be like the guy who emailed me: "They just don't realize how incredible the songs are and are fools for not buying." In other words, it had nothing to do with how he was distributing, marketing, or promoting his product—it was the world's fault, not his.

A better approach would be to figure out why it isn't working so you can begin to identify what it's going to take to fix it.

What Do You Have to Toss, and What Can You Keep?

This might mean a new logo or changing promotional items. It might mean a new Internet marketing plan or a different way of soliciting for gigs. You have to be very honest with yourself in this phase. While it's good to look at things that have been effective, don't sugarcoat them. Twenty great reviews from Facebook but no sales means something is not working. Knocking the socks off an audience for a night with no sales and not being invited back or offered another booking could be your fault and not theirs. Maybe you are playing too often in an area. Maybe you're getting great bookings but not selling anything at shows. So, booking method is working, but you need to figure out how to make sales at the gig. Maybe you're not working well with the venue or doing things wrong that you might not be aware of. You may need to look at your relationships, too.

This is not to say that everything is your fault. Some things that you're doing might be successful. If so, look at how and why they're working and keep them on track while you concentrate on the parts that aren't. It boils down to this: Having the humility to admit "It may be me and not them" can enable you to find out what will make things better for your shows, your sales, and your career.

Fix it right the first time. Don't use those small or rare successes as an excuse to shortcut or only partially repair. In some ways it's like a tire with a hole in it: Constantly putting air in it is going to be taxing and won't actually take care of the problem. It may fix it for a moment, but the problem will only reappear later. The most effective approach is to identify the problem and solve it for right now, next week, next month, and next year. It might take some time, some investment, and some changes, but it will be worth it. When things are more fluid and consistent, it allows you to spend time on your creativity, your music, and the things you enjoy most. A little more work now to make it right will save you time later.

What Path to Choose? Who to Listen To?

Figure out who can help you. When people have legal issues, they go to lawyers for advice and guidance. If it's something that has to go to court, they might hire that lawyer for a longer period of time. When people have car troubles, they go to a mechanic. When people are sick, they see a doctor. The same goes for musicians: Maybe you need that lawyer, that mechanic, or that doctor—in the form of a music producer, a music business consultant, or an entertainment lawyer. Find the right pro who can help you get on the right track. Make sure it's someone who knows what they're talking about and has a track record with the issues that concern you.

In a lot of ways, solving problems can be seen as a learning experience. If you can truly gain expertise from a situation, then the experience—no matter how good or bad—is not all in vain. Think of it as tuition in the school of music success.

But whatever you do, don't half-ass, don't cut corners. More than likely that's why it went wrong the first time. Avoid the easy fix; they usually cause the most problems down the road. Take the time, have the patience, and put the work into doing it right this time. You are not starting from scratch, but you have to forget the previous start and the things you did or used that were wrong. Reset the plan to fix the problems completely and as best you can instead of just putting more air in a tire that already has a hole. Whether you need a whole new tire or just a professional patch job, make the fixes to get you back on the right track toward the results you wanted in the first place.

WHAT HAPPENED TO THE WORK ETHIC OF MUSICIANS?

Whatever happened to true effort, the desire to learn and develop one's ability? Where did all the problem solvers go? What happened to the hunger that fired the effort to do extra work, take extra steps, or go above and beyond? When did the laziness and complacency set in, and where did the expectations come from, where some think it should simply come their way?

This may relate to other areas, professions, and people, but right now let's direct it at musicians and artists in particular. This is not pointed at everyone, but so many musicians these days lack that basic drive; they do not know how to work for their dream.

Blaming Due to Laziness

"It is the industry's fault." "It is harder to do in this city/genre/time . . ." There are any number of pointless, pathetic excuses used to justify bullshit. Sure, sometimes there are reasons why something goes wrong—legitimate hurdles and roadblocks—but the question is, how are you going to shift things to get what you want?

Don't be one of those bitching on Facebook about the music industry, file sharing, royalty issues, or which venue, label, or management that supposedly screwed you over. Are you pissed off at the RIAA, the National Association for Recording Arts and Sciences, this booking agent, or that venue? Okay, what are you doing to change things? This "repost this message on Facebook if you agree" crap is not helping to bring about change. Instead, post a link for people to read detailing a potential plan. Set up a document that allows electronic signatures to be sent to the entities you are hoping to inspire to change. Some people actually think posting a message on a networking site will change the world. That's not a bad thing; it's just not enough.

The Real Problem

I think it comes down to these key deficiencies:

- We are lazy.

- We are undereducated.

- We do not know how to win and we certainly do not know how to lose.

- We do not have social skills.

- We are afraid of confrontation.

- We are spoon-fed with the notion that we "can be anything" to the point that we don't put forth the effort associated with being successful.

Then, at the first sign of hardship or challenge . . .

- We are ready to give up at the drop of a hat.

- We think a positive attitude is all it takes.

- We don't think about the details; instead, we just believe in the best-case scenario.

- Our egos have been boosted, but our confidence is walking on eggshells.

- We want instant gratification and lack the patience required for true success.

What does it stem from? Some will say it is TV; others will say it is the schools and the fault of teachers who are too afraid to point out a child's areas of inefficiency. Even more will say it is parenting. Regardless, it comes down to children growing up and not understanding what it means to do what it takes.

When I was a kid, I played outside, climbed trees, and rode bikes—we were active. A lot more children today are less active and want to play on their PS3/Xbox/Wii, be on the computer, or be inside. Addiction to television and video games and the increase in obesity clearly shows we are less active. This suggests a lack of effort.

Are we undereducated as a whole, or are we learning from the wrong people? When a young musician begins to study drums with a freshman in college, how much is he learning that is positive and how much is negative? The college kid wants to make a few extra bucks but could be implementing bad habits and incorrect elements that will ultimately have to be unlearned. I know this firsthand. It took a good deal of time to unlearn and relearn things that were hurting me more than helping me.

We are losing an understanding of good sportsmanship: how to be a good winner *and* a good loser. I believe that confidence and growing healthy self-esteem and worth are good things. But we have gone overboard, not allowing children to differentiate between their strengths and weaknesses.

So, yes, I'm comparing musicians to children who have been coddled and told they are good at something in order to keep them from getting their feelings hurt. Sometimes your music is not good—not all art is subjective—and you need to know why, lest you pave the way for ridicule and worse, for not being the best you can be.

I remember a game of kickball in sixth grade. The teams were picked pretty fairly, but the score was 11–0; we got killed, fair and square. The team that won did not overly gloat, though they celebrated, and we did not sulk too much.

By contrast, a friend recently shared with me this odd experience with his child's softball team. At the end of the game, they called everyone a winner. While I am all about positive reinforcement, these kids were being told they were amazing when, in fact, they played awfully!

Isn't there a middle ground where a child can be told he or she is good, smart, and doing well while adding encouragement and lessons in how to improve? Hell, maybe this is where the ego issues come from with artists who think they are so incredible when they truly suck. Maybe there was an excess of support that became a liability and kept the musician from actually doing the work required to get better and improve.

Still, with all this positive reinforcement, confidence can be broken in an instant. I was working in the studio with a drummer, and I asked him to change up a pattern. He gave it a shot for maybe five minutes, and then he was in tears—literally! It was clear that he had played and performed in a safety bubble; the moment he wasn't doing something correctly, he was a wreck. We had to take a break, and we ended up keeping his part that didn't work in the first place. Later I overheard him telling other band members how I had been asking for the "stupidest pattern," and how in spite of the fact that he could actually play it, it didn't work and it was terrible. I was not digging into him in the least. But he chose to blame me! An ego that doesn't allow for growth isn't a healthy ego.

We think drive, determination, and a positive attitude is all it takes. So many people talk about going after your dreams, yet there is little focus on the hard work and necessary adjustments involved.

Drive and determination must be accompanied by *action*!

Too many artists don't want to hear the truth. It is one thing to identify a problem and another thing to actually take action and solve it. I do not claim to have all the answers, but I do know you must take a hard, cold look at yourself, your music, your band, and what you are doing, while assessing those things you might need to change and those things that should remain the same. What are you doing every day to get you closer to what you want? What has worked for you or brought small successes? Analyze it, work on it, and see if you can apply it to other areas that are not working.

No one is perfect; I have to address these issues just like everyone else. Surround yourself with the hardest working, strongest communicating, and best musicians you possibly can. Respect the business side just as you respect the art side, and you will have a bigger chance in an industry where the chances of success become slimmer and slimmer day by day.

LAZY WORK: DON'T TRY TO REINVENT THE WHEEL

I'm often amazed by the effort many artists will put into making things easier, faster, and quicker. Yet when it comes down to doing the real work, the time just isn't available. They are trying to reinvent the wheel, and while coming up with new ideas and effective methods to save time is a great thing, more often than not, it seems that they are avoiding the real work they have to do.

Lazy Work Doesn't Work

I am all about time management, but I have worked with artists who claimed to be so driven to find a different way to do something that they would not commit a single hour, week, or month to trying it in the best way available right now. Reinventing-the-wheel approaches and shortcuts end up shortcutting the real work that needs to be done. Nobody likes the load-in and load-out, and while it might be easier and quicker to throw the cases down a stairwell, is that really a good idea?

Sure, save time where you can, but put the real effort into the work that must be done the right way. Some tasks are not going to be fun, but if you are doing the work the right way, the right results will follow. Watch out for the lazy work that is not delivering the results, and give the effort, the time, and the work ethic that your dream deserves.

HOW WOULD YOU RATE YOURSELF AS A BOSS AND AS AN EMPLOYEE?

Much of my work as a music consultant is less about telling artists what to do and more about finding out how they approach a task. In fact, most answers to the questions concerning being a professional musician, working full-time, and bringing in profit can be answered by the musicians and bands themselves. They just don't realize that they already know a lot of these answers. One of my favorite tricks is to ask an artist to "rate yourself."

First, imagine yourself as if you were the boss, rating your work, commitment, drive, efforts, and results from the standpoint of an employer. While you might say that you did all you could, maybe when you look through the eyes of a boss, you might see a better way, a different way, or a more effective way. A boss wants results or movement toward results. Looking at your work, productivity, and results from this viewpoint may open your eyes to other ideas. This is also the place where a consultant or coach can help as well.

Then try looking from the point of view of an employee. Even though artists are working for themselves in most cases, ask yourself, are you working toward your goals as if you were working for someone else? Sometimes, as employees, we cut corners when the boss isn't looking. In the same way, because we aren't reporting to anyone, we can start to cut corners as artists.

Try holding yourself accountable to yourself. If you had to give yourself a daily, weekly, or monthly report, would you be proud to talk about what you had done, or would you need to be prettying up things, bullshitting, or lying to keep your job?

Trying this exercise from both angles can be a great way to review yourself and look at a few areas where you may be able to improve.

TAKING RESPONSIBILITY: ACCEPTING THE CONSEQUENCES FOR YOUR ACTIONS

While working with different people in different cities with very different viewpoints, I noticed one very similar theme: The people who blamed everything and everybody else for their lack of success tended to continue to have a lack of success. By contrast, those I talked to who were proactive, problem-solving minded, assertive, and responsible were all on a better path in their career (maybe not successful yet, but on the right road). I would put money down that if they keep that mindset, they will achieve some level of sustainable success.

So the economy is bad; do you want to spend the energy bitching about it, or spend the energy to find the ways to sell, perform, and draw in fans? Sure, there are labels, managers, and agents with horrible contracts. But . . . know what? If you signed that contract, took that deal, and went with it, it is as much your fault as theirs.

Everyone makes mistakes, but it is the trait of successful people to learn, problem-solve, and not repeat the mistakes they made.

A few years back I made a big mistake that cost me a great deal. A number of people warned me how wrong this person treated me. I agreed, but it was as much my fault for the contract I signed. This person did me wrong, but I was also responsible, and I took the steps to make things better after it went down.

Do you want to be a part of change? Then take the steps to take care of yourself, protect yourself, and share your experiences with others so you can learn from their successes and their mistakes as they learn from yours. Put your energy into finding new and different ways to attack your dream while taking care of yourself and your art. Cut out the excuses. Take responsibility for your actions and put your energy into being an assertive, proactive problem solver and a humble student of the music industry. You will see the results a great deal faster than if you are weighed down with excuses, blame, whining, and all the other crap. Your career is depending on it!

CLOSING THOUGHT

A successful career in the music business of today comes down to patience, attention to detail, follow-through, and thorough research of any contract, deal, offer, or proposal. In the end, it is your responsibility to read the small print, whether it is for gig contracts, record contracts, investors, management, booking agents, or anything else. You can blame everyone else for your mistakes, but when *you make them, you end up being the one who has to pay.*

Care for your career in the same way a good parent cares for a child. Wouldn't it be interesting if artists treated their dream or goal like a living, breathing baby in need of attention, support, and love? I wonder, then, if we would see laziness replaced with commitment; passive mindsets replaced with assertive action; shortcutting replaced with total attention to detail; procrastination replaced with a must-do-now approach. Step up for your dream; respect your dream. Do what the Staple Singers said: Respect yourself—and the work that it will take to get there.

Either be a good parent to your career, or just give your dream up for adoption. Do something else and stop wasting your time, your effort, and your breath. It's fine to do music part-time. It's fine to do music as a hobby, but if you're going to tell the world and yourself that this is your dream, your goal, your life, and there are no other options, then learn the steps, create the plan, and do the work that sets up the best foundation for a solid career.

Things will go wrong; it will be a hard road at times. But if a career in music or the arts really is what you need, what you can't live without, and what you have to make happen, *then make it happen*. It's your choice. It's your career.

CONCLUSION

———•———————————•———

Waiting to be discovered, hoping to be seen, wishing someone else would do the work, wanting to make it big while dreaming of being rich and famous just like your heroes is submissive, passive, foolish, weak, and ineffective. Take your desire for your dreams, your goals, and your ambition, then make them fuel for the fire to light your ass up, to get to work and on the path to make it happen. Energy, effort, execution, and actions make dreams come true. Following through, applying the work ethic, and having patience delivers more results. Learning, empowering, studying, practicing, and not repeating the same mistakes will help you move forward, move up, and move on to where you want to be.

Use the tools, ideas, and concepts in this book; apply and customize them to create your plan of action. This will allow you to be someone who drives for that dream, lives for the goal, and will not settle, lose, or let anything get in the way of success. Keep the waiting, wishing, wanting, hoping, and dreaming in check. Too many focus too much time and energy in areas that do not allow for growth. Don't just call for change; make change happen.

Talk less and do more. Commit to your dream and stand out from others who just talk. I know of no other profession where so many people talk so much about how badly they want success and how driven they are. Yet the bulk of these people do little work and constantly look for the easiest and cheapest route to get where they want to go. Are shortcuts, delusions, lack of work ethic, absence of problem solving, and low attention to detail why you still have your day job and still haven't reached your goals? Is your career standing still?

There is a difference between standing still and standing your ground. Your solid footing in your dream, your honor, your morals, and your plan—in good times and bad—will showcase who you are. If you don't stand your ground, honor your successes, and work to fix and pay for your mistakes, how can you expect anyone to trust you, stand by you, and give you that same respect?

I have made mistakes in my career. I have won, but also lost. I have failed, but I take full responsibility for all of it. There are some situations where I am still working to make right what went wrong. As your career grows, do not forget those who were there for you, who took a chance on you, and who stood behind you. The road will be long and challenging. But the work, the effort, and the commitment to doing the right thing reveals the true character and heart of a successful and honorable person.

It's time to respect yourself and your dream; both truly deserve that respect.
Be the person you would do anything for. Be the person you will not let down.
Be the person you would never give up on.

Photo taken by Roy Wells

ABOUT THE AUTHOR

Loren Weisman is a music consultant, music producer, and business coach who works to help, assist, and consult independent artists, musicians, bands, labels, and other businesses to achieve sustainable success. He has been a part of over seven-hundred albums as a drummer and music producer.

Loren also maintains television productions credits for three major networks and serves as a media consultant for many businesses in and out of the arts and entertainment fields.

Weisman has seen and stayed up to date with the constant changes in the music industry over the past two decades and has kept up with the pulse and motion of marketing, promotion, and social media in today's world.

For more on Loren's speaking engagements, seminars,
consulting, coaching, or other services, visit:

lorenweisman.com • facebook.com/lorenweisman • youtube.com/lorenweisman
twitter.com/lorenweisman

INDEX

———— • ————

NOTES

NOTES

NOTES

NOTES

NOTES

NOTES